D1234160

> *Divide each problem into as many parts as possible; that each part being more easily conceived, the whole may be more intelligible.*
>
> — DESCARTES
>
> *Discourse on Method*

THE
NAZI
SEIZURE OF
POWER

William Sheridan Allen was born in Evanston, Illinois, and studied at the universities of Michigan, Connecticut, and Minnesota, and in Germany at the Free University of Berlin and the University of Göttingen. *The Nazi Seizure of Power* is his first book; he is at work on a study of underground resistance to the Third Reich. Mr. Allen is now Professor of History at the State University of New York at Buffalo.

THE
NAZI
SEIZURE OF
POWER

THE EXPERIENCE OF
A SINGLE GERMAN TOWN
1930-1935

BY

WILLIAM SHERIDAN ALLEN

卐

NEW VIEWPOINTS
A Division of Franklin Watts, Inc.
New York, 1973

First NEW VIEWPOINTS edition published 1973 by Franklin Watts, Inc.

Library of Congress Catalog Card Number 65-10378

Standard Book Number: 531-06439-5

Manufactured in the United States of America

TO MY FATHER,

who taught me love of learning

PREFACE

This is a history of a single small town in Germany during the last years of the Weimar Republic and the first years of the Third Reich. It is an attempt to understand one of the central political and moral problems of the twentieth century: how a civilized democracy could be plunged into a nihilistic dictatorship. I chose to approach this problem by studying a single town partly because no close study of the local aspects of the Nazi Revolution existed. A book has been written on the State of Brunswick's Nazi-Conservative coalition, and another on the Nazification of the Schleswig-Holstein provinces * (both halting before the actual seizure of power), but before I undertook this present study there was no work written covering the entire period of the Nazi Revolution or focusing on a limited locality.

Yet Nazi measures on the local level were a key to the establishment of totalitarianism in Germany. Before Hitler came to power he gained great support through the virtuosity and adaptability of his local party organizations. The actual seizure of power in the spring of 1933 occurred largely from below, though it was facilitated and made possible by Hitler's position as Chancellor of Germany. The *Fuehrer* reached the pinnacle of power because his followers were successful at the lowest level, at the base.

A single unit can never adequately reflect the whole. The subject of this book was not, in many ways, an average German town. It was heavily middle class; it was more closely tied to the country-

---

* Ernst-August Roloff, *Bürgertum und Nationalsozialismus: Braunschweigs Weg ins Dritten Reich* (Hannover, 1960); Rudolf Heberle, *From Democracy to Nazism* (Baton Rouge, 1945).

side and less to industry than most German towns; it was over-whelmingly Lutheran; it turned to Nazism earlier and more strongly than most of the rest of Germany. Yet it does show representative characteristics: in the activism of the Nazi party, in the sociological strengths and weaknesses of the Social Democrats, in the attitudes of the nationalistic middle class, in voting trends, in the growth of political activity and partisan violence, and perhaps in other ways that will become apparent only when other towns are studied in similar detail. In this sense it is not a true microcosm, though it can be instructive of broader trends. I offer it as at least one concrete example of what the Nazi Revolution meant in all its varied aspects in one confined area.

If a microcosm has the drawback of being non-representative, it has the advantage of permitting a close and detailed study. The smaller number of actors makes it possible for the historian to come near to knowing them all. Variables are limited and there is a comprehensible and relatively constant background. Immediacy and reality are enhanced. One can fit actions into the pattern of daily life and thus determine why individuals acted as they did, why Germans made the kind of choices which let Hitler into power. It was this possibility, more than anything else, which led me to re-search into the fate of a town which would otherwise not deserve even a footnote in a general study of the rise of Nazism.

The ravages of revolution, terror, war, and occupation severely limited the number and type of source materials available for this study. Thanks to the cooperation of the townspeople, however, most of the public and private documents that survived were put at my disposal. Enough of the people of the town agreed to be inter-viewed so that I was able to interrogate most leading figures and also obtain an acceptable general cross-section. Their recollections and impressions were then checked against the contemporary docu-ments and newspaper accounts. The result was a considerable col-lection of detail, much of which had to be omitted from this book but which is to be found in my doctoral dissertation.*

When the idea for this study first came to me, I was given essen-

---

* Available from University Microfilms, Inc., Ann Arbor, Michigan, No. 63-1188.

tial encouragement by Dr. Harry Marks of the University of Connecticut, for which I thank him. The research was made possible by a grant from the Federal Republic of Germany. Dr. Heinrich Eggeling gave me valuable advice and practical aid, while Dr. Karl Roskamp provided me with the benefit of his experience in the labyrinth of German tax statistics. Various revisions were suggested by my two excellent teachers at the University of Minnesota, Professor Harold Deutsch and Professor William Wright, by my two kind colleagues at the University of Missouri, Professor David Pinkney and Professor Roderick McGrew, by Professor Gerhard L. Weinberg, and by Professor Raul Hilberg. My wife, Luella S. Allen, lent a critical ear and much moral support. While I acknowledge their separate kindnesses gratefully and affirm the collective nature of whatever insights this work may possess, the actual formulation and therefore the responsibility for any defects rests with myself alone.

Small towns the world over have two aspects in common: little privacy and much gossip. Before I ever began my research I came to the conclusion that not only should the names of informants and other principal characters be kept secret but the actual name of the town would have to be disguised. Consequently anyone who looks on a map or in an encyclopedia for "Thalburg" will not find it. This precaution was also part of a promise which I made to the city fathers and to all those interviewed. Scholars who want to pursue the matter will find the identity of the town plus a list and identification of sources on file at the History Department of the University of Minnesota.

There is a descriptive list of persons interviewed appended for reference. In addition, each person interviewed will be described in a note on the page where he first appears. No person from Thalburg mentioned in this study has been given his true name. Inventing so many names taxes the imagination; should any reader find his name in these pages I hope he will understand that it is pure coincidence.

W.S.A.

Columbia, Missouri, 1965

CONTENTS

Appendices

PART ONE

The Death of the Democracy

卐

January, 1930, to January, 1933

CHAPTER 1

THE SETTING

Drink and Eat
Forget not God
Protect your Honor
No one will ask more of you than that.
—MEDIEVAL INSCRIPTION ON A
THALBURG HOUSE

If you open an atlas to the map of Central Europe and put your thumb down on the center of pre-war Germany, the chances are good that you will land on Thalburg, a town in the former Kingdom of Hannover. In the days of the Weimar Republic it was still a small town, with a population of about ten thousand. There were close to a thousand towns of this size in Germany then; about one of every seven Germans lived in them.[1]

In 1930 Thalburg was the kind of town that English tourists were fond of discovering: provincial and off the beaten track, semi-medieval, set in quiet and pleasant surroundings. It nestled against one of the series of low, wooded foothills that frame the valley of the Grade River. Since the valley was only a few miles wide and very flat, a person standing in the slanting fields above Thalburg could see across to the hills on the other side; it gave the town a sense of being snug, enclosed, protected from the outer world. The placid Grade River was joined at Thalburg by another river, the Muhle, which had carved out a narrow valley immediately north of the town. The confluence of the rivers and their valleys created the town, for from the days of the Hanseatic traders the town had been a minor east-west, north-south junction point. From the hills above the town you could see the main railroad line stretching up and down the Grade River Valley, just touching against the perimeter of Thalburg, and the spur-line swinging around under the city walls to follow the Muhle Valley towards Berlin.[2]

There actually were walls around part of the town. They enclosed the medieval inner town which was the core of Thalburg. Here, within an oval about six hundred yards long, was a neat but imprecise jumble of half-timbered houses with steep red-tiled roofs along winding cobblestone streets. One street that ran through the town was three lanes wide (and therefore called "Broad Street"): the main commercial avenue with shops in every house. In the middle of the town was a large square, used for the weekly market and also suitable for open-air meetings. The only other clear areas within the walls were a small War Memorial on one side of Broad Street, a small space in front of the Town Hall, and another in front of the great sixteenth-century Lutheran church. The rest of the inner town was filled with narrow streets, with houses built to the very edges, jammed side by side, the front of each decorated with timbered beams of various geometric patterns, the upper stories marked by irregular, small-paned windows, the whole surmounted by steep roofs in a skyline diversified by angular gables and chimneys. There were over five hundred houses in the old part of Thalburg; almost half of the townspeople lived there.[3]

Outside the medieval oval were various residential areas, built mainly in the period from 1870 to 1914. The most desirable district was on the hillside above the old town. There one found large, one-family dwellings, schools, broad asphalt streets, spacious lawns, shade trees, and shrubbery. From these houses there was a good view of town and valley, and in the summer breezes kept this area cooler than the rest of Thalburg. Here dwelt the town's upper class.

On the other side of the medieval section, across the spur-line of the railroad, was the Muhle Canal, dug in the Middle Ages to power a grain mill. This narrow strip of water created an island closed off by the Muhle River. There were apartment houses, small dwellings, and a large circus grounds on it. At one end of the circus grounds was a large meeting hall, called the *1910er Zelt*, suitable for dances, festivals, and mass meetings. A bridge, called the "Long Bridge," spanned the Muhle River. On the other side

OLD ARMY
COMPOUND

MUHLE RIVER

GRADE RIVER

1910er
ZELT
and
CIRCUS
GROUNDS

MUHLE CANAL

MEDIEVAL INNER TOWN (COMMERCIAL)

TOWN
HALL

FACTORIES
and
RAILROAD
YARDS

WAR
MEMORIAL

MARKET
SQUARE

BROAD ST.

LUTHERAN
CHURCH

CATTLE
AUCTION HALL

RAILROAD
STATION

THALBURG in 1930

LOWER CLASS RESIDENTIAL AREA

MIDDLE CLASS RESIDENTIAL AREA

UPPER CLASS RESIDENTIAL AREA

lay a former Army compound backed up against foothills. In 1930 the compound housed a variety of state houses, including the employment office, a factory, emergency low-rent dwellings, and a youth hostel.[4]

On the side of the town towards the Grade River were nondescript residential dwellings, a few industrial plants and a sugar beet refinery whose ugly smokestacks spoiled the skyline, and the railroad station with extensive yards and maintenance buildings. Thus around the old inner city were three areas where the town had expanded: up the hill and towards each of the two rivers, one district for the rich and two for the lower classes. But the center and essence of Thalburg remained the old medieval city surrounded by the slowly crumbling walls.

The history of the town, like its physical setting, shows an interplay between isolation and involvement. Thalburg was founded in the time of Charlemagne, but from then to the thirteenth century it was little more than a blockhouse, a monastery, and an appended village. In those early days Thalburg enjoyed some moments of national eminence, for one of its counts was a military leader strong enough to do battle with the Holy Roman Emperor himself, though with disastrous results to his own family's fortunes.

The future of the town lay in more prosaic areas of endeavor. Beginning in the twelfth century merchants settled before the monastery walls, and it was under their leadership that Thalburg was granted a city charter by the Welf Dukes in 1252. In subsequent years the town grew rapidly. A town wall was built with battlements, towers, and moat; immigration swelled the population; the Muhle Canal was dug; and Thalburg joined the Hanseatic League. By the fifteenth century the town was almost completely independent of the Welf Dukes and even coined its own money. This was the period of Thalburg's flowering. An ancient engraving shows it to be one of the richer and larger cities of its time.

The period of medieval splendor and independence for Thalburg came to an end with the Thirty Years War. The town had become Lutheran during the Reformation, and when it was ordered to open its gates to the Catholic Army under Tilly, the city council refused. A bitter two-year siege followed. Within Thalburg there was an intense factional fight. The upper classes favored surrender while the lower classes chose to resist the Catholic Army. In 1627 the peace party turned the town over to Tilly, who punished Thalburg severely for its former resistance.

Thalburg emerged from the Thirty Years War small and weak: "The shadow of its former strength." [5] It had been occupied by both sides, beleaguered, plundered, and burned. In 1648 over three hundred houses were empty and only about seven hundred inhabitants were left in the town. The Duke had revoked its rights, stripped away all vestiges of independence, and placed a permanent garrison in the town to intimidate the burghers.

Recovery came very slowly; it was not until the time of the French Revolution that Thalburg regained the number of inhabitants it had had in the fourteenth century—about 2,500. Though the merchants still predominated, economically and politically, the town had become only a local market center exchanging handicraft products for agricultural ones.[6] It was not until 1817 that the first house was built outside the city walls. The mainline railroad was built through Thalburg in 1857, and ten years later the east-west line through the mountains turned the town into an important traffic point. Now government offices began to find it a convenient location. The former Kingdom of Hannover was incorporated into Prussia, bringing new uniforms to the garrison troops and laying the basis for more rapid development. By the 1870's the town had acquired a variety of technical academies and college preparatory schools. In 1886 it was named a county center. Railroad maintenance shops were built and several small factories were founded. The town acquired a working class who brought with them the new doctrines of Karl Marx. Owing to the influx of teachers, artisans, government officials, and railroad personnel, a Catholic church could be opened in Thalburg. The railroad had brought the outer world with it.

The last vestige of medieval ways ended in 1900 when a sewage system was introduced. Prior to that, Thalburg had cleaned its streets by opening the upper moat every Saturday. The waters would flow down the slight incline, coursing over the cobblestones towards the Muhle Canal, and housewives would follow with their brush-brooms. The sewage system was expensive, but the Germany of Kaiser Wilhelm II was prosperous and required symbols of prosperity. In Thalburg a fountain was built on the Market Square with a copper statue of the ancient Count of Thalburg, at a cost of 9,000 marks. The War Memorial, built to commemorate those Thalburgers who had fallen in the short war between Prussia and Hannover in 1866, was now topped with a bronze "Germania."

Both of these symbols of present affluence and past military glory were soon to be lost, however, and many more names were to be added to the War Memorial. When World War I erupted, the statues were melted down to help supply Germany's need for metal. In return, the central government provided the town with an Army school for noncommissioned officers, with a permanent compound located across the "Long Bridge." Two hundred and fifty-three Thalburgers gave their lives to defend the Reich.

Yet despite these efforts, and for reasons mysterious to many Thalburgers, the war was lost, and with it also a whole way of life, for in the wake of defeat came a revolution led by the working class which overthrew the Kaiser and established a democratic republic in Germany. The revolution of 1918 was accomplished peacefully in Thalburg, with the troops arranging matters with the officers. The following year, however, the local workers-and-soldiers soviet forced the commander of the garrison to resign, and in November, 1920, the army withdrew from the town completely.[7] There were Thalburgers who refused to accept the new state of affairs; the town soon became a relatively strong center for the violently rightist organization, *Jung deutsche Orden*. In 1922, shortly after nationalistic terrorists assassinated the Republic's Foreign Minister, Walther Rathenau, the *Jung deutsche Orden* decided to stage a nationalistic drama in Thalburg. Socialists from Thalburg and neighboring areas determined to stop the play. In response, nationalist-minded farmers flocked to Thalburg and a column of students from a nearby university also marched on the town. When they met they fought wildly with cobblestones and beer bottles as weapons. The police were roughly handled before the town was restored to order, and practically every shop window on Broad Street was broken in the mêlée.[8]

As in the Thirty Years War the town was rent by strife and inner cleavage. An indication of Thalburg's political division, even in the settled middle years of the Weimar Republic, comes from election statistics. In the presidential election of 1925, the Socialist candidate received 2,080 votes; Hindenburg (running for the rightists) got 3,375 votes; the only other candidate, a Communist, polled 19 votes.[9] Despite its Grimm's Fairy Tales appearance and apparent remoteness, Thalburg contained all the conflicting loyalties and tensions of Weimar Germany.

CHAPTER 2

THE ANATOMY OF
THE TOWN

"Then," said I, "suppose we should imagine we see a city in the making, we might see its justice, too, in the making, and the injustice?"
—SOCRATES, in Plato's *Republic*

Even so small and apparently integrated a community as Thalburg has its elements of strain and disintegration. In normal times these may balance; in times of stress they may pull the community apart; a demagogue may exploit them, driving wedges into existing social gaps. Thalburg was a remarkably complex community for its size and some of its sociological and economic aspects bore directly upon the growth of Nazism in the years after the onslaught of the depression, and on the eventual ease with which the Nazis introduced totalitarian reorganization.

There were political divisions between left and right; there were class lines between worker and bourgeois; there were occupational lines between the stable and the insecure; there were areas of exclusion between the relative newcomers and the old families; there were religious and social divisions. There were also areas of common interest, such as city government; and instruments of cohesion, such as schools, clubs, and interest groups; and there were primary loyalty groups from families to circles of close friends.

Despite its antiquity, Thalburg was essentially a product of the nineteenth century. In 1871 the town had 4,700 inhabitants; by 1930 it reached exactly 10,000. Half the increase came from an increased birthrate, but the other half came from immigration. In the late 1930's, the composition of Thalburg was estimated as follows, counting back two generations: [1]

Born in Thalburg	25 per cent
From rural Thalburg County	26 per cent
From the rest of Hannover	34 per cent
From all other parts of Germany	15 per cent

The rural hinterland, with its strongly nationalistic prejudices, had made a considerable impression on the town. But more important was the natural division between these newcomers and those whose families were Thalburgers running back for several generations. Most of the "old Thalburgers" lived in the inner town. A list compiled in 1932 of the most common family names in Thalburg shows how interwoven these families were. Excluding the usual "Muellers," "Meyers," and "Schmidts," one finds 109 names, each of which was shared by five to ten families. Some twenty-five names were each shared by ten or more families. Three particularly localized names were shared respectively by twenty-two, nineteen, and eighteen families each.[2] The "old Thalburgers" knew each other quite well; most of them had become related by marriage down through the centuries. There was thought to be neither special fellowship nor common political outlook among them, though they would present a common front against "outsiders." [3]

The whole area where Thalburg was situated has a reputation for being *stur:* stubborn and reserved, as New Englanders are said to be. One man who first came to Thalburg in 1930 found that it took him two years to get to know anyone well and to be accepted in social circles, even though he was fairly extroverted and held a job of high prestige.[4]

If Thalburgers were divided as to origin, they were united in religion. Despite changes wrought by the nineteenth-century influx, 86 per cent of the townspeople were Lutheran, only 6 per cent Catholic, and the rest consisted of various sects and those of no faith. This was substantially the same proportion that existed at the turn of the century and that was to be found in Thalburg County. There were only 120 Jews in Thalburg, approximately the same percentage as the national average for urban areas.[5]

In occupation, Thalburg looked upon itself as a city of civil servants: about one-third of its seven thousand adults were in the public employ, most working for the railroad. An additional fifth were widows or pensioners, so that close to half the townspeople had fixed incomes. One out of every seven persons was a higher civil servant. Stability and dependence on the state ran high.[6]

The large proportion of civil servants conditioned the town's economic structure. There was little industry, and what there was depended either on the rural hinterland or the railroad. The government offices brought farmers to town and Thalburg's merchants and artisans supplied them with goods. As long as farmers prospered and as long as the government kept its offices in Thalburg the town could expect to maintain economic equilibrium. Furthermore, the cost of living was low in Thalburg: in 1931, per capita expenditures for staples were 25 per cent less than the national average.[7] Many Thalburgers kept pigs or other animals and many had small vegetable gardens. Barring catastrophe, Thalburg was economically secure.

In 1930 the depression had just begun and its economic effects were scarcely noticed in Thalburg. The number of motor vehicles in the town increased by about 15 per cent between the summer of 1929 and the summer of 1930. Savings deposits in the City Savings Bank rose by almost a half-million marks in 1930, and the number of accounts was increased by about five hundred. In that bank alone there were close to 3,600 savings accounts with an average of 537 marks per account. The average per capita savings in Thalburg was 20 per cent greater than the average for all Prussia.[8] Thalburg was at the top of its class of cities in new dwellings constructed for 1930. Alarmists might note that there were 329 registered unemployed at the beginning of 1930, but that was less than the average in Thalburg's governmental subdistrict as a whole.[9]

If the town seemed sound even in the face of depression it was because there was so little industry. A sugar beet refinery, a dairy products plant, a grain mill, a brewery, two sawmills, and a cannery made up the industries dependent on the rich land of the Grade Valley. In addition, there was a construction firm, two brick factories, a road building company, a cigar manufacturing plant, a paper sack factory, and a tiny cement works. None of these were large undertakings. At a moment when all were operating at once they could employ about 1,125 people. But between one-third and one-half of the work force depended on seasonal employment; when the sugar beet factory shut down in December of each year, for example, almost three hundred people were thrown out of work. Over three hundred more depended upon construction, and an equal number, employed by the cigar factory and the cannery, were women. Industry was the weakest factor in Thalburg's economy, but it was also the smallest factor.

The rural-connected industries, the many governmental offices, and the good road and railroad connections all drew farmers to Thalburg and made the town a center for retail trade. In 1930 there were about a hundred shops with perhaps five hundred employees. The largest was a dry-goods store employing about thirty people. Most were small family shops, with very moderate incomes, passed on from father to son.

The artisan shops were also family businesses. In 1930 one iron-worker celebrated the 300th anniversary of the founding of his smithy; he was the tenth generation of his family to serve the town.[10] It was a rare artisan who could not trace his shop back at least three generations. Thalburg's artisans were organized in guilds, which were mere shadows of their medieval precursors, being essentially professional societies. There were seventeen guilds in 1930, representing about 150 small shops. The artisans and retail traders dominated the commercial life of the town, although there were also several credit institutions: branches of three national banks, a local bank owned by a Jew named Braun, a local stock bank, a County Savings Bank, and the City Savings Bank.

Most of Thalburg's middle class consisted of government civil servants. The list of government offices in Thalburg in 1930 was extensive, the most important being the County Prefecture which administered the eighty towns and villages of Thalburg County for the Prussian government. The Reich government maintained nine other offices in Thalburg, such as the post office, district court, employment office, etc., which employed about four hundred persons and served several counties. But the government service with the largest number of employees was the railroad, with its switchyards, maintenance shops, tie-dip, and bus system. Altogether, the railroad station gave work to about a thousand people and was the dominant economic force in the town.

The city itself maintained a considerable bureaucracy. In addition to the customary functions such as police and fire departments, street cleaning, and garbage disposal, it produced gas, electricity, and water for the town and maintained a construction office and a hospital. It owned numerous nongovernmental enterprises, such as a slaughterhouse, an icehouse, a cemetery, and a brewery. These were money-making enterprises and they tended to spawn others. The city owned considerable forest land in the hills above the town and so maintained a forest administration, which ran a gravel pit that then led to a small cement-making plant. The welfare office not only supplied payments to the disabled, the poor, and the unemployed, but also operated two small old-age homes, a soup kitchen, and emergency low-rent housing units for those who would otherwise be shelterless. Also under control by municipal authorities was the local Health Insurance Office, which, since its director happened to be a Social Democrat, was known as the "red" Health Insurance Office.[11]

In this way the city added over two hundred civil servants, not counting the seasonally recruited casual laborers. There were so many employees of central and local government that they formed their own political party for local elections, the Civil Servants party, which held the balance of power in the City Council. Not all were of the middle class, though a civil servant of full rank was well paid and occupied an enviable position in German society. A worker, on the other hand, even if employed by the government, was viewed by others and by himself as a proletarian. The railroad workers formed the core of the Socialist vote in Thalburg and the bulk of the city workers were also Social Democrats.

Class structure, though strongly affected by income, is really contingent on an attitude of mind. Every year the city published an address book, and from the titles individuals gave themselves, one can make the following calculation: [12]

Lower class   37 per cent
    (unskilled and semi-skilled workers)
Lower middle class   32 per cent
    (skilled workers, white-collar workers, farmers, and
    pensioners)
Upper middle class   27 per cent
    (craft masters, civil servants, and businessmen)
Upper class   4 per cent
    (businessmen, self-employed, and professionals)

Though this is a very rough approximation it leads to the conclusion that Thalburg had an exceedingly strong *petite bourgeoisie:* the raw material from which Hitler forged his movement. The relatively even distribution does not mean that great differences in income were nonexistent. One laborer at the city gas works with over fifteen years' seniority earned 1,500 marks a year.[13] A man in the medical profession had an annual income of 9,600 marks.[14] When a worker with a good job saw a rather ordinary professional man earning six times as much as he did, he was bound to reaffirm whatever concepts of class struggle the Social Democratic party might have instilled in him.

In Thalburg, as in most other places in the Germany of the Weimar Republic, the working class formed a definite community, almost a sub-culture. Workers had their own social clubs, economic organizations, and their own party: the Social Democratic party *(Sozialdemokratische Partei Deutschlands).* The SPD's organization was complex. It consisted of a number of different groups, all nominally independent of one another, but all facets of the working class and all actually working together. A list of the leaders of the various organizations showed so many duplications that for all practical purposes one composite committee could have been made of about fifteen persons, which would have included the key officers of all the groups. It would have included union secretaries (especially of the railroad workers' union), chairmen of sport societies, the workers' first-aid society, workers' choral groups, workers' shooting societies, and the like. There were officers of the "Common Good Construction Club" and the "Householders Consumers' Cooperative," the latter with a membership of 1,275 families and gross annual sales of a third of a million marks.[15] The former built low-rent housing; with 128 members it did over 600,000 marks worth of business in the depression year of 1932.[16] Then there were the direct adjuncts to the SPD: the youth group ("Young Socialist Workers"), the children's group ("Red Falcons"), the Women's Auxiliary, and proliferating committees of all kinds. There was the *Reichsbanner,* a paramilitary corps for the defense of the Republic, which though theoretically open to all, was actually staffed and peopled almost exclusively by Socialists. From the Infants' Aid Society to the Workers' Funeral Savings Association, the SPD permeated and unified the working class of Thalburg.

Class consciousness was not the only unifying bond, for the SPD also provided a common ideology—essentially, commitment to democracy. This, plus overlapping leadership, made it possible for the SPD's minor solar system to revolve smoothly. Each organization had its own needs and aspirations, however, so that cooperation necessitated compromise and adjustment. Since the nineteenth century, when it was founded, Thalburg's SPD had not only provided excellent practical training for democracy; it had become a way of life to the working class of the town.

For Thalburgers who were neither workers nor Socialists, the real social cohesion was supplied by clubs. There is a proverb: "Two Germans, a discussion; three Germans, a club." This was almost true of Thalburg, where, in 1930, there were no fewer than 161 separate clubs, an average of about one for every sixty persons in town. There were twenty-one sport clubs, forty-seven with an economic or occupational function, twenty-three religious or charitable societies, twenty-five veterans' or patriotic associations, and forty-five special interest and hobby groups. With hardly an exception, they followed the town's class lines. Of the two soccer clubs, one was middle class and one was composed mainly of workers.[17] Of the gymnastic clubs, two were middle class and one was worker. In the economic or occupational associations the class line was even clearer and occasionally became political. The thousand-member Railroad Club, with a social as well as an occupational function, was SPD-oriented. The County Farmers' League and the County Artisans' League, on the other hand, both sponsored rightist speakers and eventually gave open backing to the Nazis and the Nationalist party, respectively.[18] Most were not so openly political, however, and one economic club deriving from medieval customs even cut across class lines.

Traditionally, Thalburgers who owned houses within the walls had certain privileges, such as free wood to repair their timber beams or a small amount of free beer from the brewery in compensation for the loss of private brewing rights. In the revolutionary atmosphere of the early twenties, which seemed to threaten these privileges, the house owners formed the "Club for the Defense of Old Thalburg Privileges" and took legal action to maintain and extend their rights. In 1930, for example, they used old documents to win a case for a free chimney cleaning once a year. Without political or class orientation, this was another instance of cohesion among the "old Thalburgers" who intermarried and stuck together, at least against the outside world.[19]

There was a bewildering array of militaristic and nationalistic organizations in Thalburg. This was not unusual for the area and the times, as comparison with neighboring towns shows. Many of the militaristic societies were affiliated with a specific branch of the armed services, such as the "Society of Former Reserve Ninety-Firsters" or the "Cavalry Association." Others were general, such as the "Warriors League," or else derived from specific experiences, such as the "League of the War Wounded." There were also nationalistic societies such as the "Association for Germandom in Foreign Lands," or youth groups such as the "Schill Free-Band." [20] When one adds to this list the organizations that were adjuncts to the German Nationalist party or the Nazis, such as the "Steel Helmet" and the "Queen Luise Society," or the "National Socialist Women's Club" and the "Hitler Youth," one can see to what extent rightist organizations dominated the social life of Thalburg's middle classes.

All of these organizations had considerable membership. The smallest ("Society of Former Artillerists") had thirty members. The "Warriors League" had over four hundred in 1930, and the twenty-three others ranged between.[21] Their activities included speeches, parades, and social gatherings, and were marked by orgies of nationalism. On occasion they joined for a "non-partisan" political effort; in 1930, for example, they petitioned the Prussian Minister of Education to ban *All Quiet on the Western Front* from school libraries.[22]

Spectacles were a definite part of the military clubs' activities. Three or four times a year one of the veterans' organizations could be counted on for a parade with bands, uniforms, and participation by all the other organizations. All gave service to the nationalist cause, and a few even came to espouse the Nationalist party, and later the Nazis, publicly. Taken as a whole, the nationalistic and veterans' clubs formed an important social element in the town. Their "stag evenings," dances, and theatrical presentations kept them in the public eye. They were primarily responsible for whipping up patriotic fervor and keeping militarism popular and vital in Thalburg.

The most clearly social group of clubs in Thalburg were the special interest and hobby groups. Despite their specific purpose they functioned essentially as occasions for social gatherings, and consequently followed class lines. Choral societies are a case in point. Thalburg had eight such clubs: seven middle class and one worker, the "Thalburg People's Choir." The upper class club was clearly the "Song Stave." In the words of a non-member, it was "really a social club composed of the better elements." [23] A former member of the "Song Stave," who admitted that he joined for professional reasons rather than from a love of singing, described its members as "directors, professional men, and entrepreneurs of larger enterprises." [24]

The size of these singing clubs varied from sixty-five to twenty-five; close to four hundred Thalburgers belonged to one or another in 1930. They met frequently to practice, with beer afterwards to cool the throat. Five or six times a year wives were brought for a concert, and occasionally the club traveled to a regional singing festival. Only the "People's Choir" had a political orientation; it performed at Republican festivals and Social Democratic gatherings.

Another vehicle for good fellowship and social intercourse were the "shooting societies," a relic of Thalburg's medieval past. In those days all burghers had been mustered through their guilds to man the city walls. An annual shooting festival kept these part-time soldiers effective. When the old guilds were dissolved, five shooting societies took their place. In 1930 they held regular practice sessions, and their three-day shooting festival with parties, dances, prizes, and parades was the social event of the year. One member described the class structure: "The 'Gun Club of 1910' was for the broad masses; the 'Hunters' were mostly middle class; the 'Free-hand Shooters' were the upper 10 per cent." [25]

While these were strictly apolitical, many of the most innocent clubs became infused with nationalism. Thus the "Gardeners' Club" gave a garden-products show in 1930 at which the speaker attacked foreign competition: "It must be hammered into every German: Eat German fruit! Eat German vegetables! Buy German flowers!" [26]

Whatever social cohesion was not provided by the various formal clubs of Thalburg came from two informal types of social gatherings. One was the *Stammtisch;* the other could be called the "beer club." The *Stammtisch* was a group of men who ate lunch together on a specified day every week at the same restaurant around the same table (hence the name). They were closed and definite groups, some lasting the lifetime of the members, all marked by close friendship and free discussion. The "beer clubs" were similar; they consisted of regular meetings at some tavern for talk, beer, and possibly card-playing. They tended to involve mainly lower class people, while the *Stammtische* were generally middle and upper class in composition. Together, these groups were the most common and closest social organizations in the town. Mutual trust was a prerequisite for their flourishing.

The many clubs and societies cemented individual citizens together. Without them, Thalburg would have been an amorphous society. Yet few of them cut across class lines.

The institution which most clearly embraced the various divisions of the town was the public school system, a part of Thalburg's remarkable educational facilities. There were three public primary schools with 1,200 pupils, arranged so that children could also secure religious orientation. *Bürgerschule I* was Lutheran, the *Katholische Volksschule* served Catholic children, and *Bürgerschule II* was non-denominational. Each school had its own School

Advisory Council, elected by the pupils' parents. By prior discussion with Social Democratic leaders, working class parents were assured representation on these councils.

The secondary system involved a boys' *Gymnasium* and a girls' *Lyzeum,* both of which had college preparatory curricula and charged tuition. Together they enrolled about five hundred pupils, half of whom were from Thalburg. Most of these students were from the middle classes and most were strongly nationalistic.[27] For children who wanted vocational training there was a Business School with over three hundred pupils, mainly apprentices from artisan shops; a Merchants' Vocational School with fifty-five pupils, maintained by the Thalburg Merchants' Association; an Agricultural School which served several counties and was controlled by the Farmers' League, and a Home Economics School which was financed by the County Prefecture and graduated twenty-five girls a year.

These various schools minimized some of Thalburg's provincialism. Their teachers, according to a former newspaper reporter from the town, "controlled, shaped, and directed the intellectual and spiritual life of Thalburg." [28] But teachers also depended on the government for their income and position, with the Thalburg City Council and the Provincial Ministry of Education dividing the functions of a school board.

Thalburg possessed other cultural facilities, though much depended on private groups such as the Lecture Society or the Museum Society. The town sponsored a city band which gave weekly concerts on the Market Square and joined in public festivals. There was a public library with over two thousand volumes, but it was not much used. Workers preferred their own library at the Union Hall. There were two motion picture theaters and, for a while, a local operetta company.

The most important cultural institutions were the three daily newspapers. The oldest was the *Gräfische Hofs-Curier,*[29] founded in 1831 as the town's first newspaper. According to its editor-publisher it "put itself completely at the service of the National German." [30] In point of fact it was an organ of the German Nationalist party, and its editor was on the right wing of that party. Bias found its way into every article and in addition it was often a day or two late with the news. It had a small but stable readership of about six hundred subscribers in Thalburg, and probably considerably more in the county. The GHC made a definite attempt to appeal to the farming community.

At the other end of the political spectrum was the *Volksblatt*. Though published in a neighboring town, it carried enough local news to compete with other Thalburg newspapers. It was an organ of the Social Democratic party and made no pretense of neutrality. More than any other newspaper (except the Nazis') it was a scandal sheet, full of scathing attacks and red ink. About two thousand Thalburgers read it. Also printed on the *Volksblatt* press was the weekly pep-sheet of the *Reichsbanner,* called the *Thalburger Echo,* with a circulation of three thousand for Thalburg County.[31]

The local Nazi publication began in the summer of 1931 and was called *Hört! Hört!* ("Hear! Hear!"). It consisted of two pages, letter-sized, mimeographed on both sides, and used brown paper (the hue evoking scatological speculations from the *Volksblatt*). Its stated purpose was to provide news of Nazi doings and to "combat the lies of the reds which the bourgeois press seems incapable of doing."[32] It was slanderous, constantly under libel action, and periodically suppressed.

The third major newspaper was the *Thalburger Neueste Nachrichten,* founded in 1909 and primarily a business venture. Its editor was a member of the People's party and national news was often taken from the People's Party Press Service; but it tried to remain as moderate as possible so as to retain a large circulation. It was always first with the news, generally accurate, and gave the most complete coverage. Its circulation in Thalburg was close to four thousand. Middle class calm and efficiency were the outstanding characteristics of the TNN; its chief editorial concern was that city government operate in a businesslike manner.[33]

The government of Thalburg was in the tradition of efficient city government that in Germany dates from the reforms of Baron vom Stein. The constitution represented a cross between aldermanic and city manager governments. Voters elected a twenty-member council which then elected four Senators. All laws were passed by the council, which also formed committees to supervise administra-

tion. A Senator was chairman of each committee and could intervene in the administration of its area of competence (for example:
police, brewery, welfare department). The formal work of running the city rested upon the Mayor, or Burgomaster, a professional administrator. He was chosen by the Senators for a term
of twelve years and could expect to be continually re-elected, the
fixed tenure protecting him from the council's extreme powers. As
a professional the Mayor was expected to be impartial and was
paid an exceedingly high salary.

This carefully balanced system plus the long tradition of self-
administration resulted in a smoothly functioning city government
for Thalburg. It was with sober pleasure that the TNN reported,
in August of 1930, that while in fifty-six German towns with a
comparable population there was an average public debt of 7.74
marks per person, Thalburg had no deficit at all. The budget for
1930 balanced at 1,385,000 marks.[34]

Indeed, when one surveys Thalburg's economic, cultural, and
governmental structure the impression is that of a balanced, self-
contained entity. The one way in which the town was not integrated harmoniously was socially, where there were distinct class
divisions in almost every sphere of activity. This disunifying factor
grew to be politically important, and under the impact of steadily
declining economic conditions, politics became radicalized. In the
years after 1930 this situation split Thalburg wide open, led to
bloody riots and the deterioration of the democratic mood, and
culminated in the Nazi seizure of power. The Nazi answer to the
problem of class division was to abolish its expression by force.

CHAPTER 3

ENTER THE NAZIS

(Spring and Summer, 1930)

> *The evil which you fear becomes*
> *a certainty by what you do.*
> —GOETHE, *Egmont*

Mass extremism, intolerance, a desperate desire for radical change —all factors that make a stable democracy impossible—are difficult to evoke. When the community is secure, political agitators find themselves ranting in near-empty halls. It takes a haunting fear, a sudden awareness of hitherto unsuspected dangers, to fill the halls with audiences who see the agitator as their deliverer.

The average Thalburger looked upon himself as a *Spiessbürger:* calm, oblivious to great problems, satisfied with life, pleasantly filled with good food, modest hopes, and a sense of simple order. On Sunday afternoon Thalburgers are wont to take family walks in the neat and ancient woods above the town, slowly strolling along the well-kept paths to points where they can look across the Grade Valley to the misty western hills. And then, Sunday dinner digested, they return to the snug town with its medieval houses. The setting gives a sense of continuity to life; the old ways can be trusted; stability is both desirable and inherent.

But in 1930 new fear began to haunt the town, for the world depression was spreading and cascading quotations on the New York Stock Exchange affected even this remote valley in central Germany. It was the depression, or more accurately, the fear of its continued effects, that contributed most heavily to the radicalization of Thalburg's people. This was not because the town was deeply hurt by the depression. The only group directly affected were the workers; they were the ones who lost their jobs, stood idle on the corners, and existed on the dole. Yet paradoxically the workers remained steadfast in support of the status quo while the middle class, only marginally hurt by the economic constriction, turned to revolution.[1]

The economic structure of Thalburg kept the middle classes from being hard pressed. Merchants lost only a small portion of their trade. Artisans, apart from those in the building trades, found plenty of work. Civil servants had their wages reduced, but none of them lost their jobs, and if their pay was less, prices also dropped so that their relative position was not weakened. Total savings increased slightly during the years of the depression in Thalburg, and the number of savings accounts also rose. By 1933 over half of the adult population of Thalburg had savings accounts, and almost half of these were for substantial amounts: from 100 to 500 marks.[2]

But the depression engendered fear. Businessmen whose own enterprises were doing well worried about the general situation in Germany. Banks which had no difficulty collecting on loans began to reduce all credit allotments.[3] Only the workers were directly hurt, but the rest of the townspeople, haunted by the tense faces of the unemployed, asked themselves, "Am I next?", "When will it end?" Because there were no clear answers desperation grew.

In this situation, the voice of the Nazi began to be heard. Thalburg had previously ignored the NSDAP * (as it had ignored other extremist groups after the *Jung deutsche Orden* battle which was largely the work of outsiders); in the national elections of 1928 the total vote for the Nazi party in Thalburg was 123, or 2⅓ per cent of the votes. In the local elections of November, 1929, the Nazis received only 213 votes out of 5,133 cast.[4] Before the depression they were an insignificant fringe in Thalburg.

This was not for want of Nazi effort, for the Nazis were tireless

---

* *Nationalsozialistische deutsche Arbeiterpartei* (National Socialist German Workers' Party).

in putting their ideas before the public. In the early months of 1930 the NSDAP held a meeting roughly every other week, advertised with such titles as "The German Worker as Interest-Slave of Big International Capitalists" or "Saving the Middle Class in the National Socialist State." Like most Nazi meetings, each of these featured an outside speaker, promised a discussion after the speech, and charged an admission price of about thirty *pfennig* (the price of two loaves of bread). The meetings were held in the Thalburg Cattle Auction Hall which, according to the Socialists, simply exemplified the Nazi slogan "To Each His Own." But the hall was well suited to Nazi needs; it was cheap to rent, emphasized Nazi connections with the rural population, and was small enough so that a poor turnout would not be conspicuous. This was important, because, in these early months of 1930, attendance at the meetings was very small.[5]

But the meetings were not without effect, for they created an image of the Nazis. To the average Thalburger the Nazis appeared vigorous, dedicated, and young. A housewife put it clearly:

The ranks of the NSDAP were filled with young people. Those serious people who joined did so because they were for social justice, or opposed to unemployment. There was a feeling of restless energy about the Nazis. You constantly saw the swastika painted on the sidewalks or found them littered by pamphlets put out by the Nazis. I was drawn by the feeling of strength about the party, even though there was much in it which was highly questionable.[6]

Thus one function of the constant Nazi activity was to demonstrate to Thalburgers that Nazis really believed in the ideas they preached. But who were the Nazis? Most Thalburgers would have found it difficult to answer this question in 1930, for individual Nazis were rarely in the public eye. Yet most Thalburgers could have identified at least one member of Hitler's party: Walther Timmerlah, the owner of a bookstore on Broad Street. Walther Timmerlah came from an old Thalburg family; his father owned the town's first bookstore. One of his brothers fought and died in World War I and another became a university professor. Walther became a high school teacher in a German school in South America, where he lived from 1912 to 1921, when he returned to take over the bookstore:

It was shortly after the *Spartakus* uprising in the Rhineland; practically every windowpane was broken on the train in which I re-entered Germany, and the inflation was reaching fantastic proportions.

I had left Germany at the height of the power and glory of the Wilhelmine Reich. I came back to find the Fatherland in shambles, under a Socialist republic.[7]

In his years abroad Timmerlah had come to admire the writings of Houston Stewart Chamberlain. Shortly before the Munich *Putsch* he heard, at a literary tea, that Chamberlain had said of Hitler, "There's a man I could follow with my eyes shut," and consequently Timmerlah joined the NSDAP as the first member in Thalburg.

Walther Timmerlah was exceedingly well liked in Thalburg. A spare, lively man, he was gentle and kindly, friendly to everyone yet thoughtful and reserved enough to hold people's respect. His bookstore was the intellectual center of the town, for he was acquainted with many of the writers and poets the town admired, and he was chairman of the Thalburg Lecture Society. In addition, he was a prominent member of the Lutheran church. "Walther Timmerlah bears a heavy burden, for it was mainly his example that led many people to join the NSDAP," remarked one Thalburger. "People said, 'If he's in it, it must be all right.' "[8]

What were the ideas that drew men like Walther Timmerlah into the Nazi movement? To most Thalburgers the NSDAP was first and foremost an anti-Marxist party.[9] When a Thalburger thought of Marxism he was not likely to think of the Communists, who in 1928 had received only 28 of the 5,372 votes cast in the town. The "Marxist" party in Thalburg was the Social Democratic party, the SPD, the Socialists. The Socialists were the dominant political force in Thalburg. In the 1928 elections they cast almost 45 per cent of the town's votes—more than the next three largest parties combined.

The fact that the SPD was a non-revolutionary party (espousing, in fact, the status quo) and "Marxist" only in rhetoric probably did not matter to most of the town's burghers. The Socialists carried a red flag. They sang the *Internationale*. There had been laws against them in the days of Germany's glory. They were associated with the cataclysm of 1918. They represented the proletarians, the unwashed workers, the restive unemployed. They preached Marxism and class struggle. Their leaders who sat in the city council were cited by improbable occupations: "oiler," "union secretary," "track-walker." One never met them socially, yet there they were in the City Hall—touchy, aggressive, demanding. To oppose these radical apostles of equality was of paramount importance in a depression environment.

This was a fact in middle class thinking which the Nazis understood clearly. The Socialists, for their part, appreciated the Nazi threat very early. In March, 1930, their militia organization, the *Reichsbanner,* passed a resolution at their Thalburg County conference which called for "an energetic stand against . . . the ruffianly behavior of the NSDAP" and demanded action; "otherwise the comrades will turn to their own solutions." [10] A month later the *Reichsbanner* combined with the unions, the SPD, and the tiny Democratic party to sponsor a mammoth rally in opposition to the Nazis. Plans called for a series of parades, a demonstration on the Market Square, and a speech in the huge shooting hall, *1910er Zelt,* on the subject "Dictatorship or Democracy?" The affair was planned for April 27, a Sunday. This was what the Nazis were waiting for, and three days after the Socialists' announcement, Thalburg's Local Group of the NSDAP advertised that they would hold a meeting on the same day with a parade led by a band, a speech on the Market Square, and a "Gigantic Meeting in the Cattle Auction Hall" featuring a Nazi Reichstag representative. Moreover, the Nazi program was geared to conflict directly with the SPD's; both parades were to start at one in the afternoon, both demonstrations on the Market Square were set for two o'clock.[11]

This confluence was too much for the police. Because of previous outbreaks of violence, Prussia had prohibited all open-air meetings and processions of a political character for a three-month period which had just ended on March 30, 1930.[12] In the week of the two announcements there had been two outbursts of violence in Thalburg. In one, which occurred in front of a tavern on Broad Street, ten Nazis and Socialists had a short fight which sent one of the participants to the hospital in an ambulance. In the other fight, which took place in the woods above the town, eleven people were involved and one emerged with a broken nose.[13] In view of the tense situation the police forbade both April 27 meetings.

This provided the Nazis with another opening. In an advertisement emblazoned *"Trotz Verbot—Nicht Tot!"* ("Despite Prohibition—Not Dead!") they announced that their demonstration would be held as planned, but in a village about two miles from Thalburg. To the meeting the Nazis brought over two thousand people, drawing on the entire district. Eight hundred Stormtroopers marched in what the GHC called "a powerfully impressive recognition of Nazi ideas." After the event three truckloads of Stormtroopers passed through Thalburg scattering leaflets.[14] By this demonstration of organizational agility the Nazis had not only blocked the Socialist meeting; they had dominated the press and "powerfully impressed" Thalburgers with their size and determination. Their mood was so exultantly bellicose that at a County Council meeting the following day, they heckled the Socialist speaker to a point almost precipitating a brawl. The Nazi image was projecting itself upon Thalburg. Perhaps for this reason, May Day of 1930 was celebrated in full strength. Workers from all areas, especially the railroad workers, were present for the march through town in closed ranks. There was much drinking, many speeches, and of course the sentimental singing of the *Internationale*.[15]

The second idea of Nazism that Thalburgers recognized clearly in these early days was their claim to fervent patriotism and avid militarism. This was a foot in the door of respectability, as the number and nature of the town's nationalistic social organizations shows. The extent to which the people of Thalburg accepted these values was demonstrated by the big event of May, 1930—a visit to Thalburg by Field Marshal von Mackensen. The occasion was the fortieth anniversary of the founding of the Thalburger "Militia and Reservist Club."

The Field Marshal arrived on the morning of May 17, by special train, and was greeted by about a thousand people at the Thalburg station. A small girl presented him with flowers while the Thalburg city band played a stirring march. After inspecting the local veterans' clubs, drawn up in uniform on the platform, the Field Marshal mounted a white horse and rode up Broad Street followed by the band and the clubs, including contingents from neighboring towns. Crowds lined his route, many houses were bedecked with the old Imperial colors, and roses were strewn in his path at the Market Square, where a rousing cheer welcomed him. His brusque speech on the importance of a strong army led to the general singing of *Deutschland über Alles.* Three days of parades and festivities followed.[16]

This spectacle could hardly be matched by the Nazis, who were still reveling in their triumph of April 27 over the Socialists. The day before the Field Marshal arrived the Nazis held another of their small meetings in the Cattle Auction Hall, entitled "What's Going on in Thalburg? Confusing Newspaper Reports, Deliberate Errors, and the Forbidding of the Demonstration of April 27." [17] In the ensuing weeks of May and June the Nazis kept plugging away with meetings on unemployment, on the "Protocols of the Wise Men of Zion," and on youth in Germany.[18] But such meetings lacked the spark of controversy and the pageantry needed to impress the public.

In 1930 the Prussian Ministry of the Interior was trying a variety of expedients to limit the violence that was corroding German life. The main contributors to street fights were Hitler's Brownshirts, the SA.* The shirt was significant, for it emboldened its wearer and was a provocation to others. Hence, in 1930 the wearing of uniforms by political groups was prohibited in Prussia. This provided the Nazis with a new propaganda tool. In the last week of June the Thalburg NSDAP again drew on neighboring areas to stage a protest march over the Prussian uniform prohibition. About four hundred SA men marched (all wearing white shirts instead of brown) accompanied by a fife-and-drum corps from a larger town about ten miles from Thalburg. On the Market Square a vitriolic speech was given by a Nazi imported from Hamburg, featuring the slogan: "Heads Will Roll in the Sand." The rest of the afternoon was given over to speechmaking in the Cattle Auction Hall.[19]

This spurred the Socialists to counteraction. On June 26 the

---

* *Sturmabteilung,* literally "Storm Section," commonly known as Storm-troopers.

SPD sponsored a meeting in the spacious *1910er Zelt* on "The Crimes of the National Socialists." Over a thousand people heard what the TNN called "an objective and calm" analysis of Nazism. There were some catcalls but no violence, and when a Nazi attempted a rebuttal he was "easily dispatched by reference to his personal record," according to the TNN. The experience must have cut the Nazis, for the following day they distributed one-page leaflets attacking the SPD's speaker.[20]

A second event growing out of the Nazi demonstration against the uniform prohibition shows how seriously the Socialists took the Nazi threat. The Deputy Chief of Police for Thalburg was Senator Wilhelm Mahner, leader of the rightist faction in the City Council. He had been present at the Market Square meeting where the Nazi speaker promised that "heads will roll in the sand." Thalburg's Socialists thought that Senator Mahner should have had the police arrest the speaker for inciting to violence. Mahner's failure to act was taken as a sign that he was partial to Nazism. Consequently the *Reichsbanner* called a special public meeting at which it was determined to send a complaint to the Prussian Minister of the Interior and the Provincial Governor (both, providentially, Socialists). Mahner was then stripped of his police powers by the provincial authorities, and Senator Karl Hengst, the leader of the SPD faction in the city council, was made Deputy Police Chief in his stead.[21]

About the same time, the *Volksblatt* began to report incidents which suggested that the Nazis were violent and vicious. For example, it reported that when a Nazi leader told some of his SA men, marching in the parade in Thalburg, that they looked like "a herd of sheep," bystanders who had laughed were threatened with assault. It later recounted that a Nazi from Thalburg, while hitchhiking into town, showed the driver his revolver, fired two shots into the air, and then fled before the driver could call a policeman.[22] Thus even before the Reichstag election campaign of 1930, the political atmosphere in Thalburg was tense and the lines were drawn between the Nazis and the Social Democrats.

The Socialists had long since evolved a method of electioneering; they had been fighting election campaigns in Thalburg since the 1870's. The method was to make every effort to fuse the working class into a solid bloc by big, impressive demonstrations and meetings, and at the same time to give evidence to voters on the periphery that the SPD was solid, effective, and responsible. In August of 1930, when the campaign for the September Reichstag elections began, the SPD was favored by the coincidence that the opening of the campaign came about the time of the annual Constitution Day holiday, August 8. This was the chief festival of the Weimar Republic, with which the Social Democrats were so closely identified.

As early as June of 1930 the *Reichsbanner* announced that it would hold a torchlight parade and a dance in the *1910er Zelt* in support of the holiday. In addition they pressured other organizations to support Constitution Day by publicly excoriating clubs which refused to participate and promising "certificates of honor" to those who co-operated in the celebration. To assure a large crowd, teachers and pupils from the schools were required to attend. The torchlight parade involved over eight hundred torches and twenty-one clubs, including the Military Club and the Naval Society. In the words of the TNN, it was "the first really successful Constitution Day celebration in Thalburg." [23]

The SPD was also active on the legislative front. By June, 1930, there were 272 registered unemployed in Thalburg, a matter of obvious concern to the Socialists, who therefore presented the City Council with petitions and concrete plans for a limited public works project. In August these efforts paid off when the council adopted the SPD's program and voted funds for the lengthening of a few streets, the construction of a playground, and the erection of two extra sets of emergency barracks for the "shelterless." [24] The SPD could now enter the election campaign countering constructive action to Nazi demagoguery.

This was important, for the Nazis, spurred by the election campaign, became increasingly active. On August 10 they held their first election meeting, with an outside speaker, on the subject: "Eleven Years Republic—Eleven Years Mass Misery." A week later there was a second Nazi meeting featuring a *Gauleiter* who spoke on: "Down to the Last Tax Penny." This drew such a large crowd that many had to be turned away from the Cattle Auction Hall. Five days later there was a meeting featuring a member of the Prussian Diet, with standing room only, and a week after that yet another.[25]

The Social Democrats held fewer campaign meetings but strove to make them more impressive. On August 24 the SPD staged a "County Party Festival" involving six hundred *Reichsbanner* men who converged in four columns upon the Market Square. After numerous speeches there was a second parade through Thalburg with 1,200 participants and five bands. The parade wound up at a beer garden where there were speeches, songs, acrobatic acts, and, in the evening, a dance. Ten days later the SPD held a second mass rally in the *1910er Zelt*. Admission was only 20 *pfennig* (unemployed free) and the hall was jammed. A series of speeches defended Social Democratic policies and attacked the Nazis, a few of whom were on hand to heckle.[26]

The efforts of other parties were far less strenuous. The German Nationalist party held only one meeting, a small one. The GHC was their main campaigning instrument; in the last two weeks before the voting it ran at least five advertisements a day for Alfred Hugenberg and the DNVP.* By election eve the paper was filled almost exclusively with Nationalist party propaganda. Page one, for example, was completely taken up with a picture of Hugenberg, a poem in honor of the party, and an appeal to vote DNVP. The People's party also made extensive use of the TNN for election advertisements, with at least one a day for the three weeks preceding the voting. The general line of the DVP ** was "Order, law, morality, and unity," which left it free to attack both the SPD (for "causing the depression") and the Nazis (for "destructive radicalism"). This was also the theme of the DVP's one meeting during the campaign, at which the Nazis were condemned in astringent terms while the People's party was extolled as the carrier of the spirit of the late Gustav Stresemann and the solid core of the middle class. It was well attended by a quiet crowd.[27] The only other election campaign meeting was held under the auspices of the *Staatspartei,* a reactionary successor to the defunct Democratic party. The speaker called for orderly, middle class parliamentary

---

* *Deutschnationale Volkspartei* (German Nationalist People's Party).
** *Deutsche Volkspartei* (German People's Party).

rule, and for laws by which "Jews would be allowed citizenship only according to their character and accomplishments." [28] There was sparse attendance.

At the climax of the campaign there occurred an event which, though not directly related to the electioneering, must have aided the cause of nationalism, and thus probably the Nazis. In the last days of August the Seventeenth Infantry Regiment, one of the crack units of Germany's tiny *Reichswehr,* passed through Thalburg on its way to fall maneuvers. One company was quartered in the town for a night and the regimental band gave a concert on the Market Square which drew a large crowd and much applause. Both newspapers gave considerable space to the event, and the TNN noted slyly that the soldiers got along well with the local girls. Many children were up with the troops at six the following morning to watch the regiment march out, band still playing.[29]

The last days of the campaign were hectic, with all parties pasting up posters and distributing leaflets. Inevitably violence flared. Five days before the voting three Communists beat up a *Reichsbanner* man because he refused to accept a propaganda leaflet they were handing out. Shortly thereafter, another *Reichsbanner* man was beaten by two Nazi Stormtroopers. Feeling ran so high that it became necessary for the leaders to insist that *Reichsbanner* men not carry canes in their demonstration parades. The state authorities had also issued ordinances requiring all meetings to close by ten o'clock and providing stiff penalties for anyone found with a knife or cane on his person at a campaign meeting.[30]

On election eve the SPD held a final mass meeting in the *1910er Zelt* with a direct appeal to its followers to vote Socialist and do away with the "unsocial bourgeois-bloc cabinet." For their last meeting the Nazis appealed to the religious element in Thalburg by bringing in a Lutheran minister as a speaker. The Cattle Auction Hall was overflowing and the speaker assured his audience that Nazis were neither economic nor anti-religious radicals.[31]

On Sunday, September 14, 1930, Thalburgers cast their first ballots of the depression period. The voting was extremely heavy: 6,235 people voted, 94 per cent of those eligible. In Thalburg as all over Germany the most amazing result of the election was the meteoric rise of Nazi strength. In the Reichstag, Nazi representa-

tion went from twelve to 107 seats. The NSDAP in Thalburg went
from 123 votes (in 1928) to 1,742 votes, or 28 per cent of the
electorate. Nazi gains did not come at the expense of the SPD
(with 2,246 votes the Social Democrats actually gained slightly) or
at the expense of the People's party (which, with 788 votes, showed
a net loss of only forty-six compared to the 1928 elections). But
805 "new" votes were cast, and the various splinter parties lost
over a thousand votes; it was here that the Nazis garnered support.[32] At least three-quarters of the new voters voted NSDAP; at
least half of the Nazi vote gain came from those who had previously voted for another party. Votes were taken especially from
the Nationalist party and the *Staatspartei*. Since there were fewer
than 350 newly qualified voters, the Nazi gain had to come from
those who were not especially young but had either voted for
another party in 1928 or had not bothered to vote at all.

Regardless of the origin of its votes, it was clear that the NSDAP
had increased its backing by fifteen-fold. Over one-quarter of the
adult population of Thalburg now placed its hopes with Adolf
Hitler. The radicals, the extremists, the advocates of dictatorship
had arrived in force.

CHAPTER 4

EXPLOITING
VICTORY

(Autumn and Winter, 1930-1931)

> Democracies are most commonly
> corrupted by the insolence of
> demagogues.
> —ARISTOTLE, *Politics,* BOOK V

Every week in September, 1930, about six thousand men came to
Thalburg. They came from four counties to look for jobs or to
receive their dole at the Thalburg District Employment Office. The
Employment Office was located in one of the barracks of the old
Army compound north of town. The other barracks served as
emergency housing for the most destitute citizens of Thalburg—
the "shelterless." The barracks of the compound formed a quad-
rangle, and it was within this small area that the bitter unemployed
milled about while waiting their turn at the Employment Office
windows. Inevitably there were jostlings, arguments, eruptions of
the pent-up energy of idle men. Most of the jobless belonged to
the SPD but there were enough Nazis and Communists to guarantee frequent fights. In the supercharged political atmosphere, the
Army compound, with its daily influx of hungry and worried men,
was a concrete example to Thalburgers of what the deepening
depression could bring.

Burghers who watched the unemployed pass through Thalburg saw them as more than the symbol of economic catastrophe and potential social degradation. The misery of the jobless evoked suspicion and disgust more often than compassion. One teacher recalled primarily that "Masses of young men stood idle on corners and made a lot of noise, often insulting people who were passing by." A housewife had similar reactions: "There were great numbers of unemployed who just stood around—the bulk of them were just lazy and didn't want to work—theirs was a sad case." [1]

There were those who did look for work, though—for example at Thalburg's sugar beet refinery, which needed an additional two hundred men each fall after the crop was in. In September, 1930, over nine hundred applied for these jobs. The *Volksblatt* claimed that the refinery favored Nazi sympathizers because they were not organized in unions. It predicted gloomily that previous gains in wages and working conditions at the refinery would now be lost.[2] Even if wages were lower, the jobs were still desired, since they reestablished the worker's right to regular unemployment benefits. The maximum period a worker could receive these was one year—less depending on how long he had previously been employed. After the regular payments were exhausted, the jobless could draw "emergency" payments for an additional thirty-five weeks. After that the unemployed worker came under the care of the city Welfare Office, which ordinarily supported orphans, cripples, and the aged. There was no limit to the length of time a worker could stay on the Welfare Office rolls, as long as he had no other income.

Normal wages of a semi-skilled worker were about 30 marks per week; regular unemployment pay was 15 marks per week, and "emergency" benefits were only slightly less. But the welfare dole was only 8.75 marks per week for a married man, and half as much for a single man. The process of moving downwards through the grades was accelerated when it was decided in November, 1930, that "emergency" payments would be made only to those who could "prove need." This dismal and elastic concept was the first of many expedients designed to ease the strains caused by unemployment on the state and local budgets. As for the jobless, a class structure had developed among them by autumn, 1930, with those receiving regular unemployment compensation being the uneasy élite.[3]

Shopkeepers and other previously self-employed persons were excluded from the stages of degradation; if they lost their income they went directly on the welfare dole. In 1930, three of Thalburg's artisan shops went bankrupt, two of them about the time of the September elections.[4] Though each was a marginal enterprise to begin with, every case must have caused reflection among the townspeople. The Artisans' League believed its workers' troubles stemmed from illegal competition from unemployed journeymen. In November, 1930, it ran advertisements beseeching Thalburgers to contract immediately for any repair work they were planning, and to abstain from hiring illegal workers.[5]

The SPD, instead of commiserating with the burghers, exploited these bankruptcies. One of the September failures, a locksmith, happened to be a Nazi. The *Volksblatt* reveled in the gory details. According to its account, the locksmith's "property was in . . . a horrible situation. There were enormous and illegal debts." The final blow came when one of the locksmith's employees absconded with the remainder of the shop's money and also with a young lady. The *Volksblatt* described the whole event as "a good example of Nazi business methods." [6]

There were other ways in which the Socialists rubbed salt in the wounds of the middle class. At the time of the visit of the troops to Thalburg, the army had advertised payments for quarters, but with few takers. The *Volksblatt* exposed this shortly after the September elections. It thought it strange that "the rightists with big houses" did not offer their extra rooms to the soldiers, many of whom had to sleep in halls. It asked: "Where are the four hundred members of the Warriors' League? The four hundred men of the Militia and Reservists Club? And the countless hurrah-patriot clubs?" [7] Nor did the SPD hesitate to attack leading nationalists openly, to the extent of provoking feckless denials. This was the case with a Nationalist leader from Thalburg County, Baron von Barten, who wrote to the GHC in September, 1930, to say that he hired only a few foreign workers on his estate, that his pension was a small one which he deserved since he was wounded in the war, and that the SPD was responsible for high taxes and unemployment.[8] Nor did the touchiness of the Socialists themselves when attacked endear them to Thalburgers. In 1930, for example, Senator Hengst sent a mimeographed copy of the Uniform Prohibition Decree to all SA men in Thalburg County and received a bitter reply from one Stormtrooper. Hengst took it to court where it was found slanderous; he was awarded 50 marks.[9]

Thus many Thalburgers felt there were good reasons to oppose the SPD, some obvious and rational, others stemming from general disquietude over the threatening economic situation. If the burghers wanted the Socialists cut down they could argue that they were simply restoring the traditional order. In Prussia, prior to 1918, towns like Thalburg were run by a closed clique of wealthy people. The instrument of exclusion was the "three class" voting system by which those individuals who paid the highest taxes controlled the City Council. The revolution of 1918 swept away all monetary suffrage distinctions and introduced direct, equal, and secret balloting. It was this that suddenly enabled the SPD, with its mass backing, to have a dominant voice in the Thalburg City Council for the first time in the town's history.[10]

The political vehicle used to combat the Socialists prior to the rise of Nazism, was the Civic Association (*Bürgerliche Vereinigung*).* If the bewildering variety of national parties had competed independently in local elections, the Socialists, with their solid block of votes, would have controlled the city government completely. To prevent this, all those who stood to the right of center joined in support of a common list of candidates. But the Civic Association was more than a local political alliance; it was also an independent entity with its own officers, treasury, and division of candidates by occupation: artisans, retail merchants, etc. The cement of the organization was, nonetheless, antipathy to the SPD.

The Chairman of the Civic Association was Senator Mahner, owner of a small business and a member of the DNVP. He was

---

* *Bürgerlich* is impossible to translate in one word, since it means "civic," "bourgeois," and "conservative" in German. Henceforth *Bürgerliche Vereinigung* will be rendered Civic Association, but the reader must bear in mind that the term also had the connotations of political and economic conservatism as well as social exclusiveness.

staunchly Lutheran and unabashedly reactionary. From 1924 to 1929 the Civic Association had the largest representation on the Thalburg City Council, which was divided among eight Civic Association councilmen, seven Social Democrats, and five from the Civil Servants party. In November, 1929, the SPD increased its representation to nine while the other two parties each lost a seat. Had the Socialists won two more seats they would have had an absolute majority.

In the September, 1930, Reichstag elections, Thalburg's Social Democrats increased their vote slightly again. The leaders began to consider new areas of activity, but the choice they made refocused the antipathy of the town's middle classes. Due in October was the election of Elders for Thalburg's Lutheran church. Like the rest of the townspeople, nine-tenths of the Social Democrats were Lutherans. Yet they had hitherto been unrepresented on the Church Board and felt, moreover, that Thalburg's ministers emphasized nationalism far too much. Hence the Socialists prepared a list of candidates for the Elders' election.

The burghers saw this as an intolerable challenge. The Civic Association called a meeting on October 23 where Senator Mahner attacked the SPD as anti-religious. He demanded a heavy vote to defeat the "Marxists." Advertisements by the Civic Association and the Evangelical Men's Club charged that "For the first time, the anti-church SPD wants to drag the hate and agitation of partisan politics even into church. . . ." [11]

Most Socialists were embarrassed by this attack. In their own meeting, held shortly before the election, the speaker began by expressing his regrets that politics had entered the church, where it did not belong. He insisted, nonetheless, that since most Social Democrats were Lutherans, they had a right to representation. The sharpness of the campaign could have been avoided if the rightists had been willing to make a compromise list of candidates with the SPD. He hoped that nothing like this would occur in the future.[12]

If the Socialists were embarrassed and the rightists outraged, the Nazis were delighted, for this gave them a new chance to portray themselves as effective opponents of "Marxism." They had by no means been inactive since their election victory in mid-September. Ten days after the election they held a discussion evening and five

days after that a member of the Reichstag was brought in for a
speech. A few days later, there were two showings of the film,
"The Growth of National Socialism," each with a speaker afterward. Finally, on October 12, a meeting featured the chief candidate in the previous elections, now a member of the Reichstag.
Thus in the month following the election, Thalburg's Nazis held
as many public functions as they had in the month preceding
the election—a prime example of their tactics of perpetual
campaigning.[13]

The September election campaign taught Thalburg's Nazis that
their best drawing cards were religion and nationalism, preferably
combined. This lesson was now put to work to exploit the middle
class uproar over the SPD's entry into the Church Elders' election.
The day before the voting the NSDAP staged a rally featuring a
Lutheran pastor who was also a Nazi member of the Reichstag.
The announced topic was "Marxists as Murderers of the German
Volk in the Pay of the Enemy." Confident of a mass audience, the
Nazis rented the *1910er Zelt,* which could contain 1,500 people.
Fifty *pfennig* admission was charged, and since the meeting was
aimed directly at the middle class, no reduction in price was
offered to the unemployed.

Nazis expectations were fully justified; so many people came to
the meeting that there was standing room only. The pastor's main
topic was the nature of the NSDAP, which he likened to the old
Imperial Army in that both represented the whole of the German
people and not any specific group. Near the close of his speech
he dwelt on the Elders' election in Thalburg which he said proved
the SPD's tyrannical motives. He exhorted the audience to vote the
"Non-Partisan" ticket.[14]

The following day, a Sunday, the elections were held. In earlier
church elections only 17 per cent of the Lutheran community had
voted; this time about 60 per cent voted. The heavy voting was
aided by a Civic Association transportation service to bring voters
to the polls. The SPD mustered only a quarter of its usual voting
strength and its candidates were defeated by a margin of five to
one. A solidly conservative set of Elders was elected.

Though they had not run candidates, the Nazis could be well
satisfied. The campaign had exacerbated the burghers' repugnance

for the SPD. The Nazis could claim a heavy contribution to the defeat of the Socialists through their meeting, which was also their first real mass meeting in Thalburg. Best of all, the burghers had been taught that the SPD could be beaten.

The remainder of 1930 was filled by the Nazis with frequent but fairly ordinary meetings, all held at the Cattle Auction Hall. On November 9 the Nazis commemorated those who had died in Hitler's abortive "Beer Hall" *Putsch* of 1923. Four days later there was a discussion evening and two days after that a speech on "The Echo in Foreign Lands of the September 14 Elections." Early in December a speech on economics emphasized Nazi ties to the lower middle class, and a week before Christmas another speech attacked the SPD. The year 1930 closed with a Nazi Christmas party for children and an "Evening of Entertainment" for the adults.[15]

For the SPD there was work to be done beyond propaganda activity and forays into church politics. In October the SPD faction in the City Council proposed an extensive public works project to get the unemployed off the streets. The plan, sections of which were used by the Nazis after they came to power, involved improvements in Thalburg's parks and streets. Its main feature was that it would provide much work and little expenditure for tools or materials. Only one measure of this ambitious program was passed—the widening of a forest path in the town-owned woods—but it was the first project to use unemployed workers exclusively.[16]

In the County Council where the SPD held ten of the twenty-one seats and, thanks to a coalition with the two "Middle Party" delegates, controlled the council, the whole SPD program was voted. By October, 180,000 marks were allocated for works projects. But it was of no benefit since by December rising welfare costs from unemployment put the county so deeply in debt that nothing could be carried out.[17] In the two years to follow, the County Council was impotent because of financial weakness. Since the voting was predictable after the formation of the SPD coalition, the Council became a sounding board for the participating politicians. In December of 1930, for example, the right faction expostulated against the *Volksblatt* and in the ensuing debate Karl Hengst attacked the Nazis so vehemently that the entire rightist faction left the session in protest.[18] The possibility of increasing taxes was limited. The mere mention of this brought a protest meeting by the Civic Association in December, 1930, which declared that higher taxes would be "unbearable." At this meeting August Thiere, a Thalburg teacher who was a Nazi, gave the Civic Association a long lecture establishing that the Treaty of Versailles was the root of Thalburg's financial problems.[19]

The growing Nazi threat caused as much concern to the Social Democrats as the depression. On November 22, the *Reichsbanner* held a crowded meeting on the subject of Mussolini's Italy. The speaker compared German democracy to the Italian dictatorship, with direct allusions to the Nazi program. Many Thalburgers sensed the danger. The *Reichsbanner,* which had numbered one hundred members before the September elections, reported that seventy new members had joined in the interim. A few weeks later, on a grey Sunday afternoon, the *Reichsbanner* held another meeting, this time on the Market Square. A parade with five flags and a fife-and-drum corps brought out a large audience. The speaker's theme was the Nazi slogan, "Heads Will Roll in the Sand." He declared that the *Reichsbanner* was ready to fight in defense of the Republic, but that it would not strike the first blow. Two days later, a members' meeting reported thirty-nine new *Reichsbanner* men in the past few weeks.[20] By the beginning of 1931, Thalburg's *Reichsbanner* counted three hundred members, including a fifty-six man Youth Section.[21] Democracy would not go without a fight in Thalburg.

Social Democratic determination did not deter Nazi intentions, nor did it lessen political tension, which rose sharply with the coming of the new year. New Year's Day, 1931, saw the first incident of violence. Three Nazis, apparently drunk, dragged Karl Hengst's teenage son into the men's room of one of the town's hotels and beat him. Several *Reichsbanner* men rushed to the rescue and only the coolness of the hotel owner averted a general mêlée.[22] Also within the first week of 1931, the SPD held a mass rally to point up the Nazi threat. The *1910er Zelt* was filled to hear a Socialist Reichstag member insist that everything must be done to keep the Nazis from getting into the government. He predicted accurately: "If that bunch ever once gets in, democracy will be lost." [23]

Thalburg's Nazis began 1931 with a Sunday afternoon meeting in the Cattle Auction Hall. It was typical of those held in early 1930. The speaker was from Hannover and the topic typical: "Enchained Justice—German Law in the Straitjacket of a Party-State?" [24] Such meetings had become unsatisfactory to Thalburg's Nazis after their experience with mass audiences the previous year and in view of the SPD's recent rally. What was needed to fill halls was an appeal to nationalism. On January 16, 1931, the TNN reported excitedly: "The NSDAP has been able to get the well-known U-Boat Captain Hersing to come to Thalburg for a speech. Hersing is the second most famous U-Boat hero of the World War and sank innumerable ships." [25] Nazi advertisements were exultant:

GERMAN PEOPLE AWAKEN!   ON TO THALBURG!
Sunday, January 25
at 3 p.m. in the *1910er Zelt* there will speak
Party Comrades:
1. Corvette-Captain (Ret.) *Hersing,* commander of U-Boat 21.
2. The famous agrarian revolutionary *Blankenmeyer* (of Oldenburg).
   Expense-contribution: Advance sales 50 pfennig at Timmerlah's Bookstore; at the box office, 60 pfennig.
FREE DISCUSSION!   OUT WITH THE MASSES!
NSDAP, *Ortsgruppe* Thalburg [26]

To add spice to the affair the Nazis told a leading figure of the Thalburg SPD that he could have forty-five minutes' time to speak at the Nazi meeting and could bring *Reichsbanner* men with him if they paid 30 *pfennig* admission. Before the meeting the SA from the whole of Thalburg County marched through the town, with the *Reichsbanner* marching behind them. Ten minutes before the Nazi meeting began, 150 *Reichsbanner* men appeared at the *1910er Zelt*. Walter Eckstein, the Nazi leader in charge of the Hersing meeting, was somewhat shocked by this and declared he would admit only twenty *Reichsbanner* men at 30 *pfennig*—the rest would have to pay the full price. This touched off a heated argument during which an additional 150 *Reichsbanner* men material-

ized. The Nazis hurriedly got the police to close the doors, whereupon the Socialists repaired to the Market Square and held a
counter-demonstration. When both meetings broke up tempers were
still high and a brawl between the SA and *Reichsbanner* was only
narrowly averted.[27]

In the two weeks that followed, two more battles almost broke
out when *Reichsbanner* men tried to stop Nazi parades.[28] On
February 8, the SPD held another mass rally featuring Professor
Eric Noelting on the subject, "National Socialism: Its Beginning
and Its End." Over a thousand republicans crowded the hall and
heard an exact description of what Hitler intended to do: "Whoever wants to make a successful *Putsch* in Germany must also hold
the power of the state in his hands. Therefore Hitler wants to get
into the government, but never *out*." [29]

The Nazis were beginning to feel oppressed by Socialist militance. Shortly after the Noelting meeting, one Nazi tore the
cockade off the hat of a *Jungbanner* member and was promptly
knocked flat by nearby *Reichsbanner* men. There was also a rash
of incidents at the Employment Office, the victims being Nazis
from other places who had come to Thalburg to collect their
compensation payments.[30] In the City Council, the SPD moved
that the town no longer buy its school books through Walther
Timmerlah's bookstore, since Timmerlah was a Nazi. Fortunately
for him, the Civil Servants party joined with the Civic Association
to defeat the motion. A conservative councilman lamented even
the suggestion, "since politics change every day in our world." [31]

The Nazi response to the Noelting meeting was to change the
title of a previously planned meeting from "The Politicos into the
Bacon, the Folk into the Pigsty," to "A Correction of the Announced Noelting Theme, namely, 'National Socialism at Its Beginning, the SPD at Its End.' " Furthermore, they cut their admission price for unemployed persons from 15 *pfennig* to nothing.[32]
But neither this meeting, nor one held a week later directed to
"young workers of the hand and brain," drew much of a crowd,
and so the Nazis turned to another of Thalburg's peculiarities, its
high proportion of government employees, for a mass meeting. The
theme was to be "The Civil Service and National Socialism" and
the speaker a railroad man, "the famous old fighter, Locomotive-

Engineer Dreher, a Reichstag representative." The *1910er Zelt* was rented and the admission price was cut to 30 *pfennig.*

The meeting drew a crowd in excess of 1,500. A strong contingent of SA was on hand and thus the atmosphere became tense when a body of *Reichsbanner* men entered the hall in closed formation, with flags flying, and proceeded to heckle the speaker, dwelling particularly on the fact that he never touched on his preannounced theme. According to the TNN, which covered the matter in an editorial appealing for political moderation, "a great tumult ensued and only the reasonableness of the leaders on both sides kept order." [33]

Socialist political activity kept pace with the Nazis during this hectic February. The *Reichsbanner* was engaged in preparing itself to thwart a Nazi *Putsch.* Shortly before the incident described above, a test alarm was held when the *Reichsbanner* District Commander made a surprise visit to Thalburg. With only one hour's notice, one hundred *Reichsbanner* men were assembled at the Market Square to hear their commander give a pep talk and to make a propaganda parade. The following week the county organization of the SPD met and was told that now was the time to defeat the Nazis. Every Socialist was exhorted to recruit one more man. A few days later, the whole county organization of the *Reichsbanner* gathered to celebrate the seventh anniversary of its founding. There was a parade of nine hundred *Reichsbanner* men, all from Thalburg County, with twenty flags, two bands, and two fife-and-drum corps. There were speeches at the Market Square and on the circus grounds, and a dance at the *1910er Zelt.* The theme expressed prevailing fears of a Nazi *Putsch:* "The *Reichsbanner* will be strong enough to protect the Republic." As though to punctuate this, a contingent of SA crashed the dance, and, after they were expelled by the police, threw a chair leg through a window of the hall.[34] Nor did the Socialists during these days forget their antipathy to capitalism. This was the subject of a play put on by the Free Unions on Valentine's Day, which drew an audience of four hundred.[35]

Not to be outdone, the Nazis staged another mass rally at the *1910er Zelt,* on February 26, with a former Army lieutenant and another speaker on "Twelve Years of Republic—Where's the Freedom?" [36] The town was becoming saturated with political activity. In the thirty-one days since the Nazi meeting which featured the U-boat hero, there had been twelve different political events: parades, rallies, meetings—six by the Social Democrats and six by the Nazis. The *1910er Zelt* was in almost constant use, and most of the events had been tinged with violence or at least extreme tension. Charges of political malpractice were also in the air. On February 27, the GHC, quoting from a Nazi newspaper article, charged that "scandalous conditions . . . rule at the Thalburg City Construction Office." The article alleged that workers who would not march in an SPD parade were "unbelievably terrorized" and that one worker had to quit his job to protect himself. Since the Construction Office was in an SPD Senator's area of competence, the GHC demanded investigations and suspensions. Unfortunately for the Nationalists, the City Council had already investigated the matter and found the Nazi allegations to be devoid of fact. The *Volksblatt* was happy to report this the day after the GHC's editorial, and went on to label the editorial "another fat bourgeois swindle." [37]

The Socialists undoubtedly felt, by the end of February, 1931, that they were successfully meeting the Nazi challenge. The arrogance of the SA had been matched by the militancy of the *Reichsbanner*. Nazi charges were refuted, Nazi plots exposed. Every Nazi meeting or rally was countered by a Socialist rally. But in the half-year since the September elections the whole political atmosphere of the town had changed. Politics was becoming radicalized, with mass meetings, demonstrations, and street clashes replacing the rather sleepy provincial approach that had been the norm in Thalburg except during election campaigns.

This shift was bound to have its effect upon the watching burghers. The times were changing drastically. In the game of matching radicalism with the Nazis, the SPD could not hope to win, for they lacked the brutality and irrationality of their opponents. Furthermore, every move in the game simply added to the troubled spirit of Thalburg's middle classes, making them more vulnerable to extremist appeals.

CHAPTER 5

AUTHORITARIANS UNITE

(Spring and Summer, 1931)

> Nazi propaganda consists entirely
> of a perpetual appeal to whatever
> is swinish in man.
> —DR. KURT SCHUMACHER (SPD)
> Reichstag speech,
> February 23, 1932

To the Socialists the Nazis were a threat only insofar as they might attempt an armed *coup d'état*. Serious politics was a matter of rational appeals and positive results. Since the NSDAP seemed incapable of either, they could not constitute a political threat. Nazi propaganda seemed to illustrate this, for it consistently pinned two labels on the SPD, *"Marxisten"* and *"Bonzen"* (approximately, "ward-heelers," with overtones of corruption). The labels are of course contradictory; it is difficult to conceive of fervid radicals who are simultaneously comfortably venal. But effective propaganda need not be logical as long as it foments suspicion, contempt, or hatred. The choice of the two words not only had that effect upon the bourgeoisie, it summed up the dilemma of the Social Democrats precisely.

The SPD was not "Marxist," though it used language that made it appear so. Thus it was doubly encumbered, for it was unwilling to be a revolutionary party at a time when the best defense of democracy may have been social revolution, and secondly, its revolutionary tradition made it incapable of seeking or receiving the support of any but the working class. Furthermore, the SPD's defense of democracy meant, in practical terms, defense of a status quo which was identified in the minds of most Thalburgers with national humiliation and economic ruin.[1]

The SPD's tradition as a proletarian party was the most serious impediment to a *modus vivendi* with Thalburg's middle classes. The town's class structure and the social antipathies felt by the middle classes contributed to this: Thalburgers resented the Social Democrats' insistent class consciousness even though it was largely a reflection of that of the bourgeoisie. Townspeople who had working contact with individual Socialists conceded that they were good and able men, but still distrusted the SPD in general.[2]

From the Socialist point of view there seemed little to gain from an alliance with Thalburg's middle classes. The town had a permanent rightist majority and the SPD often felt oppressed by it. Especially after 1930, the bourgeois elements in Thalburg seemed bent on weakening the SPD and willing to back the Nazis to accomplish this. To Thalburg's workers, the town's businessmen seemed exclusively Nazi.[3] By tradition, organization, and ideology, the workers expected to rely upon themselves alone. Why should the SPD appeal to the middle classes at the risk of losing the allegiance of their main support, the workers? If the SPD relaxed its ritualistic radicalism, the Communists were there to lure off dissidents. Thus neither the Socialists nor the moderate middle class worked for a rapprochement.

As the depression deepened, it was no longer radicalism that alienated burghers from the SPD but the rhetorical quality of that radicalism. No one believed that the Socialists would really attempt fundamental economic changes. Many blamed the Social Democrats for not being radical enough (in economic matters) while still resenting their social composition and "leveling" goals.[4] Thus the SPD could not keep the middle classes from flocking to the banners of the NSDAP, for the Nazis were known as real radicals. It was not enough to preach loyalty to democracy or to the Republic. Most Thalburgers obviously felt no reason to respond to such an appeal. The way to undercut the Nazis was not by blind opposition but by a counter-program sufficiently attractive to awaken in the hearts of the bourgeoisie the kinds of hopes that the Nazis were able to arouse.

Instead, the Social Democrats concentrated on holding the loyalty of the working class and saw the Nazi threat in terms of armed rebellion. Thus, no matter how hard they tried, Thalburg's Socialists did not provide effective opposition to the Nazis.

Most of Thalburg's SPD members were born into the working class. Belief in Socialism tended to come more from family background than from subsequent conviction. The typical SPD member's father had worked at the town's railroad yards, had been a follower of the SPD since before the turn of the century, and had reared his children as Socialists. Thus the average Social Democrat had the almost unconscious commitment to Socialism that the average American worker seems to have to trade unionism.[5] Nazism made few gains among these people. Almost all Thalburgers knew this and voting statistics demonstrate it.[6] Far from joining or backing the Nazis, Thalburg's workers were known for their extreme anti-Nazism. As one SPD leader put it when his wife questioned him about the dangers of his opposition to Nazism, "I'd rather lose everything than my freedom." [7]

This sober determination characterized most Social Democratic leaders. They were not flamboyant men. They rose through the ranks to posts as union secretaries, consumers' cooperative chairmen, and other roles in the Socialist *Apparat* on the basis of their ability and seriousness, not because of charismatic qualities. When they were young men, one of the key slogans of the Socialist movement was: "Knowledge Is Power!" In toilsome hours after their regular workday, the youthful energy of the aspiring Socialist leader was spent in studying economics, history, or social welfare laws. To those whose social position made them disparage the proletarian party, these men might easily appear to be *Bonzen,* for they were certainly not revolutionaries.

Three of Thalburg's SPD leaders stood out among their quiet colleagues—Karl Bette, Willi Brehm, and Senator Karl Hengst. Bette, the *Reichsbanner* leader, was described by a non-admirer as "a brutal and inconsiderate man." [8] He was short and powerful with a voice that had been made hoarse and weak by a gassing in World War I. Though his official occupation was *Krankenbesucher* (i.e., he investigated insurance-receivers in the town hospital), he was essentially a politician. In addition to his work with the *Reichsbanner* and the offices he held in the SPD Local and other worker organizations, he was Speaker of the City Council and a delegate to the County Council. Touchy and aggressive, he alienated many people by his roughness, but he was very much respected by the workers and was cool in a fight.

His assistant and leader of the *Reichsbanner* youth section, Willi Brehm, was just the opposite. Tall, slim, and exceedingly boyish, he had a clear and winning speaking voice. He had once intended to be a singer and had received vocal training, but he gave it up to become a clerk in the county administration. While the County Prefect was a Social Democrat, Willi Brehm was given as much free time as he wanted to work for the *Reichsbanner,* though this ended when the county received a conservative Prefect in 1932. Honesty, modesty, and kindliness shone from Willi Brehm's face; most Thalburgers liked him.

The real leader of Thalburg's SPD was Karl Hengst. He was chairman of the Thalburg SPD Local and of the county organization, too. He was Senator in the Thalburg city government and SPD majority leader in the County Council. He was also delegate to the Hannoverian Provincial Legislature and a member of its twelve-man executive committee. To many he was the embodiment of the Social Democratic party in Thalburg.

Karl Hengst was not a worker. He owned a small tobacco shop in the heart of the old town. He was rather distinguished looking, with sandy hair and a florid face. The conservative County Prefect, von Altberg, described him as "a man of great natural talent, but violent; he imparted a violent character to the whole SPD Local." [9]

Senator Hengst was that rarity, the completely partisan man. He was capable of the most oily political double-talk but managed to make it sound forthright and honest. He had great self-confidence, courage, and presence of mind (his record in the war was distinguished), but could also use refined invective and vituperation. With all this he was a good judge of character and believed in the ultimate triumph of rationality and love, though only in the misty future and not without a struggle. Most Thalburgers accepted him for what he was—the complete politician—but the town's workers idolized him. Finally, he possessed two other attributes: full commitment to democracy and considerable common sense. He was superbly fitted to lead Thalburg's SPD but totally incapable of building a supra-Socialist alliance. His opponents hated him but gave him grudging admiration. Few underestimated Karl Hengst.

This, then, was Thalburg's Social Democratic party, the town's only defenders of democracy and its only bulwark against Nazism. They failed the test they were put to in the years before 1933. That they were incapable of victory did not mean, however, that they were without courage and dignity.

After its vigorous efforts in January and February of 1931, the SPD no longer attempted to match the Nazis meeting for meeting. The Nazis, however, did not relax their agitational pace. In the first week of March they held a different type of meeting, an "SA Recruitment Evening with Theatrical Presentations and a German Dance." [10] Five days after that, another famous personage was brought in for a speech: "Edmund Heines (member of the Reichstag), the Chief Defendant in the . . . Stettin Feme Murder Trial." Heines had been in the highly nationalistic Free Corps in the early twenties, where he had "executed" a "traitor" after a kangaroo-court trial, and had gone unpunished in a trial before rightist judges. This meeting was held in the *1910er Zelt,* and according to the GHC, the audience all cheered when Heines got to the point in his story where he shot his victim, and after that, there was a mounting wave of applause, culminating in a final storm of hand-clapping, cheers, and the "Horst Wessel Song." [11]

By way of contrast to such bloodthirstiness, the Nazis next decided to arouse the populace against Orthodox Jewish methods of cattle slaughtering. Consequently they sponsored a speech on this subject, with color slides, by the chairman of a Hannoverian society for the prevention of cruelty to animals. At the speech, Thalburg's Nazi leaders put themselves on record as being opposed to such practices.[12]

The *Volksblatt* was quick to point out the almost comical irony of "the Nazis screaming about 'cruel Jewish slaughtering methods as the greatest cultural disgrace of the twentieth century,'" while they were also "constantly talking about 'heads rolling in the sand.'" But apparently some people took the Nazi charges seriously, for the *Volksblatt* also devoted a long article to refuting the specific charge that animals were being cruelly handled by the rabbi in the town slaughterhouse. It also noted that "Nazi elements frequently hang around the slaughterhouse and are discourteous to Jews there." This brought results; the SPD Senator in charge of the slaughterhouse brought suit against the Nazi newspaper which made the original charge of "Gruesome Torture of Animals at the Thalburger Slaughterhouse," while the Thalburg Senate issued a warning to two Nazis that if they were discourteous to Jews again they would be forbidden to enter the slaughterhouse.[13]

The incessant agitation drew other parties into activity, especially the Nationalists, who felt that Nazi success could be matched by a similar appeal. Already in February, the *Stahlhelm* (which locally stood in the same relationship to the DNVP as the SA to the Nazis) held its first meeting in Thalburg in over a year, featuring "His Excellency von Henning auf Schoenhott." As was to be the case with almost all Nationalist functions, the affair was held in the town's best hotel, the Georg-Friedrich, and admission was free. (The hotel was owned by a member of the DNVP.) The speaker, in addition to attacking Liberals, Marxists, Jews, and the SPD, proclaimed that Hitler was the "drummer of Nationalist ideas" and that "Bismarck was the first National Socialist." Thirty new members joined the *Stahlhelm*. A month later the DNVP held a meeting featuring a Nationalist party Reichstag member. Three weeks after that there was another *Stahlhelm* meeting, this time with a motion picture as a drawing card.[14] Furthermore, the Civic Association held an open-air meeting in March at which Senator Mahner attacked the Treaty of Versailles and prophesied that when Germany became internally united she would once again become a world power. A band was present to lead the crowd in singing *Deutschland über Alles*.[15]

The Communists also were active, holding their first parade and meeting in Thalburg. For their meeting they rented the Riding Hall, which, while it was mammoth, was not really a meeting hall. Fewer than one hundred people came to the Communist meeting.[16]

Thalburg was beset by so many differing political points of view that it is hard to imagine anything approaching common political action. Yet in March, 1931, an event was at hand which would show that the Communists and the Nazis, the Nationalists and the People's party could all join hands—at least for purposes of opposing the SPD.

The bastion of democracy in Weimar Germany was the State of Prussia, which in Germany's peculiar federal system constituted three-fifths of the population and land area of Germany. Prussia was ruled by a coalition of the Catholic Center, which drew its strength from the Roman Catholic Rhineland provinces, and the SPD, whose support came from the industrial areas of the Ruhr, Silesia, Berlin, and the Hanseatic harbor towns. As long as the SPD-Center coalition conducted the government in Prussia, democracy was safe.

After the first hard winter of the depression, both the Nazis and the Communists believed they had enough increased support to break the coalition's majority, if elections were held. To have elections, however, the Prussian Parliament would have to be dissolved, which the governing coalition refused to do. The Weimar Constitution provided another way. If enough signatures could be gathered on a petition, a referendum could be held, and if enough votes were gained on the referendum, dissolution of the Prussian Parliament would be forced despite the government's majority within the Parliament.

The Nazis conceived the idea, and the Communists were quick to support them (following the Comintern's tortured thinking that defeat of the Social Democrats was the prime goal). The Nationalists, the Hannoverian party, and the People's party also pledged aid, though at least one Thalburg People's party leader refused to join in this purely negative maneuver.[17] Most of the welter of splinter parties followed suit. The Civic Association also participated; Senator Mahner explained that while it existed for local politics, a change in the Prussian government would have a decisive effect on local government too.[18]

Nazi meetings slowed down during the petition campaign, which absorbed most of their energies. To be effective the campaign required an actual gathering of signatures; propaganda would not

have been enough. Nevertheless, the Nazis found time to hold at
least one public function, a speech at the Cattle Auction Hall on
"Position of Civil Servants and Government Employees on the Petition to Dissolve the Prussian Parliament; also, The End of Unemployment." The speaker was a former Prussian civil servant
who was now a Nazi Reichstag delegate.[19] The Civic Association's
meeting during the campaign was a larger one, held at the *1910er
Zelt*. Senator Mahner attacked the SPD and its government in
Prussia as "dictatorial." He urged all Thalburgers to sign the petition and "break the power of the SPD." [20]

The Socialists were concerned by the petition campaign, primarily because they feared Nazi pressure tactics. No ballot booths
were involved and the voter, confronted with a Stormtrooper on
his doorstep, had to say "yes" or "no" openly. The *Volksblatt*
charged that the Nazis were using the petition lists to boycott any
businessman who did not sign. The SPD was especially concerned
about Nazi intimidation in the somewhat isolated villages of Thalburg County. Later, when the referendum was held, the *Volksblatt*
was able to show that in some villages in Thalburg County fewer
people voted "yes" than had signed the petition.[21]

The Social Democrats' answer to this was to increase the activity of the *Reichsbanner*. On March 24, a week before the campaign opened, the *Reichsbanner* held a meeting in the Market
Square. Bette was the speaker, and he pulled out all stops. He
referred to Hitler's cowardice at the time of the Munich *Putsch,*
reviewed Nazi political assassinations, and castigated the murderer
Heines, whom the Nazis had featured as a speaker. Two days thereafter one hundred Thalburg *Reichsbanner* men undertook a thirty-
five kilometer march through the county with speeches afterwards
in the Market Square. A few days later it was announced that the
Reichsbanner had acquired twenty-two additional members and
expelled one who was a spy for the Nazis.[22]

In the very midst of the signature-gathering for the petition, on
April 10, the *Reichsbanner* made another demonstration. About
two hundred *Reichsbanner* men marched, with a fife-and-drum
corps in the van. The parade was led directly through the hillside
residential district and also stopped twice in front of the offices

of the Civic Association to hoot and shout. Behind this was the anger of SPD leaders over the conservatives' collaboration with the Nazis. In the Market Square, Bette gave what the TNN called an "incendiary speech" against the Nazis and the Nationalists. A second speech, before the Town Hall, commemorated the fall of the Spanish dictator, Primo de Rivera.[23] The *Reichsbanner* was making its presence felt.

The *Volksblatt* also charged that Nazis were violating the uniform prohibition decree and provoked the government to a reiteration of the ban on brown shirts. The Socialist Governor of Hannover Province, Noske, prohibited the transporting of participants for political gatherings in trucks or buses, since it had been noted that fighting elements (especially the SS) were frequently brought to political meetings and inclined more to street fights than the local contingents. Noske also—acting on the basis of a private theory—forbade the use of the color red in all posters except official ones.[24]

Despite these measures, the increased tension inevitably led to violence. On April 8, there was a fight between two Nazis and four *Reichsbanner* men, with the Nazis getting the worst of it. A week later the *Volksblatt* reported that a Nazi had slapped the wife of a *Reichsbanner* man; it threatened to take matters into its own hands if more police protection were not forthcoming. At the climax of the campaign the TNN reported that two young Nazis mishandled a woman Socialist, that two *Reichsbanner* men ripped the swastika insignia from the coat of a lady who was a member of the Nazi Women's Auxiliary, and that members of the youth section of the *Reichsbanner* jeered at some children on their way to church. The *Volksblatt* denied the latter two incidents.[25]

The campaign atmosphere also led to some scatter-shot propaganda by the *Volksblatt*. On April 1, it reported that the son of a pastor from Thalburg County received a scholarship intended to enable poor but gifted students to attend the *Gymnasium*. It pointed out that the pastor earned 800 marks per month while an unemployed worker got 60 marks a month at the highest; readers were then invited to draw their own conclusions. Two days later it noted that three copies of the Nazi *Völkischer Beobachter* were found on a table in the Thalburg City Library. It thundered editorially: "What is this subversive newspaper doing in the public library?" [26]

If the Socialists were seeing Nazis everywhere it was because of the extent of middle class collaboration with the Nazis in the petition campaign. On April 19, 1931, all groups supporting the petition joined for a mass rally. Official sponsorship was given to the *Stahlhelm,* and the speaker of the evening was a member of its youth section. But the meeting was also backed by all political parties involved (except the Communists) and by almost all right-wing organizations in Thalburg: the County Agricultural Society, the Pan-German League, the National Association of German Officers, the Savings Depositors' League, the German National Apprentices' Society, and finally, the Civic Association. The *1910er Zelt* was packed. The *Stahlhelm* provided a band from a neighboring town and its own Thalburger fife-and-drum corps, while the Nazis provided SA contingents. The main speaker pronounced a lengthy curse on the "godless movement," by which he meant the SPD, and went on to say that the SPD-Center party coalition was a league between "Rome and the Reds." The meeting closed with the enthusiastic singing of "The Watch on the Rhine" and the national anthem.[27]

The gathering of signatures lasted only two weeks and demonstrated considerable organizational ability on the part of the Nazis, who were the driving force behind the campaign. In the first ten days almost one-fifth of Thalburg's qualified voters (1,275) signed up. Then the Nazis put on a spurt of energy and in the last four days collected almost as many signatures again to bring the total up to 2,246, one-third of the town's voters. In the rest of Prussia enough signatures were gathered to insure that the referendum would be held, with the date set for August of 1931.

Certainly many Thalburgers signed the petition because of the concurrent signs of economic construction. On April 2, Thalburg's branch office of the *Commerz und Privatbank* closed permanently. A week later occurred the worst calamity to befall the town's middle class during the depression: the collapse of the Enterprise Bank, a locally financed cooperative bank which was the pride of the lower middle class. Bankruptcy was declared on April 9,

1931, although the liquidation extended into 1933 and caused considerable bitterness. The collapse of the Enterprise Bank was not due to the general economic situation, but was the result of poor management, especially in interest policy. Meetings of the creditors were acrimonious and the matter became a political issue. The Nazis claimed that the bankruptcy was due to the Versailles Treaty and the republican form of government, while the Socialists gleefully pointed out that the board of directors was composed of Nationalists and Nazis, and listed some of the blunders which had caused the bank's failure. After 1933 the Nazis tacitly acknowledged the element of mismanagement by instituting legal action against the former director.

About 15 per cent of the town's small businessmen were decisively affected by the incident and at least one man later declared himself bankrupt because of it. Many others had to struggle for existence thereafter.[28]

Under these circumstances, protests became more bitter. At a meeting of the Thalburg Housewives' Club held on April 7, the speaker ranted against "the Americanization of the economy" and against department stores, consumers' cooperatives, and foreign imports. He exhorted women to buy only from small dealers.[29] The Nazis, in their catch-all propaganda, promised to aid the small businessman, but until the millennium arrived businessmen were pressed hard to contribute to the Nazi cause. By the end of April, 1931, the *Volksblatt* charged that Thalburg's Nazis had not paid their bills and had no money to pay them. It warned businessmen not to extend credit to the NSDAP, but suggested that the Nazis frequently threatened businessmen with boycotts in order to extort credit or contributions. At least one Thalburg businessman later verified the charge.[30]

Businessmen were the last to suffer from the depression; by April, 1931, the number of unemployed registered at the Thalburg District employment office reached twelve thousand—double the number of the previous autumn. Other workers suffered pay cuts or shortened hours. The town's cigar factory (with 250 employees) had been on a reduced work-week for over four months.[31] The *Volksblatt,* in reporting the death in a farm machinery accident of a ten-year-old boy from Thalburg County, noted parenthetically that the boy had been earning more than his father.[32] Under these circumstances hardly any workers left their jobs for the May Day celebration, which in 1931 fell on a Friday. There was a pitifully small parade led by only three red flags and a placard inscribed "We demand the 40-hour week." The town band played a few marches in the Market Square, but that was all.[33]

In general, political activity abated after the petition campaign, though the Nazis attempted to keep up the pressure. On May 2 they brought in a Reichstag delegate for a speech and a few weeks later staged a parade with six hundred Stormtroopers, a concert, and a meeting in the *1910er Zelt*. About 1,300 people attended, and the only thing to mar what the GHC called "one of the greatest successes of the NSDAP" was actually the sort of thing the Nazis felt added spice: a short fight with some *Reichsbanner* men during the parade.[34] Early in June there was another varied program in the *1910er Zelt* with a concert, dramatic presentations, speeches, a raffle, and dancing. This also drew a large crowd which apparently enjoyed itself, though the "dramatic presentations" consisted solely of scenes of SA men beating up Communists.[35] Four weeks after that the President of the Prussian Parliament spoke in Thalburg for the Nazis and a week later, in keeping with the relaxed summer atmosphere, the SA band gave a concert at the ruins of an old castle outside Thalburg.[36]

The Nationalists also relaxed. Apart from a recruitment evening in May, which gave the *Stahlhelm* ten new members, their only other activity in the early summer of 1931 was a June garden party in honor of their national commander's fiftieth birthday, with a concert and other light entertainment.[37] There was only one unpleasant incident to bother the conservatives. In May, Senator Mahner had charged that the SPD used Welfare Office funds to show one of their propaganda films to some pensioners. Mahner was promptly sued by an SPD leader and was required to publish an advertisement in the TNN declaring that: 1) he had not really made the accusation; 2) he took it all back with an expression of deep sorrow; and 3) he would pay all the costs of the trial.[38]

The pace of SPD activity also slowed in the late spring and early summer. In early June the *Reichsbanner* staged a demonstration parade and in a speech at the Town Hall Willi Brehm dwelt on the miseries of the Italian working classes and emphasized that Socialist ideology thrives only in a democracy. A few days later the SPD sponsored a mass meeting in the *1910er Zelt* featuring the exiled Italian anti-fascist, Professor Mario Cofi. A good-sized crowd heard him talk on "the bloody and shameful regime of Italian Fascism." The lecture was significantly entitled "Swastika Wonderland." Some Nazis were present but none tried to speak.[39]

A few days after that Thalburg was invaded by groups of "Young Socialist Workers" for a two-day conference. The SPD Local took advantage of their presence for a parade and meeting on the Market Square. The TNN thought the boys and girls made a handsome parade with their blue blouses and red ties, their songs, and their bright red flags.[40] Another pleasant interlude was provided a week later by the celebration of "Workers' Sport Day" on June 15. Proletarian sport clubs paraded with the city band and the *Reichsbanner* fife-and-drum corps, and then held a variety of athletic contests. At night there was a torchlight parade, songs by the Workers' Choir, and a speech on the Socialist import of sport. The day ended with cries of *"Hoch der deutschen Republik!"* and the singing of the *Internationale.* A few days later the SPD tried more low-pressure propaganda as it sent a loudspeaker truck through Thalburg with only a few slogans and mostly light, non-political airs.[41] The depression even abated during June of 1931; unemployment in the Thalburg District dropped to eight thousand, the lowest it had been since the previous October.

As the heat of the summer bore in, though, there was a new economic crisis. The American stock market crash led U.S. banks to call in loans they had made to Germany. The credit crisis became acute by mid-1931 and in July the major German banks began to close. The government declared a bank holiday on July 14. In Thalburg there was no real run on the banks. A former director of one of the banks recalled that "only a few people came in to withdraw their money, and they later returned it with sheepish excuses." [42] Yet the town's leaders were concerned. The City Council decided unanimously not to attend the annual festival of the shooting societies. Its reasoning was that the general economic misery made festivals inappropriate. This decision was extremely unpopular, since the populace took the opposite view, holding that beer and skittles were needed especially to take one's mind off the depression. The Council did not repeat its mistake the following year, though the economic crisis was even graver by then.[43]

The Social Democrats also displayed concern, especially over the possibility that the Communists might make inroads among the unemployed. In June the Free Unions called a special meeting to discuss countermeasures against KPD * activity among the jobless. Within a week the *Volksblatt* was able to report that through SPD city councillors the town of Thalburg had made potatoes and other food available to the Free Unions for distribution and had also arranged the free use of the town's swimming pool for jobless persons. The *Volksblatt* also issued a vehement denial that the Communists were making inroads among Thalburg's "Young Socialist Workers." [44]

Along with economic concern came rising political tension, especially with the August 8 Referendum for the Dissolution of the Prussian Parliament in the offing. In mid-July there was a rumor of a Nazi *Putsch* and the Thalburg *Reichsbanner* was mobilized, but the evening passed with nothing more than a parade and a speech on the Market Square. A week later the *Reichsbanner* was called out again to give a protest demonstration over the murder of a *Reichsbanner* man in Hannover. The Thalburgers probably remembered a nasty incident that had occurred in their own town in June when two Stormtroopers had trampled a Socialist with their boots and then cut off his fingers with a sickle. In their protest demonstration the *Reichsbanner* marched to the Market Square, led by their fife-and-drum corps, to hear Willi Brehm promise that they would defend the Republic and to have Bette lead them in a *"Frei Heil!"* for democracy.[45]

The August referendum drew together all the anti-Socialist forces that had backed the April petition. Nationalist propaganda became the prime content of the GHC, while the TNN ran a *Stahlhelm* advertisement for twelve consecutive days preceding August 9, calling on people to vote "yes." As before, the Nazis were the driving force. On August 1 they held a meeting in the Cattle Auction Hall preceded by a parade of about four hundred

---

* *Kommunistische Partei Deutschlands,* Communist Party of Germany.

SA, SS, and Hitler Youth, plus a band. They also had the honor of the election-eve rally.[46] The Civic Association's turn came on August 5, when Mahner called for a "common front against Bolshevism" (ignoring the fact that the Communists were also supporting the referendum). At this meeting a car pool was arranged to help get out the vote.[47]

Again the *Reichsbanner* focused its efforts on the remote villages of Thalburg County, using trucks for transportation. Meetings were held in each village under the slogan "Republicans are ready to fight." One trip ended with a march past the Cattle Auction Hall, prompting admonitions from the TNN. In repeated speeches on the Market Square, "against the destruction of Prussia," Bette emphasized that Nazis and Communists were working together to break the SPD supremacy.[48] The SPD also held meetings in outlying areas of the county, places with a thoroughly Nazified peasant population. The *Reichsbanner* from Thalburg usually went along to provide protection, and wives of Socialist speakers waited up until their men came home.[49] On one occasion Karl Hengst was able to save himself from a beating only by prolonging his speech until *Reichsbanner* reinforcements arrived from town. As it was, the SA was just beginning to interrupt when police and *Reichsbanner* arrived simultaneously.[50] In other parts of the county Socialists were living in a virtual state of terror. In one village a twenty-two-year-old worker died as a result of a beating given him by Nazis in the spring, and in August, Nazis led a mass assault on a few *Reichsbanner* men in the same village. The event was carefully noted in Thalburg, especially when some thirty Nazis received fines and prison sentences totaling 128 months for their part in the attack.[51]

There were also rumors of an impending Nazi *Putsch*. Rumors of this sort were frequently spread. A year before, after the September, 1930, elections, the TNN took pains to point out that rumors about a Hitlerian *Putsch* were false and that the Defense Minister had said he was prepared to nip any revolution in the bud.[52] Behind it all was the fact that Hitler had one attempted *Putsch* on his record—the Munich "Beer Hall" fiasco of November, 1923.

A few days before the election Thalburg's *Reichsbanner* took to patroling the streets in groups of five. The Mayor, as chief of police, immediately warned the *Reichsbanner* not to do this. In reply, the *Volksblatt* published a belligerent open letter demanding better police protection and refusing to stop the patrols.[53] The Thalburg police also prohibited a planned Nazi parade on election eve, fearing it would "pose a danger to the public peace." [54]

In the last few days before the election, haying was completed in the rural areas around Thalburg, enabling numerous SA men to come into town and thus raising the political temperature. Tempers were honed to the point where the slightest incident became a cause for violence. The day before the election, for example, an SA man entered a tavern and announced "Make way—the SA is here!" A *Reichsbanner* man immediately knocked him unconscious. No wider violence came of this episode at the time, though it helped set the stage. That same day, a Thalburg Nazi named Tumpelmann hit a member of the Workers' First Aid Society on the head with brass knuckles, sending him to the doctor for stitches.[55]

In short, everything was conducive to a major battle, which occurred the evening of election day, August 9. During the day both *Reichsbanner* and SA were in a state of full alert. In the subsequent trial the Nazi attorney produced the following secret order which indicates the mood of the day:

Reichsbanner Black-Red-Gold 10th District
To all Local Groups of the 10th District

Comrades:
All local Groups of the 10th District will place themselves in full alert. Any moves of the enemy which indicate *Putsch*-intentions are to be reported immediately to the District Leader. Local Groups [X, Y, and Z] shall each provide a motorcyclist to maintain contact with the District Leader. These contact-people are to present themselves on Sunday the 9th at 7 P.M. at the residence of the District Leader. They are to appear completely in civilian dress without any insignia. All other Local Groups are to make certain that they have further motorcyclists or bicyclists ready so that in the event of a disruption of telephone communications, contact will be maintained with the District Leader. For security reasons all orders will be delivered orally. Telephone calls

from Sunday evening after seven o'clock only at the Thalburger *Ratskeller,* Number 204. After 10 o'clock that evening, at the City Construction Office, Number 357.

Frei Heil!
Bette, District Commander,
the 10th District.[56]

In Thalburg the *Reichsbanner* gathered in uniform at the *Ratskeller* café, while the SA maintained headquarters at another tavern two blocks up Broad Street. Dusk came at eight o'clock, and both groups began their patrols through town. Inevitably the two patrols met head on between the two cafés. In the Nazi group were Kurt Aergeyz, Deputy Leader for Thalburg, and Tumpelmann, about whom the *Reichsbanner* had been talking all day because of his brass-knuckles attack the previous evening. Words were exchanged, and the Nazis struck the first blow. The noise attracted attention in both cafés and in a minute Broad Street was filled with fighting men. Leaders on both sides wanted to halt the battle, but when the *Reichsbanner* saw two of their comrades lying on the ground bleeding while Kurt Aergeyz was beating one with a cane and shouting "I'll beat you to death," there was no holding them back. The Nazi leader phoned the state police, who arrived ten minutes later and broke it up. Men from both sides were hospitalized with knife wounds and broken heads; many were cut and bruised.

Investigation by the police led to the indictment of the three Nazis in the original patrol on charges of assault with a deadly weapon. Two trials were necessary because of the confused and contradictory testimony. The court found all three Nazis guilty. Aergeyz was given two months in prison, a fine of 300 marks, and three years' probation. Tumpelmann was given four months in prison, as was the third Nazi, who had been indicted for a murder in the interim and had fled the country. In its decision the court declared that the *Reichsbanner* was not entirely without guilt for the "Referendum Day Battle," as it came to be called.[57]

The actual referendum was a failure throughout Prussia, and the SPD-Center coalition continued to govern. In Thalburg, the SPD made no effort to "get out the vote" since not voting was equivalent to voting "no." The Nazis had worked hard, and over a thousand more Thalburgers voted for the referendum than had signed the petition. Yet the total "yes" votes barely exceeded the total vote that parties supporting the dissolution had won in September, 1930.

While the vote was not a Nazi victory, since it failed to topple the government, the NSDAP could be well pleased with the atmosphere created by the spring and summer campaigns. Not only had all parties succumbed to Nazi leadership; the political process had been further radicalized, and by means of a constitutional provision designed to assure maximum democracy. The violence in Thalburg was especially gratifying since it was another step towards bringing the town's troubled burghers over to Hitler's side. Dictators are nothing if not good policemen.

CHAPTER 6

THE DEPTHS OF THE DEPRESSION

(Autumn and Winter, 1931-1932)

> No higher being will come to save us,
> No God, no Kaiser, nor Tribune.
> If we want freedom from our misery,
> We'll get it only by ourselves, alone.
> —German Socialist version of the *Internationale*

The split lips and broken heads, the ragged cuts and throbbing lumps that were the heritage of the "Referendum Day Battle" had at least one beneficial consequence. They cleared the air of violence and sated the hotheads on both sides. There were no more incidents of physical violence in Thalburg for almost three months following August 9.

This does not mean that all tensions abated immediately, for there was still a backwash of accusations and suspicion left from the campaign. Three days after the referendum the GHC charged that Karl Hengst, as chairman of the vote-watching committee, had permitted voters to use a booth in which an election slogan had been scrawled. The City Council investigated the charge, found it incorrect, and the GHC withdrew its accusation and apologized. A relatively mild riposte from the *Volksblatt* followed.[1] Actually the GHC was routed from the field of polemics less by the *Volksblatt's* barbs than by the appearance of a competitor whose attacks were without restraint: the Nazi newsletter *Hört! Hört!*, the first issues of which appeared in early August. Every issue contained furious attacks on the SPD, especially upon city operations within areas of competence covered by SPD Senators, and above all upon the "red" Health Insurance Office. The weapon was the same type of rhetorical question that the *Volksblatt* used so skillfully. For example: "How can the Health Insurance Office send *three* men and a car to a convention? Or are they incapable of saving money?" [2]

The *Volksblatt,* for its part, focused most of its efforts upon Senator Mahner because of his collaboration with the Nazi effort to dissolve the Prussian Parliament. It charged that Mahner was a Nazi dupe and that the Civic Association's election-day car pool was used by the Nazis to build up their own prestige. It accused Mahner of writing articles for *Hört! Hört!* and of diverting funds from the Civic Association's treasury into Nazi hands. This was the beginning of a campaign to destroy Mahner, which eventually succeeded.[3]

Another by-product of the bitterness engendered by the referendum campaign was the neglect of the annual Constitution Day celebration. The public meeting was held in one of the schools and the assembly hall was only two-thirds full. The *Volksblatt* complained that very few civil servants, who presumably owed allegiance to the Republic, were present. In the evening there was a torchlight parade with only the *Reichsbanner* and the Free Unions marching. The GHC charged that because the Socialists had insisted on having the *Reichsbanner* head the parade, none of the clubs or guilds would join.[4]

There were other signs of the ominous effects of the "Referendum Day Battle." At the next meeting of the City Council the SPD demanded an annual subsidy of 25 marks for the Workers' First Aid Society. Thalburg was already subsidizing the Voluntary First Aid Society of the Red Cross, but Karl Hengst threatened to block further grants to that organization if the Council did not pass his motion. The Civil Servants group reluctantly helped the SPD override the Civic Association and the subsidy was passed.[5]

Measures of a preparatory nature were also taken by the

Stahlhelm. At a meeting in September, featuring two outside speakers, a *Stahlhelm* leader declared that there would soon be civil war in Germany "between the Bolsheviks and the National Opposition" in which "there will be no neutrality." The following morning the youth section of Thalburg's *Stahlhelm* held "defense-sport" exercises. A week later, a thousand *Stahlhelm* men were expected in Thalburg for similar activities, but the police were afraid of trouble and forbade it. By now the *Volksblatt* was aroused and reported that "some *Stahlhelmern* practiced hand-grenade throwing Sunday morning in the Thalburg park and called it 'sport.' Also at 2 A.M. they marched through the streets singing songs. Will the police do something about this?" [6]

As the first autumn winds swept over the north German plains these matters were thrust aside, for another depression winter was moving upon the town. Unemployment figures followed the seasons, cresting in the winter. By October there were over nine thousand registered unemployed coming to the Thalburg Employment Office each week. In the town itself there were 418 unemployed. This was not many more than there had been the previous year at the same time, but whereas in October, 1930, two-thirds of the town's unemployed were still on regular unemployment compensation, by October, 1931, only about a third were; the rest were drawing emergency benefits or the welfare dole. The difference was the measure of despair.

Again there was an enormous press of applicants at the sugar beet factory. The *Volksblatt* reported that a worker who had been employed every harvest season for the past twenty years was now turned down because he was a Republican. The worker stated that the employment chief told him he would have to change his politics if he wanted work. [7]

As the misery of the unemployed increased, there were attempts to mitigate it through private charity. In October of 1931 all of Thalburg's charitable organizations (Nazis and *Stahlhelm* excepted) decided to work together with a common treasury. This *Hilfsbund* included Lutheran, Catholic, and Jewish charities, organizations of the left, such as the Socialists' Workers' Welfare, and of the right, such as the Fatherland's Women's Club. It also received public support from the County Prefect and the

Mayor of Thalburg. The *Hilfsbund* undertook street collections and distributed food, clothing, and fuel. By the end of November 1,350 marks had been collected. In addition, merchants contributed clothes, while grocers, bakers, and butchers promised weekly deliveries of food. The Jewish merchants in the town were among the heaviest contributors. The Free Unions sponsored a Welfare Party which drew a large crowd at 75 *pfennig* per person. There was music by the Workers' Choir and the city band. Various local comedians performed and the Workers' Gymnastic Society gave a show. From this alone 350 marks was earned for the *Hilfsbund,* and the Workers' Welfare Society also held a sale of homemade Christmas presents, with proceeds going to the unemployed. By November 27, 1931, 250 unemployed had applied for help. They also asked for four representatives from their own ranks to help supervise the distribution of aid, but this was unanimously refused.[8]

In support of the general effort, coal dealers reduced the price of lignite bricks for all unemployed and the Thalburg Bakers' Guild cut the price of bread by 8 per cent. It was more than altruism that prompted the bakers, for the *Volksblatt* had conducted a relentless attack against their pricing policy, comparing it unfavorably to that of neighboring towns. When the December, 1931, price cut came, the *Volksblatt,* instead of applauding, simply noted that the price of bread in bakery shops was now the same as that of the consumers' cooperative. Since Thalburg's bakers "made Nazi propaganda," workers were advised to shop at the cooperative even without the advantage of lower prices.[9]

The city also helped to mitigate the lot of the unemployed. Beginning in February, 1931, free "cultural" movies were shown at one of the public schools. The following autumn the town began vocational training courses for young unemployed persons and also offered to lease several acres of city-owned garden land to unemployed families. During the winter of 1931-1932, needy unemployed were issued certificates enabling them to buy up to two hundred pounds of coal a month at 30 *pfennig* a sack less than normal prices.[10]

Despite all these measures, the pace of the depression increased.

There were six bankruptcies in 1931, double the number of 1930, and in December, 1931, one of the town's larger businesses, a paper sack factory, closed down and prepared to move from Thalburg.[11] ·By the end of the winter there were 704 unemployed in Thalburg. There were over thirteen thousand in the Thalburg Employment Office District, which meant an average of two thousand a day tramping through Thalburg to the old Army barracks. To complete the misery created by the economic situation, nature added woes. In January of 1932 the Muhle river flooded, doing great damage to the workers' district north of the railroad tracks. Even the emergency dwellings for the shelterless in the old Army compound were flooded. Total damage in Thalburg County was estimated at a quarter of a million marks.[12]

Banking began to show signs of constriction also. With the bank holiday of the previous summer, the City Savings Bank lost 50,000 marks' worth of accounts. This was less than 3 per cent of the total, but it was enough to make Senator Mahner urge that members of the Civic Association keep their money in the City Savings Bank, since the bank was perfectly safe "despite vicious rumors." He was speaking to the right people, since it was the large accounts, those over 500 marks, that had left the bank. By the end of 1931 the City Council, County Prefect, and twelve economic organizations signed a large advertisement telling Thalburgers not to hoard their money but to put it in banks, where it would be safe.[13] Though it was not reported in the press, this worked; by the end of 1932 not only had the large accounts returned, but many new small accounts were opened, so that the City Savings Bank showed a net increase over the three years of the depression. At least a quarter of the town's adult population had savings accounts of over 100 marks in the City Savings Bank, and this did not include money put in other Thalburg banks or invested in stocks and bonds. The middle classes were hardly touched by the depression in Thalburg, except psychologically.[14]

The Nazis, with their feel for effective agitation, moved to exploit the deepening of the depression. In the wake of the referendum there had been a reversion to old-style meetings. One at the end of August, held in the Cattle Auction Hall, featured a former army officer and a former Communist who spoke on "Our Gigantic Advance to the Great Victory! The Red Terror!" A week later a Hitler Youth Leader spoke on "The Murder of the Youth." Shortly thereafter the Nazis rented the *1910er Zelt* for a theatrical presentation: "National Socialism is trying to rescue German art and make it German again. Therefore the N.S. Stage Group will present the play 'Poison Gas 506'. . . ." Attendance was not noteworthy despite the bait of "Famous Actors; Cheap Prices." Apparently the town could stand only so many "evenings of entertainment," for later in September the Nazis took part in one put on by the *Stahlhelm* rather than give their own.[15]

In October the Nazis began to work on the town's concern over economic matters. During the first week there was a speech on "What Will Winter Bring Us?" A fortnight later, the chief Nazi economic theorist, Gottfried Feder, came to Thalburg to speak on "Financial and Economic Policy in the National Socialist State." He drew an enormous crowd to the *1910er Zelt,* including many middle class people who were interested in the Nazi economic program. They got, instead, such generalities as "no nationalization of the productive free economy" and "organic economic leadership." Nevertheless, this was one of the Nazis' most effective meetings.[16]

The rest of 1931 was filled by the Nazis with fairly ordinary events: a play, the annual commemoration of the Munich *Putsch,* a welfare concert, and the Christmas Party. The only mass meeting was held on November 26, featuring a Prussian Parliament member who attacked the SPD as responsible for the current economic distress and promised that when the Nazis came to power they "would not use soft gloves." [17]

The Nazis also went beyond propaganda in exploiting the depression. In the late fall of 1931 they opened a soup kitchen to feed the unemployed. It was located in the former factory of a canning company which had gone bankrupt in 1929; the owner supplied the rooms free. Hitler had formed an alliance with the Nationalist party—the so-called "Harzburg Front"—in October, 1931. Hence the way was open for closer cooperation on the local level and the soup kitchen was a joint Nazi-*Stahlhelm* venture. Since it was in competition with the *Hilfsbund,* the Nazis attempted to discredit the town's general relief effort:

The worst winter in 100 years! State and Reich refuse to help! Germany will only be saved from all misery when no heart closes itself to this cry of need! Every man must give as much as he can spare. The majority of the *Volk,* represented by the National Opposition, will master the distress by standing together, all for all. Contributions may be given only to the representatives who have our card.

Stahlhelm (League of Front Soldiers)
NSDAP, County Thalburg [18]

Enough contributions came in so that by mid-December the kitchen was feeding two hundred people per day, including forty families, twenty single people, and numerous SA men. Most of the food was donated by peasants and by some of Thalburg's grocers, bakers, and butchers. The Nazis claimed that they charged only those who could pay and gave food to all regardless of party affiliation, but at least one worker was refused food because he was a "leftist" and the *Volksblatt* claimed that only unemployed Nazis were fed.[19]

By the end of 1932 the Nazi kitchen had given out twelve thousand dinners, but welfare operations were not its only function. Some rooms were set aside for the SA (the *Stahlhelm* was elbowed out early in 1932 after the "Harzburg Front" collapsed) and the factory became Thalburg's SA headquarters and "barracks." Within a fortnight of its opening, a swastika flag waved from the highest chimney of the factory. Since the Nazis were forbidden to display party symbols in Prussia, the *Volksblatt* was quick to ask what the police intended to do about it. Nothing was done, however, until the short-lived dissolution of the SA in the late spring of 1932, when the flag came down upon police order, but only for a few days. In a country preoccupied with symbols, the constant flying of a swastika over Thalburg must be counted as another step towards convincing the wavering middle class that the Nazis were the party of the future.[20]

By the end of 1931, Thalburg's Nazis could look back on a busy year. The number of meetings was not greater than in the previous year, but their character had changed. In the first place, the NSDAP was able to draw upon the pool of Reichstag delegates elected the previous year. No fewer than five Reichstag delegates appeared on Nazi platforms in 1931, in addition to the President

of the Prussian Parliament and the Nazi parliamentary leader of
that body. This was a rich selection of speakers for a town of ten
thousand, especially since it also included Gottfried Feder, who in
the eyes of the general public was a top Nazi leader. Furthermore,
the NSDAP was beginning to play upon the militaristic yearnings
of Thalburg's citizens. During the year they provided three former
officers as speakers and staged five paramilitary parades. But the
most striking difference was the size of Nazi meetings. The Nazis
had been able to rent the *1910er Zelt* only once in 1930; in 1931
they filled it no fewer than ten times—true mass meetings, with
over a thousand people on each occasion. There were also fourteen
meetings in the Cattle Auction Hall. In other words, almost every
other meeting was planned for a mass audience. Finally, 1931 also
saw the beginning of Nazi "evenings of entertainment": infused
with as much pageantry as politics, but of varied appeal and a
distinct change of pace from the usual three- to five-hour speeches.

The Nazi record of activity becomes even more astounding when
one considers that Thalburg had only about forty actual members
of the NSDAP prior to 1933. They were aided by many party
members from the county, and also by many fellow-travelers, but
the core was a strictly limited one. A limited core was not a limiting factor once the movement achieved a mass following, which
it clearly did in Thalburg by mid-1930. Furthermore, not many
Thalburgers suspected how few dues-paying members there were
in the town. The townspeople believed that the Nazis were numerous and young.[21]

As far as the youthful aspect is concerned, this was probably
correct. Students at the Thalburg *Gymnasium* were strongly attracted to Hitler. Most of the work done in public was done by
young people in the SA or the Hitler Youth. A former member
of the Hitler Youth in Thalburg still has vivid recollections of
painting swastikas and slogans on sidewalks and walls and distributing leaflets and pamphlets.[22] Despite their reliance on the
spoken word, the Nazis often distributed such literature, and especially at election times delivered party newspapers, broadside
leaflets, and free tickets to their meetings to almost every house
in Thalburg.[23] Though the Hitler Youth was used for this, most
of its program was not directly tied into Nazi party activity. A

former member described Thalburg's Hitler Youth in the years
before 1933 as follows:

There was no pressure put on me by my father or anyone else to
join the Hitler Youth—I decided to join it independently simply because I wanted to be in a boys club where I could strive towards a
nationalistic ideal. The Hitler Youth had camping, hikes, and group
meetings. I was number 9 in the Thalburg group when I joined in
1930. There were boys from all classes of families though mainly
middle class and workers. There were no social or class distinctions,
which I approved of very much. There was no direct or obvious political indoctrination until later—after Hitler came to power. Without
really trying to get new members, the Thalburg Hitler Youth grew
rapidly. I think most of the other boys joined for the same reason I
did. They were looking for a place where they could get together with
other boys in exciting activities. It was also a depression time and
there were many evil influences abroad from which decent boys wished
to escape. In any event, I don't think the political factor was the main
reason boys joined. We did march in parades and hated the SPD, but
that was all general, not specific—it was all a part of it. We weren't
fully conscious of what we were doing, but we enjoyed ourselves and
also felt important.[24]

By the end of 1932 the Thalburg Hitler Youth had grown to
about seventy-five members.

The real workhorses of Thalburg's Nazi organization were the
members of the "Storm Section": the SA, or "Brownshirts." Not
all members of the party were in the SA, nor were all Stormtroopers party members, though there was some cross-over. In
Thalburg there were not more than fifty members of the SA before
1933, though it seemed to most townspeople that there were any-
where from three to eight times as many. Whenever the Nazis
held a public function in Thalburg they called in SA men from the
rural countryside for protection and to impress the populace. Much
of the day-to-day work of the SA was also done by these men
from the farming villages of Thalburg County. Whenever they
came to town they gathered either at the soup kitchen or at Thalburg Nazi headquarters (in a tavern on Broad Street), and in
addition to drinking and talking politics they were available for
any tasks. They were frequently seen on the streets and made

themselves conspicuous by shouting insults at Social Democrats or *"Heil Hitler!"* to one another. Thus there appeared to be many more Stormtroopers than there actually were.[25]

There was much for the SA to do. Many Nazi meetings were held under their auspices and almost all required their participation for protection, music, or entertainment. It was their job to put up posters and in general to conduct publicity. The SA also undertook all sorts of actions as a result of either boredom or animal energy. Thus in 1931, two SA men crept up to the house of a Thalburg SPD leader and painted a swastika on his door with the words, "Under this sign you'll bleed, you red pig." [26] Thalburgers frequently saw slogans painted on walls or telephone poles, "Throw the Jews out!" or "The Jews are our misfortune!" and these too were the casual work of the SA.[27]

If there was nothing else for the SA to do, there were always lists of potential pro-Nazis to work on. The Nazis kept close track of whoever came to their meetings and afterwards worked hard to get such people to join, contribute to, or at least vote for, the NSDAP.

Many Stormtroopers were rough types, and at least some were former Communists. Thalburg's workers were likely to beat them up, and furthermore SA discipline systematically promoted nihilistic brutality. The SA generally incorporated weapons into their uniforms. Leather shoulder straps were made detachable and the buckles were weighted. Many SA men carried blackjacks, brass knuckles, or *Stahlruten*. These last were ingenious weapons consisting of a short length of pipe open at one end inside of which was a spring with steel balls attached. The pipe was the handle; the spring and balls the weapon. When swung, the balls came out on the spring and struck with the leverage of their extended distance, yet the whole contraption fitted neatly into a pocket. The presence of a group of rough, armed, and bored SA men, many of whom came from outside Thalburg, was the prime cause of violence in the town.[28]

Many SA men were unemployed and could not afford to buy the uniform. Usually a wealthier Nazi would fit out five or six SA men in addition to buying his own uniform. Like the whole of Nazi operations in Thalburg, the SA was financed exclusively from local sources; far from receiving money from the national NSDAP, it was constantly called on for contributions. Money came from dues, contributions, and from the proceeds of meetings, where an admission fee was always charged.[29]

Thalburgers saw the SA most frequently when the Nazis held parades. The newspapers generally commented favorably on their drill order. But the SA was determined to be more than good parade soldiers. Already in 1931 the *Volksblatt* reported that people passing by the Cattle Auction Hall could hear the sounds of military exercises. By autumn, 1932, Thalburg's SA members engaged in extensive public maneuvers in a nearby forest, followed by a "Maneuver Ball." By late 1932 training courses were instituted, and the SA was able to set up its own *Standarten-Heim* in an abandoned factory, moving from the soup kitchen.[30] In short, by the end of 1932, Thalburg's SA, composed mainly of young farmers' sons, had developed into a formidable instrument: well trained, equipped, and housed; spirited and under the iron discipline of the Nazi party. The knowledge that people had of the existence of this corps was to be an important factor in the opening months of the Third Reich.

The Nazis also had an organization for women, set up early in 1931 with a starting membership of twenty-two. Most, but not all, of its members were the wives of Nazis. Internal bickering characterized the Women's Auxiliary in Thalburg primarily because of the personality of the chairwoman, who despite her unpopularity was perversely supported by the local Nazi leader until early 1933.[31] Finally, there was the League of German Girls, the female counterpart of the Hitler Youth. It became active in propaganda work and developed a membership of about thirty-five.

The whole network of Nazi organizations was supervised by two officials—the County Leader, Walter Eckstein, and the Local Group Leader, Kurt Aergeyz. While the Local Group Leader was theoretically subordinated to the County Leader, in practice they were equals since the Local Group Leader's control over day-to-day operations in the town gave him considerable leverage.

Walter Eckstein, the Thalburg County Leader, was well known in the Nazi hierarchy, since he had been one of the earliest members in Germany. He was of the lower middle class, an unsuccessful salesman. His great weakness was alcohol, which he consumed prodigiously and which finally killed him during World War II. He often spent his days sitting around the baggage room of the Thalburg railroad station, drinking from his private flask and telling the workers Rabelaisian jokes. After the first Nazi election successes, Eckstein became a full-time paid executive of the NSDAP. Supervising the county organization was a big job, but Eckstein approached it in an easygoing way. A sentimentalist, he was at his best when joking with SA men. He was never much of an orator and often lamented the passing of the old intimate meetings in the Cattle Auction Hall. Though capable of ruthlessness, he was never brutal, and even his opponents conceded that he had a warm heart, albeit a crude manner.[32]

Kurt Aergeyz was a different sort of person altogether. Chunky, with fair hair, a ruddy complexion, and pale blue eyes, he was enormously energetic. The kindest thing said of him was that he was "an unpleasant contemporary," which at the least was the reaction of most Thalburgers, including Walter Eckstein. With his brother, he inherited his father's small hardware shop. Another brother had died in World War I. Kurt Aergeyz was cold, cynical, crude, ruthless, and brutal. He was a failure as a businessman but showed enormous talent as an administrator and politician. He drank heavily and when drunk was generally morose. His most common emotion was anger, which could develop into blind rage. Many Thalburgers still quail at the recollection of his pulsing red face and mordant language. Devoid of sentiment and consumed by ambition, he was chiefly responsible for the driving energy of the Thalburg Nazi group.

Aergeyz had joined the Nazi party in the late 1920's and rapidly became Deputy Group Leader. In 1931 he became Local Group Leader when the previous holder of that office left Thalburg after a business scandal. Generally unknown, even to some Thalburg Nazis, he rapidly imposed his cold and driving personality upon the organization. Even before 1933 many of Thalburg's NSDAP members had misgivings about Aergeyz. To most Thalburgers he was identified with the rough, undesirable aspect of Nazism.[33]

"There were two groups of Nazis in Thalburg," said a former civil servant, "the decent ones and the gutter type. In the end the gutter won out." [34] This was the feeling of many Thalburgers, for even those who voted for the NSDAP had mixed emotions. But then there were Nazis like Walther Timmerlah, and indeed many respectable Thalburgers were Nazis: the owner of one of the town's hotels, the director of the *Lyzeum*, about three teachers, both judges at the County Court, and several high officials of the railroad directory. And of course a leading Nazi who lived in Thalburg County was the Baron von Barten, a man of impeccable credentials—nobleman, landowner, and Major in World War I. When he quit the Nationalists to join the Nazis, it was page one news for both the GHC and the TNN. [35]

Another ambivalent aspect of Nazism for most Thalburgers was the party's anti-semitism. Social discrimination against Jews was practically non-existent in the town. Jews were integrated along class lines: the two wealthiest Jewish families belonged to upper class circles and clubs, Jews of middling income belonged to the middle class social organizations, and working class Jews were in the Socialist community. Yet abstract anti-semitism in the form of jokes or expressions of generalized distaste was prevalent, approximately to the extent that these things exist in contemporary America. If Nazi anti-semitism held any appeal for the townspeople, it was in a highly abstract form, as a remote theory unconnected with daily encounters with real Jews in Thalburg. Thalburg's NSDAP leaders sensed this, and in consequence anti-semitism was not pushed in propaganda except in a ritualistic way. (The chief exceptions to this were the chalked or shouted slogans of the SA and their acceptance by peasants and by some of the rowdier employees of the artisan shops.) Thalburgers were drawn to anti-semitism because they were drawn to Nazism, not the other way around. Many who voted Nazi simply ignored or rationalized the anti-semitism of the party, just as they ignored other unpleasant aspects of the Nazi movement.

Thalburgers joined the NSDAP for many reasons in the years before Hitler came to power. One man and his wife were moved by "social" reasons: "We believed the common people should have a better life and that socialism was essential. We were idealists. In fact we were among the few people who had something to lose, for my business was successful." [36] Others joined because it looked

as though the Nazis would be victorious and they hoped to profit.
This was notoriously the case with a teacher at the *Gymnasium,*
and indeed, when the Nazis came to power he was promoted.[37]
Another man, who owned a printing shop, joined for business
reasons:

> It was the depression and business was bad. The Nazis used to ask
> my father for contributions and he refused. As a consequence of this
> he lost business. So he joined the Nazi party. But this lost him other
> customers, so he was discouraged by the whole situation. He probably
> wouldn't have joined of his own choice.[38]

In the opinion of a keen observer, "Most of those who joined
the Nazis did so because they wanted a radical answer to the
economic problem. Then, too, people wanted a hard, sharp, clear
leadership—they were disgusted with the eternal political strife of
parliamentary party politics." [39]

Yet most Thalburgers were dubious. "My previous experience
showed me that the ranks of the NSDAP were mostly filled with
incompetents and bankrupts." [40] This was the opinion of the conservative Prefect of Thalburg County (an opinion he later
changed). "The Nazis were bankrupt people prior to 1933—full
of the poor, the thieves, and the morally and financially bankrupt,"
said another who later joined the NSDAP.[41] And of course the
Social Democrats were uniformly of this opinion.

Most Thalburgers had little idea what the Nazis would really
do after they achieved power. Even Jews had no notion that the
Nazis really meant what they said.[42] This was not for lack of
information. Anyone who went regularly to Nazi meetings, or read
the pamphlets, or even the slogans chalked on the walls, should
have been able to discern the vulgar and violent aspects of the
NSDAP. Thalburgers could find out directly by reading the Nazis'
own publication for Thalburg: *Hört! Hört!* Every article in it
derided some individual, and it was readable only because of
variety in the forms of derision. Sarcasm and gutter language were
the rule. Not one single issue of the paper contained a positive
idea.

One series of opinions on what kinds of individuals were Nazis
was available to Thalburgers through the columns of the *Volks-*

blatt. Nor did Thalburgers have to subscribe to the SPD to hear the stories, for they were generally so juicy that they went around by word of mouth. The *Volksblatt's* stories attempted to show that Thalburg's Nazis were ridiculous, crude, venal, and brutal. If a delivery boy fell off his bicycle while trying to manage the Nazi salute, that made the *Volksblatt*.[43] If the SA put swastika stickers on the tombstones of the cemetery, the headline was "Nazi Respect for the Dead." [44] Since the *Volksblatt* believed most Nazis were thieves, it always reported stories like "B———, writer for *Hört! Hört!* . . . and pillar of the Nazi party in Thalburg, who was recently given a three-month sentence for libel against Governor Noske, has now betrayed the confidence of his landlady and stolen money from her. Another Nazi has thus proved himself a common crook. Who'll be next?" [45]

In addition to seeing the Nazis as foolish, crude, and greedy, the *Volksblatt* portrayed them as violent and vicious. Story after story built up this image: of a four-year-old boy admitted to the Thalburg hospital after having been beaten by his Nazi stepfather, of a sixteen-year-old Hitler Youth member who shot his grandmother while trying to rob her, and, most scabrous of all, of a Nazi carpenter in a neighboring town who tried to rape a married woman who was dusting the altar in the town church.[46] The other newspapers did not report incidents of this sort. The editor of the GHC, though a Nationalist, was favorably disposed toward Nazism. The TNN considered such stories in bad taste; if it had to report unpleasant incidents it avoided mentioning names but used the person's occupation and first initial of his last name. The worst one could read about the Nazis in the TNN were reports of their being jailed for violating the uniform prohibition, or of the suppression of *Hört! Hört!* for libel (both frequent occurrences). By late 1932 the editor of the TNN became increasingly anti-Nazi, but he was also a careful businessman with no desire to lose circulation or advertising, with so many people voting Nazi.

Thus unless Thalburgers believed the Socialist press, which was probably the case only for those townspeople who were already Socialists, they had little chance to hear unfavorable opinions of the NSDAP. Enough of the character of the Nazis was apparent in their words and actions to make even those who voted for them dubious, but the fact remains that few Thalburgers had any real conception of what the Nazis would do if they ever came to power. Thalburgers were mainly aware that conditions were currently very bad and that the Nazis were a young, energetic group pledged to rectify the situation.

The only Thalburgers who clearly apprehended the Nazi threat were the Social Democrats. After the August referendum the Socialists were relatively inactive. In October the *Reichsbanner* staged another march through the county and in December held a public meeting with about six hundred attending. The speaker attempted to show that a Nazi-bourgeois coalition in Braunschweig worked to the disadvantage of the middle classes, but his only recommendation was that the middle class join the SPD. One final event of the year was the showing of an anti-Communist film.[47]

But public meetings were not the only work of the SPD in 1931. During that year the Socialists held seven membership meetings in Thalburg and sixty-three in the county. Finances came from dues and the small admission fee charged for some public meetings. Income of the Thalburg Social Democratic party in this depression year was 1,841 marks; expenditures, 1,762 marks. In addition, the Workers' Welfare section was active with four meetings, three children's excursions, 206 Christmas packages to poor families, sixty-seven packages to old folks, and 350 articles of clothing made. It took in 2,125 marks and disbursed 1,859 marks, an effort which put it ahead of all other private welfare organizations in town. The Socialist Women's Group held fifty meetings over the year and increased its membership to 130. The Young Socialist Workers held eighty-five meetings, showed films, and gave a "parents' evening" in addition to working for the party. The SPD Children's Friends Movement visited thirty-five children to make sure they were well cared for. Politics was almost a sideline for the SPD.[48]

The year 1932 was the last year of democracy in Germany. Thalburg's Social Democrats could not know this, but they did have a sense of crisis. An indication of this was the decision, made nationally in response to the Nazi-Nationalist "Harzburg Front," to amalgamate all anti-Nazi groups into one organization to be named the "Iron Front." In Thalburg a new executive committee representing all workers' organizations called a mass meeting in late January in the *1910er Zelt*. The hall was so crowded that many had to stand. The black-red-gold flag of the Weimar Republic was prominently displayed and music was supplied by the *Reichsbanner* fife-and-drum corps and two workers' choral societies. A trick film, "In the Third Reich," was shown. There were four speakers, including Bette and Karl Hengst. The speeches were militantly anti-Nazi, though one also emphasized SPD achievements and Nazi-capitalist connections. Three weeks later another mass meeting heard a general denunciation of the NSDAP and a promise that the Iron Front would be victorious. At the SPD County General Meeting on February 16, all agreed that Nazism was the prime foe, and that it was "do or die" this year against Hitler.[49]

With the beginning of 1932 the Nazis also moved into high gear. On January 25 they held a "Big Army March and Concert Evening" with gymnastic presentations and an SA *Oberfuehrer* as speaker. The *1910er Zelt* was full until one in the morning. The very next day there was another mammoth rally with three speakers including a member of the Reichstag and of the Prussian Parliament. For five hours the audience heard speeches on agriculture, the middle class, and "the struggle against Marxism and Liberalism."[50]

The Nazis did not neglect their appeal to the religious element in Thalburg, either, in which they were aided by Lutheran fears of the SPD. The previous autumn the county church convention had heard a pastor from Hannover warn the faithful against the Social Democratic party, which he characterized as "fundamentally anti-church." His speech was seconded by the Baron von Barten, who directed the assembled ministers to struggle against "Bolshevism." At a meeting of the Thalburg Lutheran parish in February, 1932, another pastor linked the SPD with the Communists as the chief force behind atheism and "free-thinkerdom."[51] The SPD simply ignored such charges, but the Nazis moved to exploit them. On February 12, 1932, they brought in a minister to lecture before a select list of "preachers, church elders, teachers, and school committeemen" on "National Socialism and Christianity" at one of the town's hotels. The speaker declared that German Christianity had received a blow from the Weimar Constitution, which he said pointed directly towards Bolshevism. He described the Nazi goal as "the folkish, organic, God-fearing man." At least one pastor challenged the speaker by asserting that the Nazi racial program would lead to "national idolatry and mass-hatred." But "when the speaker denied this heatedly, the audience applauded warmly." [52]

Nationalism was also promoted. On February 12, a packed *1910er Zelt* heard the Braunschweig Nazi Minister of the Interior spend two hours attacking the "Pan-Europe" movement.[53] The DNVP pushed a similar theme at a meeting in the Hotel Georg-Friedrich where a retired lieutenant general described how the German army would have won World War I if it had not been stabbed in the back by traitors at home. Nineteen new members of the *Stahlhelm* youth section were sworn in and the meeting closed with the singing of *Deutschland über Alles* and an oath of allegiance to the black-white-red Imperial flag.[54]

Against this background the SPD could score one success. Since the August referendum, the *Volksblatt* had been relentless in its attacks on Senator Mahner of the Civic Association. Among the Senator's areas of competence in the city government was the Thalburg Brewery. Late in 1931, the *Volksblatt* reported persistent rumors that the brewery's bookkeeper had embezzled funds. The editorial queried gleefully: "Can it be that Senator Mahner has not kept careful watch?" Within a few months the whole story was out: since 1924 the bookkeeper had stolen 90,000 marks. The *Volksblatt* warmed to its task: "Were there no auditings of the books? Did Senator Mahner take adequate precautions against embezzlement? When will there be a public hearing?" A few weeks later the *Volksblatt* reported with unspeakable joy that the book-keeper was a member of the German Nationalist party, just like Senator Mahner.[55]

The Senator was eventually driven to despair by the *Volksblatt*'s incessant attacks. At practically every Civic Association meeting he railed against the paper and tried to get Thalburg's businessmen to stop advertising in it. He vigorously denied that he was a mem-ber of the NSDAP, saying that he was above parties (*"Bürgerlich und daher überparteilich"*). He explained to the general meeting of the Civic Association of February 26, 1932, that the brewery bookkeeper had repaid all that he had embezzled and the City Council had unanimously decided not to prosecute. After this explanation, Senator Mahner declared that he could no longer bear the attacks of the *Volksblatt* and that he was therefore resigning as chairman of the Civic Association. His fellow members defended him and later tried to re-elect him, but he refused to serve any longer. The fight had gone out of him; he never made another speech and was inactive thereafter.[56]

Even this did not mollify the *Volksblatt*. As long as Mahner continued to hold his Senatorship, the assaults upon his character continued. In April it was charged that the brewery supplied free beer to a Nazi Stormtroopers' school in a neighboring town. In August the *Volksblatt* charged that the brewery automobile had been given a faulty repair job but that 1,000 marks had been paid to the garage owner anyway. In December, 1932, Mahner was charged with hiring "double earners" instead of unemployed persons for some city work.[57]

All of this made interesting reading for Thalburgers and possibly increased the *Volksblatt*'s circulation. In some cases it might even have affected votes. But its chief effect was to debase the nature of politics and to destroy the foundation of trust and mutual respect without which democracy cannot succeed. When politics becomes a matter of vilification and innuendo, then eventually people feel repugnance for the whole process. It is the beginning of a yearning for a strong man who will rise above petty and partisan groups. The Nazis were to exploit this feeling fully, and though they contributed richly to the rise of partisan acrimony, they were also the first to pronounce "politician" with every possible tone of scorn and sarcasm.

CHAPTER 7

POLITICAL CRESCENDO

(Spring, 1932)

> *Elect Hindenburg! Elect our best.*
> *He is not the servant of any party*
> *—he follows only God and his*
> *conscience. . . .*
> —Advertisement of the German
> People's Party (*DVP*), Thalburg,
> in the *Thalburger Neueste Nach-*
> *richten* on March 11, 1932

By the end of the winter of 1931-1932, conditions in Thalburg were favorable to the rapid advance of Nazism. The depression was at its worst, violence was becoming more frequent, and the twin passions of nationalism and class antagonism were at their height. Thalburg's Nazis had established themselves as both respectable and radical. They were seen as patriotic, anti-socialist, and religious. They enjoyed the apparent blessings of the conservatives. But at the same time the Nazis appeared to be vigorous, determined, and, above all, ready to use radical means to deal with the crucial problem—the depression. Ordinary measures had been proved sufficient for welfare efforts, but only extreme measures would end the depression and only the Nazis were thought of as sufficiently extreme. All that was needed to complete the favorable situation was the whip of new election campaigns.

The propitious circumstances were not, of course, predominantly local. Despite its constant activity in Thalburg, the NSDAP won its first successes there only after democracy deteriorated on the national level. Beginning in 1930, a stable majority was unobtainable in the Reichstag and the Chancellor, Brüning, began to issue laws over the head of the Parliament by using Hindenburg's presidential emergency powers. Though Brüning's decrees were unpopular with the SPD, the Socialists refused to topple Brüning because they feared that the turmoil of elections would result in further Nazi and Communist gains. Hence a queasy stalemate existed in Germany from the spring of 1930 to the spring of 1932: the country was ruled by unpopular laws, issued not on the authority of a democratic Parliament, but on that of the aging Field Marshal who had been elected President in 1925.

The only justification for such a debilitating procedure would have been success in dealing with the depression. But Brüning's harsh deflationary measures, based on economic orthodoxy, actually intensified the effects of the depression, and the Nazis successfully labeled him the "Hunger Chancellor." The only benefit of Brüning's semi-authoritarian rule was political stagnation in the sense that new elections were avoided. In 1932 even this came to an end as Hindenburg's term ran out. The final condition for Nazi growth in Thalburg was thus present.

The presidential election was set for March 13, 1932. Hindenburg stood for re-election and was backed by Republican parties from the SPD to the People's party. The Nazis ran Hitler, and the Communists also entered a candidate—the veteran Stalinist Ernst Thaelmann. The Nationalists, unwilling to support Hindenburg because he had not subverted the Republic, and not yet willing to throw in their lot with Hitler, nominated the deputy commander of the *Stahlhelm,* Duesterberg. There was also a crackpot named Winter who managed to get on the ballot. But almost every German saw the essential contest in terms of Hitler *versus* Hindenburg.

In Thalburg the first, almost predictable sign of the impending election was an upsurge of violence. Since the "Referendum Day Battle" of the previous August, there had been no political fights in the town, except a minor tavern brawl in early December.[1] In the last week of February, 1932, however, there was a knife fight near the railroad station and two other fights on Broad Street between Nazis and *Reichsbanner* men.[2] A week later an irate Thalburger wrote to the TNN to say that even children were becoming involved. He had observed a group of boys describing Hitler in filthy terms (with the encouragement of their parents) before the newly opened Nazi election headquarters. The *Volksblatt* countered this by reporting that three Nazi youths followed some working women home shouting foul language at them. It identified one of the boys as a clerk at Otto Made's store. It also reported that a woman taking her child to church on a Sunday morning was struck in the face by a bundle of political leaflets when she refused to accept one from a young *Stahlhelm* member.[3] These incidents found their way into the newspapers, but exchanges of taunts and insults between *Reichsbanner* men and Nazis were daily occurrences.

Behind part of the bitterness was the economic distress, since the election campaign came at a time when the greatest number of Thalburgers were unemployed during the entire depression era. In the town there were over seven hundred registered unemployed in March and April, 1932, an increase of almost 50 per cent over the previous year at the same time. Furthermore, from this time on the number of men on the welfare rolls regularly exceeded the number of those drawing unemployment insurance. To the District Employment Office in the old Army compound, almost fourteen thousand registered unemployed were making their dismal journey every week—double the adult population of Thalburg. Two bankruptcies occurred in February, and a government proposal to lower the price of beer brought such heated protests from the Thalburg County Tavern-Keepers Society that the authorities were forced to abandon their plans. Even the widows and orphans rose in protest. In early February a mass meeting of War Widows and Industrial Accident Victims was held to protest the lowering of pensions. Because the meeting was dominated by Socialists, World War I and not the Republic was blamed for the existence of so many widows and orphans, but the audience was in a bitter mood.[4]

It was also in March, 1932, that the saddest blow of all came to some Thalburgers when the Workers' Funeral Savings Society collapsed. It was a result of embezzlement by the Society's treasurer, though the loss could have been withstood if new subscribers had been joining. The 470 members each were reimbursed only a small portion of what they had put in over the years. As the older workers and their wives filed out of the hall they knew that in addition to everything else they now faced a pauper's grave.[5]

Such frustrations were easily channeled into aggression by the partisan press. The Nazis concentrated on accusations of corruption, even if there was none. By the opening of the election campaign, *Hört! Hört!* was being sued by the Thalburg Senate for a libelous article on the City Hospital, by the County Prefect for having slandered a county official, and by the Health Insurance Office for publishing false reports. The *Volksblatt* was less clumsy but equally vicious. Among other things it took note of the fact that a leading Thalburg conservative ("that great enemy of socialistic laws") had sent his daughter to draw unemployment pay. The *Volksblatt* expressed the fervent hope that the Employment Office would scrutinize this case with extra care. Similarly, fresh instances of Nazi crudity and bloodthirstiness were sought out and published.[6]

Though the SPD supported Hindenburg's re-election solely because he was the "lesser evil," it conducted a vigorous campaign in Thalburg. On March 6, the new Iron Front staged a mass demonstration with the town band, the *Reichsbanner* fife-and-drum corps, and twenty-five flags and banners. At the Market Square little was said about the benefits of Hindenburg but much was said about the drawbacks of Nazism, including, according to a woman speaker who bolstered her assertions by quotations from the writings of Goebbels and Strasser, the probability that "women would be breeding-slaves in the Third Reich." [7]

The second SPD meeting for Hindenburg had to be held in the Riding Hall, since the *1910er Zelt* was unavailable. Over 1,200 people were present to hear Karl Hengst and Bette attack the Nazis and the Civic Association and also call for Hindenburg's re-election.[8] The People's party, officially backing Hindenburg, limited its support to advertisements in the TNN proclaiming Hindenburg to be above parties.[9]

The spur of electioneering even brought the Communists to

Thalburg. In February their district brass band came to town for a parade and a meeting in front of a tavern. Just before the voting the KPD staged another parade led by a ten-year-old boy wearing a red tie. The atmosphere became a bit tense when a strong contingent of *Reichsbanner* men joined the parade; the Communists rapidly decided to end their demonstration with a concert by the brass band instead of speeches in the Market Square.[10]

The Nationalists were in the campaign primarily to retain their identity. They also hoped, by increased activism, to regain the allegiance of their former followers who were drifting into the Nazi camp. Their first election meeting featured a lieutenant colonel who adopted a peculiar hedging stance on Nazism, saying that the DNVP was "against Hitler's politics, not his person." This was followed by a *Stahlhelm* "Theater Evening" with a century-old comedy of manners, and two other political meetings in the last week before the election. One, featuring a DNVP Reichstag member, who spoke of experiences during a trip to the USSR, drew a sizable crowd. The second meeting, poorly attended, heard a member of the *Stahlhelm* attack Hitler vigorously, claiming that he wanted to dissolve the *Stahlhelm* and institute Socialism.[11]

This extensive political activity was as nothing when compared to the Nazi effort. A month before election day the NSDAP brought the Nazi Minister of the Interior of Braunschweig to Thalburg for a mass meeting.[12] But instead of following this up, Thalburg's Nazis attempted a new tactic. No further meetings were held until early March, but then the Nazis rented the *1910er Zelt* for eight days running. Mass meetings were held on four different evenings, and daytime demonstrations were used to keep the town saturated with Nazi propaganda. It was an all-out campaign and it completely eclipsed the efforts of the opponents of Hitler.

The first mass meeting was held on Sunday, March 6; the speakers included the pastor who had spoken at the church-oriented gathering the previous month, and a Nazi member of the Provincial Parliament. There was an enormous crowd. The general theme was the desperation of the middle classes and corruption in Berlin. Two evenings later a mass meeting was directed towards workers with "the former red sailor, party-comrade Madel, and the former Communist miner, party-comrade Knauth" speak-

ing on "The Treason of the SPD and KPD to the Workers. Marxism Our Death, Only National Socialism Our Salvation." Poor
weather caused a poor turnout, which was probably just as well
for the Nazis, since the second speaker had some nasty things to
say about "indifferent bourgeoisie who won't help the workers,"
words of doubtful appeal to the overwhelmingly middle class following of the NSDAP in Thalburg. Both of these meetings had
cut-rate admission: 30 *pfennig* and unemployed free.[13]

Thursday, March 10, was given over to the SA. By full use of
all Stormtroopers in Thalburg County and neighboring areas, the
Nazis were able to stage an hour-long parade with band, fife-
and-drum corps, and close to 1,500 SA and SS men. The streets
were packed with friends, enemies, and the curious, and the
marchers were greeted alternately by cheers and catcalls. At the
Market Square numerous Communists were massed. The Nazis
sang the "Horst Wessel Song" as they passed, accompanied by
hoots and curses from the crowd and finally by the *Internationale*
as a riposte. Thalburg's police, heavily reinforced by state troopers,
managed to get the Nazi parade past this narrow passage without
incident. The Brownshirts wound up their demonstration in front
of the *1910er Zelt* with a speech. But when the Nazis started to
march back through the center of Thalburg, they found their way
blocked at the railroad tracks by an enormous crowd, well leavened
with Communists. The crowd disdained police orders to clear
the area, whereupon the police moved on them with nightsticks,
arresting many. This led to new difficulties as the crowd attempted
to recapture the prisoners. The police, almost powerless in the
face of such a mob, finally released the prisoners in the Market
Square, where they were greeted by cries of "Red Front!" Through
all this the Nazi Stormtroopers kept perfect order in their ranks
and eventually dispersed quietly.

Socialists were particularly incensed by the day's happenings
because on the previous Sunday the *Reichsbanner* had been forbidden by the police to sing songs or wear uniforms in their parade,
while on this occasion the Nazis were allowed to do both. The
SPD contended that all difficulties could have been avoided if the
police had been firm with the Nazis. This charge deftly obscured
the main effect of the violence, which had been to make Nazi

charges against the "Marxists" appear reasonable in the eyes of the bourgeoisie.

In any event, by evening the town had cooled off and there were no further difficulties. The NSDAP filled the *1910er Zelt* for film-slide lectures on "How They Lie" and "The Braunschweig SA March" plus a speech on "Money Measures in the Third Reich." [14]

Nothing had been planned for the following day, Friday, but nonetheless there was a big event when Adolf Hitler passed through Thalburg at noon on his way to a neighboring town. He was met and cheered by a group of Nazis, and paused to express his thanks before driving on. Tempers were still high enough from the previous day so that the *Fuehrer's* reception was not altogether friendly. His car was forced to stop at the railroad crossing, where a crowd of unemployed greeted him with cries of "Red Front." His SS bodyguards cleared the way by displaying pistols, which prompted the *Volksblatt* to ask rhetorically: "Are we already in the Third Reich?" [15]

The final Nazi event was an "Evening of Entertainment" on Saturday night (election eve) with a band concert and the *Gauleiter* of Hannover speaking on "Into the Final Flight." It was well attended.[16]

This kind of electioneering—by last minute saturation—may or may not have won votes. It is impossible to say whether or not the votes gained by the Nazis in the election reflected primarily these tactics or the accumulation of other factors. In any event, it was a most impressive display of power, imagination, and energy. The mass meetings were varied and interesting, the street demonstrations were orderly and powerful, and the timing skillful (from straight speeches down to pure entertainment). This was an example of Nazi agitational and organizational ability at its best.

The resulting election statistics indicated for the first time how much the Nazis had gained since the Reichstag elections of September, 1930. They had approximately doubled their support in Thalburg. With 3,261 votes for Hitler, the Nazis now had 51 per cent of the townspeople behind them. The parties of the so-called Hindenburg bloc (the SPD, the Center party, the People's party, and most of the splinter parties) had together polled almost 4,000 votes in 1930; now they lost over 1,100 to Hitler. The Nationalists, despite vigorous electioneering, saw their voting totals cut in half. The Communists gained sixty-seven votes (but were to lose them within a month). The Nazis had gained their increased support by winning at least three-quarters of the three hundred or so "new voters" and by drawing from the other parties, especially those of the bourgeois center.[17] The NSDAP could now boast an absolute majority in Thalburg.

It would be hard for the Nazis to surpass the impact of this campaign, yet this was exactly what they were then asked to do. In the March 13 election, Hindenburg had received a clear plurality, but not a majority (nationally, Hitler had received only 30 per cent of the vote). Thus a second election had to be held, on April 10, four weeks after the first. Since Hitler ran for the presidency again, Thalburg's Nazis had to begin their campaign all over again. Moreover, their campaign began under most inauspicious circumstances, since they had been discovered preparing for a *coup d'état*.

Rumors of an impending Nazi *Putsch* were especially numerous immediately before the first presidential election. The TNN declared that these rumors were unfounded but pointed out also that the police and state troopers had canceled all leaves and were on the alert to maintain peace and order. The *Reichsbanner* had by this time stepped up its campaign of readiness for a counter-stroke. By the beginning of 1932 there were four hundred trained *Reichsbanner* members in Thalburg, which was also the headquarters of the Tenth *Reichsbanner* District (Thalburg plus three other counties), which numbered about two thousand members. *Reichsbanner* strategy assumed that the workers would be armed by the undersized German Army in the event of an uprising by Nazi Stormtroopers. Hence they undertook frequent covert military maneuvers and rapid mobilization tests; within a half-hour they could assemble the entire Thalburg force, without using telephones, automobiles, or bicycles, as their repeated "test alarms" proved.[18]

On March 13, 1932, the Thalburg *Reichsbanner* was in a state of alert and watching Nazi actions very closely. In the evening, a considerable number of Nazi Stormtroopers, instead of listening to the election returns, gathered in the woods above town in uniform. *Reichsbanner* men were dispatched to keep tabs on them and were able to creep within fifty feet of the assembled SA. The police were then informed and promptly came out from town and dispersed the Brownshirts. Some of the Nazis regathered at the SA soup kitchen where they were joined by a number of other Stormtroopers from neighboring villages. About three in the morning the police raided the soup kitchen and ordered the Stormtroopers to leave Thalburg. The rest of the night was uneventful.[19]

This might be dismissed as romantic shenanigans except for a simultaneous event in a town about ten miles from Thalburg. There, on election day, the police intercepted a truck loaded with five rifles, eighteen helmets, eighteen new rucksacks (each with two-day rations), two hundred rifle bullets, and a thousand cubic centimeters of explosives plus two detonating lines. The rucksacks were marked with the names of local Nazis; consequently the local NSDAP headquarters was searched, yielding twenty-eight additional helmets and several thousand more rounds of ammunition. The police also discovered that the town's Nazis had plans to assemble in a nearby woods. The whole story was prominently reported in the TNN.

By now the town began to take on an atmosphere of civil war. Over the previous weekend both *Reichsbanner* and SA had instituted "patrols" through Thalburg's streets and had maintained standing forces at their respective headquarters, even after the election. The police became so nervous that they called in state troopers for reinforcement and cleared out both headquarters. In addition, the Mayor of Thalburg (and of the neighboring town) and the Thalburg County Prefect joined to issue a blanket prohibition of "alerts" in political headquarters and of all "patrols." Henceforth both sides had to be more circumspect.[20]

Because of their suspicious actions on election day, the NSDAP was under a temporary cloud in Thalburg. Official Nazi sources promptly disclaimed all knowledge of the arms discovered in the neighboring town and then later stated that they had expelled those guilty of the action. The leader of the local SA group issued a statement declaring that all SA actions were defensive, being designed solely to protect the lives of its members against the Iron Front. The SA *Oberfuehrer* gave his oath that no *Putsch* had been planned for the day of the presidential election. Within a few days Thalburg's Nazis advertised that their district propaganda leader would speak on the subject, "Not Civil War; Rather the Renewal of the Republic." Though the meeting was to be in the *1910er Zelt,* admission was cut to 30 *pfennig,* with unemployed admitted free. But Thalburgers never heard this speech, since another speaker was substituted and delivered the standard diatribe against internationalism, freemasonry, conservatives, and the "system." There was a good crowd and the matter of the rucksacks, helmets, bullets, explosives, and nocturnal gatherings in woodsy spots was never brought up again by anyone but the Socialists.[21]

The new election campaign also served to draw attention away from the *Putsch* alarms. Hindenburg had come so close to re-election that the SPD did not put much effort into the second presidential campaign. It held only one meeting, under the auspices of an *ad hoc* "Hindenburg Committee." The speaker was a member of the People's party, Professor Percy Schramm of the University of Goettingen, who gave a calm talk entitled "Why Hindenburg?" During the discussion period, Kurt Aergeyz, the local Nazi leader, gave a bitter speech in opposition. When he finished, all the Nazis present left the hall singing the "Horst Wessel Song." An eighteen-year-old Nazi called out "Croak Hindenburg," for which he was promptly arrested.[22]

The other parties were similarly inactive. The Nationalists, who had decided to back Hitler in the second elections, held only one meeting for this purpose. Apparently there was some grumbling over DNVP tactics at this time, since its "non-partisan" women's auxiliary, the Queen Luise League, inserted the following unique advertisement in the TNN:

QUEEN LUISE LEAGUE
The Local Group leadership calls on its members to
PARTICIPATE IN THE REICH PRESIDENTIAL ELECTION
on this Sunday.

Even though the League officially withholds its voice and, on the basis of its constitution, which provides for a strongly anchored non-partisanship, exercises no pressure, nevertheless this does not mean that you need not vote.

This second election also counts in the struggle against Marxism for the freedom of the *Volk*. Therefore, on April 10, EVERY VOTE TO THE CANDIDATE OF THE HARZBURG FRONT, *ADOLF HITLER,* no matter what national party individual members otherwise feel themselves drawn to.[23]

The lack of electioneering did not mean that the mood of violence had subsided. By 1932 Thalburg resembled two armed camps bivouacked in one confined and tension-laden area. If constant police vigilance prevented most major battles, it did not eliminate individual violence, which hardly abated at all between the elections. Two days after the first election the police had to go to the Employment Office to rescue Tumpelmann (who had not yet been jailed for his part in the "Referendum Day Battle" of the previous August) from an angry crowd. Just as the police arrived, Tumpelmann clubbed a Socialist with his cane. The crowd followed the police all the way to the city jail and were dispersed only with difficulty. A week later there was a barroom brawl involving about fifteen people, which was prevented from developing into a major battle only by rapid police action. Both sides began carrying side-arms. Early on the morning of the second presidential vote a Nazi was arrested for having fired his revolver at a Communist on the main street of Thalburg. That same day, a *Reichsbanner* man was arrested for having an army pistol and five bullets on his person.[24]

Under these circumstances no political parades were permitted in Thalburg, which prevented the Nazis from staging another SA spectacle. Nevertheless the NSDAP attempted to repeat its last minute electioneering tactics. A week before election day the first of the mass meetings was held, featuring the team that had spoken in the previous campaign, Knauth and Madel. This time the weather was good; they drew a full house. Both attacked "Marxism," which Madel characterized (in mirror image of Socialist charges) as being a threat to women, especially mothers. Knauth developed the thesis that "Marxism" was anti-national rather than international and claimed that Hindenburg was being "duped into saving the system." Five days later there was an "evening of entertainment" with a four-act play ("1914, 1918, Corruption, Nazi Victory") plus song and dance. The final meeting came on election eve and consisted of a speech directed to the only group to whom the Nazis had not yet made a specific appeal—pensioners and war widows. Such persons were admitted free and attendance was excellent.[25]

This was a commendable effort—four meetings, with three held in the week before election day—but it definitely lacked the punch of the previous campaign. Particularly missing was the pageantry of mass parades. Nevertheless, in the vote of April 10 Thalburg's Nazis gained 435 votes over the election of a month earlier. Over half of the Nazi gain came from the newly won support of the Nationalist party (240 votes). The Hindenburg Bloc lost only twelve votes while the Communists lost fifty-five; all of which must have gone to Hitler as must also the 106 new voters whom the Nazis had gotten out by vigorous campaigning. Hindenburg was re-elected by a comfortable margin, but nationally the Nazi vote had risen to about 37 per cent of the German people.

The electioneering of this incredible spring was not yet ended. There still remained the election of a new Prussian Parliament, scheduled for April 24, in which about three-fifths of the German people would vote.

The SPD, at last able to campaign for candidates they endorsed wholeheartedly, set to work for the Braun-Severing government. Two meetings were held in the two weeks available, both under the auspices of the "Thalburg Iron Front" and both in the Riding Hall. Over a thousand came to the first meeting at which a Reichstag member from Berlin spoke on the election, while Thalburg's Karl Hengst, himself a candidate in the election, attacked the "Thalburger Nazi lies." The second meeting had poor attendance because of rain. The speaker, an SPD Reichstag delegate, compared the Prussia of the three-class vote to that of 1932 and exhorted the audience to vote SPD so as not to lose all the good things gained.[26]

Two of the splinter parties also entered the campaign. The *Staatspartei* held a meeting entitled "We Want No Hitler-Prussia," but about the only people present were a strong contingent of *Reichsbanner* men who turned the meeting into an anti-Nazi demonstration. After this experience, the *Staatspartei* gave up activity in Thalburg.[27] The other splinter party active in the campaign was the German Hannoverian party, a cranky and reactionary states rights group. Their slogan for the campaign was "Against Prussia to the German Reich." [28] The faltering German Nationalist party also held a meeting during the two-week campaign, stressing its demand for a balanced budget and an end to the dominant SPD-Center party coalition in Prussia.[29]

The Nazis showed no signs of the weariness which might have been expected. They inaugurated their third campaign just four days after the final presidential election with a mass meeting featuring Gottfried Feder, who had done so well in Thalburg the previous year. Advertisements announced "Password Prussia." There was a huge audience and the Nazi claque kept up a rolling applause as Feder used heavy sarcasm to attack the newly reelected Hindenburg. The reaction of some townspeople to this was distinctly negative.[30] Eight days later, and just before the election, there was a final meeting, with a Reichstag member, at which all effort was given to attacking the SPD. Despite rain there was a full house. This made a total of ten meetings during the eight weeks of electioneering for the Nazis, almost all strongly attended.

Much Nazi effort was also devoted to their rural strongholds in Thalburg county. The few Socialists who lived in the surrounding villages felt terrorized, so much so that the *Volksblatt* reminded its rural readers no fewer than three times during the two-week Prussian Parliament campaign that the vote was secret.[31] In Thalburg itself the period of intense political activity came to a climax on election day with a major battle between Stormtroopers and *Reichsbanner* men. Teams of both were out hanging election posters that morning, and a fight involving about twenty-five men developed when the Socialists began to rip down Nazi posters. Neither side had weapons with them, but a picket fence was rapidly stripped to provide clubs. Contrary to explicit police instructions, both paramilitary forces had units on alert at different spots in town and within a few minutes each side was reinforced by sixty or seventy men. Fortunately the police arrived in time to limit the outbreak, though several men were badly wounded. Subsequently five *Reichsbanner* men were indicted for assault, but four were acquitted and the fifth received a suspended sentence. This did not put an end to the destruction of opponents' placards, but it did lead to its being done more covertly.[32]

The voting showed little change from the second presidential election. The total vote dropped by only fifteen while the Nazis lost only seventy-six; in other words, they held tight to virtually all the gains they had made in the presidential elections. With 3,620 votes out of a total of 6,585 cast, the NSDAP now represented 55 per cent of the people of Thalburg. Behind them were the Social Democrats with 2,024 votes or 31 per cent (down 222 votes since 1930). The remaining 14 per cent was divided among the Nationalists, Communists, and the splinter parties.

As these figures suggest, Nazi gains had come at the expense of the small parties of the center and the moderate right. In 1928, these parties had had the backing of almost half the voters of Thalburg. But these voters divided their allegiance among no fewer than ten parties, including such esoteric groups as the Farmers, House-and-Landowners party. By the Prussian Parliament election of April, 1932, these parties had been reduced to the point where, between them all, they controlled no more than about 450 votes. By the summer of 1932 they were whittled down to 200 votes, even though the total votes cast had been increased by over 1,200. Their erstwhile supporters were voting Nazi.

In Thalburg the most important of the minor parties was the People's party, the DVP. In 1928 it was second only to the SPD in size, with 834 votes. In 1930 it withstood the Nazi onslaught better than all the conservative parties, losing only forty-six votes. But by the time of the Prussian Parliament election the DVP too had to surrender its electorate to the Nazis and was left with only 154 votes. By the summer of 1932 it lost half of these, and with sixty-nine votes became totally insignificant.

If the DVP was the most popular bourgeois party in Thalburg during normal times, this was probably because of the civil service element in the town. Its realistic acceptance of the Weimar Republic, its generally non-demagogic character, and its connections with Gustav Stresemann appealed to the solid burgher. Yet the DVP was unequivocally capitalistic and nationalistic. In Thalburg the leading personalities of the People's party were very solid citizens: the director of the Grain Mill, the publisher of the TNN, and two highly respected teachers at the *Gymnasium*. In the eyes of most Thalburgers, this was essentially the party of the middle way as exemplified in the persistently calm and generally moderate propaganda of the TNN.

What destroyed the DVP in Thalburg was its ambivalent attitude towards democracy and its antipathy to the Socialists. When it combated the Nazis openly, as it did in the September, 1930, elections, it was able to retain its followers. By the following spring, however, it joined in the drive to dissolve the Prussian Parliament, putting its enmity for the SPD ahead of its repugnance for the Nazis. A year later, the DVP switched sides again and allied with the Socialists to back Hindenburg.

The basic ambivalence of the People's party was well exemplified by a meeting which it held for the Prussian parliamentary election of April, 1932. The speaker was a retired admiral who declared his opposition to splinter parties, to unscrupulous radical propaganda, to the Nazis, and to the Social Democrats. He was especially opposed to the Communists, to "emotion in politics," and he excoriated Brüning for not admitting Hitler to the government. It was not wholly clear what he favored.[33] In subsequent campaigns the DVP was more explicit. What it wanted was an authoritarian state based on the power of the president, which would "destroy the awful party politics of the Reichstag." [34]

The DVP's contribution to the cause of democracy was indeed dubious. It did oppose the Nazis, but mainly for their "radicalism." The TNN also clucked its tongue over excesses of every sort. This was, just as in the time of Aristotle, a good viewpoint, and one well suited to periods of normality. But these were radical, excessive times, as attendance at Nazi meetings showed. The TNN's prissy moderation served essentially to relax its readers after supper; it could not combat Nazism effectively. Had the DVP and its organ pushed for a reasoned and progressive democracy, the NSDAP might have found it a more dangerous opponent than the SPD. But by its fuzzy opportunism and blind "anti-Marxism" the DVP in Thalburg not only proved incapable of dealing with the Nazi threat but also probably denied Thalburg's middle class the only feasible alternative to the NSDAP.

In 1928 the third largest party in Thalburg was the Democratic party. At that time it polled about five hundred votes, close to 10 per cent of the total. Thalburg was exceptional in this respect, for nationally the Democratic party fared so poorly that it went out of existence even before the great Nazi electoral surge. It had been the party of non-Socialist, non-Catholic backers of the Weimar Republic. At its demise some of its members voted for the SPD and some for the DVP, according to their feelings on "Marxism." [35]

There had existed in the Democratic party an extreme right wing which founded a successor party called the *Staatspartei* (State party). In Thalburg it manifested itself as anti-Nazi but also as authoritarian, hyper-nationalist, anti-Socialist, and anti-semitic— a poor imitation of Hitler's movement. Since Thalburgers preferred the real thing, the *Staatspartei's* voting totals dropped from 246 in 1930 to 105 at the time of the Prussian parliamentary election. By autumn, 1932, only thirty-four people voted for the *Staatspartei;* it served only to clutter the ballot.

The final splinter party of any consequence in Thalburg was a peculiarity of the area formerly encompassed by the Kingdom of Hannover and reflected the xenophobia of some of its inhabitants. This was the German Hannoverian party (DHP), which was created in the Bismarckian era as a protest against Prussian dominance in Germany. The goal of the Hannoverians was to "rectify the crime of 1866," i.e., to separate the lands of the former Kingdom of Hannover from Prussia (which had incorporated them after the Austro-Prussian War of 1866). That this remnant of nineteenth-century particularism had no relevance to the problems of Weimar Germany goes without saying; nevertheless, the DHP did have views on other subjects and it did have a following. Its position was nationalistic, conservative, authoritarian, and anti-Socialist. Its following was provincial, cranky, and old-fashioned. What is amazing is that the DHP had so strong a following. In 1928 it had 455 votes—over 8 per cent of the total cast. As the realities of the depression bore in on the people of Thalburg, these rapidly melted away. By April, 1932, the DHP registered only sixty-two votes, which represented the hard core of "Hannover Firsters."

The DHP's contribution to the political struggle in Thalburg was essentially negative. Being opposed to the SPD, it backed the Nazis at the time of the attempt to dissolve the Prussian Parliament, though it voted for Hindenburg in 1932. It publicly opposed a dictatorship and radicalism in general, but even in the momentous year of 1932 the DHP proposed, as its key plank, the separation of Hannover from Prussia.[36]

Thus by backing a program hopelessly out of touch with reality, the DHP provided the Nazis with some four hundred votes—its own followers who deserted because they had not been provided with an adequate political understanding of what was wrong with Nazism. Like the other splinter parties it had paved the way for Hitler by promoting nationalism and anti-Socialism. In fact the essential contribution of the splinter parties had become wholly clear by April, 1932. They served as the repository of potential Nazi backers.

The failure of the middle class parties to withstand the Nazi electoral drive was caused by many factors, some of which have been mentioned. But overriding them all was the inadequacy of their followers' commitment to (or understanding of) democracy. The German middle classes hardly wanted a nihilistic dictatorship, but their ideological heritage from the days of Bismarck and Kaiser Wilhelm II left them ill prepared to appreciate what Nazism would mean or to develop a viable alternative to it. In the panic atmosphere of the depression they responded to Nazi symbol manipulation out of ideological poverty. In this sense the growth of Nazism was as much the product of two generations of the erosion of democratic values as it was of the constellation of circumstances present in the years of Hitler's drive to power.

One final item emerged from the voting totals for the three elections held in March and April, 1932. The Communist party went into these elections with 115 votes, rose to 182, and then dropped again to 117 in the Prussian parliamentary election. From this it seems clear that at least sixty-five Thalburgers switched from the Communists to the Nazis. Subsequent elections were to show increasing numbers switching back and forth between the two totalitarian parties.[37]

Obviously some Thalburgers were ready, by 1932, for any dictatorship, as long as it guaranteed revolution.

CHAPTER 8

THINGS FALL APART

(Summer, 1932)

Things fall apart; the centre cannot hold;
Mere anarchy is loosed upon the world,
The blood-dimmed tide is loosed, and everywhere
The ceremony of innocence is drowned;
The best lack all conviction, while the worst
Are full of passionate intensity.
　　　　　　　　—W. B. YEATS, *The Second Coming*

When relative calm descended on Thalburg after the elections of
March and April, the average citizen (who had probably voted
Nazi) could take time to consider what the depression had done
to his town since 1930. The first fact to emerge from various newspaper reports was that people were spending less. In the town's two
secondary schools the number of students had dropped from 472
in 1930 to 387 in 1932. This was clearly a matter of parents
saving money, for there was a simultaneous rise in the number of
students in the public schools. In the vocational schools, where
tuition was only 16 marks a year, enrollment had fallen by a
quarter since 1930. It was an ominous sign when parents saved
at the expense of their children's future.[1]

Thalburgers retrenched sharply on any unessential spending.
The secretary of the Museum Society reported that membership

dropped by 12 per cent in 1932 because people were unwilling to pay the annual dues of 2 marks.[2] The number of passenger cars owned by Thalburgers dropped to 143 by 1932, which brought the total back to the 1929 level.[3] Between 1930 and 1932 receipts from dog licenses fell by a third, as did entertainment tax receipts, and even the number of bath tickets sold at the public bath house. The townspeople even economized on the cost of gravestones and burial plots at the town cemetery, where receipts were cut almost in half between 1930 and 1932.[4]

A more serious manifestation of economic atrophy appeared in housing construction. In 1930 there were sixty-eight new dwelling units built; in 1932 there were only sixteen, twelve of which were publicly financed. This was despite a mounting housing shortage. Already in 1930 there were 136 families who needed new apartments either because they were living with relatives, or in condemned buildings, or had registered as "shelterless" and were housed by the authorities. Some of the latter paid 5 marks a month to live in the old Army compound. Others were put in emergency barracks and paid no rent at all. In 1930 a monthly average of fifty-one persons were so housed; by 1932 the average number rose to 114. Not only did this create an explosive social situation by compressing destitute people in a small area; it was basically irrational. There were many large apartments in Thalburg too big to be rented, which the "shelterless" could have afforded had these been subdivided.[5]

Even more ironic is the fact that there was capital available in Thalburg to finance the subdivision of apartments or the construction of new ones. In the City Savings Bank alone there were at least 1,500 accounts with over 100 marks each and another eight hundred accounts with over 500 marks each.[6] Beyond this were the savings Thalburgers had invested in stocks, bonds, and the other banks of the town. The more Thalburgers became concerned about the depression, the more they curtailed their consumption in favor of savings. The depression thus affected their emotions more than their pocketbooks, and if spending in Thalburg fell it was not because the middle classes were hurt; it was because they were hoarding their cash.

Two groups were hurt by the depression—the small artisans

connected with construction, and the workers. Artisans in the building trades were definitely pinched by 1932, though they were able to keep operating on a reduced basis. By the summer of 1932 a convention of craft masters in Thalburg called for a public works program and bitterly denounced both illegal competition and the capitalist system. There were, nevertheless, few artisans who were actually driven out of business, unless they were inefficient to begin with.[7]

It was different with the town's workers, especially those already unemployed. Customarily, unemployment abated in the summer months from the crest of the late winter. There was no quick summer recovery in 1932; the high level of unemployment persisted. The only change in the statistics was an ever-widening gap between the numbers of those unemployed and those receiving regular or "emergency" compensation. Furthermore, new rules went into effect in June, 1932, limiting welfare payments to those who had previously been on regular payrolls. Many young people were thus excluded from all support and there were bitter protests.[8] By July only a third of those registered at the Thalburg District Employment Office were actually receiving payments there. Most of the rest had been without work so long that they were wards of official charity, men who had forgotten what it was to work, men without a future.

For these men the summer of 1932 was dry and barren rather than fruitful. This was literally so since heat records of a hundred years were broken in July. There was also a major increase in the incidence of polio that summer.[9]

Despair was bound to register politically, even in the working class with its solid ties to Social Democracy. In the spring elections of 1932 the SPD showed its first losses of the depression era. Only 222 voters were lost (an eleventh of the previous total, most of whom apparently voted Communist though some must have gone Nazi), but even this was portentous for a party that had been growing steadily for decades.

To the stolid Socialist leaders the solution had to strike at the roots of the problem and hence could only take the form of a massive public works program. But Thalburg had no money for this. The town's budget had balanced for the first two years of the depression, but only because it was steadily cut. By 1932 the budget came to only one million marks, whereas in 1929 it had been a million and a half. Even then there was a fifty-thousand-mark deficit envisaged for 1932, and both the beer and head tax had been raised. Not only were welfare costs increasing enormously, but tax sources threatened to reduce their yield. In 1931 and 1932 the business tax percentage was the same, but the yield from the profits tax was only half as much in 1932 as it had been the previous year. The German tax system, which allowed the collector to charge on the basis of capital holdings where profits taxes were insufficient, kept this drop in profits taxes from cutting the total business tax income, except by about 5 per cent. But it was clear that tax receipts were not rising to meet the rising welfare costs, and that a continued tax on capital rather than profit might be dangerous.[10] Nor could the town borrow money for public works projects, since by 1932 the various emergency decrees of the central government prohibited this.[11]

Nevertheless, the Socialists insisted constantly that public works be inaugurated far beyond what had been done in previous years. In April, 1932, the SPD faction on the City Council brought forward a new detailed works program involving mainly road construction and other projects which would require minimum outlays for materials and maximum for employment. Council members from the middle and right were dubious in view of the town's financial situation. In May the *Volksblatt* published a scorching editorial demanding that the Socialist plan be put into effect and asking what had been done with funds previously reserved for such a program. Finally and grudgingly, in June, 1932, the Council approved a limited program involving three of the SPD's projects.[12]

Over that same summer some of the central government's plans for works projects began to be realized. A unit of the Voluntary Labor Service *(Freiwillige Arbeitsdienst)* was formed in Thalburg. Its first project was to be a large sport field which would involve 5,500 workdays. This would begin to make a dent in the town's unemployment rolls, but it was too late to take effect in 1932. Moreover, the possibility of the Reich's financing large projects deterred local action. After desultory discussion the Thalburg City Council finally postponed all works projects until government funds would be available. They were granted in January, 1933—two weeks before Hitler became Chancellor.[13]

The most promising public works scheme came from the unemployed themselves. This was developed by a "Settlement Club" which was founded in Thalburg in the spring of 1932. The plan was to build inexpensive one-family houses on unused land belonging to the provincial monastery office, using unemployed workers for labor. The same workers who had built the houses would then live in them. An unemployed architect drew blueprints of a house which would be easy to build and would use very little material. The central government would lend each settler 2,500 marks if the city would provide materials and 500 marks per house. The only problem was that the monastery administration would not give up the land until the money was granted, and the Reich would not lend the money until the free land was assured.[14]

By August this impasse was overcome and the Thalburg City Council voted funds for the first thirty houses, although it was stipulated that the cost per house must be within the amount of the government's loan. The city also agreed to supply free sand, gravel, and wood from its forest. Rightist members of the Council added a proviso that all other materials had to be purchased from Thalburg business people. The next step was simple approval from the County Council, where the plan was backed by the SPD-Middle coalition. But the Nazis were very much against it.

The Nazi leader in the County Council condemned the whole settlement idea as "socialistic" and moved to postpone indefinitely consideration of the plan. The resulting debate was a violent one and at one point the whole SPD faction left the room in protest over the kind of language employed by the Nazis. At that moment the Nazis called for a quick vote and killed approval of the plan.

These tactics were then challenged by the Middle party and on a second ballot the plan was approved. An SPD motion to guarantee against a loan default by any settler fell, through Nazi opposition, since it required a two-thirds majority. At this Karl Hengst exploded and his speech against the Nazis was so strong that the County Prefect had to summon police to prevent physical violence.[15]

The Nazis later asserted that they actually favored the settlement plan but that the time was not ripe. As far as a county guarantee for the settlement was concerned, that was true, for at that point the county had an uncovered deficit of over 200,000 marks and was applying to the Prussian government for aid in view of the imminent collapse of its treasury. The deficit was mainly due to soaring welfare costs.[16]

It was now up to the town of Thalburg to guarantee the loans since the county had refused. Again the Socialists backed the plan vigorously and the right opposed it. Karl Hengst called attention to the pressing housing shortage and pointed out how even this minor expenditure would be good for the town's economy. The only argument the right brought against the settlement was that the children would have over a mile to walk to school. With the support of the Civil Servants party the SPD overrode the right in the City Council and the town became patron of the settlement.[17]

But it was already autumn, 1932; the days were growing shorter and the work could not begin. The unemployed would have to live on hope until the following spring. By that time the Nazis had seized power, inaugurated the settlement, and claimed full credit for its success.

If the town's workers were desperate over their economic plight, that was only half the story. The other half was that the Nazis, flushed with their electoral successes in the spring elections and armed with an absolute majority in Thalburg, began to apply an inexorable political and economic pressure upon the SPD's followers which the Socialists were powerless to resist.

The process was the more excruciating because, in the beginning of the spring of 1932, the hopes of anti-Nazis were momentarily raised by an action of the Reich government. In April the Brüning cabinet issued decrees disbanding the SA. The day before this occurred the *Volksblatt* gave its opinion of the Stormtroopers:

> In *Hört! Hört!* we read a note by Hitler giving the Thalburger SA the tradition of the old Hannoverian *Garde-Kürassiere*. Should one laugh or cry? The ranks of the SA are filled with thieves, crooks, and worse. The old Guards would throw them all out if they knew about this.[18]

The following day the SA was officially prohibited. In Thalburg the police, reinforced by state troopers, raided the Nazi head-quarters and searched the homes of SA and SS leaders. No weapons were discovered, though perhaps some might have been found if a policeman had not tipped off the head of the Thalburg SS a few hours before the raid. But the Socialists had the satisfaction of seeing the Nazi soup kitchen-SA barracks closed and the swastika flag that had fluttered over Thalburg since the previous fall hauled down by the police.[19]

Any rejoicing was premature. Within a few days the police permitted the Nazis to reopen their soup kitchen and the swastika was promptly raised again. Furthermore, the SA was disbanded only on paper. Within a week of the dissolution decree the *Volksblatt* discovered that "the last emergency decree seemed to have no effect in Thalburg, where Nazis in SA, HJ, and SS uniforms stroll through the town. When will the long arm of the Prussian Ministry of the Interior reach into Thalburg?" [20]

The Social Democrats nevertheless felt there was cause for extensive celebration on May Day. The *Reichsbanner* fife-and-drum corps marched all over town early in the morning to remind people what day it was. There was more music on the Market Square by the town band, and in the afternoon a stately parade wound through the town with numerous flags and banners to a beer garden. There the workers heard songs by the People's Choir, saw acrobatic acts by Socialist youth groups, and consumed much beer. A speech against capitalism brought loud hurrahs for German and International Socialism. The *Volksblatt* interpreted the event as "a turning point in the workers' struggle against Nazism." [21]

The NSDAP was at least quiet during May. The first week of that month it staged a relatively unpolitical "May Walk" in which about 250 men, women, and children made an excursion to the woods above Thalburg and then returned to the City Park for coffee and *Kuchen* in the evening. Though the Nazis' next meeting, held a week later, was boldly advertised as "The Struggle Continues," it consisted only of a talk on how the Nazis hoped to overcome unemployment by a lightly inflationary credit program.[22] Violence also abated in Thalburg, though in mid-May there was a fight between eight people in which one was seriously wounded, and in June a Nazi beat a young man into senselessness.[23] By late

May, however, the interlude of hope was over and the Nazi jugger-
naut began to grind forward again.

Nationally a cabal of Junkers and Army leaders forced the
resignation of Brüning. General von Schleicher then secured the
appointment of the right wing authoritarian, von Papen, as Chancellor in a cabinet which had not even a shadow of parliamentary
support. One of von Papen's first acts was to rescind the ban on
the SA, and for good measure he also tore up the decrees prohibiting the Nazis from wearing uniforms.

In Thalburg the Nazis chose the late spring of 1932 to oust
the SPD from its subsidiary positions of power, notably the School
Advisory Councils. This was a telling blow since the SPD had
long worried over the composition of Thalburg's schools. As early
as December, 1930, the *Volksblatt* charged that students at
the *Gymnasium* regularly greeted each other with *"Heil Hitler!"*
Ten months later the *Volksblatt* reported that two Nazified *Gymnasium* students threw a stink-bomb through the open window of
a house. It editorialized, "What are the school authorities going
to do about all the Nazi ideas in the children's heads?" [24] Though
the principal of the *Gymnasium* forbade students to give the Nazi
salute and provincial authorities prohibited student membership in
the Hitler Youth, the SPD did not relax its concern. By the end
of 1931 the *Volksblatt* charged that *Bürgerschule I* was a "Nazi
stronghold." It implied that several teachers were Nazis and noted
that the buildings and lampposts around the school were " 'decorated' with swastikas." [25] Thus the Nazi decision to expel Socialists
from the School Advisory Councils came at exactly the moment
when the Socialists were most concerned about the influence of
Nazi teachers.

In the beginning of April, 1932, the SPD initiated a campaign
to purge the schools of Nazi teachers. The *Volksblatt* charged that
August Tiere, a teacher at *Bürgerschule I,* was a radical Nazi who
read *Hört! Hört!,* taught politics in class, and wrote Nazi slogans
on blackboards, all of which was true.[26] Since it was illegal in
Prussia for teachers to belong to the NSDAP, this was a serious
matter. A few days later, the *Volksblatt* attacked two other teachers, charging one with being drunk at three in the morning and
shouting *"Heil Hitler!"* as he staggered through the streets of Thal-

burg, and the other with giving the Nazi salute during instruction and allowing pupils to carry swastika pennants on a school excursion. For the latter charge there was an eyewitness.[27] At the end of April the Socialists on the City Council formally demanded that Tiere and another Nazi teacher from *Bürgerschule I* be discharged as subversives. The Mayor ruled, however, that such action was beyond the competence of the Council.[28]

If the Socialists thought that these exposures would win them the support of the middle class they were mistaken. The SPD tried to arrange a common list for the new School Advisory Council elections, but it was turned down. As the *Volksblatt* put it:

> The bourgeoisie have decided on a "Christian-National" list made up almost exclusively of Nazis and also some former Communists who went over to the Nazis. Naturally a counterproposal must come from the workers.[29]

The Social Democrats contested the election only at *Bürgerschule I* and *II,* where their lists were called "Social-Republican Progress." Both the TNN and GHC threw their weight against the Socialists. Both reported an SPD proposal to the City Council to curtail the town's subsidies to the Lutheran Church; both reported (in the *local* news section) that the SPD had voted for a Communist proposal in the Prussian Parliament to tax away all income above 12,000 marks.[30]

The Nazis led the attack. At the end of May a Lutheran pastor who was also a Nazi Reichstag member addressed a mass meeting in which he attacked the SPD savagely and demanded that it be outlawed in Germany. In addition to claiming religious support for Nazism he also insisted that the German Army was solidly behind Hitler's movement. A week later there was an "evening of entertainment" in the *1910er Zelt* which the GHC reported was "truly Germanic." A week before the vote the Nazis demonstrated their concern for the young by holding a Hitler Youth conference in Thalburg with parades, bands, and sports events. Then, on the eve of the election, another Lutheran minister spoke at a mass rally for the Christian-National list. The speaker declared that Liberalism and Socialism were poisoning the youth, that "Evangelical [Protestantism] and German Folkdom are insepara-

ble," and that "in the National Socialist movement Christianity will
celebrate its resurrection." The meeting closed with the singing
of the "Horst Wessel Song" and repeated *Sieg Heils.* There had
been an enormous turnout.[31]

The voting was heavy in both schools. At *Bürgerschule I,*
located in the hillside residential district, the Nazis won ten of the
fourteen representatives. At *Bürgerschule II,* located on the north
side of the railroad tracks, the vote split and five representatives
apiece went to the Socialist and the Christian-National lists.[32] The
impotence of the SPD had been demonstrated on its own ground.
The following day, June 22, the Nazis celebrated by holding a
mass march in Thalburg County in honor of the old tribal-Ger-
manic festival of the summer solstice. Three bands and twelve hundred SA men from three counties combined to make it an impressive event.[33]

The Nazi victory in the school elections was depressing but
hardly catastrophic to the Socialists. What was serious was Nazi
economic pressure. The core of Socialist strength in Thalburg was
the railroad workers. In 1930, the elections for Works Council
members was won by the Socialist union with a ten-to-one margin.
In the spring of 1932 the Nazis moved to break the union and
coerce the workers into at least outward acceptance of Nazism.

The first indication of what was happening came in a *Volksblatt*
report in mid-May. The Thalburg Railroad Office was firing many
men, some of whom had worked there as long as twenty years.
Salaried workers with tenure were made to sign a release by which
they became hour-wage workers and lost their tenure. Nine men
refused to sign and were immediately fired. At the same time,
wages were reduced to 50 *pfennig* an hour.[34] A former railroad
worker, Hans Leidler, described the process:

In the spring of 1932 the Nazis made their first attempt to organize
the railroad workers. Nazism was already strong among the directory,
control offices, bureau workers, etc. It started with the highest officials
and worked downwards. From 1931 on, the officials saw to it that
those workers who belonged to the Brownshirts got privileged treatment. . . . There were often excited arguments and even some fights.
When I argued with workers against the Nazis I was ordered by the
directors not to speak during working hours. . . . In the late spring of

1932 all Socialist workers were made to sign a release removing them from tenure. The bulk of them signed rather than lose their jobs. The pressure began to be applied to the other workers and the final step was "either join [the Nazi union] or be fired." I was the only one who held through and stayed [openly] with the SPD.[35]

The process continued throughout the summer and in September there was a new wave of firings, including Leidler. For his obstinacy, Leidler was discharged without papers, which meant that he would be ineligible for either new employment or unemployment compensation. The yards director personally promised Leidler that he could keep his job if he joined the Nazi union, but Leidler felt safe because, as a works councillor, he could not legally be fired. When this happened nonetheless, and when the national offices of the union proved powerless to reverse the process, it convinced the other workers that they were defenseless.[36]

The struggle was a silent one, for apparently the Socialists were unwilling to expose their weakness, while the GHC printed the official explanation of "seasonal layoffs." The Free Unions did arrange a mass meeting in July, where the workers might expect that some stand would be taken on the matter. Instead the speeches simply emphasized the need for a defense of the Republic and the ultimate achievement of Socialism. The only reference to the immediate needs of Thalburg's railroad workers was an appeal by a union secretary for proletarian solidarity.[37]

After the second wave of dismissals at the railroad yards, elections were held among *tenured* employees for the Works Council. The day before the voting the district railroad office announced it would hire a thousand workers in the Thalburg area to replace 85 per cent of those who had been fired. In the elections Nazi representatives won four of the six seats and the Socialists won none. Results were the same throughout the district, and a man who was to become local leader of the "German Workers Front" in the Third Reich was named district representative from Thalburg. In November, 1932, thirty new workers were hired at the Thalburg railroad station.[38]

The general economic situation rendered the Socialists helpless. With thousands of workers waiting for every job, a strike would have been impossible. Legal action, even in Leidler's clear-cut case, would have foundered through a lack of witnesses; the officials were in collusion, the workers already terrorized. As a result, the only action the SPD took was to call for a boycott against all Nazi stores. The *Volksblatt* published a list of shops owned by Nazis and suggested sarcastically that "Republicans will make sure that these stores survive." [39] The boycott never took hold. Since almost all of Thalburg's merchants were Nazis, the worker had little choice. On the other hand the SPD's following of impoverished workers simply did not have the economic strength to make any decisive impact by means of a boycott, and the most politically conscious were already shopping through their consumers' cooperative.[40]

In any event one could hardly boycott the railroad, and it was there that the workers were suffering. The sense of hopelessness that the workers acquired through this experience engendered a mood of rage and despair over the summer of 1932 and led ultimately to a feeling of resignation that helped insure a frictionless seizure of power in Thalburg after 1933.

There was one final blow which the Socialists received that summer. The inevitable result of von Papen's permissive attitude towards the SA was a wave of violence in Germany. Seizing this as a pretext, von Papen then executed a *coup d'état* in Prussia on July 20. The SPD-Center government was deposed and an authoritarian commissar replaced it. The Socialists chose to take the matter to court rather than fight. The bastion of German democracy was breeched without a shot being fired in its defense.

The Nazis not only attacked the subsidiary strongholds of the SPD in the summer of 1932, they also used their new majority to infiltrate the conservative Civic Association. Since the Socialists forced the resignation of Senator Mahner, a new executive had to be elected in July and Thalburg's Nazis were there in force to see that it was the right one. At least six of the nine new executive committee members were Nazis, including the Chairman, Vice-Chairman, Secretary, and Treasurer. The new Chairman's first act was to call on all members of the Civic Association to vote NSDAP in the coming Reichstag elections. The new Vice-Chairman, who was Kurt Aergeyz, Local Group Leader of the Nazi party in Thalburg, added that the Nazis were the sure defense of the middle class, while the Nationalist party was controlled by Big Capital. The round of applause that he drew for this statement was probably not joined by the Nationalists, who had hitherto been the backbone of the organization.[41]

The final aspect of the Nazi attack came in July of 1932, with the *Reichstag* election campaign. The election was set for July 31, but the campaigning began at least a month beforehand, with predictable results.

The constant political activity of 1932 had already brought the town to the end of its tether. Political division had spread into all areas of life. The schools were disrupted by it. Families were split on the issue of Nazism. By summer, boys in the Hitler Youth were afraid to go home alone after meetings, yet to wear an anti-Nazi insignia (such as the three arrows of the Iron Front) was also to invite attack. Political violence was becoming a permanent institution.[42]

July, 1932, brought with it not only the election campaign, but also hot, muggy weather. The SA, recently permitted to wear their uniforms, were in a belligerent mood. Socialist workers who had "hungered through" the winter found it impossible to pick up even short-term jobs. All over Germany violence erupted on a mass scale. Between July 1 and July 20 there were 461 political riots in Prussia in which eighty-two people were killed and over four hundred seriously injured.[43]

In Thalburg a mood of arrogance settled over Hitler's followers. The SA readied itself for armed uprising. The *Volksblatt* reported in June that eighty uniformed Nazis were holding military maneuvers in the woods above Thalburg and had roughed up a *Reichsbanner* man who "happened to be out for an evening stroll." Action was demanded of Thalburg's chief of police.[44] The first Nazi campaign meeting stressed the mystique of the uniform:

Saturday, July 2, 1932, in the *1910er Zelt*. ARMY MARCH EVENING with SA RECRUITMENT. The Army March music will be presented by the 44-man strong Music-train of Standard 82. ***All kinds of [Entertainment] presentations by the SA. *** Standard Leader X will speak on "The Will to Defense—The Way to Freedom."

—The SA as bearer of the spirit of 1914.
—It will be an experience for soldierly hearts.
—The evening will begin by a Propaganda March through the city.

Sturmbann I/82
Standarte 82

Advance ticket sales at Timmerlah's and at the Business Office of the NSDAP.[45]

The event fulfilled Nazi expectations as over five hundred SA and SS men marched. The *1910er Zelt* was crowded with an enthusiastic audience which applauded the SA's acts (gymnastic exhibitions) and especially the music, which, according to the GHC, "had the true ring and high spirit of Nationalism."

Four days later the Nazis held another mass meeting geared directly to the impending elections. The speaker was a Reichstag member and the topic, "Brüning—Never Again! Von Papen—a Transition! Give Hitler the Power!" The speaker clearly dissociated the Nazis from the von Papen government, insisting that "without Socialism, Nationalism is impossible." He also swore that Hitler would come to power legally but that "the November criminals and SPD murderers" would "answer for their crimes." The *1910er Zelt* rang with applause and, finally, with the strains of the "Horst Wessel Song." [46]

The Socialists, struggling to retain the allegiance of the working class and to hold back the Nazi tide, responded with extreme militance. The day after the SA's "Army March Evening," the Thalburg Iron Front held a countermarch led by the town band, two fife-and-drum corps, and many flags emblazoned with the three arrows. The speech on the Market Square was again in defense of the Republic. Five days later the Communists also held a propaganda parade with about fifty men and some red flags. The following day the Socialists marched again in an enormous demonstration sponsored by the Iron Front. The mood of militancy was reflected in advertisements for the event:

To all Republicans of Thalburg County! On Saturday, July 9, 7 P.M. in Thalburg: Demonstration of the Republican Workers of Thalburg County against Fascism. The streets belong to the Republicans! Therefore all Republicans must march! [47]

The parade lasted over an hour and a half and was led by thirty flags and the two fife-and-drum corps. In the Market Square a speaker castigated the von Papen government and closed with the cry "Let us not be beaten by the swastika in the Reichstag elections!" [48] The very next day there was another mass meeting, this time of the unemployed and sponsored by an *ad hoc* "Committee of the Unemployed" which was controlled by Socialists. Demands for better pay for the jobless were expressed and plans were made for a vast protest march in Thalburg during the coming week.[49]

July 10 was memorable for more than the SPD's meeting, however, for this was the day that the swelling pustule of violence finally burst in Thalburg. Early in the morning six Nazis beat up a member of the Iron Front who was wearing the "three arrows" pin. This set the stage for the real battle, which came about seven o'clock in the evening. About twenty-five *Reichsbanner* men were marching towards Thalburg from the Employment Office and had just started across the "Long Bridge" when they were met by a column of sixty SA men who were crossing the river in the opposite direction. The heads of the columns passed each other without incident, but the rear ranks fell to exchanging curses. The passage on the "Long Bridge" was narrow and the insults led rapidly to a general battle. Clubs, canes, bicycle pumps and other improvised weapons were used by both sides. When the "shelterless" inhabitants of the old Army compound at the north end of the bridge saw what was happening they rushed out to help the *Reichsbanner*. By the time the police arrived and broke up the battle there was a surging crowd of about eighty persons pelting the Nazis with stones. Even while the police were trying to keep the opposing sides apart, individual fights broke out and the crowd began to hurl stones over the heads of the police into the ranks of the SA. This continued until a policeman drew his gun and fired over the crowd. Both sides were finally dispersing when two SS men rode up on the Employment Office side of the bridge and the crowd let fly the last of their stones. The SS beat a hasty retreat.

As a result of the battle, three men were hospitalized and many others received light wounds. By the time the wounded *Reichsbanner* men passed through Thalburg, the news of the battle had brought out a hostile crowd and they were jeered all the way to the hospital.

In the subsequent trial, held in Thalburg a month later, nine *Reichsbanner* members were indicted for assault with a deadly weapon. Four were acquitted; the others were given prison terms ranging from two to six months. In passing sentence the judge declared that neither side was exclusively at fault and regretted that there was insufficient evidence to prosecute some of the SA men.[50]

Four days after the battle of the "Long Bridge," on July 14, Bastille Day, the protest demonstration of the unemployed was staged. Though planned by the SPD, the march was infiltrated by both Communists and Nazis. The day before, the Communists held a parade with a hundred men, and speeches calling for a united front with the SPD against Fascism. That evening the police arrested two Communists in the woods above Thalburg; both had revolvers and ammunition.[51]

The July 14 demonstration of the unemployed involved about five hundred men and women. It was immediately dubbed the "Hunger March" by the newspapers. Its prearranged objectives were to protest the low dole rates and to make specific demands on the City Council, such as free baths and an end to compulsory labor.

The parade assembled at the City Hall after marching through the streets of Thalburg with signs, placards, and a black flag (symbolizing a general mood of sorrow and extreme distress, as is still carried at funerals all over Europe). During the march the jobless grew restive and began to shout "Hunger!" and "Give us bread and work!" At the City Hall the cry went up for the Mayor to come out and talk to them. When he refused, angry muttering commenced and one man cried out "What shall we do with the Mayor?" The crowd shouted back: "Hang him!" Then the front line started up the steps into the City Hall.

The police immediately unsheathed their nightsticks, but some were grabbed and held while others were struck or kicked as the crowd surged forward with one man screaming, "We're coming in no matter what the cost!" When a policeman drew his gun he was told by one of the marchers, "You'll shoot only once."

Once inside the City Hall the jobless had no idea what to do next. There was a confused scramble and the police kept them from advancing beyond the first floor. One of the original leaders of the demonstration, a union secretary and local leader of the SPD, gave a short speech persuading the crowd to leave the building. Once outside they formed again and marched in an orderly manner to the County Prefecture where the Prefect came out and told them that he would like to raise the dole but that the county was almost bankrupt. Thereupon the parade dissolved.

The following day the jobless were still in an ugly mood. The GHC had written a sarcastic account of the occurrence and an angry crowd gathered before its editorial office and began knocking on the window. The police arrived in time to prevent violence. Later in the day one of the *Reichsbanner* men who had been in the fight on the "Long Bridge" was released from the hospital and was immediately set on by a Nazi and brutally beaten. The same day also saw a political brawl between two women.

Eight of the "Hunger Marchers" were subsequently tried in Thalburg before the circuit court. The trial dragged into November and was marked by more excesses. The courtroom had to be cleared repeatedly, and at one point the judge threatened to arrest the whole audience. Later he sentenced one of the defendants for contempt of court. Both the Nazis and Communists provided defense lawyers. Seven of the defendants were found guilty and given sentences ranging from six to nine months. When the sentence was pronounced one of the Communist defendants cried out from the dock, "The 'people down below' in Germany will soon give another judgment. You can lock up my body; my spirit stays free!" At this the audience in the courthouse broke into the *Internationale* and it was with extreme difficulty that the police were able to clear the room and disperse the crowd outside.[52]

After the tumult of the "Long Bridge" and the "Hunger March" the Nazis were relatively quiescent. Their sole activity came on July 18 when the SA staged a propaganda march through Thalburg County after which their choir serenaded an SA man and his new bride with the "Horst Wessel Song." [53] This lack of activity was due to preparations for the biggest event in the Nazi repertoire— a speech by Adolf Hitler.

The speech was not held in Thalburg itself, but in a neighboring town about ten miles away. To bring Thalburgers and others there, the railroad scheduled several special trains. The meeting was to be in the open air, with room for a hundred thousand in the audience. Hitler was to be preceded by Dr. Frick who would begin at eight o'clock in the evening. The grounds were to open at three. Hitler would arrive by airplane.

By early afternoon almost all seats were taken. The speakers' tribune was a mass of swastikas and flag after flag was visible behind it. The local SA served as ushers while squads of SS and Hitler Youth stood in groups. War injured were brought to the front for special places of honor; then the sick were carried in, including (it was announced) one dying man whose last wish was to see Hitler. During hours of waiting the tension grew. Suddenly at eight the crowd broke into shouts as Hitler's airplane flew over from Braunschweig where he had spoken before. There were cries of *"Heil!"* and handkerchiefs were waved as the plane flew on to the airport.

Then Dr. Frick began to speak. "If the police say they can't protect the SA, we'll protect ourselves. Just give us the same weapons which our opponents have used against us for so many years." At nine forty-five he stopped and the crowd waited, murmuring restively. A light rain began to fall. Suddenly Hitler appeared on the platform, to be greeted with a roar of joy and spontaneous *"Heils."* With a few brusque words he ordered the umbrella over the rostrum removed so that, like the audience, he would stand with bare head in the drizzle. He spoke approximately as follows:

There are moments in the history of nations when a decisive instant comes. The coming vote is not an election but a decision between two worlds—the world of Internationalism and that of the true German spirit. One must decide between a Germany riven by classes, parties, religions, and the Germany of one will, one goal. The last thirteen years have brought misery, destruction. No one else could have destroyed the national wealth, created millions of unemployed so well. These thirteen years have led to thirty parties all arrayed against one. All elements have their parties, only the German *Volk* has none. But the National Socialist

German Workers party will never give up the struggle, for only it has the courage and will to act.

As he left the tribune, there were rolling waves of furious applause interrupted by volleys of *"Heils"* and, finally, the spontaneous singing of the "Horst Wessel Song." "Everyone went home wet but full of hope," reported the GHC; "street lamps were out near the railroad station—we hear that the Marxists cut the power." [54]

Although after Hitler anything would have been an anti-climax, the Nazis still had to fill out the remaining ten days of July with election meetings. They were able to hold two meetings, neither especially distinguished. On July 25 a Viennese Nazi was brought to Thalburg for a talk against the Jews, and on election eve an "evening of entertainment" featuring 'talkie" movies of Hitler, Goering, and Strasser was held in the Cattle Auction Hall.[55] To fill the gap the Nazis turned to slanderous accusations in their newsletter *Hört! Hört!*

It is probable that press vituperation had already reached a point of diminishing returns. A case in point is the clerks at the Thalburg Post Office. A year before, the *Volksblatt* had labeled them Nazis but subsequently retracted the charge. Now, in July, 1932, the Nazis attacked the same men for being Socialists. The clerks finally responded by instituting legal action against the Nazis, forcing them to publish a public correction and apology. The clerks then made a notarized declaration that they belonged to no political party and were thus left in peace.[56]

But Nazi mud slinging worked in the case of the Thalburg Health Insurance Office. This institution, controlled by the Socialists, had been under constant attack by the Nazis since the first issue of *"Hört! Hört!* in August, 1931. A week before the Reichstag elections of July 31, 1932, the Health Insurance Office Directorate published an open letter explaining that its lawsuit against *Hört! Hört!* had fallen through because the court ruled that no reader could possibly find meaning in the tortured prose of the Nazi articles, but that since *Hört! Hört!* had renewed its attacks a new lawsuit had been instituted. The new charges, widely publicized in the TNN, were that the Health Insurance Office had permitted various labor organizations to use its mimeograph machine. *Hört! Hört!* discovered this from an employee of the office, who had subsequently been fired. The Socialists insisted that there was nothing improper in this, that the same thing had been done at the City Hall and County Prefecture for years, and that the use of the machine was paid for in every instance. The matter was speedily clarified when the County Prefect and a board of examiners went over the case and declared the Nazi allegations to be slanderous. The commission exonerated the Health Insurance Office completely on all counts and approved the dismissal of the employee who originally betrayed the matter to *Hört! Hört!* But this news was published only in the *Volksblatt,* and *after* the election. Thalburgers went to the polls with the Nazi charges fresh in their minds and probably also with the impression that somehow, as a result of all the noise, there was something wrong with the Health Insurance Office and its Socialist directorate.[57]

The Socialists also indulged in wild charges on the eve of the election, including the claim that the Nazis would pay 3 marks to any worker who would walk around town in an SA uniform and 50 marks to any man who would become a Stormtrooper. In addition the SPD held two final meetings. One, sponsored by the unions and held six days after von Papen's coup in Prussia, sent protests to the government over this. The second came two days before the election. One speaker at this meeting was the chief Socialist candidate, who gave an objective analysis of the difference between Nazi promises and performance. The second speaker was a local union secretary who refuted in detail the Nazi charges against the Health Insurance Office. Thus the meeting differed considerably from the original advertisements which had proclaimed: "We are attacking! At the enemy!" There was, however, excellent attendance.[58]

All other parties had been reduced to insignificance and hence did not campaign, with the exception of the Nationalists. Though von Papen was not a member of the DNVP, he certainly represented its point of view; hence it was the only party to back him in the Reichstag and felt that this gave it renewed political possibilities. In Thalburg the DNVP held one campaign meeting, two days before the voting, at which members carefully dissociated themselves from the NSDAP. The Nationalist speaker said he admired the Nazis for their patriotism but opposed their program, especially its "socialistic" aspects. He also condemned Hitler's wish to destroy all other parties, for "German culture has grown through diversity." The meeting was poorly attended.[59]

On Sunday, July 31, 6,730 Thalburgers went to the polls— 96 per cent of those eligible. The Nazis received 4,195 votes: an increase of five hundred over their previous high. They now represented 62 per cent of Thalburg's electorate. They had gained all of the "new" votes and had also drawn from all of the other parties. The SPD lost 385 votes in this election and now represented only a quarter of the townspeople. The only party besides the Nazis to register gains were the Communists, who doubled their vote; still they had only 285 votes, or 4 per cent of the electorate. This made them the third ranking party in Thalburg. Even allowing maximum switching of SPD votes to the Communists, at least two hundred former SPD votes must have gone to the Nazis. Suffering and a sense of helplessness had begun to overtake the erstwhile followers of Social Democracy.

The Nationalists held their own in Thalburg. With slightly more than two hundred votes they were climbing up from the nadir of the Prussian Parliament elections. While this was hardly a cause for wild rejoicing, there was much happening to encourage followers of authoritarian conservatism. Since von Papen's *coup* put the Prussian state under his control, he could now proceed to purge Prussia's administration of Socialists and replace them with conservatives. In Thalburg the Civic Association immediately arranged the removal of Karl Hengst as Deputy Chief of Police, with Senator Mahner taking his place. It also attempted to vote censure of the *Volksblatt* in the City Council, though unsuccessfully, since the middle refused to agree. Most important, however, was the removal of the County Prefect, his replacement with a Nationalist, and the dissolution of the County Council.[60]

The previous County Prefect, though a Socialist, was a man of monumental calm; he was so objective that even the Nazis were sorry to see him leave in 1932. He remained unruffled even when Karl Hengst, in the heart of a verbal battle, forgot that they were both Socialists and called him a dictator. The new County Prefect, Franz von Altberg, was a conservative anti-Nazi with doubts about democracy and a distaste for Socialists. His appointment also meant the end of the Socialist majority in the County Council, since the von Papen government decided to join Thalburg County with a neighboring one, retaining Thalburg as the county seat but dissolving the Council. A provisional committee took its place, composed of two SPD members, two Nazis, a Nationalist, and a moderate rightist.[61] The Socialists had been expelled from yet another position of power.

The symbol of all these changes was the August, 1932, celebration of Constitution Day. There was no parade. A small meeting was held in the Auditorium of *Bürgerschule I,* but the schools were not even let out for the day. Late in the afternoon there were swimming races, but that was all for this chief annual holiday of the democratic Weimar Republic.[62]

In view of what had happened over the summer, there was little to celebrate.

CHAPTER 9

THE LAST WINTER
(Autumn and Winter, 1932-1933)

> *"I am hungry! I have hunger and nothing else!"*
> —Shouted by an unemployed worker arrested for disturbing the peace, as reported in the *Thalburger Neueste Nachrichten*, December 6, 1932

Despite the crushing series of blows delivered to the Social Democrats, and despite the Nazis' decisive majority gained in the July Reichstag elections, the political situation in Thalburg slipped into stagnation after the summer elections. There was little for the Nazis to do; they were at the apex of their popularity but still without power. The same situation existed nationally. The Nazi "triumph" of 230 seats won in the Reichstag in July proved, upon closer inspection, to be hollow. The NSDAP had only 37 per cent of the vote—a proportion that had not increased since the second presidential election. When Hitler presented himself to von Hindenburg on August 13 with the demand that he be allowed to form a cabinet, the old man not only refused, he implied that he would never allow Hitler to become Chancellor. If the "legal way to power" seemed bankrupt, force was equally out of the question. When the SA unleashed a wave of terror in August, 1932, the von Papen government responded with emergency decrees under which five SA men were condemned to death for murder, and the Army told Goering that in the event of an attempted Nazi *Putsch,* they would shoot.

In this stalemate the Army seemed to have all the advantages. In Thalburg the key event at the beginning of autumn, 1932, reflected this, for it was a visit to Thalburg of troop units from the Seventeenth Infantry Regiment engaged in fall maneuvers. The town received four hundred soldiers and six officers with open arms. The newspapers were filled with descriptions of the maneuvers, the Regimental Band gave two concerts, and there were numerous "Maneuver Balls" held in various taverns. The TNN reported that the town's children were especially delighted to hear the old soldier songs, since they had a love of the military in their blood. To further their education, the children were all let out of school to watch the second day of the war games. In short, the town reveled in the pure military spectacle.[1]

On a minor scale the same sort of thing had occurred frequently before. In November, 1930, a bicycle platoon visited Thalburg and had a "comradely evening" drinking beer with members of the Thalburg Society of Former Reserve Ninety-Firsters. In May, 1931, a small motorized detachment spent two days in Thalburg on simulated maneuvers. Apparently Thalburgers were so desperate for military life that they were happy to see even police units come to town. In 1931 a party was given in honor of a troop of police who stopped in Thalburg, and in June, 1932, a "Maneuver Ball" was staged when police units visited Thalburg. It should be noted, too, that several Thalburgers were volunteer members of the illegal army (*Schwarze Reichswehr*),* for there was a unit stationed about fifteen miles east of the town.[2]

Commitment to militarism went beyond watching soldiers march. The fantastic celebration touched off by Field Marshal von Mackensen's visit to Thalburg in 1930 demonstrates this amply. In 1932 the former Field Marshal passed through Thalburg again, on his way to visit his old friend Baron von Barten (a top local Nazi),

---

* The "Black Reichswehr" was a segment of the regular Army which was concealed from the public in order to evade the restrictions of the Treaty of Versailles.

whose estate was near Thalburg. He requested that no fuss be made over him, but nevertheless he was met at the railroad station by 150 representatives of the *Stahlhelm* and presented with flowers by the Thalburg Queen Luise Society. He drove through Thalburg in the Baron's limousine (many houses had hung out flags in his honor), and was met by a *Stahlhelm* guard of honor at the "Long Bridge." The *Stahlhelm* marched behind the automobile all the way to Baron von Barten's estate before being reviewed and dismissed. Later the local Cavalry Club was invited to tea at the Baron's mansion in order to meet the old warrior. Thalburgers who delighted in this could hardly be pleased when the *Volksblatt* published a half-page photograph of the Baron's manor house, showing the servants' quarters, stables, etc., captioned: "Here lives the Baron von Barten—leader of the workers—leader of the NSDAP —further commentary unnecessary." [3]

The persistent nationalism which Thalburgers showed in the years of the depression must be taken as a political constant, but one which few could exploit as skillfully as the Nazis. Even entertainment was affected by it. The Lecture Society frequently had military speakers. Over the Christmas holidays, 1931-1932, the film "Reserves at Ease!" (*Reserve hat Ruh'!*), a military farce, broke all records for Thalburg movie houses and ran a full two weeks. It outdrew such stalwarts as Tom Mix and Harry Piel. Nor was it a tolerant nationalism. In August, 1931, the TNN reported that a small balloon from Belgium, with a postcard attached asking date and place of discovery, had been found near the town. "Many people think such things are a meaningless joke," editorialized the TNN, "but since so many of them come asking questions about wind, weather, and place of discovery, one can assume that the senders are seeking strategic information. Therefore do not send the postcards to France or Belgium. . . ." The GHC noted that the Thalburger boy who climbed the tree to get the balloon had ripped his pants; it proposed seriously that the French pay for a new pair of trousers for him. The story drew no comment from the *Volksblatt*.[4] Religion was also used to foster nationalism; though the churches did not celebrate Constitution Day, they did hold services commemorating Bismarck's establishment of the Reich and in October, 1932, they celebrated President von Hindenburg's birthday.[5]

It was in this atmosphere that Nazi appeals to nationalism and militarism, however crude, could have effect. Socialist charges that the Nazis were militaristic, on the other hand, were valueless, especially when they contained implied threats of violence. By late autumn, 1932, the *Volksblatt* was driven to demanding action of the town government against Nazis wearing uniforms and marching through the town with flags. It called such activities "provocations to violence." [6] The town's Nazis knew, however, that these were precisely the kinds of gestures that appealed to their followers in Thalburg. Thus, instead of attempting to combat the nationalistic, military-based government of von Papen, the Nazis turned the new emphasis to their own advantage.

On September 17, Thalburg's Nazis held their first meeting after the July 31 Reichstag elections. It was advertised as a "Big Army March Evening" and featured a "Sport Show by the SS." A good crowd was on hand to watch the SS perform, though their "Sport Show" turned out to be an exhibition of what were euphemistically called "defense sports," i.e., military exercises. Two days later the SA held extensive public maneuvers in the forest near Thalburg, followed by a "Maneuver Ball." Events of this type held much more appeal than another meeting, held a week later, in which "Workers of all classes! Businessmen! Artisans! Farmers!" were invited to "Storm with us with elemental rage against Marxism and Reaction!" According to the *Volksblatt,* the Nazis had only one-tenth of their usual attendance. [7]

By October, 1932, Thalburg faced a new election campaign— the fifth in eight months. The Reichstag elected in July had held only one business session, in which "no confidence" was voted against the von Papen government by a margin of over ten to one. Von Papen, who had no intention of ruling on the basis of parliamentary confidence, promptly dissolved the Reichstag and called for new elections on November 6. While it was clear that the government was supported only by the authority of von Hindenburg and the bayonets of the Army, there was no possible combination within the Reichstag that could have formed a government; 319 of the 608 seats were held by Nazis or Communists. They could not rule together, but together they could keep anyone else from ruling.

Thus in many respects the autumn Reichstag campaign was devoid of either hope or meaning. This did not prevent the Nazis from fighting the campaign with their customary skill and energy. On October 8 the first Nazi mass meeting was held—again a mixed affair rather than a straight speech. There was a lottery, music by the SA band, and a play by the Hitler Youth entitled "In the Enemy's Gold." Three days later a Nazi member of the Prussian Parliament spoke on "Down with the Dictatorship of the Money-Bags." His whole effort was aimed at von Papen and the Nationalists, and he promised that the Nazis would crush this "class-war party of capitalism." Attendance was good at both events.[8]

With the new campaign came the dreary increase of violence and vituperation. Throughout August and September the town had been quiet. The only exception came in early September when that inveterate Nazi brawler, Tumpelmann, beat up a Socialist, for which he was fined the token sum of 10 marks. On October 23, however, there was a fight between two *Reichsbanner* men and a Nazi, in which the Nazi's head was broken open. In the same week the courts fined an Iron Front member for insulting a policeman, and a Nazi for insulting a town councilman.[9] Comic relief was eventually supplied in the "Battle of the Bands" on October 10. The town band (which the Nazis considered Socialist since it frequently rented itself for SPD gatherings) was giving its usual weekly concert in the Market Square when the SA band arrived. Through police bungling the Nazis had also been given permission to play at the same time and place. The audience on the square rapidly aligned itself politically and exchanged shouts of *"Freiheit!"* and *"Heil Hitler!"* To avert violence the police drew a line down the middle of the square and manned it while the bands attempted to out-blast each other. Under the urgings of the police both bands finally packed up and the crowd dispersed quietly. Thalburgers had probably had their fill of music that day anyway, since the Communist brass band had been through town earlier on a truck.[10]

The SPD began its campaign with a mass *Reichsbanner* meeting on October 22. The featured speaker was the National Leader of the *Reichsbanner,* Karl Hoeltermann, and the meeting was preceded by a parade and a concert in the Market Square by the *Reichsbanner* band from Hannover. Since men from the entire

Tenth *Reichsbanner* District came to Thalburg for the event, the parade was impressive. Hoeltermann's speech, entitled "Our Freedom at Stake," consisted of a vehement attack on the Nazis. The whole affair was a considerable demonstration of strength. A week later the SPD youth section held a demonstration with songs and an anti-Nazi play. The final demonstration came on November 4 and featured Otto Grotewohl, who attacked both the Communists and the Nazis in an extremely emotional speech.[11]

The Nationalist party held two meetings in the campaign, both in the final week, both attacking equally the Nazis and parliamentary government.[12]

The Nazis began the final electioneering with a mass meeting featuring the League of German Girls. A speech by the Thalburg leader stressed "love of Fatherland, Folkish Community, Germanic consciousness, and German morals." Three days later a dual meeting was held appealing to "Rentiers, Pensioners, and War Invalids" and to "German Artisans and Businessmen." Prices were cut to 20 *pfennig,* the lowest amount ever charged for a Nazi meeting. In the morning the SA, SS, and Hitler Youth went to church *en masse,* and at noon the SA band gave a concert. Two days later a Lutheran minister spoke for the Nazis. Again the price was cut, though the Nazis were in financial trouble, for they made a public appeal for funds. The minister attacked the von Papen government, though as usual he stressed religion and nationalism: "There is only one God in heaven whom we serve, and only one Fatherland that we love." There was a big, enthusiastic crowd. Finally, on election eve, the Hitler Youth and League of German Girls joined to sponsor an "evening of entertainment," with songs and a dance as well as speeches by local leaders.[13]

In this election, for the first time since 1930, the Nazis supplemented their meetings with newspaper advertisements. For the week prior to the election, large advertisements appeared daily in both the TNN and GHC, consisting of short slogans such as: "Fourteen Years Misery, Shame, and Dirt! Defend Yourself!" or "Our daily bread is the prime need. We want bearable living conditions!" In addition, all sections of the party were put to work distributing literature and tickets to meetings. The Nazis were clearly running scared.

The election, on Sunday, November 6, showed the first drop in Nazi support in Thalburg. Some of this is attributable to "election weariness"; though only a hundred fewer people voted, these must have come from the NSDAP's totals, which fell by 267 votes. The main gainers were the People's party and Nationalists, though the Communists also added about fifty votes. The SPD seemed to have leveled off. Though it lost a dozen votes in Thalburg, it actually gained in Thalburg County. Yet despite the Nazi drop-off, they still controlled 59 per cent of the popular vote while the Socialists had only 24 per cent. Nationally the NSDAP seemed to have passed its zenith. It fell from 230 seats in the Reichstag to 196, while the Communists rose from 89 to 100. Yet the election solved nothing, for the Nazis and Communists still maintained their "negative majority" and authoritarian government continued.

As if to make this clear, von Papen issued a decree on election day prohibiting *all* political meetings, everywhere in Germany, for a twelve-day period. Even this did not prevent violence; two days after the election there was a fight between several SA and *Reichsbanner* men, though no one was seriously injured.[14] In the dangerous political sterility there was only one cause for optimism. By autumn, 1932, it appeared that the depression had passed its worst period and recovery could now be expected, even without governmental action. Thalburgers who studied the local unemployment figures that were published twice a month in each newspaper could see that the high point of unemployment reached in the spring of 1932 barely exceeded that of the previous year. They could note that unemployment was not increasing as rapidly in the fall as it usually did. Already in October, 1932, the district Industrial and Trade Council came to the conclusion that economic revival was underway. A statement to this effect, the first hopeful statement of the depression years, was issued to the press with evidence to back it up.[15]

This brought little cheer to the unemployed, however. Even those who found work at the sugar beet factory in autumn, 1932, earned only 2 marks a week more than unemployment pay; the wage rate was exactly half of what it had been in 1929. In November, 1932, a young woman welfare recipient began shouting "Hunger!" in the City Hall because her needs could not be met by the Welfare Office. She continued until the police expelled her. Later in November a local court sentenced a worker to a month's imprisonment for having cried "To the barricades! To civil war!" in anger over finding that the unemployment payments for his large family had been reduced. A near riot ensued at the City Hall when welfare recipients learned that the dole had been cut. Early in December an unemployed man became so incensed at the Welfare Office that he refused to leave and had to be arrested. All the way to jail he kept shouting: "I'm hungry! I have hunger and nothing else!" At the same time the Association of Industrial Accident Invalids and Widows sent a demand to the government for better and more equitable pensions.[16]

The city did what it could to help. The unemployed were offered inexpensive meat, or if one of them had a pig, the city would slaughter and dress it free at the town abattoir. Some potatoes were on hand for emergency cases, and those without any food could have free meals at the town's soup kitchen (an average of thirty-seven a day were given out in 1932). The city bath house offered warm baths at 10 *pfennig* a person, and in especially needy cases the unemployed could bathe free. A warming hall was also established for the unemployed.[17] The city took such action partly because private charity failed. The "Charity Union" of 1931 was not repeated in 1932, "so as to avoid the difficulties they had last year." Exacerbated political rivalries made cohesion among the separate charitable societies impossible.[18]

In the last two months before Hitler came to power, the Socialists were gripped by a peculiar fatalism. Since the summer they doubted their ability to control events. No public meetings were held, though the *Reichsbanner* continued its preparations for a fight in case the Nazis should seize power. In their Berlin headquarters a secret short-wave radio station was built and, after November, manned round-the-clock so as to be able to flash the signal when the Nazis struck. In Thalburg the mood of the men became more belligerent the longer they waited. *Reichsbanner* leaders warned incessantly against precipitate action. They were eager to fight and yet they had little hope of winning. A union leader burnt his membership lists in December, 1932. A *Reichs-*

banner leader from a suburb immediately adjacent to Thalburg had difficulty holding his men back from an independent strike against the Nazis, but at the same time he took the precaution of destroying his membership rolls, also in December.[19] A common worker summed up the general feeling. He saw the Nazis possessing overpowering strength, mainly financial. He would not cower before them—in fact he was one of the leaders in a fight with some SA men, for which he was sentenced to jail—but he did feel that the Nazis would come to power and that he could not prevent this. After all, he was "just a small figure." [20]

The townspeople were also convinced of the inevitability of a Nazi victory. It was widely believed that the NSDAP had already compiled lists of how positions of power would be distributed in Thalburg. Non-Socialists did not believe the *Reichsbanner* would fight; they argued that its leaders were pacifistic and lacked personal courage.[21] This despite the fact that most of Thalburg's *Reichsbanner* leaders had war medals to prove their courage (Karl Bette held the Iron Cross, First Class). But while the town waited for the Third Reich in December and January, nothing happened.

The senseless round of political activity did continue, however. The Communists persisted in agitating and distributing leaflets among the jobless in the Army compound. Communist slogans were found traced in the sidewalks with a brown oil dye that caused city workers endless trouble to remove. In January the KPD led about eighty demonstrators in a parade with placards which bore the slogans: "Open the Cupboards! Out with the Coal, Potatoes, and Bread!" This also gave the townspeople something to think about. The *Volksblatt* twice issued vehement denials that the KPD was making inroads among the Young Socialist Workers.

Contrary to popular opinion about the Socialists, the Communists were considered serious revolutionaries who would fight if the Nazis came to power. In fact, Thalburg's Communists were not prepared to fight. When Prussian police searched the homes of all leading Communist functionaries in Thalburg County in August, 1932, the total of weapons from sixteen houses consisted of one pair of brass knuckles, two "daggers," four "clubs," and a revolver.[22] But the possibility of Communist growth in Thalburg continued to provide the Nazis with a whipping boy, the middle class with new reasons for concern, and the Socialists with another cause for a siege atmosphere.

The Nazis also continued their agitation over the dead winter months. Early in December they held two events, one with propaganda films and one with diverse entertainment. In January an SA propaganda march was held and also a mass meeting in which their speaker described the NSDAP as "the last tortured cry of a *Herrenvolk*." Perhaps many of the unemployed, who were admitted free, came mainly because the Nazis had advertised that "the hall is well heated." Finally, at the end of January the SA gave another "Army March Evening" coupled with a presentation of the play "Brown Heroes." These activities did not stem from élan, as had been the case earlier, but from grim determination and inertia. The mood of the SA became increasingly ugly. A week before Christmas one of them beat an elderly Socialist so severely that he blinded him in one eye. In January, 1933, the first serious faction fight broke out in the Thalburg NSDAP with charges of financial corruption being answered by summary expulsions.[23] Like a vessel wallowing in the Doldrum latitudes, the town had cast off from democracy but as yet had no sight of the new order.

The factors that brought Thalburg to the brink of the Third Reich with a three-fifths Nazi majority (almost double the national average) were not numerous, but they were complexly interrelated. Paramount among them was the depression. Though only the working class suffered physically in the three-year crisis, the town's middle class was more decisively affected through fears that an ultimate catastrophe would thrust upon it the same fate as the "shelterless," or that social revolution would destroy its status. More important than the actual misery caused by the depression was the constant flow of news items stressing that misery.

There were only seventeen bankruptcies in Thalburg in the entire depression era, eleven of which befell small, marginal shop owners, and the other six for causes dissociated from the depression. But the bankruptcies were strung out over a long period of time and each involved lengthy and dolorous legal proceedings, all faithfully reported in the press. At the high point of unemployment, in April, 1932, only 8 per cent of the townspeople were unemployed, but the constant protests, fights, demonstrations, and the endless stream of grey-faced workers coming to the District Employment Office kept unemployment uppermost in the minds of the town's middle class. Nazi agitation drew upon this mood and intensified the unsettled atmosphere.

The despair of the unemployed not only terrified and repelled the middle class, it also destroyed the self-confidence of the workers. Years of idleness sapped their discipline; the destruction of the power of their unions left them exposed to crude economic pressures. Wage gains acquired over a decade were swept away, and even those who still held jobs lived in fear of losing them.

The depression not only created the climate of fear in which the Nazis throve, it also embittered political processes. Political rivalry in turn prevented the cooperation that was needed to mitigate the effects of the depression. In Thalburg the politics of crisis took the form of a general class war. The town's middle class had never accepted the SPD as an institution; now with the rise of Nazism it was offered a method of destroying Social Democracy. One response by the SPD was to increase the vicious ness of attacks in the *Volksblatt* against some of Thalburg's leading citizens. Responses in kind by the GHC and *Hört! Hört!* only succeeded in degrading politics and adding to the tension. Ultimately the Nazis proved the most capable at vituperation, which would have been held against them in normal times, but which was to their credit in the welter of mud slinging. Only the moderation of the civil servants bloc in the City Council made effective city government possible amid the maneuverings for partisan advantage. It was hatred for the SPD that drove Thalburgers into the arms of the Nazis. Few of the conservatives realized that after the Nazis had destroyed the Social Democrats, they would turn on their erstwhile allies and smash them.

But the Nazis never would have been chosen as the instrument to subdue the SPD if they had not been otherwise acceptable to the burghers. The attributes which made the Nazis respectable were their intense nationalism, their manipulation of religion, and the support given them by the conservatives.

Thalburg was a nationalistic town long before 1930, though as the depression wore on, commitment to nationalism and militarism increased. Outside forces contributed to this, as did Nazi propaganda, but by manipulating the symbols of patriotism the NSDAP in Thalburg associated itself with an important tradition. The same applied to the Nazis' exploitation of religious feelings, especially their use of Lutheran pastors as speakers in Thalburg. The association of the German Nationalist party with the Nazis was also a reciprocal one. The DNVP and NSDAP were more or less in alliance throughout the entire pre-Hitler era in Thalburg. The only period of real bitterness between the two came under the von Papen government, when counter-charges of "reactionaries" and "socialistic radicals" filled the air. Then, in January, 1933, the Nazis and Nationalists acted in concert again, since the Hitler government was originally a coalition.

The Nazis and the DNVP had much in common: hyper-nationalism, fanatical anti-Socialism, and commitment to the destruction of the Weimar Republic. In Thalburg, leading Nationalists were pleased by Nazi successes despite the frequent and clear signs of contempt which the Nazis showed them. The GHC gave them editorial support, reported frequently and favorably on Nazi doings, and apparently provided cut-rate or free advertising space. In the early years of the Nazi growth the GHC printing press was available for Nazi pamphlets and posters and its columns were the only way the Nazis could reach a mass audience.[24]

Though the DNVP had a small following in Thalburg they had two assets which benefited the Nazis. One was money. In Thalburg most of the members of the DNVP were either high-ranking civil servants, entrepreneurs, or noblemen. The other asset was respectability. Not only were the "best" people members; the party bore the tradition of having firmly supported the monarchy in the golden days of Germany's greatness. Finally, it seemed to have an intimate connection with the Army, through the *Stahlhelm,* whose honorary national commander was von Hindenburg. By giving enthusiastic support to the Nazis and by limiting its opposition (in the periods when the parties were at odds) to Nazi social goals, the DNVP helped pave the way for Hitler. To Thalburgers it was clear that the best people were for the Nazis except where it might affect their moneybags.

A further factor which aided the rise of Nazism in Thalburg was politicalization. The yearnings and needs created by the depression, class antagonisms, and resurgent nationalism all seemed capable of political solution. Constant elections meant constant campaigning and each campaign spurred bitterness and radicalism. From the local elections of November, 1929, to the Reichstag elections of November, 1932, there were nine major campaigns, five in 1932 alone. Thalburgers voted heavily in all of these. This followed the pattern of the whole electoral district, which had the second highest voting participation record of Germany's thirty-five electoral districts.[25] In Thalburg, between 94 per cent and 97 per cent of those eligible voted in each of the major elections. Since registration was automatic, only the sick and feeble-minded stayed home. The rest were involved in politics, which is to say that political passion pervaded almost all areas of human existence in Thalburg.

All of these factors contributed to the Nazi success in Thalburg, but even favorable circumstances do not explain the remarkable Nazi leap from 123 votes to almost 4,200 votes in three years' time.[26] To understand this one must consider the skill and effort which the Nazis put into campaigning. Quantity was the first component. In the three-year period from January, 1930, to January, 1933, the Nazis averaged close to three meetings per month in Thalburg. As the years went on, the number, size, and variety of the Nazis' public functions increased. High points were reached during election campaigns; in July, 1932, there were six Nazi functions: three meetings with speeches, two parades followed by rallies, and one "evening of entertainment." Furthermore, activity was constant; throughout the entire three-year period there were only two months without Nazi meetings (August and November, 1932).[27] Vigor was the strongest impression.

Nazi propaganda efforts in Thalburg went beyond pure activism. Persistent, imaginative, and driving effort was coupled with a shrewd appreciation of what was specifically suitable for Thalburg, and for each element in the town. Aside from general speeches on nationalism, Jews, and "Marxists," there were meetings devoted to artisans, businessmen, civil servants, pensioners, and workmen. Thalburg's local peculiarities were taken into account; there was little real anti-semitism in the town, hence this was soft-pedaled. But the townspeople were strongly religious and this was exploited to the hilt. When there was no specific group to be appealed to, the Nazis relied on pageantry, "evenings of entertainment," film showings, plays, acrobatic acts, lotteries, dances, sport exhibitions, military displays, recitals by children, and other expedients from a seemingly inexhaustible bag of tricks.[28] They drew the tortured masses into the mammoth meetings where one could submerge oneself in the sense of participating in a dynamic and all-encompassing movement geared towards radical action in fulfillment of every need. The enemy was defined in similar terms: he was the Jew, the Socialist, the godless one, or, if one preferred amorphous generalities, the System which was to blame for everything from the collapse of the Enterprise Bank to the Treaty of Versailles.

In short the NSDAP succeeded in being all things to all men. This was even reflected in the use of the name in advertisements, which were signed "National Soc. German Wkrs. Party," "Nat. Socialist Germ. Workers Party," or other variations according to the needs of the moment. From the morass of propaganda the Nazis emerged as devout, serious, impeccably patriotic, the archenemies of "Marxism," "Socialistic" only so far as it served the needs of Nationalism, and (if you ever attended their "evenings of entertainment") obviously hail fellows. But the prime effect attained by the Nazi meetings was achieved simply by their numbers. If you wanted an energetic party this was it.

Despite their efforts, the Nazis would not have succeeded as well as they did had there been any effective opposition to them in Thalburg. The various right-wing splinter parties were no competition since they agreed with the Nationalism and anti-Socialism of the Nazis and were at best highly doubtful of the merits of democracy.[29] Only two parties had an unqualified commitment to democracy and a clear appreciation of the dangers of Nazism. These were the Catholic Center party and the SPD. The Center party had a small following in Thalburg because of the religious complexion of the town, but it was stable—180 votes in each election, give or take ten. The Socialists remained remarkably stable too, considering the fact that the depression bore directly upon their followers. They showed no losses at all until the spring of 1932. In the spring and summer elections of 1932 the SPD lost 28 per cent of its votes but then stabilized itself. The social homogeneity that was the source of the SPD's strength was also the source of its inability to combat Nazism effectively. Had the

Socialists mended fences with the non-Nazi bourgeoisie they might have prevented the growth of Nazism. The town's social traditions prevented this. Had the Socialists presented a revolutionary program they might have stolen the banner of radicalism from the Nazis. Their own reformist tradition prevented this. But the basic error in strategy was to assume that the threat of Nazism lay in its potential for armed uprising. The Socialists were prepared to counteract this; what they did not counteract was the Nazi *political* threat. Instead their approach was wholly negative.

The SPD emphasized the evils of Nazism but had no alternative program. It defended the Republic but could not promise a better future. The mood of SPD, *Reichsbanner,* or union meetings was wholly defensive, even to the extent of using mass rallies in national campaigns to deal with Nazi attacks on the local level. In the ideology of Socialism the SPD had a superb weapon for dealing with the depression, but in Thalburg there was never any effort to use this weapon except for the crude vilifications of the individual bourgeois printed in the *Volksblatt.* Taken as a whole, the work of the SPD may serve as an example of the fecklessness of even the most dedicated activity without an effective strategy behind it. Furthermore, the more the SPD strove to match the Nazis in determination the more they drove the middle class into the Nazi embrace. Socialist militancy simply increased the political tension in Thalburg without diminishing the Nazi appeal.

The factors conducive to the rise of a radical mass party of the right were thus abundant in Thalburg: economic misery which seemed to grow progressively worse, a traditional division along class lines which became exacerbated by political intolerance, intense nationalism and fervid militarism, an ineffectual but belligerent left, and a splintered, indignant, insecure right. In addition to its own propaganda the NSDAP contributed one other ingredient to this witches' cauldron—the breakdown of civil order.

From 1930 to 1933 there were no fewer than thirty-seven political fights in Thalburg. Of these, four were general mêlées. These figures do not include the near misses—times when only the vigorous action of the police or the restraint of opposing leaders prevented fresh outbreaks of physical violence. There were also many times when the police forbade meetings, when contingents of state police had to be brought to Thalburg as reinforcements, and when the newspapers reported the presence or lack of violence in almost the same tone as the weather or auto accidents. Police rules and regulations, government edicts and emergency decrees, none of these sufficed to eradicate the almost daily street fights in Germany, the classic land of tight laws and strict order.

The root of the problem was the division of the town into two groups of absolute opponents, each of which meant to destroy the other, the one to institute a dictatorship, the other to save the existing, if battered, democracy. This clash of views led to mutual vilification, first by the parties, then by individuals. Libel suits became commonplace. Taunts and insults by word and deed fostered arrogance. Terrorism, especially in Thalburg County, became a standard weapon; knives, blackjacks, even guns became standard equipment. Beyond this there were the persistent rumors, some based on fact, of an impending Nazi *Putsch*.

From a sleepy provincial town, Thalburg became an explosive center of violence. It is possible to construct a "fever chart" composed of political activity and street fights.[30] It would show a direct correlation between election campaigns, frequency of political meetings, and physical clashes. All three increased yearly. Furthermore, the courts were generally lenient so that hotheads on both sides were encouraged. The culmination of this attitude came on January 20, 1933, when a general amnesty was granted to all those convicted in the "Hunger March" and "Long Bridge" battles. Thus they were free to participate in the events following Hitler's accession to power.

The heritage of three years of violence, the fruits of numerous broken heads, split lips, and black eyes were manifold. Nothing, of course, was settled by any of the fights, which were the result rather than the cause of political tension. But from them the town accumulated a full measure of bitterness. Since peaceful settlements proved impossible, Thalburgers grew accustomed to expect a violent resolution of political differences. Orderly-minded people were sickened by the recurrent fights, but finally became inured to them. Thus the way was paved for the systematic use of violence and terror by the Nazis after Hitler came to power, and for their relatively indifferent acceptance by the people of Thalburg.

PART TWO

Introducing the Dictatorship

卐

January, 1933, to January, 1935

CHAPTER 10

THE LAST
ELECTIONS

(February and March, 1933)

*If this cancer of the German peo-
ple was not all too obvious at the
beginning, it was because there
were enough healthy energies at
work to restrain it. But as it grew
and grew and at last, by a final
piece of knavery, came to power,
the cancer burst and made foul the
whole political body. Then the majority of those who had opposed it
went into hiding. . . .*
—GERMAN RESISTANCE LEAFLET DIS-
TRIBUTED IN 1942 *

The month of January,. 1933—the last few weeks before Hitler
became Chancellor in Germany—was a hard one for almost all
Thalburgers. The weather was cold and damp with that peculiar
marrow-chilling quality that one finds in the north German plain.
The slate sky gave greyness to the old buildings and cobblestone
streets and the very air itself seemed grey and dull. To the unemployed the barren branches of the trees and the frosty mud of the

---

* Desmond Flower and James Reeves, editors, *The Taste of Courage:
The War, 1939-1945* (New York, 1960), p. 400.

fields must have symbolized their own situation: stretched on the rack of despair, frozen in the mire of endless and pointless idleness.

Some had been unemployed for three years and more; others had found work only intermittently. Still others were perhaps more unfortunate: they had just reached the age when they would normally be getting their first jobs, but there were none, and it seemed as though there never would be any. To the store owner standing beside his idle cash register, to the artisan—with the proud title of "Master of his Craft"—sitting in his shop, waiting for the orders to come, it was an evil winter. Not even the children were merry, for there was a flu epidemic so severe that the schools closed, and to the ordinary man's worries were added the sight, at the end of his empty day, of his feverish children and his harassed wife.

What emotions were possible for the Thalburger in this, the winter of the depression? Even the Nazi answer—hate—seemed lackluster, as attendance at Nazi meetings fell off and the SA men stood forlorn and miserable in their haughty uniforms, shaking collection cans on the street corners. In Thalburg the Nazis appeared to have passed the zenith of their power. They had the votes of more than half of the town, but how long could they keep them when nothing happened? In the latest election (November, 1932) it was all that Thalburg's Nazis could do to retain the electoral gains they had made. Nationally the Nazi tide gave signs of receding. In Thalburg itself the Nazis seemed to be engaged in ritualistic acts: small meetings in the Cattle Auction Hall, plans for another of the repetitious speeches or "evenings of entertainment." Determination to hold on, not the élan of victory, seemed to be the characteristic note in January, 1933.

Nor did the Social Democrats of Thalburg have reason for elation. They had lost heavily in 1932. There were ominous signs of increasing interest in the Communist party among the unemployed of Thalburg. Many expected a Nazi takeover. They planned to fight, but it was no longer fully clear what they were fighting for. For the Republic of General von Schleicher or von Papen? For democracy under rule by presidential emergency decree? During the grey January of 1933 Thalburg's SPD held no meetings, sponsored no speeches. What was there to say?

The town government carried on, however, trying to deal with the depression. The City Council met on January 13, and Mayor Johns was able to announce that the budget would balance for 1933. This was accomplished by raising the town's taxes by 35 per cent. In another effort to ameliorate the lot of the poor, rents on garden lands owned by the city were reduced 25 per cent. Finally, Thalburg's share of the central government's public works money had come through and amounted to over 60,000 marks. Plans were in the making to put the money into employment-creating work. Before the meeting adjourned, Senator Hengst took a moment to accuse the Nazi newspapers of slander.[1]

By January 27 the city administration had completed its plans for utilizing the public works money. A new street would be built and several others would be repaired. The shooting societies asked the town for a new rifle range since this was a precondition for the expected holding of the North German Shooting Society convention in Thalburg in 1933. The SPD was indifferent to pleas from the town's businessmen about the money this would bring into town and refused to allocate funds, thus provoking some bitter words.[2]

In the last days of January the TNN ran a curious story. An old Jewish cattle dealer named Moses had died. He had once been well-to-do, but his fair-weather friends helped him squander his wealth and now he was to lie in a pauper's grave. On this mildly anti-semitic and moralistically lugubrious note, January, 1933, was coming to an end in Thalburg.[3]

Then, on the last day of the month, the news burst over Thalburg that Adolf Hitler had been appointed Chancellor of Germany. To all Thalburgers it was clear that the pointless wanderings of national politics were over and that at last something was happening.

The news caught Thalburg's NSDAP unprepared. The Nazis were not even able to organize a victory parade immediately after the event. However, on the weekend thereafter (Saturday, February 4, 1933) a "German Evening" complete with speeches and a military concert had been planned. And on Sunday, February 5, a conference of all Nazi Local Groups in the county was to be held in Thalburg. Now these plans took on new significance; apathy was swept away and Thalburgers flocked forward to buy tickets. A torchlight parade was hurriedly improvised for Saturday, February 4. Thalburg's *Stahlhelm,* now in coalition with the Nazis, agreed to join. The victory parade was exceedingly impressive. In addition to the fife-and-drum corps and flags of the *Stahlhelm,* there were the flags, band, and fife-and-drum corps of the SA. Nazis and Nationalists from all over the county were in Thalburg for the event. If the GHC's figures are correct there were over eight hundred Nazis and two hundred *Stahlhelmern.* It took a quarter-hour for the whole mass to pass by. The streets of Thalburg were packed with onlookers and in the Market Square there was an enormous crowd, "bigger than any heretofore seen," said the TNN. Speeches were given on the unity between Nazis and Nationalists and on the perfidy of Communism.

Most of those who had come to Thalburg for the parade left immediately afterward, but enough went on to the *1910er Zelt* for the "German Evening" so that people had to be turned away. There was enthusiastic celebration, speeches by County Leader Eckstein and other Nazis, and jubilant toasts by the *Stahlhelm* leaders on how good it was to be back with the Nazis as comrades. The Nazi talk of "reactionaries" and the DNVP charges of "dictatorship" and "proto-socialism" of the previous summer and fall were as forgotten as the vanished foam on the beer.

The following morning the Nazis sobered up to complete a strenuous series of activities connected with the county conference. In the morning the fife-and-drum corps marched through the town bright and early while a wreath was laid on the War Memorial by Walter Eckstein. There was a parade and then conferences in the Cattle Auction Hall, two hotels, and a café. In the late afternoon there was a round of speeches, particularly against Communism, at the *1910er Zelt.* The Nazis gave the impression that Thalburg was completely theirs.[4]

Repression went hand in hand with celebration. To Thalburgers the justification was the prevention of violence: within the first ten days of February there had been two fights in the old Army compound.[5] With Goering in control of the Prussian Ministry of the Interior, however, there was to be no violence, except that which was officially sanctioned and directed. On February 2 all public demonstrations by the Communist party were forbidden. The following day Thalburg's police, under orders from Berlin, raided the homes of local members of the KPD, though without finding, as the TNN reported, any "forbidden literature." By successive orders the Communists were forbidden to distribute any literature, solicit contributions, or hold meetings in homes or in public places.[6]

The Social Democrats were dealt with in a more piecemeal manner. On February 18 the Thalburg police, prodded by new Nazi officials in the Prussian Ministry of the Interior, confiscated that week's issue of the *Thalburger Echo,* the organ of the "Iron Front." The grounds were that it had ridiculed Hitler in one article and called the swastika "the bankrupt symbol" in another. This was significant news for the timorous, especially since it was intimated that the paper would soon be suppressed altogether.[7]

The full meaning of the new order came to the SPD on February 19. On that day the "Iron Front" planned a demonstration in the Market Square in Thalburg. As usual, the police had been notified beforehand. Early in the afternoon, members of the Thalburg *Reichsbanner* gathered at the old Army compound near the Employment Office. By the time the parade started out for the Market Square there were about four hundred participants plus the usual flags and musicians. At the same time about 150 SA men gathered inside the old city on Broad Street, "under alarm, and to protect the houses and the swastika flag from attack." As the Socialist parade came up to the old city walls, it was stopped by the police. Leaders of the SPD were told that there had already been clashes between SA men and *Reichsbanner* members in Thalburg. The police suggested that public security and order were threatened and ordered the parade to turn around and meet at a nearby beer garden, rather than attempt to go to the Market Square.

At the beer garden (which had aspirations to respectability) the Sunday afternoon "Coffee Concert" was being held. The nodding burghers were rather shocked to have their repose broken by four hundred *Reichsbanner* men surrounded by the police. There, isolated by the high walls of the garden and by the police cordon,

Thalburg's Social Democrats held their last political meeting, while the Stormtroopers marched freely through the streets of the town.[8]

The effect of this occurrence upon the rank-and-file of the town's SPD was enormous. On the evening of this incident Hans Leidler folded his *Reichsbanner* flag into a coffee can and buried it in a field. Others in the SPD knew the game was up, too. They pinned their hopes on the German Army. If the Army gave the word, they would fight; if not, Germany would go Nazi without organized armed resistance by the *Reichsbanner* or other worker organizations. The membership of the *Reichsbanner* was still willing to fight, but it was clear to them that unless the word was given soon they would be picked off individually by the Nazis.[9]

The Nazis now proceeded to harass the Social Democrats openly. On February 24 a Socialist pamphlet for distribution to the unemployed was confiscated by the police ". . . for ridiculing the Reich Chancellor" (i.e., Hitler). On the same day the police forbade outright a planned torchlight parade by the "Iron Front," on grounds that it would "endanger security and order." Nazi parades, of course, were permitted.[10]

Despite the absence of competition on the left, Thalburg's Nazis did not relax their agitational efforts. One of the Hitler government's first acts had been to arrange for new elections to the Reichstag, knowing that this time the campaign would be conducted on its terms. In Thalburg the first mass meeting was held on Saturday, February 25. One speech was directed to war veterans and the second was entitled "Reckoning Up with the Marxist Criminals." The speaker called on all Germans to have the same kind of faith in Hitler as had been shown by "the men of 1914" who "went to death believing in victory." The *1910er Zelt* was jammed full. On the following day the Nazis made an appeal to Thalburg's religious sensibilities by sending two hundred uniformed SA men to the town's Lutheran Church. Following the services the SA band gave a concert in the Market Square, which attracted many Thalburgers out for their Sunday constitutionals.[11]

The Nationalist party joined the campaign with a *Stahlhelm* parade followed by a "German Evening" at the *1910er Zelt*. The speeches stressed the closeness of the Nazi-Nationalist coalition and excoriated the "Party-State," i.e, the Weimar Republic. Even the People's party held a meeting, though the message was, as usual, ambiguous. The speaker insisted that the DVP would continue to be important "under the Black-White-Red [Imperial] flag." He registered his opposition to "state socialism," stressed the need for "freedom from Versailles," and concluded with an appeal to "strengthen the left wing of the Black-White-Red Front." Twenty persons attended the meeting.

On March 2, the People's party took a stronger stand. In an advertisement in the TNN on that date, the DVP reminded Thalburgers that "violence and force will neither bring economic peace nor solve the problem of unemployment." It called on Thalburgers to help ensure a strong DVP representation in the Reichstag:

That is the best assurance for the maintenance of a free citizenry and civil service, maintenance of the middle class and the working industry, maintenance of private enterprise, of a National and Liberal conscience. Those who want to hinder absolutism and want to close the ranks of all national forces, vote DVP.[12]

The allusion to "absolutism" was timely. The burning of the Reichstag building on the night of February 27 gave the Nazis a new excuse for repression of the left, and the emergency decree which followed suspended all civil liberties in Germany and thus gave the police virtually absolute power. The beginnings of informal social reinforcement of the terror system date from this event. The morning after the Reichstag fire the son of one of Thalburg's Socialists was overheard insisting to his classmates that the Nazis were responsible for the fire. Prompted solely by his awareness of the new atmosphere, the non-Nazi principal of the school suspended the boy. There were long telephone conversations with the Mayor's office and it was nip and tuck as to whether the boy would be allowed to take his final examinations a few days later.[13]

The newspapers also did their part to help create an atmosphere of terror following the Reichstag fire. For example, the TNN, on March 3, reported:

The blackest rumors have been continuously spread these days about Communist misdeeds, destructions, incendiary acts, etc. . . . They

serve to increase the general tension which has already set in before
the election. We have made inquiries to the proper authorities and
have been informed that there is not a single word of truth in these
rumors. One should strike energetically at such rumormongers. Naturally precautionary measures have been taken. The local police and
the railroad guards have been strengthened and are in a state of pre-
paredness, watching the bridges, buildings, and grounds of our railroad
station, and also certain track stretches.

In addition to the rumors there were concrete examples. On
March 1 the police confiscated "forbidden newspapers and pamphlets of the SPD and KPD" after raids on private dwellings in
Thalburg. It was also announced that a worker had been arrested
the day before for "distributing an SPD election leaflet despite the
prohibition." The instruments of repression were also increased.
On March 1, thirty SS and SA men were deputized as police. Their
uniform was the regular Nazi brown shirt with a white armband
marked *Hilfspolizei* (Deputy Police). They immediately began
patrolling the streets of Thalburg. Since these were the same men
who had repeatedly fought with *Reichsbanner* men in the previous
years, it can be imagined what their concept of law enforcement
was. The Stormtrooper achieved his dream: the chance to do violence without fear of police hindrance. The Nazis not only controlled the police—now they *were* the police.

The new police swung into action immediately. The very afternoon they were deputized, Stormtroopers raided the house of the
local leader of the KPD. Though the house was thoroughly and
violently searched, no incriminating material was found. Nevertheless a warrant was issued for the arrest of the Communist
leader, since it was suspected that "he had distributed forbidden
leaflets." Raids were also made on the homes of other Communists
and Socialists.[14]

At the same time that force was being applied to silence the
SPD, the Nazis undertook to spread slander about them. On
March 3 and 4 the Nazis published the following advertisement
in the TNN:

RESIDENTS OF THALBURG!
You want to continue your work in peace and quiet! You've had
enough of the impudent behavior of the SPD and KPD! You want

the red *Senators, Councilmen, and Reichsbanner Generals* with all their armed followers to go to the Devil! Remember the disgraceful behavior of these hordes last year! The red Messers *Hengst, Brehm, Bette* [etc.] attempted a civil war! The distribution of packages of bandages from the Health Insurance Office was a clear sign of the bloodthirsty intentions of these members of an international *Criminal Party,* named SPD and KPD. The former red Police Senator lay heavily armed with his armed hordes ready. In the barracks were brutalized Communists, armed with military rifles—the comrade-allies of Hengst and Co.—waiting for the bloody work in the streets of Thalburg. *Thalburg was to drown in blood and horror! Hitler was your savior!* The NSDAP, the SA, the SS are fighting for you, even here in Thalburg!! *Tomorrow is the day of the awakened nation!* At the ballot boxes the German *Volk* thanks the great *Fuehrer* for its salvation in the last hour! A storm will sweep through Germany! Germany Votes List 1! Heil Hitler!

NSDAP, Local Group Thalburg.

Bette, Hengst, and Brehm immediately drew up a reply to this advertisement. The TNN, however, refused to publish it. Hence it appeared in a newspaper published in a neighboring town:

RESIDENTS OF THALBURG! A CORRECTION!

Through an election advertisement yesterday the Local Group Thalburg of the NSDAP accused the undersigned of having intended a "Civil War" a year ago, manifested by "impudent," "disgraceful," and "criminal" behavior. We were supposed to have expected a blood bath in the streets of Thalburg. "Thalburg was to drown in blood and horror."

To this we declare, that we who were named in the advertisement are almost all "front-soldiers" whose bravery in action has been recognized by the awarding of Iron Crosses, first and second class, and other medals. Some of us suffered severe war wounds for the Fatherland.

It was we who, in the postwar days, regularly protected peace and order, and even in critical times restrained any of our comrades who became restive.

We and our friends have rejected civil war. We proved that not only in 1918 but also on every other occasion.

We call on our friends not to lose their calm reasonableness, despite this advertisement of the NSDAP.

We gladly leave the question of whether or not we belong to an "international criminal party" to the decision of the populace.

Thalburg, March 4, 1933.
Karl Hengst, Karl Bette, Willi Brehm [etc.] [15]

There were some people in Thalburg who read the newspapers from the neighboring town, but not many. The SPD's own newspaper, the *Volksblatt* (with its Thalburg supplement) had been "temporarily" suppressed. Thus for all intents and purposes the Nazi charges went unanswered. Nor were there any other Socialist advertisements in the Thalburg newspapers, nor public meetings, nor leaflets distributed. Social Democracy had been silenced.

The Nazis, on the other hand, were in a position to subject Thalburg, in the week before the last free Reichstag election, to the most intense electioneering the town had ever experienced. From March 1 to 4 (election eve) there were radio loudspeakers set up in the Market Square and on Broad Street, and every evening the voice of Adolf Hitler boomed across the town. During the days Stormtroopers passed out literature. On March 2, the *1910er Zelt* filled to hear Elisabeth Zander, the National Leader of the Nazi Women's Auxiliary. After Hitler's radio speech, Frau Zander spoke, affirming that now the whole world would know that Hitler was serious about "eradicating Bolshevism." Henceforth the task of women would be to buy only German goods when shopping and to instill "religion, morality, discipline, and love of Fatherland" in the children.

The great effort was reserved for election eve, March 4, a Saturday. On that night the Nazis held a torchlight parade with over six hundred uniformed SA, SS, Hitler Youth, and *Stahlhelm*. The parade ended in the city park around a large bonfire. There the crowd listened to Hitler over the radio loudspeakers, which were playing also in the Market Square, on Broad Street, in front of the church and the town hall—in short, wherever there was room for a crowd to gather.

At the park the light of the fire illuminated the many swastika flags. There were also many Black-White-Red banners, and flags of both kinds were hanging in front of the stores and from the houses in the old town. Hitler's speech could be heard at the *1910er Zelt,* too, and after it was over the crowds sang *Deutsch-*

land über Alles and the "Horst Wessel Song." Then a short speech was given by Kurt Aergeyz, after which Roman candles and multicolored rockets were fired. Finally, the crowds were allowed to go home to sleep before the voting.[16]

On election Sunday the town was, in the words of the TNN, "astonishingly quiet." The swastika and Imperial flags were still out. Nazi and *Stahlhelm* election autos brought people to the polls while units of SA and SS marched through the streets. About noon a three-plane squadron flew low over Thalburg to advertise the Nationalist party. Otherwise there were no unusual incidents.[17]

The voting was the heaviest Thalburg had experienced, with 6,802 people casting ballots—seventy-two more than the previous record set in the summer of 1932. The Nazis surpassed their previous high (from the same election) by seventy-three votes, while the Nationalists polled 105 more than they had in November, 1932. The other parties stood more or less as they had in the fall of 1932, except for the SPD and the KPD. The Communists lost 110 votes, but were still the fourth largest party in Thalburg with a total of 228. The Social Democrats lost 157 votes from their returns of November, 1932. Both Communist and Socialist votes must have gone to either the Nazis or the Nationalists, though the numbers involved are so small that analysis is problematical. In any event the Nazi-Nationalists had a clear majority. The Nazis had 63 per cent of the town's votes, the Nationalists 6 per cent. The SPD still had 22 per cent, while the KPD was fourth with 3.5 per cent.

The figures are instructive in that despite intimidation and intense electioneering, the Nazis were unable to raise their percentage of support in the town from the previous high-water mark set in July, 1932. Indeed, these figures probably represented the highest support the Nazis would ever have. This was nevertheless enough; it represented almost two-thirds of the town's voters, an ample majority for most purposes and wholly adequate for the Nazi purpose. For the Nazis knew that their goal was not to win elections but rather to secure enough popular support to work their will without serious public outcry. In Thalburg this was the case, but the Nazis, being what they were, were not content with this expression of confidence. During the ensuing critical months every effort was made to maintain and increase public support. The recipe was the continued application of both force and propaganda.

Before the Nazis could relax their actual electioneering work they had to conduct one final campaign. This was the local election set for March 12, 1933, a week after the Reichstag voting. At stake was representation in the Town Council, the County Diet, and the Provincial Diet. To some extent the Nazis could expect to ride the crest of the enthusiasm engendered by their victory on March 5. It was hardly to be expected that voting preferences would vary much in a week's time.

The mechanism of terror and the demonstrations of enthusiasm from the previous election campaign were still paying dividends. Thus the TNN reported, during the week between the elections, that seven Thalburg Communists had been arrested. The arrests followed raids on the homes of these people, in the course of which ". . . sharpened iron bars, *Stahlruten,* rubber truncheons, side-arms, daggers, ammunition, etc., were confiscated." On the Tuesday following the Reichstag election the Nazis flew swastika flags from the town hall, County Prefecture, and other state buildings, by way of celebrating the victory. The following day, by order of von Papen, there was a school holiday all over Prussia in honor of the "national victory." [18]

In the week-long campaign before the local elections, Thalburg's SPD was not allowed to hold meetings or pass out campaign literature. They did manage to place one advertisement in the TNN, but, doubtless because of their previous experience of being refused advertising space, the SPD made that a very cautious, almost perfunctory notice, in language that contrasted so sharply with previous Socialist advertisements that its publication probably did the SPD more harm than good:

To the voters of Thalburg! On Sunday, March 12, important elections will be held, namely for the Provincial Diet, County Council, and City Council. The SPD has presented its own list for all these elections, which bears the number "2." We call upon the populace all to vote, to vote early, and to vote, in each case, for the List "Hengst," List number "2."

SPD, Thalburg Local.[19]

While the SPD entered the lists under its own name, the Nazis did so only in the case of the Provincial and County elections. In the elections for the City Council, the Nazis ran under the name "National Unity List." Since the Civil Servants did not put up a separate list of candidates (as they had since 1924), the voters' choice was essentially between this "National Unity" slate and the SPD.

This represented a distinct advantage to Thalburg's Nazis and one that they brought about through skillful manipulation. The local elections of March 12, 1933, were announced on February 6, only a little over a month before the voting was to be held. Parties were given three weeks in which to prepare their lists of candidates, the deadline being February 25. The Nazi executive committee of the Civic Association did not hold a membership meeting until eight days before the list of candidates was due. At the meeting, the Nazi chairman gave a short speech on how all members should vote *Buergerlich* in the forthcoming elections and announced that the executive committee had drawn up a list of candidates called "National Unity" representing "workers, civil servants, craft artisans, craft masters, businessmen, farmers, white collar workers, and the free professions." He called on all members of the Civic Association to stick together so that the town could have "a bourgeois majority."

When this was announced there were cries from the older members: "Who are the candidates?" Thereupon the Nazi chairman announced that "for reasons of campaign tactics" he would not be able to divulge the candidates' names. This called forth vehement objections which Kurt Aergeyz then silenced by saying that anyone could make nominations from the floor if he wished. A number of nominations were made, but all those nominated refused to accept the honor, and the Nazi majority then voted to close the nominations (i.e., leave the matter in the hands of the Nazi-dominated committee). The conservative members of the Civic Association were clearly outmanuevered; though they protested strenuously, they had no choice but to accept the situation. One of the Nazi executive committee members closed the matter by remarking loftily that the names were not important; what mattered was the common viewpoint which would clearly be directed towards "German Community Spirit." After the meeting was given the sad news that the North German Shooting Society would hold its annual meeting in Bremen rather than Thalburg because the Town Council had refused money for new target ranges, it adjourned with the singing of the national anthem.[20]

The conservatives still had a week in which to get the list of candidates made public so that there might be a chance to get at least a few non-Nazis on it. Four days before the deadline the GHC published a "Letter to the Editor" signed by "several members of the Civic Association" demanding that the list of candidates be immediately announced. The GHC also attempted to keep the matter before the public eye by pointing out that the DVP had recently decided to support "Bourgeois Unity Fronts" in the coming local elections.[21]

All of the protests of conservative members of the Civic Association were to no avail. The deadline passed and Thalburg's conservatives now had no choice but to vote for a list of candidates handpicked by the Nazis. The GHC did not take this without protest. When the "National Unity" list was finally printed, it was labeled "NSDAP (??)" in the GHC. This brought a vicious letter from Kurt Aergeyz threatening the GHC with legal action unless it printed a correction with the proper title. The GHC blandly explained that it had gotten the title from the Thalburg Senate, that the question marks signified the GHC's own disbelief, and that by the time the error had been discovered, the edition had been printed and sold.[22]

Since the Senate at that time included two Social Democrats, a member of the Civil Servants party, and Senator Mahner, one can easily see how this little gibe was arranged. Thus the whole town learned that the Nazis had done the conservatives in the eye, and that "National Unity" was a euphemism for "Nazi." This was counteracted by a shrewd Nazi maneuver. The list of candidates contained mainly Nazis, but there were also several non-Nazis. The non-Nazi candidates, however, were carefully picked; they were all men who could be induced to join the NSDAP, men who in fact were ready to join but had not yet done so. The town's conservatives could therefore vote for the "National Unity

List" thinking that there were non-Nazis on it. But by the time
the town council convened, every man who had been elected from
the "National Unity" slate wore a brown shirt.[23]

This was the end of the Civic Association, whose *raison d'être*
had been to oppose the SPD. By its vehement opposition to the
only effective group in Thalburg which was devoted to democracy,
it had helped bring the Nazis to power. And once the Nazis had
used the Civic Association for their own purposes, they promptly
discarded it. It held only one more meeting in Thalburg, in
October, 1933. The purpose of the meeting was to dissolve the
organization since "its purpose had been achieved." [24]

Although they were running on a "National Unity" ticket, Thalburg's Nazis conducted the campaign for the local elections under
their own name. Apart from extensive advertising in the local
press, the Nazi campaign in Thalburg consisted of only one meeting, held the evening before the voting. The featured speaker was
Kurt Aergeyz on "The Significance of the Communal Elections"
and on "Political Matters in Thalburg." It was also promised that
"the candidates you will elect" would speak on their "goals in the
town hall."

The *1910er Zelt* was overflowing and Kurt Aergeyz was in good
form. He expressed the hope that this would be the last vote in a
long time, but should there ever be another vote he hoped that
people would be compelled by law to vote so that there would
be no neutral Germans. In the new order there would be no more
parliamentarianism but rather corporations, like those in the
Middle Ages. That was an old Germanic custom and best for
Germany.

A week ago, continued Aergeyz, a new Germanic spirit swept
through Germany, that of National Socialism, for National Socialism and Germany were now coterminous. What was needed
now was to cleanse Thalburg, too, from Marxist corruption. There
would be no more use of Health Insurance Office automobiles for
private purposes and then setting back the speedometer. For the
town's pool there would be no more diving tower from Amster-
dam which cost 90 per cent more than it should have. There would
be no more false credit and big loans at the City Savings Bank.
There would be no more cloak of silence over the brewery scandal.

That would be completely hashed over and the guilty punished. Consumers' cooperatives, so injurious to the small businessman, would disappear. Polish Jews would be sent back to where they belonged, since Thalburg's clothing goods stores had competition enough already. And the Jews who contributed money to the *Reichsbanner,* and thus to Germany's misery, would be taken care of.[25]

After Aergeyz was through, the candidates spoke. One lamented the crowding in the schools. Another called for a better tax policy and for Thalburgers to do their buying in their own town. A third revived some accusations against the SPD that had been made in 1929. Finally the police secretary (also a candidate on the "National Unity" list) promised to make sure that the police did their duty. There were no other speakers, so Aergeyz led a *Sieg Heil!* for Hitler and Fatherland and the meeting closed with the "Horst Wessel Song." It had been devoid of positive program.

The final shot in the Nazi election campaign was an advertisement in the TNN the day before the voting. The advertisement was clearly an attempt to get non-Nazi elements in Thalburg to back the "National Unity" list:

Citizens of Thalburg! For 14 years you were the plaything of the red Marxist system! For 14 years you had to look on while they governed Germany into the dirt! Last week's election cleared the way for recovery in the Reich and in Prussia! Tomorrow you must carry out your national duty in our town, Thalburg. This is the last chance for a long time that you will have, by casting your ballot, to end the Marxist rule of force of Karl Hengst and make the work of national recovery possible in Thalburg. Personal crankiness must give way before this great goal. Tomorrow will see *nationalist Thalburg* oppose the beaten remains of Marxism *in closed ranks! Away with Hengst and his red clique! For Thalburg's recovery in a Free Germany!* Vote the "National Unity List"—List 1!

—Civic Association, NSDAP, *Stahlhelm,* DNVP, DVP, Hannoverian party, Small Businessmen's League, County Artisan League, Agrarian Society, Farmers Club, Tavern Keepers Society, German Nationalist Merchant Apprentice Society, National Railroad Employees, Local Cartel of the German Civil Servants League, Unemployed Committee for Thalburg, town and county.[26]

After this only the voting remained. The results are given in the following table: [27]

Party	March 5, 1933	March 12, 1933		
	Reichstag	Town Council	County Council	Provincial Parliament
Nazi	4,268	4,565*	4,273	4,246
DNVP	406	*	456	339
DVP	101	*	——	49
SPD	1,470	1,677	1,650	1,592
Catholic Center	183	——	——	124
KPD	228	43	——	64
Others	146	*	3	81
Totals	6,802	6,285	6,379	6,495

* "National Unity" List

Outstanding in these election returns is the failure of the Nazis to gain votes. This was perhaps because the total vote cast in the local elections was about three hundred to five hundred less than in the national elections a week before. But, although all three ballots (town, county, and provincial) were cast at the same time, the provincial votes totaled 210 more than the votes for the town council. Yet it was on the provincial ballot that the Nazis showed a drop.

This may have been because it was only on the provincial ballot that the voter had a full range of choice among parties. On the town and county ballots the choice was limited and thus some two hundred people did not bother to mark their ballots. The same people did vote in the provincial election where they could cast a ballot for their own specific choice. And clearly, for some, where there was a wider choice, the non-Nazi parties were preferable to the NSDAP (though in local elections the Nazis were preferable to the SPD or Nationalists).

Secondly, one notices that despite the terror and adverse campaigning conditions, the SPD actually gained 207 votes (though, like the Nazis, they fared somewhat worse in the slightly heavier county and provincial balloting). Two facts emerge from this. One is that, in the town elections, the majority of people who voted Communist the week before decided to vote for the SPD. The other is that there was a solid core of SPD voters unintimidated by the mounting terror and unimpressed by the intense propaganda and pageantry.

In the town election the "National Unity" list received 4,565 votes. This was 297 more than the Nazis alone had received a week before. But it was also 456 *less* than the parties endorsing the "National Unity" list had cast a week before. Thus it was clear that many of the members of the parties supporting the "National Unity" list had, when it came time to cast ballots, refused to back this Nazi-dominated slate of candidates. Some spoiled their ballots, some turned them in blank—altogether over two hundred people. Some did not even bother to go to the polls at all. But some went so far as to give their votes to the Social Democrats (though most of the gain made by the SPD can be accounted for by vote transfers from the Center and Communist parties).

If any generalization can be made on the basis of these two elections, held only a week apart, it would be that the Nazis were clearly not increasing their popularity, and that the SPD was just as clearly not losing its solid backing. The townspeople also showed some confusion in their voting, some resentment over the Nazis' high-handed tricks with the "National Unity" list. Finally, the fact that over 90 per cent voted should be weighed against the fact that voting participation fell off in just a week's time, despite all Nazi efforts. Was this the beginning of a reaction against the politicalization of life, or just a case of what the Germans call *Wahlmuedigkeit* ("election weariness")? It is hard to tell, since this was the last free election in Thalburg for fifteen years.

CHAPTER 11

THE USES OF ELECTORAL SUCCESS

(Spring and Summer, 1933)

> *I run things here—all by myself—
> and it's because I'm Local Group
> Leader!*
> —Statement of KURT AERGEYZ,
> Deputy Mayor of Thalburg and
> Local Group Leader for Thal-
> burg of the NSDAP

The first task of Thalburg's Nazis after the local elections were over was to convert the town's mechanisms of power from demo-cratic, pluralistic ones into instruments of dictatorship. This in-volved a purge—of the City Council, of the administrative officials, and of the rank and file city workers. The precondition was abso-lute control over the Council.

As a result of the March 12 elections, the Nazis received fifteen seats and the Social Democrats five seats in the twenty-man Thal-burg City Council. This was certainly a working majority for the NSDAP, especially since under the "Leader Principle" all Nazi representatives had to vote as they were told by the Local Group

Leader. Nevertheless, a three-to-one majority was not enough for the Nazis, since if the SPD had even five seats they could legally demand that at least one Social Democratic city councillor be included in each of the standing committees. This would have been intolerable to the Nazis since their goal was absolute control over the town's affairs. If the SPD had only four representatives, though, they could, with complete correctness, be excluded from all committees.

The Nazis dealt with this problem with their customary thoroughness. On the one hand they were able to persuade one of the SPD representatives to declare himself "neutral," i.e., disavow the party under whose name he had run for office. How the Nazis managed to do this was never made clear. This particular Social Democrat had always been vehemently anti-Nazi; hence his defection was characterized by the other Social Democrats as the act of a Judas. It was a hard blow to them, though they realized that the Nazis had many means of persuasion.[1]

This reduced the Socialist delegation to four. As insurance, however, the Nazis arranged to have Bette (one of the four remaining SPD councillors) arrested the afternoon of the first meeting of the Council. Thus if the Social Democrat who had been persuaded to be "neutral" should change his mind in the actual session, the SPD would still have only four councillors and could still be excluded from committee seats.[2]

The first meeting of the new City Council took place on March 28. Contrary to all previous custom the meeting was not held in the room in the City Hall appointed for this purpose, but in the ballroom of Thalburg's largest hotel. Long before the opening of the meeting the hall was packed with Nazis, including many SA men. The SS helped the police keep order.

Shortly before the Council session was to open, the fifteen delegates of the "National Unity" list arrived in a body, all wearing brown shirts. They were greeted with applause and then with *"Heil Hitler!"* Almost immediately thereafter the four SPD councillors arrived. On their way to the meeting from Karl Hengst's house (where they had held a pre-session caucus) the police had seized Bette. When the others arrived they saw the packed hall, well sprinkled with brown and black uniforms. The hall itself was draped with laurel boughs and on the back of the stage there were enormous pictures of Hitler and Hindenburg, flanked by the swastika and Imperial flags. Two tables stood on the stage, one long one for the Nazi councillors and, over to one side, a small one for the representatives of Social Democracy.

Twenty-five years later, Karl Hengst still retained vivid memories of one incident. As soon as he sat down at his assigned place, Hengst took out a big cigar and lit it. Immediately an SA man came over to the SPD table and said, "Put that out! You can't smoke here!" Hengst exhaled slowly and surveyed the Stormtrooper. Then he leaned forward and said: "Now listen closely. Are you SA people running the City Council or are we city councillors? I'll smoke here if I like." The SA man turned on his heel and walked away.

Mayor Johns opened the meeting. He was a courtly man, noted for his dry and legalistic personality. After calling the session to order he spoke of his hopes that the new rise of patriotism would reflect itself in solid work for the good of Thalburg. He enumerated the difficulties that lay ahead, mentioning especially the budgetary problems. After congratulating each new councillor personally, he gave the floor to Kurt Aergeyz for the first speech.

Aergeyz began by asking everyone to ponder that, in this hour, how Germany had been governed in the last fourteen years. The military collapse had brought unspeakable unhappiness to Germany. It was the SPD that had been responsible for the misery. Furthermore it had not even hesitated to rob its own workers. Today the time had come to settle up:

We haven't forgotten a single thing. Nor will we hesitate to pay them back for every bit. In the reckoning up it won't be the poor people who were blinded by them, it will be the seducers themselves that we'll settle with, down to the smallest party hack. In locked concentration camps they'll learn how to work for Germany again!

There was more to say. Democracy was finished; from now on a dictatorship would rule and it would hit every enemy, no matter where he came from. The struggle against the Jews would be taken up anew. They would be met head on. Remembering Hitler's campaign pledge, "The common good goes before that of the individual," National Socialism was moving into the Thalburg town hall, conscious of Germany's great past, to which Thalburg had also contributed.

Next, August Tiere, the new Speaker of the Council, read a list of committee appointments as determined by the majority in its caucus. All were Nazis. The floor was then given to the SPD member who was to play the role of turncoat. He declared that he was now "neutral" and had left the SPD "since with the dawning of a new era I can no longer belong to this party." The audience cheered this announcement and it was to cries of "Bravo!" that the former SPD representative moved to the big table.

After the applause ended, Karl Hengst rose to his feet and asked for the floor. Tiere replied, "For fourteen years you wouldn't listen to the NSDAP and now we won't listen to you. I refuse to give you the floor." Hengst spoke anyway: "You have a majority in the Council and in addition you won't even allow us to speak. I see, therefore, no further possibility of representing the interests of my constituents. If you will not give us the floor, then we will leave this session." The other two Social Democrats rose beside him and, accompanied by the hoots and catcalls of the audience, marched out of the hall. As they were walking down the aisle, SA men on each side spat upon them.

The rest of the meeting was more prosaic. The Nazi nominations for Senators were unanimously accepted. A loan for public works, which the old Town Council had prepared, was approved and allocated in such a way that it appeared to have been done entirely by the new council. Finally the new Speaker, Tiere, closed the meeting with these words: "Everyone will surely have noticed that from now on a new wind will be blowing. The tasks ahead will require the entire strength of every individual, but we will fulfill them, inspired by the great idea, and by the spirit of Adolf Hitler." The crowd responded with the "Horst Wessel Song" and a triple *"Sieg Heil!"* The first session of the new Thalburg City Council was ended.[3]

This session set the pattern for all which followed in the first six months of Nazi rule in Thalburg. The features were to be persistent harassment of the Socialist members, apparent vigor in dealing with the economic situation, and the theatrical exposition of measures pre-determined in the Nazi caucus.

Thalburg's Nazis had a free hand in dealing with the Socialist councillors. According to a circular from Goering's Prussian Ministry of the Interior, representatives elected on an SPD ticket were not to be "hindered from fulfilling their duties," though this was not to preclude police action against them. If the SPD representatives were not "cooperative," however, then they were to be "furloughed immediately (if this has not yet occurred)." They were then to be replaced by temporary appointees, to be chosen by the appropriate Nazi District Leader.[4]

On April 7, Bette gave up his councillorship, since he was still in jail. On April 12 (the day before the City Council's second meeting), Karl Hengst resigned. Hengst and Bette were replaced by two Nazis. Thus the SPD delegation was reduced from four to two.[5]

At the second session of the Council, the SPD turncoat requested that he be allowed to serve on the Council's Economic Planning Committee, since he had nine years' experience on it. Speaker Tiere refused this but urged him to keep trying to cooperate with the Nazis. Next the NSDAP proposed, and it was unanimously enacted, that Hindenburg, Hitler, and Goering be made honorary citizens of Thalburg. The NSDAP's second proposal was also unanimously accepted. This was to change several of the street names. The new names were "Adolf Hitler Strasse," "Goering Strasse," "Hindenburg Strasse," "Darré Strasse" (for the Nazi Minister of Agriculture), and finally "Elisabeth Zander Strasse." It was announced that the next two new streets built in Thalburg would be called "Schlageter Strasse" and "Horst Wessel Strasse." Before the session closed one of the two remaining SPD delegates made two motions. One was for free books for school children whose parents were unemployed. The second was for a solution to the "settlement" question. Both motions were immediately tabled.[6]

Despite this kind of treatment, the two remaining SPD councillors continued to hold their posts. Thus they were present at the third meeting of the City Council on April 28. Most of the session was given over to listening to a report by the Mayor on the state of the budget. The Mayor explained how Thalburg would be able to have a balanced budget in 1933 by dipping into the capital reserves of the various town-owned enterprises to the extent of about two-thirds of their total sum. By this expedient it would be possible to cut the business tax by about 16 per cent, and to cut the town income tax by about 35 per cent. This plan was accepted by the Council without discussion. Then they proceeded to vote subsidies. The Volunteer Labor Service, which was doing work for Thalburg, was given 1,100 marks. The shooting societies were given permission to build their new rifle ranges and provided with free material for them. The Young Naval Society was given 70 marks' worth of wood for a boat they wanted to build, and 300 marks were given to the Hitler Youth so that they could attend a regional convention. The Council also voted 100 marks to help defray the cost of celebrating May 1 and agreed to pay for the use of the *1910er Zelt*. Finally, a salary of 50 marks per month was voted for each of the four Nazi Senators. The entire meeting lasted only forty-five minutes.[7]

The next session took place on June 7. In the interim Mayor Johns had gone on his vacation and Kurt Aergeyz now presided over the meeting. The first motion was to halt pension payments for city workers, "since the Reich intended to take over this cost." One of the two remaining Socialist representatives suggested that the town wait until the Reich had begun its payments and *then* cease. The original motion was then carried, over the opposition of the two SPD representatives, with Aergeyz remarking that the city would continue to pay pensions to some workers, he himself deciding which ones would get their pension money. The rest of the meeting was taken up with routine business, mainly granting financial aid to, or withholding it from, various organizations.[8]

This was the last session the Socialists participated in. Since the SPD had been dissolved in the interim, its remaining councillors had to resign by June 27, including "those who were elected as such but had since left the SPD"—in other words, the one turncoat. Nazis were appointed in their stead. Henceforth, sessions of the City Council were used solely for the purpose of announcing measures previously determined by the Nazi Local Group Leader and Deputy Mayor Kurt Aergeyz. On one occasion, one of the handpicked Nazi Senators actually spoke up, to the great embarrassment of Aergeyz. It was on July 18, 1933, and the session was being used to explain the new public works projects planned. After all the money had been allocated, Senator Blanck, who had a farm outside of Thalburg, suggested that some of the money be spent to build a sidewalk from the town out to his farm. This was voted down and the meeting was immediately adjourned by Aergeyz.[9] Henceforth, the councillors and Senators kept absolute silence in session meetings.

A similar series of events took place in the Thalburg County Council. The Nazis were unable to create a "National Unity" list, hence they were not in a position of overwhelming strength after the election. In fact, the Nazis were even incapable of presenting a united front for this election. The source of this anomaly was that during the previous summer the Prussian government had determined to unite Thalburg County with a smaller neighboring county. Local chauvinism was aroused by this measure, particularly in the neighboring county which was to lose its identity. Hence, when the time came to draw up a list of candidates, the members of the supposedly monolithic Nazi party presented two lists: the "NSDAP List" (Thalburg County Nazis) and the "Hitler-Movement List" (Nazis from the neighboring county). The SPD and the Nationalist party each managed to present a united front.[10]

The Nazis nonetheless gained an absolute majority with fifteen of the Council's twenty-five seats (ten from Thalburg, five from the other county). The SPD won eight seats, the Nationalists two.[11] Even before the County Council met for the first time the Nazis began arranging affairs to their own benefit. Sixteen SPD village councillors in Thalburg County were suspended from office. The county's contract for publishing official notices with the *Volksblatt* was severed. The *Volksblatt* was already suspended, so this was mere legalistic neatness. It also enabled the county to award the contract to the new Nazi newspaper, the *Thalburger Beobachter*.[12] Finally, the Nazis forced the County Prefect, Franz von Altberg, to join the NSDAP.

The Prefect's attitude toward the Nazis was mixed. He was convinced that increasing unemployment was driving people towards Communism and therefore that Nazism had saved Germany.

But he would never have joined the NSDAP freely, because "previous experience led me to believe that its ranks were filled with incompetents and bankrupts." This aloof attitude was not long permitted him. On the afternoon of March 29, just before the County Prefecture was closing, Walter Eckstein came into von Altberg's office. Taking off his own silver swastika pin, Eckstein tossed it on von Altberg's desk and said, "Put that on. If you don't, you won't be County Prefect tomorrow." So von Altberg joined the Nazi party.[13]

The first meeting of the new County Council was, like the first meeting of the Thalburg City Council, largely a ceremonial affair, open to the public, and with the County Hall decorated with flags, pictures, and bunting. It did not have the tension-laden atmosphere of the Thalburg City Council's opening meeting largely because the personalities of the Nazi leaders (Walter Eckstein, the County Leader was jovial and folksy; Baron von Barten, Majority Leader in the Council, coldly aristocratic) were different from the personality of Kurt Aergeyz. Nonetheless, Karl Hengst took von Barten aside before the meeting started and said, "Look, if we're going to have a farce like the City Council meeting, then the SPD is going home right now." He was assured by von Barten that decorum would prevail.[14]

The meeting opened with a speech by von Altberg in which he expressed himself in accord with the various Nazi measures and finished by calling for a triple *"Sieg Heil!"* for "the Fatherland, for President Hindenburg, and for Chancellor Hitler." Next a speech was given by von Barten, who declared that the Socialists were there on sufferance and would be tolerated only if they conducted themselves with extreme objectivity. (The position of the SPD was already tenuous. Two of their representatives had refused to take up their mandates and a third, Bette, was in jail.) No "Marxist" would be allowed to hold any office in the county, and SPD representatives would not be allowed to serve on committees.[15] Then he read the committee assignments from a prepared list. All went to Nazis.

Karl Hengst limited his reply to stating that the SPD had no choice now but to bow to the will of the majority. What this was to mean was made immediately manifest, for von Barten's first motion was that all county contracts be taken away from Jews and that Jews be expelled from the County Old People's Home and deprived of other county services. The motion was "referred to committee" and the session ended.[16]

The County Council was only infrequently convened after that. Most Nazi sniping was directed at the Nationalist members of the County Council, von Barten making statements such as: "You're like a cork on a champagne bottle. We touch you, you fly into the air with a bang, and then you're finished." The SPD passed silently out of the picture. By the beginning of June there were only two SPD representatives left; the others had resigned except for one who joined the Nationalists. It hardly mattered, since, like the City Council, the County Council had become primarily ceremonial, with all decisions resting with the Nazis, and all speeches being made by them too, since the other delegates were afraid to give speeches. By July all non-Nazi delegates were required to resign.[17]

With virtual control over the administration of Thalburg and Thalburg County, the Nazis undertook the first and most obvious task: cleansing the city and county offices of actual or potential opponents. This was part of a pre-arranged plan, for as early as 1932 it was known that Tiere, the Nazi teacher, had a list apportioning the various offices and jobs among members of the NSDAP. There was no attempt to hide the fact that a purge was taking place, and the townspeople were clearly aware of it. The Nazis considered the "general cleaning action" one of their foremost accomplishments. It was so described in a special commemorative issue of the *Thalburger Beobachter* in 1936, and when Kurt Aergeyz made a report of his activities during the first two years of the Third Reich, it was the first thing he mentioned.[18]

Although the Nazis generally claimed to have dismissed a total of thirty workers and employees (*Angestellter*), the figure was actually higher. The sum of individual instances listed in contemporary newspaper accounts was forty-three, and this did not include persons edged out of their jobs with various other reasons given. In the latter category would be, for example, Mayor Johns, his assistant Dieter Thomas, and probably others. Of the forty-five persons fired, most were workers but some were tenured employees, and a few were professional civil servants with full tenure. Together, they constituted approximately a quarter of the employees of the City of Thalburg. The basis for the purge was Hitler's "Law for the Reconstruction of the Professional Civil Service," promulgated under powers given the government by the Enabling Act, on April 7, 1933.[19]

The first wave of dismissals came in mid-April and involved Socialists in minor positions: a gas works employee, an accountant, and the manager of the city's swimming pool. At the end of April there was a second round of firings which affected fifteen workers from the Construction Office, seven from the brewery, and four more from the gas works. In addition seven union shop-stewards were dismissed. A week later the Nazi ax fell on the "red" Health Insurance Office. The board of directors was ousted and its functions taken over by Walter Eckstein as "commissar." He immediately fired the business manager and two employees. To forestall resistance the offices were occupied by the SS. In place of the dismissed employees, three Nazis were hired and later a new board of directors was appointed with Walter Eckstein as Chairman.[20] The impact of this particular "cleaning action" can be judged by the recollections of a former reporter for the TNN:

When the Nazis cleaned out the Health Insurance Office, they naturally fired the Socialist business manager, a competent fellow. In his place, Aergeyz put a Nazi named X. Now X had just been released from jail where he had served a term for—embezzlement! And his previous embezzlement had been from the State Sickness Insurance Office!

Naturally this stank. It stank so much that [the head of one of the guilds] went in to see Aergeyz and raised holy hell and pounded on the table until Aergeyz took the job away from X. But later X got another job with the city as director of the *Ordnungsamt*.

The Nazis were bankrupt people prior to 1933. Afterwards they all got jobs. The party in 1933 was full of the poor, the thieves, the morally and financially bankrupt. X is a typical example of the type of people the Nazis put in positions—people with the poorest reputations.[21]

The series of political dismissals was finally ended in mid-May with the firing of two city employees: a messenger for the City

Savings Bank and a night watchman. There were, however, other dismissals which took place without political reasons being given. In April a policeman was dismissed from service in Thalburg with no reason supplied. Later, extraordinary promotions and reinstatements occurred. In June, the night watchman who had been fired in May was rehired, according to the official announcement, "since he petitioned for this giving certain assurances." His reinstatement necessitated the dismissal of his erstwhile replacement. Later in the same month, one policeman was promoted and three others given tenure. This was an unusual and unprecedented series of moves.[22]

A similar pattern took place in the county. The only person recorded to have been fired officially for his political opinions was Willi Brehm. Nevertheless, as a result of the union of Thalburg County with the neighboring county, a number of offices (and therefore jobs) became superfluous. The decision as to who would be retained and who would be transferred, pensioned, or simply fired lay with the all-Nazi executive committee on the County Diet. Needless to say, politics played a part in such decisions.[23]

To Kurt Aergeyz the most important single office to be transferred after the seizure of power was the mayorship of Thalburg. As far as political control was concerned, it was hardly necessary for Mayor Johns to be removed from office. As Walter Eckstein put it in a conversation with Dieter Thomas:

I can't understand Kurt Aergeyz. He and I are both businessmen and not civil administrators. I think we both have our hands full with just party matters. Now I'm sure that if I wanted to, I could have von Altberg's job right now and be County Prefect myself. But I don't want to. As it now stands, he does what I tell him to in political matters and runs the administrative part quite well. Surely it is possible that Aergeyz could make some arrangement like that with Mayor Johns, don't you think? [24]

As a matter of fact, Aergeyz could have eased Mayor Johns out of his position with very little effort if he had not tried to use underhanded tactics. Johns was sixty-one years old in 1933 and had been Mayor of Thalburg since 1903. In a private conversation with his assistant, Dieter Thomas, he confessed that he would have retired voluntarily and instantly if he had been approached decently, but that he would not bow before a smear campaign.[25]

Since Aergeyz never tried anything except dirty methods, each new move he made simply hardened Mayor Johns's resolve. Johns could not be removed simply on grounds of "political unreliability." He was cold, objective, juristic. He was a conservative and in fact a member of the Nationalist party, but he suppressed his politics so completely that no one thought of him except as a professional administrator. Since Aergeyz could not use customary methods he developed a complex attack upon Johns. It took the form of trying to provoke Johns into acts or statements that could be used against him, attacking his subordinates in order to frighten him, intervening with higher officers to have him removed by administrative fiat, slanderously charging him with incompetence and bringing him to trial on trumped-up charges of administrative malpractice, and, finally, getting him and his assistant dismissed with the elastic (and patently false) reason, "in order to simplify the administration." [26]

In Aergeyz's plan of action, Mayor Johns was to be provoked into imprudent statements or actions through one of Aergeyz's good friends, August Blanck. Blanck, though a citizen of Thalburg, had a small farm a short distance from the city. He was a rough and uncouth man, a peasant in the pejorative sense of the word. He was constantly involved in legal squabbles with the town of Thalburg, which brought him into bitter contact with Mayor Johns. He was so well known in Thalburg for this that a joke went the rounds: "If August Blanck ever forgets to put his boots on in the morning, they automatically find their way to the County Courthouse." One of the things he was supposed to have done was move the boundary stone on his farm so as to encroach on city-owned land. His dealings with the pre-Nazi Thalburg Senate eventually became so acrimonious that the Senators took the extraordinary step of refusing to rent him any land under the control of the town.[27]

This was the man who was to provoke the Mayor. This became manifest by the time the Nazis composed their list for the division of elective offices in mid-March. At that time Kurt Aergeyz insisted that August Blanck be made a Senator. The other Nazi members of the City Council objected to this because of Blanck's bad reputation. Kurt Aergeyz overrode their objections:

"I need Blanck as a fighter. The era of Mayor Johns is absolutely finished. Blanck will be the one to drive his fist to the Mayor's heart." And when the councillors still refused to do as he wished, the Local Group Leader declared: "As Local Group Leader I declare that Blanck is Senator!" [28]

It was immediately apparent to many that this was Senator Blanck's function. It was hard to imagine what other functions August Blanck could possibly perform in view of his low-grade intelligence. It proved a problem what "areas of competence" to assign him as a Senator. He was finally given only three: City Gardens, City Field Lands, and Garbage Collection. All this was clear to Mayor Johns and he maintained an attitude of cold correctness toward Senator Blanck in the face of the most vile harassment.[29]

With the failure of these tactics, Aergeyz began to attack Johns's subordinates, primarily his protégé and right-hand man, Dieter Thomas. Thomas, as City Inspector, was the town's second highest administrator. He had attained this position in 1932; in a rare moment of complete accord the City Council had voted unanimous approval of his selection. Shortly after the Nazis came to power, Thomas learned that the Senate was petitioning Johns for his removal. Since each Senator refused to explain why, Thomas went directly to Aergeyz, who also refused to explain. When Thomas expressed indignation over this, Aergeyz exploded. Pounding the table he shouted: "I want to tell you something! If you think you can hide behind the Mayor's skirts, you're wrong! I run things here —all by myself—and it's because I'm Local Group Leader!" [30]

This again hardened Mayor Johns's resolve not to be dislodged and not to permit Dieter Thomas' career to be ended. Near the beginning of June, Johns went on vacation and Aergeyz, who now sat behind the Mayor's desk as Deputy Mayor, was determined to make the vacation permanent. On June 28 Aergeyz took direct action. The minutes of the relevant Council meeting read, in part:

The National Socialist Faction, which today makes up the entire City Council, has determined in its meeting of today:

1. Mayor Johns no longer possesses the confidence of the City Council. The City Council refuses, therefore, any further collaboration with him.

2. The City Council concurs with the decision of the Senate to petition the *Regierungspraesident* to forbid Mayor Johns any further official activity and (in accordance with the decree of *Ministerpraesident* Goering) to strip him of police powers and to transfer these to Police Secretary Deuvelman.[31]

This, plus some intensive lobbying by Aergeyz at the upper levels of the government, resulted in the repeated extension of Mayor Johns's vacation. In the interim Aergeyz used the supine Senate to lodge formal charges that Johns and Thomas, as directors of the City Savings Bank, had conspired with Hugo Spiessmann, the manager of the bank, to give improper credit concessions to various Thalburg businessmen. Johns, knowing that Spiessmann (a March, 1933, member of the NSDAP) might perjure himself under the kinds of pressure that the Nazis were capable of, finally permitted himself to be dismissed. Dieter Thomas was suspended and then discharged "to simplify the administration." In return, the charges against both were dropped. (Hugo Spiessmann, an unwitting tool in the process, was dismissed as Bank Manager but given a job with the NSDAP.) Shortly thereafter Kurt Aergeyz became Mayor of Thalburg.[32]

This resolution came only in 1934, but by June, 1933, Aergeyz was in the Mayor's office and Thalburgers simply assumed that he was there to stay. Most Thalburgers (excepting, as will be seen, a significant group) had no idea that there was even a struggle in the City Hall. What the townspeople did know was that by the summer of 1933 the local political situation was radically different from what it had been before Hitler. It was clear that, whether as Deputy Mayor or as Local Group Leader of the NSDAP, Kurt Aergeyz was firmly in the saddle. Not only had the Nazis gained absolute control of Thalburg's Council, Senate, and Executive, they had also conducted a thorough purge of the city's administration. All actual or potential dissidents from Nazi goals and methods were eliminated or under control. The astute Thalburger, surveying his city government at the end of June, 1933, could not but see clearly that it was exclusively a Nazi instrument.

CHAPTER 12

THE TERROR
SYSTEM

(March to July, 1933)

> *Cruelty impresses. Cruelty and raw
> force. The simple man in the street
> is impressed only by brutal force
> and ruthlessness. Terror is the most
> effective political means.*
>
> —ADOLF HITLER *

Control of the city government was one thing; absolute power in
the town was another. Control of the city government made it possible to reward friends and punish enemies. It also involved control
over the local police.[1] But that was not enough. The Nazis had to
prove in the first months after the appointment of Hitler as Chancellor that they were willing to use the power apparatus in a ruthless and effective way. If this could be done, if Thalburgers came to
believe implicitly that they might expect no mercy from their new
Nazi rulers, then later terrorism would not be needed. The initial
investment of terror would multiply itself through rumor and social
reinforcement until opposition would be looked upon as wholly
futile.

This is precisely what the Nazis of Thalburg did. Roughly by
July, 1933, any Thalburger who had his wits about him knew that

---

* Hermann Rauschning, *Gespräche mit Hitler* (Zurich, 1940), p. 81.

he no longer lived in personal freedom, that if he were even in-discreet the whole arsenal of the police state might be used against him. At the very least he might expect a raid and search of his house, at the worst the dread but largely unknown experience of the concentration camp.

It might have been possible for the Nazis to have created a system of terror without giving any justification for it, but this would have been risky. Hence, one of the first things that was done was to provide an excuse for the various repressive measures. Part of the justification had already been developed—the suggestion that the Communists and Socialists planned to overthrow the state by force. This had been bolstered by the Reichstag fire. Nevertheless, Berlin was far away from Thalburg and a justification closer to home was needed. Thalburg's Nazis provided this by finding var-ious arms and weapons in and around Thalburg and by publishing these findings in the local newspapers.

This was all the easier since there actually *were* many weapons in Thalburg. There were, of course, the usual hunting rifles and shotguns that one might expect to find in any town. Since hunting tended to be a prerogative of the wealthy, such weapons were generally not found in the homes of supporters of the KPD or SPD.[2] Secondly, the shooting societies of Thalburg also had arms—some very fine and expensive weapons. But again, these belonged mainly to middle and upper class people whom one could hardly connect with an attempt to overthrow the state.

But there were also weapons belonging to workers. Some vet-erans of World War I brought rifles or pistols home with them, or acquired them in the confused period following the Armistice. Others, who were members of the *Reichsbanner,* took the threat of a Nazi *Putsch* seriously enough to gather guns and ammunition for the counter-strike. They did this without the consent of the *Reichsbanner* leaders, but nevertheless they possessed such weap-ons. And some of the workers who had weapons were extraordi-narily careless about them. One worker frequently carried around with him a pocketful of high-caliber rifle bullets and another boasted openly of having a dozen hand grenades at his home.[3]

Thus the Nazi police undoubtedly could point to bona fide reasons to justify their repressive methods. Whether or not all the weapon discoveries reported in the local press were authentic is unimportant. The newspapers reported whatever they were told by the police, and what people believed was more important than what was true.

In the week before the March elections the Nazi Deputy Police had already made a number of raids, especially on the homes of known Communists. According to the TNN, these raids yielded several weapons, mostly of a makeshift kind, but also some "side-arms." The report was extremely vague about the actual type and number of weapons confiscated by the police.[4] More concrete reports found their way into the press about the end of March. Then throughout April a series of specific discoveries was prominently publicized.

On March 30, 1933, it was reported that children playing near a beer garden had found sixty rounds of Army-issue rifle ammunition. The speculation was that Communists had buried them there after the police raids began. On the same day it was reported that a *Reichsbanner* man voluntarily delivered to the police "a pistol, a saw, and a set of brass knuckles." Five days later police raids at the apartments of "leftists" in the old Army barracks yielded "a carbine, a saber, a side-arm, and a revolver." This apparently spurred the police to greater efforts, for four days later a series of extensive searches was undertaken. But the only weapons found were old, and probably unusable. Two days after that the police ransacked the city Construction Office and found two pistols (one of military issue) and also "a large bundle of propaganda material, several flags, placards, etc." It was also reported that the police had established that a member of the *Reichsbanner* had thrown an Army rifle and several hand grenades in the Muhle River. A week later new police raids yielded only rifle ammunition, but strollers along the Muehle found a carbine and ten bullets. Four days later the police announced the discovery of an Army pistol under the woodpile of a home they were searching, though the owner of the home denied any knowledge of how the pistol got there. Four days after that the police dragged the Muhle on the basis of a tip, but without success. Six days later, however, they fished sixty-one rounds of Army-issue rifle ammunition out of the river.[5]

Thus throughout a six-week period spanning April, Thalburgers were given the impression that the town was a veritable arsenal. It was easy to reach two conclusions: first, that only vigorous action by the Nazis had prevented a civil war, and second, that it was extremely unhealthy to have any sort of weapon around the house.

After the rash of reports in April there was hardly any further mention of weapons finds. In July the Muhle Canal was drained to be deepened and "a limited cache . . . of weapons and ammunition . . . was fished out. Probably these things were thrown into the water out of fear that they might be discovered." Finally in August a worker was given three months in prison for possessing a pistol. "The police discovered it through an anonymous accusation. . . ." Though the police claimed to have found 3,015 bullets in various places during that month, the great weapons discovery was over.[6]

This was all first-class justification for the repeated police raids and arrests. Furthermore, the Nazis were able to point out that there were no more political fights; the violence of the pre-Nazi period had come to an end. That this was an excellent propaganda point can be seen from the following report (on Easter Sunday) in the TNN:

> . . . For the rest, the Easter celebration took place in peace and quiet within Thalburg's walls, as it did everywhere in the Reich. There was not the slightest news of any political fights or other disturbances. The calmness in domestic politics, which the reordering of things has brought about, has shown itself here in an example as clear as it is beneficial.[7]

With the propaganda justification for police action firmly established, the Nazis in Thalburg made use of the familiar tactics of repression and terrorism. The homes of potential or actual opponents were repeatedly ransacked and various people arrested. This was done under the public eye, to increase its deterrent effect. In the first six months after Hitler became Chancellor, the local press in Thalburg reported, on fourteen different occasions, that house searchings had taken place. It also listed at least twenty-two people who had been arrested for political reasons, most by name.[8]

Not all arrests and house searchings were reported in the press, but enough were made known so that the public received a good general impression of what was going on. Furthermore, the way in which police actions were reported was enough to give Thalburgers an idea of the generally arbitrary nature of such actions.

Thus it was reported on March 14 that Bette, the leader of the Thalburg *Reichsbanner,* had been arrested "for reasons which in consideration of the investigation must be kept secret." The next day he was released with no further explanation. He was then arrested again on the afternoon of the first meeting of the City Council, and this time the reason given was that he was "suspected of having spread reports of an anti-governmental nature obtained from the newspaper from the Saar which he receives." [9]

Most persons arrested in the early months of the Nazi regime were taken to the county jail. Exactly what happened to them there was not clear to Thalburgers, but it was clear that it was something extraordinary. In mid-March the GHC reported:

As we hear, eight of the eighteen *Communists* who are presently in our county jail (all from Thalburg) have applied for membership in the NSDAP. Is it possible that the good influence of our hard-working jailer X who watches over them has succeeded in making itself felt? In any event, they seem to have "broken fully and finally with the unholy Bolshevism." [10]

Whatever went on in the county jail was probably considered preferable to other possibilities. Already in March the GHC published a picture of the first concentration camp (at Dachau) with a text noting that there was room for five thousand political prisoners. By the end of that month the Thalburg county jail was full and three Communists had to be taken to the "Moringen Workhouse." What this meant was only rumored, but by mid-July it was reported that "nine prisoners . . . were taken this morning by the Thalburg police to Moringen where seven were delivered to the Concentration Camp and two to the Workhouse." [11] Henceforth Thalburgers knew that there was a concentration camp within driving distance.

The press reports also made it clear that if the Nazis were after someone, they would get him on one account or another. Such was the only conclusion to be drawn from the case of a worker who was arrested and apparently promised his liberty if he revealed where guns and ammunition were hidden. He gave this information to the police and was then set free. The police were unable to find the guns at the place he indicated, however, and thus he was arrested again. A short time later he was sentenced to prison for "insulting a police officer." [12]

The reasons given for arrest were very minor, which created the impression that anything worse would be all the more severely dealt with. In June, for example, one of the two remaining SPD councilmen was arrested for saying that the *Stahlhelm* would soon be strong enough to "cut the SA to pieces." A few weeks later a woman peddler was arrested for "spreading false and agitational political rumors." It was suggested that she might possibly be a Communist and that perhaps this might be part of a Communist campaign "to make the people restive." At the end of the month a worker was arrested for "profane statements about National Socialism." [13]

Thus it seems clear that the public in Thalburg had a good idea, by mid-summer 1933, that even to express oneself against the new system was to invite persecution. In fact, not only were Thalburgers aware of this situation, but by their very awareness they reinforced the actual terror apparatus. Each time someone in Thalburg cautioned his neighbor or friend, he was strengthening the general atmosphere of fear.

This happened frequently. A teacher remembered that the mother of one of his pupils complained about the book burning. He agreed with her but also warned her not to try to tell other people, lest she get into trouble. The principal of the high school remembers that he used to buy cigars at a certain store and along with the cigars usually received the advice to be careful. The general feeling was that the Gestapo was everywhere. At least five people were identified as being "Gestapo agents," though in point of fact there was probably only one for the whole town, Otto Made.[14]

Other people claimed to know of the existence of a "list" (though they had never actually seen it) of people to be proscribed at some future date. "It was a blacklist; there were eighty people on it." [15] "It was made up of four groups: A, B, C, and D. The A people would be shot; the B people put in concentration camps, etc. . . ." [16] "I never saw the list myself, but everyone knew it existed." [17]

Thus the Gestapo became extraordinarily efficient by reason of rumors and fears. It was unnecessary for the Nazis to suggest that someone who had no swastika flag buy one. Maria Armkerl, in her kind neighborliness, took care of that for them by cautioning the flagless person, "letting her in on what one had to do." Given the atmosphere of terror, even people who were friends felt that they must betray each other in order to survive. Thus very early in 1933 there was the case of a Dr. X who went to a party and, after one drink too many, sought to entertain people by imitating Hitler's way of speaking. The next morning his hostess reported him to Nazi headquarters. Word of this spread quickly and soon Thalburgers saw that it was better not to go to parties at all. "Social life was cut down enormously—you couldn't trust anyone any more." [18] Or as someone else put it:

It wasn't so much that criticism was dangerous; it was pointless. Still I never felt free to say what I wanted, never felt a sense of personal freedom . . . It was well known that Otto Made kept himself informed on what Thalburgers thought.[19]

Even if one were not actually arrested it was clear that one could easily lose his job or simply be excluded from any of the normal factors and considerations that ordinarily make society function smoothly:

In general all people who were independent or who stuck to their own opinions were roughly handled or put to the side when the time came for favors. You could be boycotted; you could be driven out of business. These things were noticed by most people, who learned from the fate of others. It was pure force applied to politics and it meant that the Nazis got anything they wanted.[20]

Under these circumstances the Nazis had very little to do to avoid resistance. They created examples on the left and right (as will be shown) and let natural social forces do the rest. Conditions reached the point where one who failed to give the Nazi salute, who left a meeting early, or who ventured a cold look at Kurt Aergeyz was thought to be displaying almost foolhardy recklessness. "There never was any opposition. The most there was was reserve. And even that was a luxury." [21]

And yet, one has to ask the question, what happened to those who had sworn resistance? What happened to the *Reichsbanner* which had repeatedly asserted, in the years before Hitler came to power, that when the expected Nazi *coup* came they would be able to defend the Republic? In Thalburg, at least, the Republic was destroyed without a single blow struck in its defense. The *Reichsbanner,* with all its plans for instant mobilization, had its members struck down one by one, its leaders imprisoned, beaten, hounded from their jobs and their homes without any resistance from the organization as a whole.

Perhaps the basic reason for this was that there was no Nazi *coup d'état*. Instead, there was a series of quasi-legal actions over a period of at least six months, no one of which by itself constituted a revolution, but the sum of which transformed Germany from a republic to a dictatorship. The problem was where to draw the line. But by the time the line could be clearly drawn, the revolution was a *fait accompli,* the potential organs of resistance had been individually smashed, and organized resistance was no longer possible. In short, the splendid organization was to no avail; in the actual course of events it was every man for himself.

The Thalburger *Reichsbanner* itself was ready to fight in 1933. All it needed was the order from Berlin. Had it been given, Thalburg's *Reichsbanner* members would have carried out the tested plan they had worked on so long—to obtain and distribute weapons and to crush the Nazis. But Thalburg's *Reichsbanner* would not act on its own. The leaders felt that single acts would come to grief, would possibly compromise the chance when it finally did come, and would, in any event, be a betrayal of discipline. They felt that their only hope was in common action, all together, all over the Reich. Hadn't the former SPD governor of Hannover, Gustav Noske, said that *only* a counterattack should be made? So they waited and prayed for the order to come, but it never did. And while they waited the Nazis began tracking them down, one by one. Finally it was clear that there would never be an order and Bette and Willi Brehm spread the word that the *Reichsbanner* was to be dissolved:

> We told them that every man would have to follow his own conscience now. If we could have maintained the organization we would have kept responsibility for our members. But when we no longer had the strength to protect them, we could no longer ask them to remain loyal.[22]

Yet most of the old *Reichsbanner* men did remain loyal to their ideals. According to Willi Brehm, perhaps ten of the former four hundred went over to the SA. Karl Hengst agrees with this. He himself had little encouragement for the *Reichsbanner* men who came to him for advice. "Join the party," he usually said. "Think of your family. There's nothing to be gained by acts of heroism." [23]

This situation, where even heroism was denied the men of the democratic left, came about in no small measure because of the failure of the Social Democrats to understand the nature of Nazism. Just as their basic premise in the years before Hitler came to power was the erroneous assumption that the Nazis were essentially *Putsch*-ists who could not possibly attract a mass following, so their basic premise after Hitler came to power was the equally erroneous assumption that his would be a government similar to the others of the Weimar period.

The most eloquent document on this was the set of instructions sent out to SPD Locals in District Hannover on March 23, 1933. It was filled with instructions about sending for handbooks on Socialist policy in communal affairs, filling out questionnaires, in short, carrying on business as usual. The only reference to the phenomenon of Nazism was contained in paragraph seven:

> *Will the election of our village and town representatives be approved?* That is a question which is repeatedly being asked. The question is unanswerable because we do not know what this government will do. However, in any case we must, now as always, select trustworthy comrades as village representatives wherever we have a majority. Should they later not be sworn in, then we will take a position on this. Under no circumstances should we value any of our rights cheaply.[24]

This at a time when SPD leaders were having their houses

searched in the middle of the night for weapons! This when the officers of the *Reichsbanner* were being herded into jail by Storm-troopers, beaten in the prisons across Germany, cast into Nazi concentration camps! The SPD, the only defenders of democracy in Germany, the men who should have been gathering guns and calling the general strike, or at least developing an underground with passwords, false names, and the other paraphernalia of effective covert resistance, were instead being urged to keep the party files in order, to avoid bookkeeping errors, and above all to purchase the latest pamphlet on parliamentary tactics in village councils.

If the central offices of the SPD did not know "what this government will do," the local Socialist leaders in Thalburg soon found out. The details of the personal experience of five Thalburg Social Democrats will illustrate the general pattern.

Ernst Meier was a long-time Social Democrat, *Reichsbanner* member, and union official. He had been an SPD representative on the Thalburg City Council from 1926 to 1930. He worked at the city gas works, where he had been employed for eighteen years in 1933.[25]

On May 12, 1933, Ernst Meier was dismissed from his job since "according to your previous political activity you do not give any assurance that you will, on every occasion, support the national state without qualification."[26] Twelve days later he was arrested and put in the county jail. He was held for three days and every day was questioned by the Gestapo for three to four hours. During the questioning he was forced to press his face against a wall and was then beaten from behind. This was some five weeks before his fifty-first birthday.

Both before and after this incident, his house was subjected to repeated searches, conducted by seven or eight armed SA men. Meier resented most that they stripped his library of some first editions by Marx and Bebel. His wife was also made to go to the police station once for two hours, but his children were never bothered.[27]

After these experiences, Meier found that most of his acquaintances in Thalburg didn't know him any more. Furthermore, no employer was willing to hire him. Finally he found a job as a house-to-house salesman, selling soap. This was very satisfactory to Meier because he used it as a means of keeping in touch with fellow Social Democrats. "If I came to a Nazi, I just asked him if he wanted to buy soap and then went on to the next house. But if I came to a comrade or a fellow union man then we always talked about how to get rid of the Nazis. Many were for an open rebellion, but most were not."

Eventually, in 1934, Meier's travel identification papers were withdrawn from him, putting an end to the soap business.[28] The only job the Employment Office had for him was in a stone quarry, about forty-five minutes by foot from Thalburg. The work was hard and Meier swallowed his pride and wrote as a veteran of World War I to the Nazi War Victims Aid Society (NSKOV), asking them to intercede for him. They did, but Kurt Aergeyz, to whom the matter was referred, refused to allow Meier to return to his old job, "since I do not intend to dismiss old SA and SS people in order to help leading SPD people."[29]

While working at the quarry Meier was arrested again, this time for having said that "von Papen and the capitalists would soon topple Hitler," but he was subjected only to an hour-long session with the Gestapo.[30] It was enough, however, to make Meier want to leave Thalburg, which he did at the end of the year. Henceforth he was gone from Thalburg until after World War II. His spirit remained cocky and buoyant, his repugnance for Nazism unabated, but he was, nevertheless, *hors de combat* as far as effective resistance was concerned.[31]

Another Thalburg worker, who can be classed as a minor figure in the Socialist community, was Benno Schmidt. He had never even been a dues-paying member of the SPD, but he always thought of himself as a Socialist. As an unskilled laborer he had found employment only intermittently during the depression, lived mainly from the dole, and eventually registered with his wife as "shelterless" and was housed in the miserable and turbulent rooms of the old Army barracks. A frequent participant in street fights, he was sentenced to prison for his part in the "Long Bridge" battle in July, 1932, though he was covered by the general amnesty and never served his term.

In autumn, 1932, he found work with the Thalburg forest ad-

ministration. When the Nazis came to power, Benno Schmidt did
not think in terms of how to overthrow them but how to keep
from being forced into the SA. He was not fired from his job but
was given the dirtiest work. His labor gang, which had been exclusively Socialist, became half-Nazi after the purge of city workers.
Schmidt was struck by the growing distrust among the workers:

> After a while nobody wanted to talk any more because of all the
> Nazis. I can still remember the "second breakfasts" in the woods—
> everybody munching and nobody saying anything. It sure made the
> work worse.

At the same time he felt the growing power of the Nazis. He
was beaten up one day for refusing to give the Hitler salute. ("I
never could *Heil Hitler*—why should I? There was nothing special
about the man.") In the summer of 1933 the police raided his
apartment and seized the money and footballs of the Worker's
Sport Club, of which he was treasurer, and also his pruning knife
and a spring from the door, which were described as weapons
and which cost him a fine of 8 marks, 50 *pfennig*. He was also
repeatedly urged to join the SA, and as a consequence quit his
job and left Thalburg to work on the Autobahn. "They didn't
bother me after that." [32]

With more substantial people, such as Willi Brehm, the Nazis
were more vigorous. His personal fate after the Nazi seizure of
power included being thrown out of work, hindered in getting another job, prevented from drawing unemployment pay—in other
words, deprived of all income. Furthermore, he was arrested, subjected to numerous house searchings, questionings, and the like,
and, finally, was repeatedly evicted from apartments by fearful or
fanatical landlords.

The Gestapo were particularly anxious to get their hands on
Thalburg's *Reichsbanner* flags and membership lists. They refused
to believe that Willi Brehm had burned them until he actually led
them to a field outside Thalburg and showed them the cold ashes.
Yet despite Willi Brehm's prominent position in the *Reichsbanner*
he was not arrested until the end of April, 1933. He was then held
for four days without charge, ineptly interrogated but not mishandled, released, and then arrested again a week later. This time

he was made to sign a statement promising not to speak of his experiences in jail and not to sue for damages:

> I said that I wouldn't sign such a statement and Police Secretary Deuvelman said: "If you don't sign that, you will be locked up again." So I said to him: "Deuvelman! You know as well as I do that that's extortion and that you could be fined or imprisoned for it! It's right in the Civil Code Book—right there on your desk." Deuvelman got up and went over to the window and looked out of it for a long time. Then he said: "I can't help it; sign or you'll be locked up again." So I said: "Give me the damned thing—I'll sign it."

While Willi Brehm was in the county jail he received notice that he was suspended from his job at the County Prefect's Office, and after he was released he was permanently dismissed on the grounds of political unreliability.[33] From mid-April to mid-May his rooms were searched seven times by the police and SA. On April 27, two days before his first arrest, he was ordered to report to the local NSDAP headquarters. There Walter Eckstein gave him a pen and paper and dictated a statement that he had resigned from "all leftist organizations and [was] applying for membership in the NSDAP." When Brehm objected ironically that the Nazis could scarcely desire a convinced Marxist and an ostensible subversive as a "party-comrade," Eckstein simply replied: "Write what I tell you or it's the concentration camp." [34]

Willi Brehm assumes that this extorted statement was used to demoralize Socialists in other towns. "The people around Thalburg knew me well enough not to believe anything like that, and besides they could see that the Nazis were hounding me almost daily."

During the following months, Brehm was frequently brought to the police station for questioning and had his rooms searched about once a month. Furthermore, he received a letter from his landlord who declared that he would no longer rent to an opponent of the regime. Willi Brehm moved and after a few months was evicted again. After the third eviction he left Thalburg. In the interim he had to live entirely on money given him by his father. He tried to find a job, but his chances were nipped each time by his record. Businessmen simply felt that hiring Willi Brehm was a needless risk.

During this period Brehm kept contact with other SPD people. Often they met at the river and talked while swimming. "The banks were flat and no one could sneak up on us." In the winter he took walks with his comrades in order to talk, and on one occasion was trailed and afterward questioned by the Gestapo. His main reason for keeping contact with other SPD members was political. But a second reason was that they were the only friends he had.

After I was arrested most of my boyhood and family friends cut me. They just ignored my existence—didn't even say "hello." I lost good friends. Only the political friends remained true. The rest were living in a cloud. My fiancée remained true too.

Perhaps it was this as much as the frequent questionings and house searchings, the repeated evictions, and the financial distress that drove him from Thalburg. In 1935 he left town to work in a factory in Hannover. He was not to return to Thalburg until 1949.[35]

Surprisingly enough, the arch-Social Democrat of Thalburg, Karl Hengst, had no really bitter experiences of the type related above. Perhaps it was because he was so well known, perhaps because he was an astute enough politician to know that the SPD was finished and to act accordingly.

Karl Hengst met the problem of Nazism with coolness and courage, as shown by his actions in the City and County Councils. His courage did not extend to what he termed "fruitless heroics"; hence, as soon as he saw what was going on in each of the organs he was elected to, he quietly resigned. In early April he learned the essential facts at a meeting of the Provincial Parliament. At its first session he was elected to the executive committee, but the new governor immediately declared him "furloughed." Thus within a short time after the elections, Hengst either gave up or was stripped of all the offices he had held.

Apparently Thalburg's Nazis originally intended to make an example of Hengst. Shortly after the local elections in March, several truckloads of SA men from a neighboring town were brought to Thalburg for a demonstration. The demonstration took the form of smashing the windows and office furniture of the "red" Health

Insurance Office. Karl Hengst's tobacco shop was located across the street from the Health Insurance Office, and Kurt Aergeyz gave a speech to the SA men, attacking Hengst. The most frequent oratorical gesture was a finger pointed across the street. Apparently Aergeyz's hope was that the SA men would ransack Hengst's shop and drag Hengst out to be a forced witness to the burning of Weimar flags which was to cap the demonstration. But the SA, either sated or ashamed, refused to take the hint and Hengst's shop was spared destruction.

The next Nazi action was to declare that Karl Hengst's shop was under boycott. This hurt his business somewhat, especially when SA men stood outside and frightened people away, but Hengst had many friends, and shopping habits become ingrained in a small town, so that his business survived. Eventually even Aergeyz forgot about the boycott.

Naturally the "Deputy Police" searched Hengst's house repeatedly, but he anticipated their action by burning his files. Furthermore, he began counteraction. After the first searches Hengst ordered a load of wood. Then he went to Aergeyz and demanded that policemen be detailed to observe the wood being stacked up so that they would not later search the pile for weapons and mess up the neat pile. He did the same when he first hoed the small vegetable garden in his back yard.

Finally he became even more aggressive. In the course of the boycott an SA man "stood guard" over Hengst's back gate one night and the next morning Hengst saw Aergeyz bright and early and told him:

> Look, I know why you've got your Stormtrooper watching my back gate! One of these nights he'll throw a weapon over the fence and then the police will "find" it the following day. You know that mastiff I have? Tomorrow night at 8 P.M. I'm going to let him out for exercise—out the back gate. I'll feed him at 9 P.M.; that is, if he's still hungry.

The SA post was removed.

This kind of personal duel had its limits, and for Karl Hengst the other side of his relationship with Aergeyz and the other Nazis was that he was absolutely dormant politically. He never said

anything against Hitler or the Nazis and in general accepted the
regime as an established, if unpleasant, fact. He was even willing
to give in if pressed in minor matters. Thus the Nazis eventually
determined that Hengst would have to join one of their affiliates,
the People's Welfare Society. Hengst finally agreed but won a sort
of personal victory by insisting that he pay half dues "since your
boycott of my business has made me poor."

In this peculiar role, a kind of tamed tiger, Hengst lived out the
Nazi era without ever suffering more than occasional petty chicanery from the Nazis. He was even able to wield some influence, as
was the case when his interventions through von Altberg secured
the release from a concentration camp of two Social Democrats
of Thalburg County. Probably the main ingredient in Hengst's
survival was his coolness and his relationship with Aergeyz, for
the two had grown up in the same block and understood each
other.[36]

A final example of the personal experiences of Social Democrats
may round out the picture. Hans Leidler was a rank-and-file member of the SPD and also of the *Reichsbanner*. He had worked at
the Thalburg railroad yards and had lost his job in the purge of
1932 and had furthermore been denied unemployment pay. Hence
he entered the Third Reich fully engrossed with the problem of
earning his daily bread.

During this period, Leidler and his family lived by working for
the peasants around Thalburg. He and his children worked all
day and received their meals in exchange. His wife was lucky
enough to find a job at the cigar factory, and thus they lived. His
family was often hungry but his father helped out, sharing what
little he had with them. Eventually the peasants refused to give
Leidler any more work because they were afraid of what might
happen to them if it were discovered that they were helping a
Socialist.

During this period the Gestapo searched Leidler's house several
times, very carefully. They cut open mattresses and thumped on
the walls and even broke open a section of the wall that happened
to be hollow. They confiscated Leidler's rifle, but Leidler hid the
Reichsbanner flag so carefully that they never found it. The
Gestapo were very angry about it. They questioned him on that
and related matters at least twenty times.

In the summer of 1933, after he had been without work for several months, Leidler was given a job in the stone quarry near Thalburg as a result of the intervention of Walter Eckstein (who had once courted Leidler's cousin), and in return for a promise to give up political activity. He found many SPD officials from Thalburg working there. Every morning they were all made to salute the swastika when it was raised. The work consisted of breaking stones with a sledge hammer and the pay was 20 marks a week, which Leidler said was like the old proverb: "Too much to die on and too little to live on." It was actually less than the dole.

For Leidler, who had worked as track repairman, the work was quite tolerable, but for some it was brutal. Leidler's cousin, who had worked in a bureau in Thalburg before the purge of the city employees, died as a result of the exposure to the weather. Eventually, in 1935, Leidler found a better job with the Autobahn construction team.

During the intervening years the house searches continued. One Gestapo commissar searched Leidler's house at least seven times, and there were others, too. "The worst was hearing the knock on the door and wondering what was going to happen this time."

He was also watched in other ways. In the winter of 1933-1934, an unknown man knocked at Leidler's door and asked for him by name. Leidler took him in. It was raining and the man was wet. The man showed Leidler a *Reichsbanner* membership book and told him that he was a fugitive from the Gestapo. He told Leidler that the *Reichsbanner* had risen in the Ruhr and was fighting the Nazis. Would Leidler have any weapons? Could he supply the names of any loyal *Reichsbanner* men in the area? Leidler answered "no" to each question and added, "I'm through, I've had the s— kicked out of me. All I can do is put you up overnight and feed you, which I'd do for any human being on a night like this."

In the morning, after breakfast, the man went to the door and, just before he left, turned his lapel back and showed Leidler an SS button. Then he left wordlessly.[37]

From these five accounts—of a union official, a workingman, a *Reichsbanner* leader, the head of Thalburg's SPD, and a rank-and-file member—the pattern emerges of how the Thalburg Nazis dealt with avowed opponents to the regime. They were, first of all, economically hurt, as far as this was possible. Most SPD members who could be forced out of a job were subsequently given the choice of either no work at all or work in the stone quarry. The latter was work designed to break their spirits. In addition they were hounded by the police with arrests, questionings, and repeated house searches. Behind this lay the constant threat of the concentration camp, the very factor of uncertainty adding terror. For one never knew whether or not the latest house searching might, perhaps whimsically, qualify one for the half-mythical KZ. Then there were the petty nuisances: the demands to join the SA or some other Nazi organization, the calumny against one's name in speeches and the Nazi press, the pressure on the landlord and (subtly) on one's friends, the silence in the tavern when one stopped for a beer.

Poverty, terror, bureaucratic chicanery, social isolation—a potent formula. Perhaps one should add what might have been the most significant factor of all: the sense of futility. What was the Thalburger Social Democrat to do? Rebel? Even if one had weapons, whom was one to shoot? Policemen? Every Nazi (including those you went to grade school with)? And when? Which one of the various small acts exactly tipped the scale toward a dictatorship? And who was to rebel with you, since the factor of distrust entered in? And what then? Was Thalburg to declare itself an independent entity in Germany?

Perhaps one should attempt first to prepare the population through effective propaganda. But Thalburg voted for the NSDAP with a 63 per cent majority, and if the SPD could not sell democracy when it had the advantages of free speech, its own press, and a party machine, what could it do with none of these?

Thus there was left only flight, internal conviction, irony, or little triumphs of the sort Karl Hengst carried off. By the time the first six months of the Nazi regime were over these were the alternatives open to the Social Democrats of Thalburg. When it is too late, it is too late.

Under these circumstances it was only a matter of tidiness that prompted the formal outlawing of the SPD. Long before that step was taken, the membership had been broken and the organization smashed. In recognition of these facts the executive committee of Local Thalburg met on April 29 and dissolved itself. The Thalburg section of the *Reichsbanner* did likewise on the same date. Before the SPD was able to wind up its affairs, the police underscored the fact of the dissolution by seizing all SPD property (including 200 marks still in the treasury) on May 11. At the same time former leaders were subjected to extensive grilling by the Gestapo, who were apparently amazed to find democratic Socialism so easy to destroy. The trade unions were dissolved and their buildings occupied on May 2. The other organizations in the complex SPD-worker system simply ceased to exist. Other parties had no local organization in Thalburg to dissolve, with the exception of the DVP, which voted itself out of existence on July 14, 1933, after turning its treasury over to the "German War Graves Society." [38]

Thus ended all formal party organizations in Thalburg whose ideology was opposed to that of the Hitler dictatorship.

CHAPTER 13

WHIPPING UP ENTHUSIASM

(March to July, 1933)

> *What a Transposition Through Divine Disposition!*
> —Title of the main speech at the Nazi Victory Celebration in Thalburg, March 19, 1933

Vigor and thoroughness were the prime attributes of the Thalburg NSDAP in the years before 1933. These qualities developed into frenzy after Hitler was named Chancellor and the way to the Third Reich seemed open at last. Not only did the Nazis seize the whip of authority and use it to beat their former opponents into submission, they intensified their propaganda efforts. Mass backing had been the Nazi forte before Hitler came to power; mass frenzy brought them their absolute majorities in Thalburg in the March elections. Through every device in the Nazi repertoire the townspeople had been convinced that a vote for Nazism meant a vote for new times, for a revolution which would sweep away all past difficulties and inaugurate the earthly millennium. But the Nazi revolution could not be accomplished overnight. So many things had to be done that the initial stage of the revolution (the establishment of the dictatorship) took at least half a year.

Hence a way had to be found to sustain enthusiasm over a long period of time. The enthusiasm not only served to make men *feel* that a revolution was occurring; it also served as mask and justification for the various components—many of them ugly—which made up the revolution. Finally, by seeming to involve everyone, the organized enthusiasm isolated anyone who might be opposed to, or even skeptical about, the introduction of the totalitarian state. Thus it was an essential reinforcement of the dictatorship.

A crucial prerequisite for effective propaganda was control of the press. By the creation of a system of terror the Nazis had already made sure that the local press would not oppose them. The organs of the opposition (the *Volksblatt* and the *Thalburger Echo*) disappeared by March; the GHC had always been favorably disposed towards Nazism, and the TNN was at first ambivalent and then acquiescent. But Thalburg's Nazis wanted more. They wanted the existing local press to be a completely pliant tool and ultimately they wanted their own Nazi-operated newspaper.

The beginnings of a Nazi newspaper went back to 1931 when the bi-weekly newsletter *Hört! Hört!* was first published. By autumn, 1932, *Hört! Hört!* began to appear as the weekly supplement to a larger Nazi newspaper which served the entire Hannoverian area. On April 6, 1933, the supplement's name was changed to *Thalburger Beobachter* (TB) and it was published three times weekly. By June it came out daily, but still as a supplement to the parent newspaper. In the intervening months the Nazis had taken over the *Volksblatt* printing plant and in July they began using this to publish the TB as an independent newspaper designed to give the Nazi point of view for Thalburg.[1]

While the Nazis were developing their own local press they sought to promote it in every way. Early in April the TB was made the official newspaper of the town of Thalburg and the sole official newspaper in police matters. A few weeks later it became the only official organ of Thalburg County. Naturally all party members were urged to subscribe to the TB, and SA men were put to selling subscriptions, apparently with phenomenal success. In May an order was sent from Walter Eckstein to all Local Group Leaders of the NSDAP in Thalburg County forbidding them to give any news to other newspapers and requiring them to support the TB with every means available.[2] In other words, one method of aiding the TB was to hurt the other local newspapers.

In the first six months of the Third Reich the Nazis turned their heaviest guns on the TNN, which then had the largest circulation in Thalburg. While the TNN was either objective or ambiguous about Nazism in the local news section, it was an organ of the DVP and hence, in national news, anti-Nazi. This apparently made little difference to Thalburgers before Hitler was appointed Chancellor. Even the Nazis found it necessary to advertise their meetings in the TNN. After Hitler was appointed Chancellor, many Thalburgers suddenly decided, either through fear or conviction, that the TNN was not the kind of newspaper they wanted to read. As the former reporter for the paper put it:

> Between Hitler's appointment as Chancellor and the March elections, people quit reading the TNN by the hundreds. They didn't just drop their subscriptions—they came into the office and vehemently demanded that the paper never be delivered to their home again, beginning tomorrow. They said they never wanted to hear of it again. Advertising fell off too.[3]

Thus by March the TNN began to be very careful about what it printed. It even screened advertisements carefully. Nevertheless the future of the paper was in considerable doubt after the Nazis came to power in Thalburg. In March, 1933, Erhardt Knorpel, the local news reporter for the TNN, talked this problem over with his neighbor, Walter Eckstein, County Leader of the NSDAP. Eckstein told him, "There is a simple solution: you join the party and then the TNN won't get into any more trouble. The TNN will have a guarantee." So Knorpel, after consultation with the editor-publisher of the paper, joined the NSDAP. He did not feel enthusiastic about it, but it seemed a matter of economic necessity.[4]

But this by no means ended the TNN's problems. It lost its position as official organ of the town and county offices, to the undisguised glee of the TB:

> It was to be expected that the TNN should lose its official character. This, at least, it deserved because of its record of struggle against our movement. In the last weeks the TNN has tried to put on a Nazi

cloak, but they still accept ads from Jews and from the consumers' cooperative. The length of the TNN's future is indeed doubtful.[5]

After this the TNN became doubly cautious and refused advertisements from Jewish firms. But toeing the Nazi line was not an easy task, as Knorpel recalled:

I remember my first mistake. I wrote a report on a meeting in which I mentioned the County Prefect first and the County Leader of the NSDAP second. There was a great stink over this—Eckstein called me up on the telephone and bawled me out. That night the publisher told me the Nazis were going to close up the paper. When I got to work the next morning he was in a state of deep depression. So I went over to see Walter Eckstein and apologized profusely and promised never to let it happen again. Eckstein said: "Don't forget it! First comes the party, then its servants in office." [6]

In addition to these direct attacks, the TNN had other things to worry about, since circulation continued to fall off. The cause of this was the Nazi campaign to sell subscriptions to their own paper, the TB. Most Thalburgers were afraid to refuse a subscription to the TB, and also felt they could not afford both the TB and the TNN. Hence they stopped buying the TNN.[7]

The TNN fought this the only way it could. In May it published a long article on the indispensable value of the local press. In July there was another article on the value of the local press, based on quotations from the Nazi provincial governor. At the same time it tried to buoy up its readers' courage. In June the TNN reported prominently that the Society of German Newspaper Publishers had passed resolutions against the "use of threats or boycotts to gain new circulation." The following month, under a big headline ("Boycott Measures Against Bourgeois Papers Forbidden"), the TNN reported that the *Reichsleitung* of the NSDAP had forbidden the use of economic sanctions against any bourgeois newspapers. A few weeks later there was another long article on unfair competition by the Nazi press against non-party newspapers. It criticized "terroristic methods of raising newspaper circulation" and bolstered this with frequent quotations by leading Nazis.[8] It is doubtful that any of this campaign was really effective.

In the course of building up the circulation of the TB, the Nazis also trod on the toes of Wilhelm Spatel, owner and editor of the GHC. As a nationalist newspaper the GHC never made any attempt to hide its admiration for the Nazis in the years before Hitler came to power. Nazi advertisements were published in the GHC (probably at a reduced rate), Spatel printed Nazi leaflets at a time when the Nazis had no other means to get them printed, and he always reported Nazi meetings with enthusiasm. But while the GHC was enthusiastic about the Nazis, the feeling was not reciprocated. To Thalburg's Nazis the GHC was to be used but not trusted, since its editor was a despicable reactionary. This attitude was made clear long before Hitler came to power.[9]

Nazi attacks on the GHC abated after the formation of the Nazi-Nationalist coalition in the beginning of 1933, but increased again when the GHC, like the TNN, began to try to protect its circulation against Nazi competition. In May the TB published the following article:

THAT'LL HAPPEN JUST ONCE. . . .

Printer and DNVPist Spatel has attacked the . . . TB, not openly but nevertheless clearly. Talks about the value of the "Local Press"! We all agree on the value of the local press, but not on the value of the GHC. Local press is not narrow "churchyard politics" but a vital connection with the basic opinions of its readers. The GHC is too old. It clearly doesn't fit into the national community of Adolf Hitler.[10]

This stung Spatel into a lengthy editorial reply. He insisted that he was proud of his role in helping to defeat "Marxism" and that he had spent his whole life combating "Marxists." He never accepted advertisements from the SPD or the consumers' cooperative "though they were repeatedly offered." As for the "churchyard politics," Spatel said he could not understand this charge. He had reported every meeting the NSDAP held in Thalburg and had even hired a Nazi party member to write the stories. He declared that "the GHC was, is, and will be a Nationalist newspaper." As for the TB's report, it was clearly a pack of lies. If the TB attacked him again, Spatel concluded, he would not stoop to answer them.[11]

This was strong talk and the Nazis obviously would not take

this lying down. The GHC's already small circulation began to dip. People who had subscribed to the GHC asked that it no longer be delivered, but instead picked it up covertly at the paper's offices.[12]

Spatel replied to this by publishing an enormous article on "illegal competition by newspapers" replete with quotations from the official Nazi *Völkisher Beobachter*. This drove the TB into publishing an article itself against illegal methods of getting subscriptions. It suggested that people should demand to see identification papers from anyone who claimed to be selling subscriptions from the TB. Finally, it declared that it was publishing this "because of the many dirty accusations the GHC is making against us." Furthermore the Prefect's office was brought into play to keep Spatel from complaining about his having lost access to official notices.[13] Spatel, in short, was undertaking a fight he could not possibly win. By the close of the first six months of Nazi rule it was clear that the GHC and possibly the TNN were going to be destroyed altogether. Thus the field would be left to the TB alone. But in neither case was this because Nazism had been challenged openly by the non-Nazi newspapers of Thalburg. In fact, the more the GHC and TNN feared for their existence the more eager they were to prove themselves enthusiastic champions of the new regime. Thus Thalburgers were incessantly propagandized by their own trusted newspapers during the initial months of Nazi rule.

Press propaganda, useful as it was, was never the real Nazi method of stimulating support. To assure mass backing there had to be active participation, even more so after the Nazis had seized power and could require participation. Thalburg's NSDAP began providing for this as soon as the March election campaign was concluded.

The first wave of mass demonstrations was connected with celebrating the electoral victory won on March 12. Election day itself provided a foretaste, since it had also been designated a memorial day for the fallen of World War I. All public buildings were required to fly flags at half-mast, with the express stipulation that the Imperial and not the Weimar flag should be flown. In the morning, uniformed contingents of all the veterans' societies joined the SA and *Stahlhelm* in a memorial service which was also a tribute to the new *Volk** community of Hitlerian Germany. Subsequently there was a mass meeting in the Market Square at which the head of the County Veterans' Society spoke on how happy he was to see the old flag flying again.

Flags were in abundance on the following days as the Nazis called for three days of flag flying in honor of the electoral victory, featuring both the Imperial and Nazi flags. This began on March 13, with a general parade around Thalburg to raise the two new flags and to burn the old flag of the Weimar Republic. The parade was composed of the *Stahlhelm,* the SA, and the SS, and was led by the SA fife-and-drum corps. It was on this day that Thalburg's police force was made to put on swastika armbands.

The first place to undergo the change was the City Hall. The Imperial and swastika flags were raised and the Mayor said a few words on the blessings of "unity" in Germany, followed by Kurt Aergeyz on a similar theme. After the speeches the Black-Red-Gold flag of the Weimar Republic was cast on a small bonfire which had been prepared, and as it was consumed by the flames, the crowd sang the "Horst Wessel Song." This same ceremony was repeated at the police station, the county building, and the post office, each time with a new speaker. Finally the parade marched to the Health Insurance Office where the flags were also raised and where Kurt Aergeyz outdid himself in condemning the Social Democrats "who considered this very building as their domain and propaganda institute." "The day is past," finished Aergeyz, "when such Social Democratic elements will have a chance to be active in this building." At last, exhausted by the orgy of symbol manipulation and speeches, the crowd dispersed.[14]

The next big event of the NSDAP was not held until the end of the week. In between, for those who wanted more, there was a patriotic speech by the poet August Winnig and a patriotic concert by the SA band. Then on Sunday, March 19, the Thalburg NSDAP gave its victory celebration, fittingly held in the Cattle Auction Hall. The hall, decorated with swastika flags, was full to

---

* A term which can be variously translated as "national," "popular," or "racial," and thus connotes all three. It was a favorite Nazi expression.

the bursting point with at least a thousand people. The chief speaker was the Nazi preacher, Pastor Muenchmeyer, and his topic: "What a Transposition Through Divine Disposition!" The whole tone of the celebration was conservative, solemn, and religious.[15]

As soon as Thalburg's ceremonial inauguration of the Third Reich was completed, it was necessary for the town to repeat the process in order to be in line with the national ceremony staged by Hitler and Hindenburg at the Potsdam Garrison Church on Tuesday, March 21. In Thalburg all public offices were closed for the day. Shops closed early and also during the period from eleven-thirty in the morning until one in the afternoon in order to hear the ceremony over the radio. Radio sets were brought into the schools where the children listened to the events in Potsdam and had the explanation given to them by their teachers that "a new epoch in German history was beginning." Then they were given a holiday for the rest of the day. All houses and public buildings were to bedeck themselves with swastika flags. After dark came a torchlight parade which wound through the whole of Thalburg. Participating were the various Nazi and Nationalist paramilitary units, all the sport clubs in Thalburg, all the various veterans' and patriotic societies, all the schools, and such miscellaneous groups as the "Artisans' Training Club," the clerks and mail carriers from the post office, and the Volunteer Fire Department. Led by the town band, the SA band, and the SA fife-and-drum corps, the parade finally came to a halt in the city park, where Kurt Aergeyz gave a speech in which he praised the new unity of Germany: "The individual is nothing; the *Volk* is everything! Once we unite internally, then we shall defeat the external foe. Then it will really be 'Germany above all in the world.'" Upon this cue the crowd sang *Deutschland über Alles* and then dispersed. Some three thousand had marched; at least as many again lined the streets to watch. "Thus Thalburg's citizenry," commented the TNN, "has proven, in its overwhelming majority, that it is ready to throw itself without reservation into the rebirth of our Fatherland."[16]

Mass demonstrations of loyalty and enthusiasm of this sort were the very breath of the propaganda campaign designed to convince Thalburgers that they were entering a new era. But in the ensuing months it was impossible to continue having great parades and mass demonstrations simply to celebrate the advent of the Third Reich as such. Concrete occasions were needed. They were supplied by three great festive events, two of them new, a third traditional. These were the celebration of Hitler's birthday, the "Day of German Labor" (a reinterpretation of May Day), and the celebration of the tenth anniversary of the death of Albert Leo Schlageter,* on May 26. By emphasizing these events, it was possible to have a major celebration about every three weeks during those crucial first months of the protracted Nazi *coup d'état*.

The first of the three great festivals was the celebration of Adolf Hitler's forty-fourth birthday, held on April 20. The day's events began at seven in the morning with a march through the town by the SA and their fife-and-drum corps. Immediately thereafter there was a small ceremony connected with installing the new street sign on "Adolf Hitler Strasse." Next came participation in church services by all the various uniformed adjuncts to the NSDAP. The Lutheran church was decorated with Imperial and swastika flags, which were also to be seen on almost every house in Thalburg. The sermon that morning stressed the heavy responsibilities that fell to Hitler and concluded by invoking the prayers of Thalburgers for their *Fuehrer*.

After the services, a parade was held, terminating at the Market Square, where a concert was given by the SA band. The Thalburg Artillery Club contributed to the occasion by firing salutes from their miniature cannon, attended by two little boys dressed in replicas of the Prussian artillerist's uniform. The afternoon was then given over to drinking beer in the various taverns of Thalburg. In the evening, festivities continued in the *1910er Zelt* with a concert of military marches, dramatic and humorous skits, dancing, and speeches. Every official in the town government, County Prefecture, *Stahlhelm,* and NSDAP was present. Kurt Aergeyz spoke on the theme "Unity Is Everything" and promised that Thalburg would soon be 100 per cent Nazi. The great hall was so full it was practically impossible to dance.

---

* An otherwise obscure nationalistic hero who was put to death by the French during their occupation of the Ruhr.

In an imaginative aftermath the newspapers announced that Thalburg units of the NSDAP had been presented with cheese, chocolate, and sausage by Adolf Hitler. These were gifts that had been sent to him for his birthday and that he then redistributed to local units in his own name.[17]

The next great celebration came on May 1, a day which a party with the name of "National Socialist German Workers' Party" could not afford to ignore, but the character of which it was determined to alter. In Thalburg, the method used to accomplish these goals was to put the May Day celebration under Nazi leadership and thus give it a Nazi tone, and to make the celebration so heterogeneous in character as to purge it of its previous class connotations.

Preparations for "The Day of National Labor" began almost immediately after the celebration of Hitler's birthday. The opening note was sounded by advertisements placed by Thalburg's Nazi Group:

The "Day of National Labor," planned by the Reich government for May 1, will bear the spirit of National Socialism in its essence. This day will bring the creative *Volk* to a recognition of the national state, as opposed to the international efforts of Marxism. At the same time it marks the beginning of the first years of planned work under the leadership of the Reich Chancellor, Adolf Hitler. We call upon representatives of all offices, economic groups, clubs, businesses, etc., to attend the planning session at . . .[18]

Shortly thereafter, Nazi County Leader Eckstein announced that the theme for the May Day celebration would be "All Germans Are Workers." Hence, the whole of Thalburg would have to be involved in the celebration. A simple system of control was devised. Every person in Thalburg was to purchase a button at the Nazi headquarters. The button would enable him to walk in the parade on May 1. A person who did not buy a button would draw attention to himself. The price for one button was 10 *pfennig;* proceeds from the sale of buttons would finance the festivities.

In addition, the regular social and economic associations in Thalburg were pressed into service to make sure that the celebration was well organized and well attended. There was a place in the May Day parade for every organization in the town, from the local office of the *Reichsbank* to the Teachers' Association. Naturally all the veterans' and patriotic societies, all the state and local government employees, all the sport clubs, all the artisan guilds, choral groups, fishing clubs, chess societies, and so forth would march in the parade. Each one of these organizations was also asked to contribute 5 or 10 marks to cover the cost of the celebration. Contributions were payable at the county headquarters of the NSDAP.

The holiday was to be a busy one. The program prescribed the following schedule:

A.M. 6:30 Fife-and-drum corps gives the signal to arise.
      8:00 Flag raising at all offices and places of business with all employees participating.
      8:45 Church services.
     10:00 Meeting of all officials of all clubs, businesses, etc., in the city park (for last-minute parade instructions).
     10:30 Broadcast by the Reich government from Berlin.
P.M. 1:15 Parade begins.
            (For the remainder of the afternoon there will be a carnival with booths and a midway at the parade grounds.)
      7:30 Radio broadcast of Adolf Hitler's speech.
            Thereafter until midnight: concert, dancing, etc.

Preparations for this fantastic program became frenzied in the last few days of April. Many organizations had to resort to newspaper advertisements in order to give all the details of what was required of their members. But thanks to these efforts the program was carried out with the precision of a Prussian drill squad. Most gratifying of all to the Nazi planners was that hardly a house or building in Thalburg was not decorated with a swastika flag.

The parade—a miracle of organization—started only fifteen minutes late. This was, after all, excusable, since five thousand people marched in it. There were seventy-three vehicles and floats (roughly half the number of all the motor vehicles in Thalburg) and the parade stretched out for nine kilometers. It took three hours for the parade to pass. Some sections were quite colorful, since almost every occupation was represented by a float. The bakers' guild, for example, had a huge pretzel, while the Settlers' Club had a model house. The parade terminated at the parade grounds where the participants sang the "Horst Wessel Song" and *Deutschland über Alles,* and then were freed to complete the rest of the day's schedule. The press reported truthfully that Thalburg had never seen anything like this before.[19]

After the exhausting experience of organizing the May Day celebration, Thalburg's Nazis were inactive for over three weeks. Then came the last of the trilogy of Nazi celebrations, "Schlageter Day." This was a new holiday, commemorating the fact that ten years before that first Nazi spring, a former Free Corps volunteer named Albert Leo Schlageter had been executed by order of a French court-martial for sabotage during the Ruhr occupation. Thalburg would honor Schlageter by dedicating a stone inscribed: "Never forget! Albert Leo Schlageter. Murdered by the French on May 26, 1923."

The ceremony was to be a double one, for after the Schlageter dedication there was to be a burning of "filth literature" in the Market Square. The material for this literary *auto-da-fé* consisted of confiscated Social Democratic papers and pamphlets, plus other works taken from the public library, such as Remarque's *All Quiet on the Western Front.* Thalburgers who thought they could contribute to the combustibles were urged to deliver their books to Senator Otto Made.

The unveiling of the Schlageter memorial was aimed mainly at young people. Thus the Hitler Youth and League of German Girls took the leading role, though the SA, SS, and SA band also contributed. A large crowd came to witness the ceremony, including all children from the grade schools. Various poems and songs of a nationalistic nature were presented and then the main speech was given by Senator Otto Made (supervisor of Thalburg's Hitler Youth). After some general remarks on the significance of Schlageter and on the necessity for the Hitler Youth to emulate Schlageter's courage, Made came to the heart of the speech:

But besides letting your courage be strengthened by his example, let the name Schlageter cause you to increase your hatred against Versailles and against the French who murdered him because—despite persecution and danger—he dedicated himself to his Fatherland. *(Turning then to the boys and girls.)* Be you his avengers! Be you the German Youth that knows how to hate foreigners! Your way leads you daily by this stone; clench your fists and think: "Never forget, revenge is mine!"

Made was followed by the pastor of the Lutheran Church who chose, in his speech, to emphasize the heroism of Schlageter and the necessity of "being worthy of him and of our *Fuehrer,* Adolf Hitler." After a hymn was sung, the ceremony came to an end.

The crowd then repaired to the Market Square, where several hundredweight of books were piled up, with a red flag and a photo of Otto Braun, former Socialist Premier of Prussia, on top. After a few words on the "un-German spirit" and on the "Jewish spirit," Kurt Aergeyz concluded his speech by promising that no German books or newspapers would be written by "racially foreign elements" any more. Then the flames crept over the pile of books while the crowd sang *Deutschland über Alles.* The double ceremony had been highly instructive for Thalburgers.[20]

These three great celebrations do not by any means exhaust the list of propaganda activities undertaken by Thalburg's NSDAP in the first six months of the Third Reich. In addition to these general activities there were other smaller events sponsored by the various Nazi sub-organizations.

The SA and SS contributed much during the first months. In March they held a concert evening in the *1910er Zelt* and also field maneuvers. A month later they conducted maneuvers again, replete with symbolism. ("Red" attacked "Blue" and was annihilated by a counterattack in the woods west of Thalburg.) These events undoubtedly helped satisfy Thalburg's apparently unquenchable thirst for militarism. This was the case also in mid-May, when a member of Thalburg's SA was married. In clear imitation of the approved military manner, Thalburg's SA formed a passageway into the church with their arms upraised in the Hitler salute. Again, in mid-May the SS band from a neighboring town provided a "Military March" evening in Thalburg, and later in the month the SA formed a cavalry unit. With the coming of summer the SA began to emphasize "military sport." Early in June there was competition of this type in a neighboring town with twenty-six medalists from Thalburg. In July, Thalburg had its own SA "military sport" day, featuring the Motor SA of the entire district. There was a parade through the town, then an obstacle-course race for motorcycles, and finally a mock tank battle. In the evening there was a dance. Several thousand Thalburgers watched the show. Later in the month the SA, SS, and *Stahlhelm* held a twenty-five kilometer pack-march race.[21]

In the general propaganda work during the period of the seizure of power, the Nazi youth organizations also did their part. The League of German Girls gave "Parents' Evenings," such as one in the latter part of April, designed to show that the League taught girls wholesome skills, such as singing and folk dancing. In May the League of German Girls undertook two well-publicized trips, one to a district Hitler Youth convention (at which the Thalburg Local Group of the League was declared the best in the district), and another, a march to a neighboring town and back.[22]

The Hitler Youth's greatest contribution to the propaganda cause was a sub-district meeting held in Thalburg on June 6, 1933. Over 1,400 boys flocked to Thalburg, camping out on the parade grounds and holding parades and sport competition during the day. The TNN (and probably many of the townspeople) appeared genuinely charmed by "the little brown soldiers." [23] Naturally these organizations contributed most of their effort to making sure that the great demonstrations and meetings were successful. The Hitler Youth and the SA were constantly active during the Nazi seizure of power, while the SA and SS made a special contribution by working as deputy police for house searches, beatings, and arrests.

As in the period before Hitler became Chancellor, the Nazis again made use of theatrical presentations and movies. One film they pushed especially was entitled "Bleeding Germany." In April the Thalburg NSDAP provided special buses for people who wanted to see a play in a neighboring town under Nazi supervision. In July a Nazi road group gave a special showing of the play "Schlageter" in Thalburg. It packed the *1910er Zelt*. Finally, even events outside Thalburg were often used to provide propaganda spectacles. On the occasion of a general Nazi meeting in Hannover in June, for example, Thalburg sent two special trains with SA parades, both on leaving and on returning.[24]

In the general propaganda effort, the DNVP (Hitler's coalition partners) and its uniformed adjunct, the *Stahlhelm,* also tried to ease the task of the Hitler government by whipping up enthusiasm. In March the *Stahlhelm* gave a series of film presentations. In late April the young *Stahlhelm* held field maneuvers and then gave a parade and a concert on the Market Square. The *Stahlhelm* also sponsored a minor imitation of the Hitler Youth Sport day in July.[25]

During the first months of the Third Reich, many Thalburgers joined the *Stahlhelm.* Generally they did so in order to avoid having to join the SA or some other Nazi organization. Between April and June, Thalburg's *Stahlhelm* added almost 150 members.[26] While this activity was going on in Thalburg, the DNVP was being maneuvered out of power in Berlin and Goebbels was beginning to charge that Communists were infiltrating the *Stahlhelm.* In Thalburg the DNVP Local Group bestirred itself enough to send a letter to Hitler expressing their loyalty to him but also insisting that "whoever fights Hugenburg fights the Hitler government." Later in June someone removed the wreath that the *Stahlhelm* had placed on the new memorial to Schlageter. Finally, the *Stahlhelm* in the Thalburg district declared (as of July 1, 1933) that they would accept no new members so that "applications could be examined more closely." [27] The Nationalists were beginning to discover the price of being fellow-travelers of the NSDAP.

While the Nazis and Nationalists were vigorously backing the new system, there was a continuation of the kind of nationalistic activities that had become so much a part of life in Thalburg in the years before Hitler took power. Near the end of June all flags flew at half-mast in the town in sorrowful commemoration of the signing of the Treaty of Versailles. In April, the *Reichswehr,* in accordance with its custom, sent a detachment to Thalburg to give a military concert. There was considerable publicity, and backing by the NSDAP, but the event was unsuccessful—Thalburgers were kept too busy by the Nazi celebrations to have time to enjoy their traditional amusements.[28]

Despite the drain imposed by the Nazis on the energies of nationalist-minded Thalburgers, at least some of the pre-Hitler nationalist societies continued their work. In May the Thalburg Navy Club sponsored a lecture by a former Navy officer, entitled:

"With U-Boat 21 in the World War." On May 8, Thalburg had its annual convention of the old guardists. As in prior years, there was a parade, a series of speeches, and finally a dance in the *1910er Zelt.* But now Nazi symbols and ideas were fused with the customary ceremony. Thus for the first time there were pictures of Hitler at the guardists' meetings, the singing of the "Horst Wessel Song," and speeches by Kurt Aergeyz. For the rest, the ceremony continued its customary path of glorifying nationalism and militarism.[29]

By far the biggest event sponsored by the patriotic societies in the first months of the Nazi seizure of power was the joint celebration of the sixtieth anniversary of the Warriors' League and the tenth anniversary of the Navy Club. The celebration consumed a whole weekend, with speeches, pageants, and flag dedications on Saturday night, and church services plus a big parade on Sunday. As in the guardists' convention, Nazis made certain that Hitler and the NSDAP were given their due on each occasion. Because of the avid participation by Thalburg's Nazis, the celebration was extremely well organized and well attended. While it thus achieved a Nazi patina, the main effect of the anniversary celebrations was, as had been true of the work of these societies before 1933, directed towards heightening feelings of nationalism and militarism. In the same vein, the Thalburg Chapter of the Society for Germandom in Foreign Lands sponsored a marathon race and mass meeting on June 25, again with considerable Nazi overtones. This was also true of the celebration of the twenty-fifth anniversary of the founding of the Thalburg Military Society, held at the beginning of August.[30]

In short, while the main Nazi propaganda drive was going on, there was also a continuation of the customary nationalist agitation. Simply by promoting the kind of background that made Nazism appear reasonable, this aided the course of the Nazi revolution. The individual events became charged with Nazi concepts and speeches. All helped to smooth the way.

In addition to the traditional nationalist groups in Thalburg, two new movements aided the cause of Nazism. The first began before Hitler was named Chancellor but originally made itself felt in Thalburg in February, 1933. This was a civil defense program, designed to teach Thalburgers how to protect themselves against air raids. Early in February, 1933, a team of civil defense experts arrived in Thalburg, led by the former *Freikorps* leader Rossbach. The assembly hall of one of the schools was placed at the civil defense team's disposal, and for a week lectures and demonstrations were given on types of bombs and measures to be taken to minimize their effects. The course of instruction was supported by the patriotic societies in Thalburg, and the press gave considerable publicity. The civil defense team itself staged a parade with muffled drums (a traditional call to arms) to promote its course of instruction. The total effect was to suggest that Thalburg might soon be in danger from an air raid. By this means the atmosphere of a nation in arms was given a boost.[31]

The second new element was the building of gliders and training of glider pilots. This also began before Hitler came to power, but was strongly publicized by the NSDAP in the first months of Hitler's regime. The Thalburg glider was prominently displayed in parades and commonly discussed as the kernel of the new *Luftwaffe*. Finally, in late June, the Nazis took over the operation and set up an "SS Flyer Group" for Thalburg. Henceforth glider exercises were pushed vigorously.[32]

Thus in the first six months of the Nazi regime, Thalburg was subjected to a veritable barrage of propaganda. While the NSDAP took the lead, all the various nationalistic and militaristic elements in the town were brought into play to support and generalize the Nazi appeal. In addition to the mass-participation events in Thalburg, there was the steady stream of national news stories, radio speeches, and propaganda in magazines and books. The total effect was to create the spirit of a revolution and to justify the kinds of steps the Nazis took to insure themselves control over the people.

CHAPTER 14

THE ATOMIZATION
OF SOCIETY

(March to July, 1933)

> Behold how good and how pleasant it is for brethren to dwell together in unity.
>
> —PSALMS, CXXXIII, 1

Very early in the Nazi era an event occurred in Thalburg which effectively fused propaganda and terror. This was the boycott of the Jews, April 1 to 4, 1933. In addition to being the beginning of that ineluctable process which ended ten years later in the gas chambers of the SS extermination camps, this particular action was also a miniature example of what the Nazis intended to do to the entire German population. For the essential effect of the boycott of the Jews was to atomize them socially: to cut them off from the rest of German society so that normal human ties could not work to restrain the dictatorship.

Thalburg had a very small Jewish population. The census of 1932 showed 120 men, women, and children professing the Jewish faith out of a total population of ten thousand. There was no significant increase in their number; a generation before there had been 102.[1] Most Jews in Thalburg were small businessmen: cattle brokers, grocery or clothing store owners, and artisans. One Jewish merchant celebrated, in 1932, the 230th anniversary of the founding of his haberdashery—during all of which time it had been located in Thalburg. There was no Jewish section in Thalburg; Jews were well assimilated into Thalburg society. The town had very little anti-semitism before the advent of Nazism. What there was expressed itself only in jokes and slight feelings of generalized distaste—in other words, the usual heritage of medieval Europe. Jews belonged to the shooting societies, patriotic clubs, and choral groups, and if they were differentiated it was by class, not religion. Some were elected to offices in their clubs, some were very highly respected, all were accepted as a normal part of the town's life.

The Nazis were determined to change this, since anti-semitism formed one of the cornerstones of their ideology. This was not generally realized by Thalburgers, especially not by the Jews, who saw Nazi propaganda as an electioneering device or a manifestation of intellectual bankruptcy, but hardly as a concrete program.[2]

There had been occasional anti-Jewish utterances in speeches by Kurt Aergeyz, but the real campaign against the Jews opened on March 29, 1933, with an advertisement in the TNN, sponsored by Local Group Thalburg of the NSDAP. It declared that "International Jewry" was spreading "gruesome propaganda" against Germany and "mishandling our German brothers in foreign lands." In response to this, declared the statement, the NSDAP was calling a boycott against all Jewish businesses: "Germany will force Judah to his knees!" Three days later a second advertisement appeared which gave a specific list of individuals and businesses to be boycotted. The advertisement, marked "Clip and save," listed thirty-five firms representing forty individuals (in other words, almost all the adult male Jews in Thalburg).[3]

The itemized appeal for a boycott was followed by action. Beginning on April 1, SA men were posted before the doors of Jewish stores or offices. This "counteraction against the Jewish hate propaganda" was, according to the statement issued by the NSDAP, to continue "until the hate campaign and boycott against German goods ceases."

The boycott was also backed by the County Agricultural Society, which urged farmers to "crown your fight for nationalism by dealing a blow to the Jews." To provide farmers with an alternative to dealing with Jewish cattle brokers, a Cattle Brokerage Society was incorporated under the auspices of the County Agricultural Society, the only organization to support openly the Nazi boycott in Thalburg.[4]

After three days the boycott was halted, ending with a parade featuring placards against the Jews. According to the TB:

> Upon inducement by the local action committee, the following telegram was sent to German consuls and embassies in New York, Warsaw, Paris, and London: "All agitation and hate propaganda of the Jews in foreign areas about Germany untrue. Peace and quiet in Germany. Halt hate and agitation propaganda immediately. The Jewish Synagogue Community, Thalburg. The Chairman." [5]

Whether or not this telegram was extorted from Jewish community leaders or simply invented by the NSDAP is unclear. What is clear is that the connection between the six score Jews in Thalburg and an international conspiracy to besmirch the name of the new Third Reich existed only in the paranoia of the Thalburg Nazis. But the effect of the telegram was a perfect solution to the propaganda problem that had been created earlier. And in the interim the position of Thalburg's Jews underwent a radical change.

The application of the boycott varied in its effectiveness. One of the firms listed in the advertisement was Braun's Banking House, a solid and well-respected establishment. There were no SA posts before its doors on April 1, 1933, and business went on as usual. In most other cases there were SA posts, but only for a few hours. No violence occurred. Some Thalburgers were actually unaware of the action. But all Thalburgers eventually came to know that Jews were now outcasts and that the Nazis were deadly serious about this aspect of their program.[6]

The effect of the boycott upon the Jews of Thalburg was cataclysmic. Gregor Rosenthal and his wife could not at first believe that it would take place. But when they saw the two SA men posted before their door the full significance of it broke upon them. They did not dare to leave their home at all that day and Rosenthal himself sat crumpled up in his chair for hours repeating, "Was it for this that I spent four years defending my Fatherland?" [7]

The economic effect of the boycott extended beyond the formal period. While Banker Braun's business apparently did not suffer at all, Gregor Rosenthal's practice declined rapidly and his income fell from 9,000 marks in 1932 to 6,000 marks in 1933. This was probably true of most Jewish businesses; as people became more fearful, dealing with Jews became more of a luxury.

The problem of Jew-as-pariah in Thalburg was not simply one of the Nazis' attempting to impose a system of persecution upon an inert mass. The Jews themselves exacerbated the situation by withdrawing into themselves while the other Thalburgers, even if they might be opposed to the persecution of the Jews, abetted the system by their own efforts at self-protection. The day after the boycott began, a chain store with branches in Thalburg placed a large advertisement in the TNN which announced that theirs was a "purely Christian family-enterprise" with no "outside capital" to mar their "Economic Independence—the Pride of Our Firm." Shortly after the boycott more stores blossomed forth with signs proclaiming "German Merchant." Once the principle was accepted it was a simple step to the poster, "Jews not admitted." Early in May the cigar factory in Thalburg announced that "a thorough examination by the NSDAP has conclusively shown that the firm is a purely German enterprise." Astute Thalburgers could also have noted that after April 1 no advertisements appeared in the TNN by any Jewish firms.[8]

As for the Jews themselves, they reacted in various ways. Banker Braun, a man who belonged to the uppermost circles of Thalburg society, ignored the whole matter as much as possible. On the occasion of celebrations he ostentatiously hung an Imperial flag before the bank. He was happy to do this anyway since he was a nationalist, a monarchist, and had served as an officer in World War I. Braun greeted friends on the street in a courtly manner by tipping his hat, thus circumventing the "German greeting" (i.e., "Heil Hitler" plus the Nazi salute). To the solicitous advice that was given him to leave Thalburg, he replied, "Where should I go? Here I am the Banker Braun; elsewhere I would be the Jew Braun." Secure in his position as a member of Thalburg's upper class, he was convinced that the trouble would soon pass. To avoid unpleasantness he quietly resigned from his shooting society and singing club, giving "the press of business" as his reason.[9]

Others were not so self-confident. Gregor Rosenthal withdrew from all social contact and crossed the street to avoid meeting erstwhile friends. His own sense of persecution intensified the growing feeling among Thalburgers that it might be inexpedient to be seen talking to a Jew. Soon Rosenthal received letters from the Veterans' Club and the shooting society dropping him from membership "for non-attendance at meetings" (a kindly euphemism). The chairman and the secretary of the Men's Singing Society of 1850 came to see him personally; Rosenthal was entertainment chairman of the club and therefore not to be dealt with by a simple letter. They urged him to attend meetings and help them keep the club going in these difficult times. Rosenthal had developed new sensitivity, and reading their faces carefully he told them that unfortunately his practice kept him so busy that not only would he have to resign his position as entertainment chairman, he could not even be a member any longer. They expressed profound regrets and left. Most of Thalburg's Jews probably reacted in this way.[10]

Some townspeople went out of their way to talk to Jews or to buy in Jewish shops, especially the Socialists. But to counterbalance this there were SA men to mutter insults at them when they passed by street corners, and yet other SA men who bought heavily at Jewish stores, running up bills which they never paid, sometimes perhaps because the bills were never tendered.[11]

Thus the position of the Jews in Thalburg was rapidly clarified, certainly by the end of the first half-year of Hitler's regime. Every speech given by a Nazi leader on the subject of the Jew as a Marxist-Capitalist international prisoner of the *Volk,* every newspaper item in the same vein, every new joke or rumor reinforced the situation. The new state of affairs became a fact of life; it was accepted.[12]

Thalburg's Jews were simply excluded from the community at large. At the same time the Nazis undertook their most Herculean task: the atomization of the community at large. Though the methods differed, the result was the same, and by the summer of 1933 individual Thalburgers were as cut off from effective intercourse with one another as the Jews had been from the rest of the townspeople. The total reorganization of society was the most important result of the Nazi revolution. Eventually no independent social groups were to exist. Wherever two or three were gathered, the *Fuehrer* would also be present. Ultimately all society, in terms of human relationships, would cease to exist, or rather would exist in a new framework whereby each individual related not to his fellow men but only to the state and to the Nazi leader who became the personal embodiment of the state.

The usefulness of a general shakeup of social organization for dictatorial control can well be imagined. In the first place it would mean that people could be more easily observed, since all clubs would be Nazi controlled. Secondly, with old social ties broken down there would be less opportunity for the spreading of discontent. Thirdly, by giving a Nazi cast to all organizations, the members would become involved in the general Nazi system.

Facilitating dictatorial control was not the only reason for Nazi reorganization of social units. There was also a tendency to simplify social organization and thus provide more efficiency and less diversity. On the one hand, for example, it was thought that by lumping together the various sport clubs one could arrive at the best combination of athletes. On the other hand, an attempt was made to amalgamate all clubs which had the same function but which were formed along class lines, since the new criteria were to be German citizenship and good Nazism, not the old traditions or class distinctions.

In the case of mass organizations such as sport clubs, fusion did not take place in order to maintain control over the societies, since they were already well infiltrated. But in the case of small class-oriented groups, fusion might be needed to end their exclusive nature so that Nazis could bring the groups under control. Thus one of the elements of the Nazi reorganization of society was a consistent attempt to subordinate and join together all communal endeavors which had roughly the same goals or subject interests.

Clubs which pursued a definite goal or purpose (for example, a chess club) continued to exist, though their form and composition may have been altered. It was their objective purpose which kept them going, perhaps with "N.S." in front of their name (for example, "National Socialist Chess Club"), but in any event, still extant. Those clubs which were formed for reasons of pure social intercourse, or which had only an incidental objective purpose, either declined, ceased to exist, or were absorbed. This was partly because of the Nazi desire to keep people from coming together merely for social reasons where discussion prevailed. It was also a side effect of the revolution, since the enormous demands on people's time and energies made purely social functions increasingly difficult. And finally it was a consequence of the breakdown of inter-human trust under the impact of terror and rumor. Nazi insistence on politicalizing all organizations poisoned the hitherto lively clubs. As one Thalburger put it, "There was no more social life; you couldn't even have a bowling club." [13]

Most of this was accomplished in the first few months of the Nazi era. Clubs were dissolved; others were fused together; others lost their purpose and went into rapid decline. All societies came under Nazi control since they were required to have a majority of NSDAP members in their executive committees. This gigantic process was all lumped together under the general term of "coordination" *(Gleichschaltung)*.

Originally, *Gleichschaltung* was a term meaning the reorganization of political representation in the federated states of the German Reich, so as to make them reflect the political representation in the Reichstag, i.e., have a Nazi-Nationalist majority. Hitler justified his decrees on *Gleichschaltung* by claiming that they would reproduce the new "national unity" in every governmental body. But most Thalburgers thought that the *Gleichschaltung* decree also applied to social organizations.[14] Even the GHC and TNN occasionally suggested this. Thus, measures taken to control social organizations were accepted by Thalburgers as being thoroughly legal, in the formal sense at least. If an organization was ordered by the NSDAP to dissolve its present executive committee and elect a new one with a Nazi majority, the assumption was that this would be necessary to comply with the law. They might have discovered differently had they challenged the legality of the order. But no one did this in the first few months of the Nazi rule, and after that it was too late. Thus the enormous social reshuffle took place without overt resistance.

The variety and number of Thalburg's clubs made this a mammoth task. The Nazis approached it without hesitation, however, and carried it through with vigor and dispatch. In some cases the process began as early as March, 1933. *Gleichschaltung* was in full flood by April and May, with organizations falling under Nazi control almost every day. By late summer, 1933, there were practically no independent social entities left, and the great upheaval was almost complete.

The most basic organizations in Thalburg were the economic ones: the unions, the business and professional societies, and the guilds. Of these the unions were clearly the most significant, not only because of the number of people involved but also because of the unions' Socialist orientation. Since one of the basic Nazi concepts was the idea that workers should be weaned away from "Marxism," the NSDAP was determined to supplant the existing Free Unions.

The way in which Nazis in higher positions at the Thalburg railroad yards broke up the railroad union during 1932 has been described above. Thus even before Hitler came to power much of Thalburg's working force was enrolled at least nominally in the Nazis' own union, the NSBO *(National Sozialistische Betriebszellen Organization)*. Among the white collar employees a parallel development took place featuring a Nazi front organization: the Working Society of Nationalist Railroad Officials *(Arbeitsgemeinschaft nationaler Reichsbahnbeamter und Anwaerter, Bann Thalburg)*. In the first few months of the Nazi era, full control was established over this organization, with the leaders emerging openly as Nazis.[15]

Thalburg's Nazis moved rapidly to organize the city employees, too. Concurrent with the Nazi takeover of the City Council and the beginning of the purge, the NSDAP set up a professional employees' group of the NSBO and enrolled a few dozen members in it. A month later the existing Society of City Civil Servants and Employees, Local Thalburg, was "coordinated" and a Nazi executive board elected by order of the NSDAP. The Nazi unionization drive was successful in two other areas as well. One was the organization of the Highway Repairmen *(Chausee und Landstrassenwaerter)*. These were mainly rural people and hence already Nazified. All that remained was to organize them into a branch of the NSBO. This was completed in March and April, 1933. Finally, the Nazis were able to win a preponderance of the thirty-eight-man regular work force at the sugar factory. During the depression years considerable political pressure had been brought on the workers at the sugar refinery. Thus the works council election held there on April 3 brought twenty-eight votes for the NSBO and only ten for an "unpolitical list" that was clearly Free Union.[16]

Despite these small successes it was clear that the Nazis were not really progressing with their own union. How far economic pressure and persuasion might have brought the NSBO is hard to say, since national events soon resolved the problem altogether. On May 4, following the pattern that had been set all over Germany on the morrow of the May Day celebrations, units of Thalburg's SA occupied the offices of the Free Union in Thalburg, confiscated the books and furnishings, and declared the unions "coordinated." A few weeks later the NSBO moved into the old union offices. It was still so weak, however, that it required the services of at least two former union secretaries in order to carry out essential duties. The NSBO also found it necessary to call mass meetings in order to condemn the old unions. The memory of freedom was harder to expunge than the fact. To supervise the entire working force a kind of super-pseudo-union, the German Workers' Front, was later created. In the early months of the Third Reich in Thalburg it was essentially a paper organization.[17]

The unions having ceased to exist, one vital group of social organization was completely smashed. Some small matters were left to clear up. The Railroad Officials' group was incorporated into a general Nazi Civil Servants' and Officials' Association, apparently for the sake of organizational neatness. The "Railroaders' Club," which had general social functions, though it drew its members from that economic sector, was "coordinated" in July with a new all-Nazi executive committee.[18] Other working class organizations collapsed with the SPD.

Simultaneously with the smashing of the unions and the building of new Nazi structures in their place, the NSDAP moved to gain full control over the Thalburg artisan associations. The County Artisan League was already favorably disposed towards the NSDAP, since so many craft masters were Nazis. In February, 1933, the annual election of officers for the League resulted in the election of a Nazi chairman and in resolutions praising the new Hitler government. The NSDAP was not wholly satisfied with this, and in April the County Artisans' League was required to hold a new election "on the basis of the *Gleichschaltung* Law" which resulted in an all-Nazi executive committee.[19]

The NSDAP also coordinated each of the individual guilds which made up the Artisans' League. A mass meeting was held in mid-April at which the various guild leaders were told by Kurt Aergeyz that they must have their new executive committees elected by May 2. This touched off furious activity, since each guild had to draft proposals, negotiate with the NSDAP, work out new compromises, and finally elect the new Nazi-dominated executive board. Questions of personality became as important as ideological ones. Furthermore, many of the guilds were convinced that once coordination took place their treasuries would be siphoned off to benefit the Nazis. Hence several guilds held mammoth parties for their members in which they drank and ate up the treasury funds. Some guilds were able to complete the *Gleichschaltung* process almost immediately. Others had to wait until the day of the deadline. But by the beginning of May there was not an artisan organization left in Thalburg that was not Nazi-dominated.[20]

Coordinating the Retail Merchants' Association took a little longer, primarily because the existing organization was completely broken and a new, purely Nazi one created—something that went far beyond the customary *Gleichschaltung*. The new organization of retail merchants was founded on May 2 with Kurt Aergeyz's brother taking the leading role. Proposing to enroll every merchant in Thalburg County, Aergeyz declared at the organizational meeting:

Admission into the new League is voluntary, but it will be expected that every merchant in town and county Thalburg who feels himself a German *Volk*-comrade will place himself without reservation at the disposal of the new association. This will make clear his determination to aid the reconstruction of the German economy.[21]

The process of persuasion proceeded apace, but not quickly enough to please the Nazis. By June they adopted more direct tactics and forced the old Retail Merchants' Association to incorporate itself and all its members into the new at one stroke.[22] Coordination was complete.

Other economic associations suffered the same fate in rapid order. On April 18 a "National Socialist Physicians' League" was founded, incorporating the prior league. A month later the "Reich Society of Dentists" became the "National Socialist Professional Dentists' Group." In April a "National Socialist Teachers' League" was created which all Thalburg teachers eventually joined in order to keep their jobs.[23] By summer of 1933 the only uncoordinated economic organizations in Thalburg were the cooperatives. These were distinctly Social Democratic enterprises and contributed considerably to the economy of the town. A good example was the "Common Good Construction Club." Its function was to build low-rent housing. In 1932 it did over 600,000 marks' worth of business, reduced its rents by 10 per cent, increased its capital, declared a dividend of 5 per cent, and increased its membership from 112 to 128.[24]

Under these circumstances no one could complain that the "Common Good Construction Club" was poorly run. But the difficulty was that its chairman and business manager was a leading Socialist. Hence when the club received the order to coordinate itself, it manipulated the election so that the Socialist was left in a position of power, but otherwise made protestations of loyalty to the new regime. The club was especially vulnerable, however, since the Nazis looked on all cooperatives as "bolshevistic." Hence the NSDAP was able to demand still more. On August 7 it was coordinated again with Kurt Aergeyz himself installed as chairman and with the Social Democrat resigning from the club altogether. It had been his life work, but he was sensitive to the possibility of the other members losing their investments if the club were dissolved outright.[25]

An even more important economic entity was the Thalburg Consumers' Cooperative with over 1,200 members. In the years before 1933 the Nazis had consistently railed against this "red" organization, because it competed with the local merchants. But after they came to power the NSDAP was in a dilemma. To dissolve the cooperative altogether would have disrupted the economy of the town rather seriously and would have embittered an enormous number of people. But to coordinate the cooperative would have been interpreted as a guarantee of its future existence, and would have embittered the burghers. Hence the Nazis tried a number of approaches. First they spread various evil rumors about the consumers' cooperative in the hopes that these would cause it to decline. Secondly, they brought the organization under control by putting a Nazi commissar in as "supervisor." And finally they suggested to private businessmen that they would "take care of" the consumers' cooperative "when the time is ripe." [26]

In contrast to the thoroughness and ruthlessness with which the Nazis dealt with the town's economic organizations, they were very cautious about the numerous patriotic societies. They created only one new organization, a National Socialist War Victims' Association (NSKOV). The previous Reich League of War Victims dissolved itself in May and merged with the new Nazi organization, but the Kyffhaeuser War Victims was able to maintain its independence, though the parent body was coordinated. Only two patriotic groups were forcibly dissolved, the "Greater German League" and the independent boys' clubs (Boy Scouts, *Freischar*, and *Jung deutsche Orden* Youth). The latter were incorporated into the Hitler Youth. Of all the other military and patriotic clubs only the Kyffhaeuser League was formally coordinated. There were enough Nazis in the other groups to dominate them already, and presumably the NSDAP did not want to stir up needless trouble. Propaganda seemed sufficient for control. In time the slower but equally effective social atrophy resulting from fear and distrust would destroy the patriotic societies as independent entities.[27]

The same general approach was used toward the various special interest clubs—the choral groups, shooting societies, and so forth. Most of the singing societies dissolved themselves rather than be coordinated. As a former member put it, "Nobody in our club had either time or inclination for it any more." [28] Before *Gleichschaltung*, Thalburg's choral societies reflected the town's class structure. The workers' singing club was the Thalburg *Volkschor*. It had been founded in 1905 as the *Handwerkergesangverein* but became dominated by workers in the 1920's. In the three years before Hitler came to power the *Volkschor* frequently sang at SPD functions. In April, 1933, the club, in an attempt to cleanse itself of ideological connotations, severed its connections with the German Workers Singers' League and promised a "complete reorientation." This was not enough for the NSDAP, which demanded that the choral director and the executive committee resign. Since these were the leading figures in the club it chose to dissolve itself completely and did so on April 22, 1933.[29]

Shortly after this all the town's singing clubs were lumped together in one organization called the "Mixed Choral Singing Club of 1933." By bringing together all those from the defunct organizations who were actually devoted to singing, a decent membership was obtained. The new club made a point of stressing that social position was unimportant in this new club; only singing ability counted.[30]

The shooting societies of Thalburg did not suffer such a shock, though their character was also altered. At the combined annual meeting of May 15, 1933, the clubs worked hard to maintain themselves. Declarations of loyalty to Hitler and *"Sieg Heils!"* poured forth. Kurt Aergeyz was elected an honorary member and immediately named Chief Captain. In his acceptance speech Aergeyz stressed the fact that the shooting societies could no longer exist just for enjoyment. They must promote the military spirit. They must also abandon their exclusive nature. The clubs promptly responded by voting a special Adolf Hitler Shoot, open to the general public, at the forthcoming shooting festival. When the festival for 1933 took place it was renamed a *Volk* festival and every citizen was invited to attend. Special competition was arranged for the SA, SS, and *Stahlhelm,* and no admission was charged. There were as many swastika flags as there were old club banners, and the most frequent song heard was the "Horst Wessel Song." [31] In short, the shooting societies were simply subverted.

The other special interest clubs of Thalburg (Red Cross, Museum Society, etc.) were coordinated in the more formal sense with new Nazi executive boards. In most cases this took place at the regular annual meeting and with little prompting needed. In some cases the stimulus came from the national or parent organization rather than from the local NSDAP. The only club given special treatment was the Beautification Club, a society which built paths in Thalburg's woods and in general tried to promote the town's park system. Since this club had considerable money, Aergeyz was interested in it. The members anticipated him and invested all the club's funds in a hunting cabin just outside the city limits, and then dissolved themselves.[32]

The biggest special interest clubs were the sport clubs. Here the Nazi emphasis was on fusion. The process began in May, 1933, when the town's two biggest gymnastic societies merged with the football club "VfB." This created an eight-hundred-man *Turn- und Sport-verband*. At the same time the other football club (*Spiel und Sport*) strengthened itself by absorbing the Thalburger Swimming Club. The next step came in July when *Spiel und Sport* and *Turn und Sport* were merged to form one gigantic Thalburger *Sportclub* under the leadership of Otto Made. Thus by July all the hitherto independent sport clubs had been fused into one. The new super-club was justified by the Nazis on the grounds that it would end "senseless competition" and provide the strongest sport club in the district. But it was also to be Nazi-oriented. Organization in the club was modeled after the NSDAP's "block" system and its chief stress was to be on military sport. The fusion was not well-liked by the component units. It had been forced on them by Made. Despite Nazi efforts, membership in the club fell off by over 50 per cent. After the end of World War II the old clubs reconstituted themselves independently and happily resumed their "senseless competition." [33]

Nazi efforts at social hegemony did not stop with the customary associations: economic, patriotic, special interest. The NSDAP also desired a dominant voice in religious and purely cultural matters. Nazi interest in religion pre-dated the Third Reich. During the years before Hitler came to power one of the strongest appeals the Nazis had made in Thalburg was through the Lutheran church, and their favorite speakers were Lutheran ministers. The Lutheran church in Thalburg played a major role in Nazi celebrations during the first six months of Hitler's regime, and the town's pastors frequently urged Thalburgers to pray for Hitler. For its part, the NSDAP promoted religion as an aspect of the struggle against the "religionless November-State" (i.e., the Weimar Republic). In contrast to the Socialist position ("religion is a private matter"), the Nazis proclaimed, "Religion is a matter for the *Volk!*" That this could cut both ways was not yet seen by Thalburg's Lutheran pastors, nor were they as yet uneasy about such peculiar things as the application of Romans 11:36 to Hitler's role in the Nazi Revolution or the statement, "God is the Sun." [34]

Thus Thalburgers were not shocked when the NSDAP began a campaign to "revitalize the church." As one letter to the GHC put it: "The National Revolution in which we are now involved signifies a complete change of our German *Volk* in all areas of life. It is not surprising, therefore, that even church life is being drawn into the stream of this powerful movement." [35] The campaign took the form of an attempt to get Lutherans to join the "German Christian Movement." This was described as a non-political movement led by religious men who were only incidentally Nazis and who were interested solely in unifying and regenerating Protestantism. The movement in Thalburg was endorsed by a variety of active Lutherans, including both pastors of the church.

To push the campaign the customary Nazi publicity methods were used. In June, Pastor Jakobshagen, who had formally been such a popular Nazi speaker, was brought in for a mass meeting at the *1910er Zelt*. About five hundred people were present, of whom about a hundred joined the movement immediately. A second meeting, held a month later, drew a very small attendance. In July, 1933, elections were held for the Church Elders. In Thalburg the German Christian Movement presented a slate of candidates. All were Nazis. The nominations were endorsed by the Evangelical Men's Club and the Evangelical Women's Club. Since these were the only nominations, the candidates were elected automatically, without a vote. Similar results obtained in churches over the whole district. [36]

The men who backed the German Christian Movement were apparently sincere in their belief that it would aid Protestantism. In later years when the NSDAP became seriously anti-religious, these same men were in the forefront of the struggle against Nazism and formed a courageous resistance. But by their blindness in the early months of the Third Reich they gave an enormous boost to Nazism. [37]

The only Lutheran organization to suffer during the first half-year of Nazi control was the "Friends of Evangelical Freedom," which dissolved itself in mid-May, possibly under threat of *Gleichschaltung*. [38]

The smooth relations between the Nazis and Thalburg's Lutheran church were not paralleled by the party's relationship with
the town's Catholic Church. The pastor was a firm advocate of the
Center party and drew Nazi fire on that score. In March, 1933,
editorials were written against him on two occasions because he
urged his parishioners to vote *Zentrum*. The situation was exacerbated in July, 1933, when the Catholic Young Men's Society was
dissolved and its property and flags were seized by the SA. Other
Catholic clubs were not disturbed, but the NSDAP could still count
on the enmity of the Catholic priest. Since only about 6 per cent
of the townspeople were Catholics, this was a negligible factor.[39]

In the schools Thalburg's teachers were drawn into a Nazi
Teachers' Association. To make doubly sure, all other Teachers'
Associations were coordinated in April, 1933.[40] Full control over
teachers would come only in time. To Nazi eyes, even more important than the teachers was control over the children. For this
the Hitler Youth was the prime instrument. The chief weapon of
the Hitler Youth was control over the school administration. This
was manifest very early. In cases where both the Hitler Youth and
the schools wanted to hold a celebration, the schools gave way.
When questions of discipline arose, Hitler Youth members could
not be punished. Even in academic matters the Hitler Youth
reigned supreme. The principal of the *Gymnasium* was directly
ordered by Kurt Aergeyz to advance any pupils who might have
"suffered" academically because of membership in the Hitler Youth
before the Nazi seizure of power. In all these matters school
authorities acquiesced for fear of losing their jobs. By the end of
the first six months of the Third Reich it was questionable as to
who was running the schools—the teachers or the Hitler Youth.[41]

The Hitler Youth was also aided by the dissolution of competing
youth groups. By the end of the summer of 1933 it was the only
existing youth group in Thalburg.

Thalburg's public library also was coordinated. By mid-May
over five hundred books were burned (one-quarter of the total
number). This "un-German, foreign-to-the-*Volk,* and worthless
literary trash" was replaced by a select list of books beginning with
Mein Kampf. The Free Unions' Lending Library was closed when
the unions were forcibly dissolved in early May.[42]

One final cultural entity that was coordinated (after a fashion) was the City Band. For a monthly subsidy the City Band gave a concert every week on the Market Square. Since the subsidy was not enough, the individual bandsmen also played at dances and on other occasions. During the years before Hitler came to power the band frequently rented itself to the SPD for its parades and meetings. By these means the band clearly became tainted with "bolshevism" and therefore had to go. Furthermore, if the City Band were eliminated, the SA band would have a clear field. Early in March, 1933, the City Band tried to adapt itself to the new order. Instead of the customary "Weekly Concert," a "Patriotic Weekly Concert" was given. But this did not suffice. The new City Council had hardly been elected before it cut off the band's subsidy. This upset the conservatives, who had gotten used to the weekly concerts. Furthermore, the Nationalists clearly felt that with a band of their own they could compete with the Nazis more successfully. Money was therefore quickly forthcoming and the City Band became the *Stahlhelm* Band. But since the *Stahlhelm* was not too active there was little for the band to do. Hence, every week, the *Stahlhelm* Band gave a concert on the Market Square. Things were back to normal. In this at least the Nazi revolution was unsuccessful.[43]

This rapid survey of Nazi inroads on the cultural and social life of the town has not included the organizations connected with the SPD. There were many and all were dissolved. Some, like the Workers' First Aid Society, simply ceased to exist. Others with a more tenuous connection, such as the League for the Protection of Mothers, collapsed only when their offices were raided and property confiscated.[44] But the great and complicated group of sub-organizations connected with the Social Democratic party and the Free Unions were all destroyed. This put an end to all organized social life among the workers of Thalburg.

Thus by the summer of 1933, the Nazis had either broken up, altered, fused, or brought under control most of the clubs and societies of Thalburg. The complex and diversified social organization of the town had been almost completely uprooted. In most cases the Nazis tried to fill the vacuum, but often people simply stopped coming together. Either there was no more club, or the attractiveness of the club had been destroyed by *Gleichschaltung,* or people no longer had the leisure or the desire to continue with their club. What social life there was continued in the most basic groupings: the *Stammtisch,* the beer-and-cards evenings, or small social gatherings in homes.

Even these were threatened as people began to distrust one another. What was the value of getting together with others to talk if you had to be careful about what you said? Thus to a great extent the individual was atomized. By the process of *Gleichschaltung* individuals had a choice: solitude or mass relationship via some Nazi organization. None of the Nazi measures in the first six months of the Third Reich had a greater ultimate effect than *Gleichschaltung.* By it the externals of the rigid class structure were destroyed, and Thalburgers were molded into the kind of unorganized mass that dictators like so well.

CHAPTER 15

THE POSITIVE ASPECT

(March to July, 1933)

*Everyone will surely have noticed
that from now on a new wind will
be blowing.*
—AUGUST TIERE, Nazi speaker of
the City Council, March 28, 1933

Of the factors responsible for the rise of Nazism in Thalburg, none
was as important as the depression. The fear it engendered made
Thalburgers amenable to radicalism in the first place. It was the
Nazi claim that they had diagnosed the cause of economic difficulties (the Treaty of Versailles and the political leadership of the
Weimar Republic) and could provide the cure (Nazi leadership)
that made so many Thalburgers vote for the party of Adolf Hitler.
Hence the Nazis knew that they must succeed on the economic
front if they wanted to win solid allegiance.

Since the problem of the depression in Thalburg was more
psychological than economic in nature, the Nazis set out to provide an appropriate solution. A short-term solution could be
quickly advanced—remove the outward sign of the depression by
eliminating large-scale unemployment. It was also necessary to give
Thalburgers the feeling that the wheel of progress had begun to
rotate again, that under vigorous leadership the town was begin-

ning to move forward. These things the Nazis did. It was their most solid achievement.

The most visible sign of the depression was unemployment. The method of dealing with the unemployed had already been developed by the SPD faction in the City Council long before Hitler came to power: public works projects. A limited number of such projects had been carried out during the initial years of the depression and in January, 1933, the town had been allocated additional funds by the central government. What the Nazis brought to public works projects was the concept of applying them so as to eliminate *all* unemployment in the town. They were able to do this because the money previously allocated by the central government became available just at the time the NSDAP came to power and because the Hitler government rushed through new funds for public works.

In January, 1933, the town had received 60,000 marks from the central government and had made plans to expend it on street repairs. By March the government gave its approval to a loan of 300,000 marks for Thalburg County. In April, Thalburg received an additional 100,000 marks from the government for public works. This money helped the town in many ways. First, it enabled the town to put the unemployed to work. By removing unemployed persons from the welfare rolls, this increased the amount of money Thalburg itself could plough into works projects; it freed almost 4,000 marks a week from the town's treasury. Finally, by the multiplier effect, it increased the general spending in the town to the benefit of Thalburg's merchants. But most important of all, it gave the new Nazi administration ample funds to carry out a crash public works program.[1]

At the end of January, 1933, Thalburg had 653 registered unemployed, of whom almost four hundred were on the welfare rolls. It was estimated that there were an additional hundred "invisible" unemployed, bringing the grand total to 750 jobless persons. Despite the Nazi desire to put all these people to work, little progress was made throughout the spring of 1933. By June 30, 1933, there were still 506 registered unemployed in the town. The decrease was due almost solely to the customary seasonal upsurge in work.

In July, however, the great campaign began. Some 450 persons were put to work on a great variety of jobs. Roads were repaired, the town's forests were worked over, and the old moat around Thalburg was drained and converted into a ring of swan ponds and parks. New groups of unemployed were set to work almost daily. By July 24, Kurt Aergeyz was able to call a press conference and make public the news that all unemployed persons previously on the welfare rolls were at work. The only people receiving welfare payments on that date in Thalburg were women, old folks, and cripples. On the same date County Prefect von Altberg announced that since March, 1933, some nine hundred of the county's welfare unemployed had been put to work and that County Thalburg too was free of welfare unemployed.[2]

This was astounding news, but more was yet to come. Throughout August the same effort was continued. By the end of the month every person in the town who had been registered as unemployed was at work. In the last few days of August over 130 people were drawn into the works projects. Even unemployed women were put to work planting flowers and pruning shrubs. What Thalburgers could hardly believe possible had come to pass. There was not a single registered unemployed person in the town.[3]

The methods used by the Nazis in accomplishing this goal were similar to those used in their other work. In the first place, preference in the works projects was given to Nazi party members, especially those with low membership numbers—the so-called "old fighters." Secondly, many of the unemployed persons were actually forced to go to work. All unemployed persons, regardless of their previous occupation, were put into what was, after all, hard manual labor. Some insisted that they be given work commensurate with their ability and experience, but the Nazi alternative was work on the works projects or no more dole. With much protesting, many of the previously unemployed persons climbed into the labor crew trucks each morning to be driven out to do road repairing.[4]

Nevertheless, many workers were pleased to be gainfully employed again, and Thalburg's middle class was enormously impressed by the Nazi success on this level. Nor were the workers the only ones who benefited economically in the first months of the Third Reich. The artisans were also aided, primarily through a program of subsidies for household repairs. In the spring of 1933, the Reich granted 21,000 marks to Thalburg for this purpose, especially to help refurbish apartments so as to ease the housing shortage. Furthermore the Reich granted another 20,000 marks for subsidies to people who wished to divide large apartments into smaller units. The city led the way by repairing all the buildings it owned. At the same time encouragement was given to new construction so that seven new dwelling houses were erected in 1933. Since construction and repair work had generally lagged during the depression, these programs and their vigorous administration were very welcome to electricians, carpenters, and painters. If the Nazi report can be believed, they were "swamped with work." [5]

Finally, the Nazis did all they could by way of propaganda and political pressure to end the depression spirit. Aergeyz was tireless in urging businessmen to expand and spend money. A "Book of Honor" was set up in the county building and the names of all employers who hired a previously unemployed person were inscribed.[6] In short, all that could be attempted in the economic sector was tackled with determination and vigor.

One measure that the Nazis pushed in the course of fighting the depression was later to become a permanent institution of the Third Reich. This was the Labor Service. Like the works projects and the household repairs subsidies, it began before Hitler came to power but was pushed with greater vigor once the NSDAP assumed direction. Originally it was a "Voluntary Labor Service" with enlistment. The NSDAP set up the organization in Thalburg in February, 1933. Its goals were described as non-economic in nature. The purpose was to enroll young people in order to "1) unite them with the *Volk*-community, 2) re-institute their connection with the soil, and 3) re-awaken a healthy military spirit." Nevertheless, the Labor Service did get young jobless men off street corners and the labor market and it also carried out various conservation projects. By late April some sixty-five young Thalburgers had enlisted. Most of them were housed in the old Army barracks. This necessitated expelling some of the "shelterless" who lived there. To provide housing for those displaced, the city offered to guarantee rent payments and to subsidize any alterations necessary to create new apartments. Eventually Aergeyz hoped to have 250

Labor Service men in the old barracks, which, he pointed out, meant 250 new consumers in the town.[7]

In addition to its economic functions and its usefulness in indoctrinating youth, the Labor Service also aided in general propaganda work. It organized frequent parades through Thalburg, with a swastika flag in the forefront, and even gave a concert of classical music in the city park one summer Sunday.[8] All told, most Thalburgers must have looked upon the Labor Service as a very good thing.

Despite their considerable efforts to end unemployment, the Nazis did not forget to push charity during their first few months in office. Some of this was purely for propaganda purposes, for example the special extra payment to welfare cases made on March 30 "in spite of the hard times, to show the social direction of the new government." Again on Hitler's birthday a special party with coffee and cakes was given for the unemployed. Charity collections for the Nazi "Winter Aid" brought in considerable amounts, and the SA soup kitchen reported that it had disbursed over 32,000 meals in the winter of 1932-33.[9]

During the first six months of the Third Reich, Thalburg's Nazis attacked the town's economic problems with the same vigor and thoroughness with which they dealt with other problems. There is no gainsaying their effectiveness and success in this area. While they did not provide new ideas, they made the most of existing ones. By temporarily abolishing unemployment and increasing the disposable income in Thalburg, the Nazis by no means ended the depression; in fact, they had to fight the battle of unemployment all over again in 1934. But there could be no doubt in the minds of most Thalburgers that the Nazis were determined to master the depression. And to many Thalburgers appearance was more important than reality with respect to the economic crisis. In short, the NSDAP in Thalburg did what it had promised to do in the economy: it exorcised the specter of the depression.

CHAPTER 16

REACTION AND RESISTANCE

(March to July, 1933)

> The true supporters of government
> are the weak and the uninformed
> and not the wise.
> —WILLIAM GODWIN, *Enquiry Concerning Political Justice, and Its Influence on Morals and Happiness*

In the first half year of the Nazi regime, Thalburg underwent a revolution. Its main components were terror, dictatorial control, unremitting propaganda, the reconstruction of social life, and economic revitalization. Its total effect was to alter the basic structure of the town in an amazingly short period. Though six months may seem a long time, to Thalburgers it must have appeared that everything happened at once, for all the elements of the revolution which have been here compartmentalized for analysis were in actuality intermingled in a chaotic jumble. One day there were arrests and the next day a big, cheering parade. Here the city employees were purged and there the Labor Service team marched to work with shovels on their shoulders. First the singing club of ancient standing ceased to exist and then came the brassy SA band. Flashes of black-white-red flags, book burnings, blaring radio speeches, school children with swastikas, booted Stormtroopers dragging a man to jail, torchlight parades with voices singing hoarse songs, the pastor blessing the *Fuehrer,* rumors of the Gestapo, hammers pounding house repairs, rhythmic volleys of *"Sieg Heil!"*—all melded in a whirling kaleidoscope, and by the end of the summer of 1933 Thalburg was so firmly in the grip of the Nazis that there was no possibility of reversing the process.

The majority of Thalburg's adults voted for this. But in the years before the NSDAP came to power it was all things to all men. Thus most Thalburgers had hardly any clear idea of what the Nazis would really do, except change things for the better somehow. It is certain that only a few members of the NSDAP itself and some of the town's Social Democrats really expected what they got. Thus a question of considerable importance is: How did Thalburgers react to the introduction of the Nazi dictatorship?

There were, of course, as one would expect in almost any society, those who simply used the Nazi revolution for their own profit. Immediately after Hitler came to power one of the town's taverns installed a radio and then advertised that all speeches of Adolf Hitler could be heard there and that the price of beer was cheap. All through March and April there were daily advertisements in the TNN offering swastika flags for sale. The City Bank urged Thalburgers to aid the great revolution by putting their money in a savings account. Even Kurt Aergeyz's brother was not above advertising his hardware store by proclaiming "Oldest Party Member in County Thalburg." [1]

Many people also felt the need to protect themselves by joining the NSDAP. In some cases club leaders or artisan masters joined so that they could stay on executive committees. Others wanted job insurance. Still others joined in response to the growth of terror.[2] The great rush to join the NSDAP began in February, immediately after the announcement that Hitler had been named Chancellor. People who had been wavering or who had held back for fear of compromising themselves now submitted applications. In January, 1933, there were fewer than a hundred dues-paying Nazis in Thalburg. By March the Nazi Local Group swelled to almost four hundred. By mid-March there began a veritable flood of membership. This great climbing-on-the-bandwagon became so pronounced that old Nazis referred to the newcomers as the *Maerzgefallene*—the "March casualties."

The NSDAP had so many applicants that it was forced to declare that it would accept no new applications after May 1, so that the existing backlog could be cleared up. This, of course, produced a still greater rush in April. Von Altberg remembered seeing bushel baskets full of applications in the Nazi county headquarters on April 20. By May 1 close to 1,200 Thalburgers had joined the Nazi party. Almost 20 per cent of the town's adults had been enrolled.[3]

Not all of these new members joined as a result of commitment to Nazi ideas. One of the Nazi methods of bringing institutions under control was to require their leaders to become members of the NSDAP. This was the case with County Prefect von Altberg and also with the TNN's reporter, Erhardt Knorpel. Both were exceedingly skeptical about Nazism and both joined because it was demanded of them. Others joined because they saw membership in the NSDAP as an indispensable prerequisite for personal advancement. This was admittedly the case with two teachers who confidently expected that by joining the Nazi party they would insure themselves a promotion.[4] Still others joined out of a pure desire to conform, i.e., to go along with the majority, as illustrated by the following story:

Hugo Spiessmann was a curious case. Until the March Reichstag elections he was in an agony of indecision. I remember him frequently asking me for advice: Should he or should he not join the party? I always told him to do whatever he wanted, but this didn't seem to help. But the day after the Nazi electoral success the SA gave a victory parade which I witnessed. At the very end of the parade was Hugo Spiessmann with a happy smile on his face. As he marched by he waved to me and yelled, "I've done it!"[5]

Many men were forced to join by the pressure put on them at home. As one man described it: "There were wives whose constant words were 'Think of your family!' There were wives who actually went out and bought a brown shirt and put their men into it."[6] Still others entered the NSDAP in the belief that what Nazism needed was a leaven of decent people and that by working from within they could steer the revolution into moderate paths.[7]

Thus, at the very least, the level of commitment varied considerably among the new members. But once they had joined the NSDAP these people were trapped. They were now under party discipline and had to aid in the whole process. The organization of the party (in cells and blocks down to the smallest unit) kept them under constant surveillance. Instead of insuring their future, they became even more insecure, for if they were ever expelled from the NSDAP they would be marked men. Furthermore their consciences were hopelessly compromised, for as members they partook of responsibility in the most immediate sense.

But if many of the Thalburgers who joined the NSDAP were still dubious, there were also many Thalburgers who never joined but were ardent supporters of the new regime. In general the burghers were enthusiastic over the parades and ceremonies and delighted by the economic action. The feeling seemed to be that an end had come to internal division and that real leadership would now be forthcoming. As one craft master put it:

I don't agree with everything that's been done, but I'm glad to see them trying things. The main thing is that people get work again and that they somehow learn to recognize a purpose and content in life again.[8]

Many of the concepts and slogans of the Nazi revolution appealed to Thalburgers. In a nationalistic era the idea of national honor and revivification was exceedingly attractive. The vigorous, purposeful, and apparently immaculate direction of city government appealed to the civic-minded. Finally, there was fascination in the concept of the *Volk*-community, which despite its mystic connotations meant an end to class divisions.[9] The middle class was especially drawn to the idea that classes should cease to exist and that there should be only Germans. This may seem incredible in view of the burghers' repugnance for "Marxism," but it was the source and reason for ending a class war that was more important than the concept itself. Socialist efforts at social equality were examples of upstart leveling. The Nazi appeal was patriotic and charitable. While the SPD threatened, the NSDAP evoked *noblesse oblige* and was concerned with appearance rather than reality. This suited perfectly the emotional needs of Thalburgers who were upset by the existing class structure; they were virtuously uplifted by the hope of creating a *Volk*-community, without actually sacrificing their own class status.

Naturally there were many aspects of the revolution that Thalburgers were dubious about. Some, especially the conservatives, simply could not accept the Nazis because of their low class. As Herr Armkerl put it, "How can a mere corporal lead the Reich?" [10] Others were disturbed by the arrests, the smashing of opposition, the destruction of social life, and especially the violence of the new anti-semitism. But there were ways of rationalizing.

Was the SPD smashed and the unions dissolved by force? They were upstart troublemakers and had it coming.

Were there arrests and house searches? Look at all the weapons that were found! The Marxists were clearly plotting violence, in accordance with their record.

Was all opposition stifled and the NSDAP made the sole legal party? The main trouble with Germany had been the senseless political strife and splinter parties. Anyone who wanted representation could join the NSDAP.

Were the clubs "coordinated"? This promoted national unity and economic revival. Germany must end internal division and pull together for once.

Were the Jews boycotted and outcast? This was an unfortunate but temporary excess similar to those which accompany any revolution. Besides, there were so few of them.

In short, there are two sides to every question: one should not make hasty judgments; give them a chance to prove themselves; you cannot make an omelette without breaking eggs; there is always some bad mixed in with the good. After all, in six short months the town had been unified, the economic problems were being dealt with, and nothing was more convincing than the shining faces of the Stormtroopers outlined by all the torches and silhouetted against the flags. The Nazi party was providing decisive leadership and was monolithic, dedicated, selfless, and purposeful.

In reality, however, Thalburg's Nazi Group was rotten and

festering within. The first and, during the initial period, the only resistance to the NSDAP came from within the ranks of the Nazis themselves. The leaders of the revolt were the old Nazis, particularly those gathered around Walther Timmerlah. Most of them were intellectuals; they included Tiere, the first teacher in Thalburg to become a Nazi, and Trautmann, the director of the Thalburg Girls' *Lyzeum*. Ostensibly they were rebelling against the leadership of Kurt Aergeyz, but in actuality they were opposed to the violence, corruption, and dictatorial methods which they naively believed to be contrary to the true principles of National Socialism.

The Timmerlah-Tiere-Trautmann "Idealists' Conspiracy" was long in brewing. Already in 1932 several Thalburg Nazis grew restive under Kurt Aergeyz's leadership. The prime complaints against him were that he was rude and inconsiderate towards party members and that he protected the leader of the Thalburg Nazi Women's Group, who apparently had misused party money (in one case to buy herself stockings). Aergeyz's rudeness kept many Thalburgers from joining the party in the last year before Hitler came to power.[11]

Throughout 1932 the idealist group grew more and more dissatisfied. At the same time, Aergeyz proceeded to build up his own following, consisting mainly of rough and violent personalities such as Otto Made and August Blanck. Two separate Nazi groups were developing in Thalburg, but of the two, Aergeyz's held the upper hand since Kurt Aergeyz himself was Local Group Leader and could maintain himself by appeals to the authoritarian discipline of the NSDAP.

In December, 1932, the first storm broke. Several of the idealist group demanded an audit of the Local Group's finances. Aergeyz apparently had misused much of the party's funds. Whether they went into his own pocket or were simply lost through slovenliness is not clear. But donations had been taken and not entered in the books, entrance fees pocketed and the applications lost, and considerable unexplained debts had piled up.[12] At first, Aergeyz was conciliatory. He needed the idealist group because they were an important source of income through contributions. In January, 1933, the idealists threatened to cut off contributions if explanations for the financial irregularities were not forthcoming. Aergeyz was forced to act. Using his position and combining bluster with lies, he expelled several of the idealists and at the same time, as a concession, withdrew his protection from the Women's Group Leader.

None of this was successful, however, and the Thalburg Nazi Group was in danger of schism when the news of Adolf Hitler's appointment as Chancellor of the Reich swept aside all internal squabblings and united the Nazis for the important work of February and March. During this time Aergeyz was able to strengthen his position substantially. Out of a spirit of enthusiasm the idealists came forward with new campaign contributions. The rush of Thalburgers to join the NSDAP made it possible for Aergeyz to demand that new applicants pay increasingly higher entrance fees. His financial problems were rapidly resolving themselves. At the same time Aergeyz used his position as Group Leader to dispense patronage *en masse* in the form of jobs with the city, replacing those fired in the great purge of city employees. A great number of Nazis were becoming dependent on Kurt Aergeyz and still more were becoming afraid of him. Using his position, he turned the City Council into a supine instrument and packed the Senate. Protests were quelled by threats.

In April, the financial matter came up again. To settle the last of the debts Aergeyz arbitrarily raised membership dues and levied a special assessment on all members.[13] At the same time the idealists became aware of other matters. Aergeyz was exploiting his position as Deputy Mayor to distribute city contracts among relatives and friends. The TB was forcing people to subscribe by threatening them. "Contributions" were being extorted from merchants.[14] The dictatorial methods in City Hall were increasingly galling. And, worst of all to the idealists, the Nazi revolution was not producing that hoped-for utopian *Volk*-community, but rather a corrupt and brutal one-man rule. The idealist opposition began to rise again.

By June, Aergeyz found the growing opposition to him so alarming that he decided to strike first. Tiere, Trautmann, and Timmerlah were threatened with expulsion. The District Nazi authorities were notified that a conspiracy existed. The City Council was forced to pass resolutions. A petition was sent to the provincial school authorities calling for Trautmann's transfer out of Thalburg, to the Senate calling for a boycott against Walther Timmerlah, and to Tiere removing him from his post as Speaker for the City Council.[15]

Walther Timmerlah was alert to what might happen. At almost the same moment that Aergeyz moved to squelch the conspiracy, Timmerlah appealed to the District Leader for a complete investigation by the "Examination and Conciliation Department" of the NSDAP (i.e., the Nazis' own intra-party court), the *Uschla*. Timmerlah was convinced that the District authorities would examine his charges closely since he had one of the lowest party-card numbers in the whole district. He was also certain that once the higher offices of the NSDAP discovered what was going on in Thalburg, they would remove Aergeyz and "restore true National Socialism" in Thalburg.

The higher officers in the NSDAP, however, knew what Timmerlah did not know—that Kurt Aergeyz was just the kind of man they wanted. Just as Aergeyz could trust his tools in Thalburg completely, so the District Leader could trust Aergeyz. The system of satrapies by which Nazi Germany would operate during the whole period of the Third Reich was being built. The only "true" National Socialism was the rule of men like Aergeyz. Anything else existed only in the minds of idealists like Timmerlah and would never be compatible with the methods by which Nazism had established itself.

The District *Uschla* proceedings against Timmerlah and Trautmann, instituted at their request, were held in Thalburg in the early days of July, 1933. The defendants were exonerated. In other words, the charges made against Aergeyz were verified. But since these charges had concerned violations of both public and Nazi party law, Aergeyz should have been stripped of his office. Instead he was simply reprimanded and allowed to continue his old ways. This convinced Walther Timmerlah that his hopes for a clean-up were wishful thinking. He remained a member of the NSDAP, because he still clung to the idea that the *Fuehrer* himself would take action some day. Trautmann and Tiere were both eventually transferred out of Thalburg, though without loss of position. Timmerlah continued to gather malcontents about him and to amass evidence against the Local Group Leader. But he was considerably more cautious, and his friends had learned a lesson.

These matters were shielded from the general public in Thalburg. People heard rumors, but the struggle went on behind closed doors, within a relatively limited circle. Thus Thalburgers could continue to believe that the NSDAP was monolithic and dedicated. And to many Thalburgers the presence of Walther Timmerlah and his friends in the NSDAP was still reassurance that there was another side to Nazism and that once the "initial excesses" were over, the party would settle down to constructive, fruitful labor. Once again, as in the days before its acquisition of power, the NSDAP would be all things to all men.

What Thalburgers believed about the NSDAP in the late summer of 1933 was fairly irrelevant anyway. For by the end of their first six months in office the Nazis had a stranglehold on the town. The city administration and the police were under Nazi thumbs. Potential resistance had been smashed. Centers of social intercourse were dispersed or vitiated. The public was organized into a periodic cheering section. Numerous examples of terror had been provided and were spread by social reinforcement. The town had become the obedient instrument of the new totalitarian state. The essential work of the Nazi revolution was complete.

CHAPTER 17

FROM ENTHUSIASM TO RITUAL

(Summer, 1933, to Winter, 1935)

You had to go to the indoctrination sessions constantly and these ideas were drummed into you. And you had to learn them because you had to be very careful about what you said.

—A THALBURG TEACHER

Certainly one of the reasons for the Nazi success in establishing a dictatorship during the first half of 1933 was the rush of events. So many different things happened so rapidly that Thalburgers were stunned. But by the summer of 1933 the action slowed down from the breakneck pace of the spring. The new dictatorship began to find ruts and settle into them. Most of the destruction and construction had been completed and it was time to make the new system work. Yet despite the need for new approaches, there was a tendency to apply the same methods. Authoritarianism was increased, mass demonstrations were made all-inclusive, and force continued to be applied to the economy. Nevertheless there were modifications, for the town had a way of reasserting its corporate personality. The modifications worked within the new dictatorship, however, and not against it.

The momentum of the Nazi propaganda effort undertaken during the spring of 1933 carried well into the summer. While there were no great festivals, there was considerable activity on a minor scale. Some was spurred by the formation of new Nazi sub-organizations, or the rapid strengthening of existing ones which, in either case, seemed to demand some sort of demonstration of vigor. Thus in August, 1933, there were large demonstrations by the Nazi War Victims' Association, the League of German Girls, and the newly formed SS Reconnaissance troop. On the occasion of the first two events there were large parades and "field church services," with most Nazi sub-organizations drawn in. The SS affair involved "maneuvers" capped by a "Maneuver Ball." [1] Similarly, some of the new Nazi officials seemed determined to prove that they were important by setting mass events in motion. Otto Made, the new Sport Director for Thalburg, did this by proclaiming a vast sport program for the town in autumn, 1933. Every day from September 10 to October 1 (except Sundays) there were sport events in Thalburg. Most activity consisted of shooting, gymnastics, and "defense sport," and to promote general sport-mindedness there were periodic parades, speeches, and other ceremonies. Naturally all buildings were beflagged during these days. No one could complain that the new regime was underemphasizing physical exercise.[2]

Meanwhile, the NSDAP, Local Group Thalburg, pre-empted one of the free September Sundays for a general members' meeting. Kurt Aergeyz took the opportunity to declare that the revolution was over; the NSDAP was now the sole owner of state power. Nevertheless, he continued, the task of educating the new Germany would now begin. All members, especially the new ones, were reminded that they must attend their cell meetings, must join the SA, the SS, or the SA Reserve. They must participate in party functions. They must go to the German Theater. Women must join the Nazi Women's Group. Above all, every member must read the TB, and not the newspapers of those who fought Nazism. In conclusion Aergeyz declared that he personally certified that the Local Group's treasury was in good order.[3]

In short, the NSDAP saw that the excitement was over and that now was the time to tighten discipline and organize the gains. With the enormous expansion of the NSDAP in the spring of 1933, it

was questionable whether the Nazis could maintain élan and co-
hesiveness. Events were in the offing that would demonstrate that
it could, but only under pressure.

In October, 1933, Hitler withdrew the German Reich from the
League of Nations. In the face of foreign reaction to this move, he
felt it necessary to give a demonstration of home support for his
leadership. The demonstration was to take the form of a plebiscite
to which would be coupled elections for a new all-Nazi Reichstag.
The first reaction set the tone for the subsequent campaign. Upon
the request of the central government, County Prefect von Altberg
sent the following telegram to Berlin: "The population of County
Thalburg unanimously approves the Reich government's actions
and calls for peace, bread, and work." Other organizations sent
similar telegrams.[4]

The plebiscite campaign itself was an excellent example of Nazi
methods. Even though the NSDAP could expect to report unanimous approval, since they alone would count the ballots, every
effort was made to have Thalburgers actually vote for Hitler's
policies. The opening of the campaign for Thalburg was Hitler's
speech in Hannover, on October 25. Special trains featuring drastically reduced fares left Thalburg for the speech. Furthermore,
Thalburgers were advised that anyone who wanted to go could, if
he applied to local Nazi headquarters. Four days later the SA and
SS held a parade in Thalburg with two fife-and-drum corps and
their band.[5]

Then the campaign began in earnest. By order of the NSDAP
no meetings were to be allowed until after election day except those
which had a political character. The first of these took place on
November 2, ten days before the election. It consisted of a mammoth parade followed by a rally. From three o'clock on, the whole
town was involved, one way or another, as requested by the
NSDAP. ("The active participation of all inhabitants is expected!
Out with the flags!") The parade itself was organized by groups,
from the railroad workers to the Queen Luise Society, and included
over three thousand people plus two bands, three fife-and-drum
corps, and innumerable flags. Two days later, November 9, was a
special day for the NSDAP anyway—the anniversary of Hitler's
unsuccessful "Beer Hall" *Putsch* of 1923. In Thalburg there was a

full celebration with all the Nazi sub-organizations participating and with a mass demonstration joined to the wreath-laying ceremony. All public officials were required to participate.[6]

The final surge came in the last two days before the voting. On November 10, Hitler was to speak on the radio, and in Thalburg the NSDAP was determined that everyone would listen. All businesses were ordered to close during the speech and all of the town's civil servants were ordered to assemble in the largest hall in Thalburg to hear it. The program was a masterpiece of coordination:

1:00 to 1:01—Siren Signal. All work ceases; all traffic stops.
1:01 to 1:10—Report of Propaganda Leader Dr. Goebbels.
1:10 to 1:55—Speech of the *Fuehrer*.
1:55 to 1:59—Horst Wessel Song.
2:00 to 2:03—Sirens; work resumes.

The audience gathered in the Riding Hall will remove itself, in a closed column, to the Market Square where it will be dismissed.

Out with the Flags!

Local Group Thalburg, NSDAP [7]

The following day, election eve, a totally inclusive demonstration was planned:

Thalburg marches for peace! The entire population of Thalburg is hereby summoned to participate in the demonstrations on Saturday at 6:30 which will end at the *1910er Zelt* where Party-Comrade Minister Klagges of Braunschweig will speak. The order of clubs and organizations will be as on May 1. The appearance of each man is an unqualified duty.

Local Group Thalburg, NSDAP [8]

A circular memorandum to all Nazi party members in Thalburg reminded them to appear at the election eve meeting, with the words: "No excuses will be accepted." [9]

With this kind of preparation, the organization of the election itself was not overlooked. Each of Thalburg's 1,200 Nazi party members was ordered to appear at the polls at nine in the morning on election Sunday, with the members of his family, his friends, and his acquaintances. After voting, each Nazi was to report to his cell leader and remain on call for further work during the entire day. Every business in Thalburg was to fill its store windows with posters; every house was to display the swastika flag. Government offices and businesses were ordered to vote in closed ranks by noon. Various clubs were to meet and vote in closed ranks. Furthermore:

Strict control will be maintained by the NSDAP to make certain that everyone exercises his voting duty. After he votes, every voter will receive a button which is to be purchased for 5 *pfg.* at the polls. At the exits of the city, railroad station, etc., there will be posts set up, who will remind everyone without a button of his patriotic duty.[10]

To make certain that Thalburgers voted in the right way there were large ads in the newspaper giving instructions: "This is how it looks if you voted correctly. The circle under 'Nein' should *not* be marked." And again: "ATTENTION! VOTERS! When you have given your vote for Hitler and voted with 'yes' at the polls, then you will receive a button." [11]

After such preparation the results were anti-climactic. Only 94.6 per cent voted and of these only 97.2 per cent voted "yes." The published results stated that, of 6,942 voters, 193 voted "no" and 68 spoiled their ballots. Curiously, in the Reichstag elections held at the same time (for which only the Nazi slate of candidates could be elected) it was reported that 321 spoiled their ballots. How these figures were arrived at is hard to say since the NSDAP counted the ballots with no one to challenge its tabulation. But no matter how they were counted, it was treated as a victory for the cause of Hitler. Church bells were rung in Thalburg when the results were announced.[12]

The significance of the election did not lie in the results but in the methods and techniques used. The campaign and the balloting showed that the totalitarian state was fully organized. For almost two weeks before election day practically all Thalburg was forced to be involved in a ritual devoid of inner content. The function of the election was not to determine or register the will of the citizens of Thalburg. It was to impress upon Thalburgers the omnipotence and determination of the NSDAP. This was accomplished, but in the course of achieving this goal the NSDAP rapidly exhausted whatever capital of genuine enthusiasm they began with. In the last days of the campaign even the members of

the NSDAP had to be whipped on by threats. The average Thalburger could not help looking upon the whole affair with increasing skepticism. The ritual was impressive but no longer genuine.
After this campaign Thalburg's NSDAP discovered that it was only
by new threats that unified action could be achieved.

Yet despite the lack of widespread motivation, mass propaganda
methods continued. The number of occasions when Thalburgers
were ordered to hang out their flags was multiplied and came to
include such second-rank events as the birthday of Herman Goering and county congresses of the NSDAP.[13] Eventually Aergeyz
began to insist that Thalburg was known throughout Germany as a
town with ingenious decorations. Instead of merely hanging out
swastika flags, homeowners were urged to ring their balconies with
a whole series of miniature swastikas, bunting, and other kinds of
decorations.

In short, local chauvinism was brought into play to bolster whatever feelings Thalburgers may have had for Hitler. The results
were gratifying to the Nazis. Perhaps the high point was reached
when a butcher on Broad Street contrived an effigy of Hitler in
lard, parsley, and sausage-ends in his store window. The effort that
had once gone into decorating the town for the shooting festivals
and other ancient ceremonies was now redirected for Nazism. But
Thalburgers entered into the spirit of it and satisfied their aesthetic
impulses in accordance with the new situation.[14]

Other native customs were also incorporated into Nazi methods
in order to aid the propaganda effort. Long before the NSDAP
appeared on the scene, Thalburgers had been devoted to honoring
the dead of previous wars. The NSDAP capitalized on this by
holding frequent ceremonies. Special monuments were erected to
honor such diverse groups as the fallen athletes of Thalburg. A
ceremony for the dead was even held on Christmas Eve and on
other non-traditional dates. These events were superimposed on the
by-now-customary Nazi celebrations (Hitler's birthday, May 1,
etc.). But already by 1934 enthusiasm for mass demonstrations
had fallen off to the point where Thalburgers made themselves
conspicuous at the beginning of celebrations and then ducked down
side streets to avoid having to listen to the speeches. Advertisements for Nazi-sponsored events made increasing use of absolute

imperatives such as: "The *entire* population of Thalburg *must* appear!" [15]

The apathy even pervaded the ranks of the NSDAP, and members were required to bring "control-cards" to meetings to be punched. Anyone who missed three meetings was threatened with expulsion. Members of the NSDAP were also required to bring others with them to meetings so that the halls would be filled. In a memorandum circulated in the summer of 1935 this concept is repeated several times:

> Every member must look upon it as a *duty* to attend and to bring several other *Volk*-comrades with him. . . . Every party-comrade and comradess has the duty of making extensive propaganda for attendance at this meeting so that the very last of all citizens attends. . . . No citizen must be allowed to stay at home. . . .[16]

Despite these measures and despite the terror that was there to enforce compliance, the history of mass propaganda in the mature totalitarian structure in Thalburg was one of increasing indifference. More and more Thalburgers were bored and exhausted by Nazi dynamism and complained about the incessant meetings, parades, and demonstrations. As for the fanatical Nazis, they became increasingly convinced that the citizens of Thalburg were hopelessly self-centered and apolitical.[17]

If enthusiasm was not voluntarily forthcoming, there were other means of evoking it. The most effective was the system of terror. Even in the late summer of 1933 there were still arrests to be made, mostly for very minor offenses. Thus in late August it was reported that a worker had shouted *"Heil Moskau!"* and had been sent to the Moringen concentration camp for it. Reports of similar arrests continued to trickle out. In September a worker was arrested for "making anti-governmental utterances." In November, 1933, two Thalburger women were arrested "for spreading false rumors about the NSDAP." [18] But eventually there were no more reports of arrests or other police action. As in other matters, the terror system was stabilizing itself. In September the TNN felt it advisable to publish an editorial against anonymous denunciations. Perhaps the last public manifestation of Nazi power came in September, 1933, when the SA and SS carried out a round-up of beggars in Thalburg. It was unsuccessful, but shortly thereafter the police conducted a similar action and managed to catch one unfortunate.[19]

Henceforth the operation of terror was undertaken by simple injunctions or by subtler and more effective means of social reinforcement. As examples of the former there were commands not to listen to Radio Moscow, to give the Hitler salute, to maintain the graves in the town cemetery. Furthermore there were injunctions to establish oneself as a good citizen by attending meetings, contributing to charity drives, and tracing "Aryan" ancestry.[20] More than anything else, rumor and social reinforcement maintained the system of terror. Occasionally overt actions would be necessary. Thus after the struggle against the churches began in 1935, a police detective was placed before the church door every Sunday, ostentatiously taking down names and, after the services began, taking notes on the contents of the sermon.[21] But such measures were exceptional. Generally Thalburgers came to know very rapidly what was expected of them and acted accordingly. While fear was widespread, there were actually no incarcerations for political offenses in the mature dictatorship, at least not through 1935.

The terror system also accommodated itself to Thalburg's peculiarities. There was the case of an old farmer who had been a member of the Hannoverian party. As long as anyone in Thalburg could remember he had always spent his evenings in a tavern drinking beer, condemning the contemporary government, and extolling the good old days under the Hannoverian dynasty. When the Nazis came to power he included them in his curses as a matter of course. But he was so much a part of the general scheme of affairs that no one ever bothered him. Thus he had the distinction of publicly vilifying the government almost every day of the Third Reich with a complete immunity.[22]

There were also a few Thalburgers who were genuinely unaware of the terror system until the summer of 1934. It was after the "Roehm *Putsch*" that the "German glance" and the general breakdown of trust appeared.[23]

In short, while threats, allusions, and rumor served to maintain control, there was no increase in actual terrorism in the first years of the Nazi regime in Thalburg. A sort of equilibrium existed whereby Thalburgers did what was expected of them and in return were spared the potential rigors of the police state. This kind of tacit agreement, based on the possibility of terror, was the essential prerequisite for the maturation of totalitarian rule in Thalburg. It was always held in reserve while the slow process of molding the various institutions in the town into acceptable instruments of Nazism went on. This process was as thorough as it was deliberate. The best example of it was in the school system.

The Thalburg city government possessed extensive power over the operation of the elementary school system, from determination of the budget to appointment of teachers. It did not have the same kind of control over the *Gymnasium* and *Lyzeum*, since these were supervised by the Provincial School Board. After the NSDAP came to power, however, the determining factor was the Local Group Leader who not only controlled the Thalburg city government but also had considerable influence, through the NSDAP, upon the Provincial School Board. It was not really necessary for Kurt Aergeyz to exercise this power after 1933, since almost all of Thalburg's teachers cooperated fully with him. Only three teachers were removed: Tiere and Trautmann from the "idealist" opposition, both of whom were simply transferred out of town, and another teacher from the *Gymnasium* with known republican sympathies who was also transferred away from Thalburg.[24]

The NSDAP was not only interested in removing opposition, however. It was also concerned that education be enlisted as a positive support for the new regime. According to the town's official historian, writing in 1936:

It is no longer the sole task of the schools to impart knowledge; next to that stands the need to make out of the growing youth men and women such as the National Socialist State desires—adults who sense the meaning of "community" and want to join it. Thus the struggle for the unity of the nation has become the basis of education . . . . To develop men with hard bodies and hard wills, who can stand up to their man in the *Völkisch* struggle of our era: that is the new task which the schools have taken over in addition to their customary promotion of general intelligence.[25]

Converting the schools into ideological bastions of the new state was a process begun almost immediately. New textbooks were brought in in 1933. The existing school libraries were stripped of "degenerate" literature and stocked with books glorifying nationalism and militarism. Teachers were given lectures laying down the general lines under which history and other sensitive subjects were to be taught. New courses were introduced in "Racial Theory" and Teutonic pre-history. The lectures and "schooling sessions" for the teachers continued incessantly. Frequently the same themes were reiterated session after session. Teachers were careful to get the general line down exactly, since the word was quickly spread that the Hitler Youth would report to the NSDAP on what teachers were doing.[26]

In addition to the new subjects and the new approach to old subjects, the schools were required to emphasize sport and physical education, especially shooting and "defense sport." In science classes, for example, pupils were put to building model gliders. Nazi propaganda films were used extensively and radios were installed in the class rooms so that propaganda speeches could be heard.[27] The extent to which life in the schools was changed can be gauged from the report of the Catholic Grade School on new acquisitions:

> Flags were acquired . . . every class put up a picture of the *Fuehrer* . . . reparations charts and hand grenades purchased . . . the school library was revised, among other things Graf Luckner's *Sea Devil* acquired. . . . School wall pictures were increased by racial tables, "Swastika in Four Centuries," genetic laws . . . a map of the World War 1914-1918 became our property . . . air rifles purchased . . . flagstaff . . . model gliders. . . .[28]

The process included all schools. The business and professional schools introduced courses in "Racial History" and "Political Education." Even the small school for the feeble-minded did what it could do to indoctrinate its charges.[29]

The Hitler Youth played an active role in all these changes. In 1934 a drive was undertaken to enroll every pupil in the school system in either the Hitler Youth or the League of German Girls. Existing school clubs were driven out of existence. By exalting the Hitler Youth, however, the authority of the teachers was considerably diminished. In the words of a former principal, "It became almost impossible to teach." [30]

Despite this program, one aspect of Nazism did not enter the schools during the first two years of the Nazi regime. This was anti-semitism. One principal recalls having had three Jewish children in his school: "There were never any difficulties with them in any way. The children graduated from school with the other children. And to the best of my knowledge the other children never insulted or harassed them in any way." [31] Later, Jewish children were systematically excluded from the schools, but not in the early years. In fact, even pupils sympathetic to Nazism felt enough of a sense of solidarity with fellow-students of the Jewish faith so that they refused to sing the "Horst Wessel Song" in their presence.[32] But in all other ways, the school children were intensively indoctrinated. More than any other institution in Thalburg, the schools became active instruments of Nazism.

If their success with the schools was a source of encouragement to Thalburg's Nazis, the same was not true of that other instrument of education, the daily press. It is true that the press was under firm control; both the TNN and the GHC were well aware of the limits upon their freedom. But in Nazi eyes the press would cease to be a problem only when it was wholly Nazi-owned.

As noted above, Kurt Aergeyz declared on September 16, 1933, in a general meeting of the NSDAP, Local Group Thalburg, that it was the duty of every member to subscribe to Thalburg's own Nazi newspaper, the TB. The TB was quick to exploit this fiat. On September 23 every Nazi member received a letter from the TB reminding him of Aergeyz's command and informing him that he was therefore a subscriber as of October 1, 1933. An agent would stop by soon to take the order formally.[33]

This was part of a general campaign to increase the circulation of the Nazi press. Beginning in 1934 the TB did not have to be concerned with expanding its readership; this function was handled by a special official in each Nazi Local Group, the *Pressewart*. The *Pressewart* had the general task of overseeing all newspapers in his area, but his special and primary task was to build up the Nazi-owned press. He was to be a general reporter for the Nazi paper in his locality, covering every newsworthy event, ". . . so that he will have the possibility of informing our press, first, of all news . . . and so that the fat burgher will know that we have eyes and ears everywhere, and on this ground alone will fit himself into the new Germany." Furthermore the *Pressewart* was to do everything in his power to aid the Nazi press and weaken the non-Nazi press. He was especially to keep the non-party press in line.[34]

In Thalburg these general rules were interpreted to mean that the TNN and GHC would be driven out of existence. With Erhardt Knorpel writing the news for the TNN, however, it was hard for the NSDAP to find anything to complain about in the TNN. After his early brushes with disaster, Knorpel became exceedingly cautious. In fact, the TNN followed the Nazi line down to every twist and wriggle. Finally, however, Thalburg's Nazi *Pressewart* found something so obvious that no one else had noticed it. Ever since the TNN was founded, it had borne the slogan, as a part of its masthead, "Fatherland above Party" *(Das Vaterland ueber die Partei)*. In Imperial and Weimar days this was presumably a statement of impeccable sentiments. In the Nazi state, however, it was treasonable, since it promoted the heretical concept that state and party were distinguishable. Had Erhardt Knorpel thought about it he would have whisked the offending slogan away immediately. But a masthead is something that everyone looks at but few see, that is, until the Nazi *Pressewart* for Thalburg saw it one day in early December, 1933.

The TNN was immediately suppressed. Knorpel and the paper's publisher had to make the most abject apologies and pull the longest strings to get permission to resume publication ten days later. Needless to say the masthead had been trimmed. The NSDAP was convinced that this temporary suspension would be the death blow.

In point of fact it gave the TNN a new lease on life. Until the suspension the TNN's circulation had fallen steadily. After the paper was suppressed subscriptions came pouring in. The paper's reporter was convinced that this was the first sign of popular discontent with the Third Reich. In all likelihood it was simply that Thalburgers had had their curiosity piqued. Whatever there was in the TNN that made it suppressable would surely make interesting reading in those days of censorship. Hence the TNN won back its readership, and, since it was still well written, accurate, and first with the news, the subscriptions were maintained.

Perhaps the reporter was right and Thalburgers read it out of protest (a magnificent irony since the last thing the publisher was interested in was becoming a symbol of resistance), but in any event the TNN was economically secure thereafter. The Nazis threw up their hands in disgust and the TNN was tolerated, though still subjected to occasional harassment.[35]

While Thalburg's Nazis were willing to tolerate the TNN, they were absolutely determined to exterminate the GHC. This was partly because of antipathy for "reactionaries" such as the paper's owner and editor, Wilhelm Spatel, and partly because Spatel had the temerity to talk back to the Nazis. Although the GHC was a dying paper anyway, Spatel was convinced that his lagging circulation was due to Nazi pressure (which was certainly also true). He even went so far as to write to the District *Pressewart* for help against "illegal competition." This stung the TB to attack Spatel repeatedly in editorials. He was charged with knowing nothing about National Socialism, with taking advertisements from Jews (he did), and with publishing erroneous reports about the doings of Thalburg's NSDAP. He was also badgered in minor ways. By the summer of 1934 the TB refused the usual courtesy exchange of papers with the GHC. Spatel was urged by minor Nazi figures to publish scurrilous poems directed against himself. He was repeatedly found guilty of minor indiscretions by the Thalburg *Pressewart*.[36]

Eventually Spatel began to write to friends for help. One editor in a neighboring town informed him that the editor of the TB had a past which included conviction as an embezzler, a perjurer, and a debt-evader, but that nothing could be done to aid the GHC. A poet to whom Spatel had written for aid went so far as to try to intervene with the District Nazi officials but was told there was no hope for the GHC.[37]

Thus no matter where he turned, Spatel was trapped. The remnants of his family fortune enabled him to continue putting out the GHC at a personal loss, but eventually the circulation shrank to the point where each issue became an exercise in futility. Early in 1937 he capitulated, sold the paper to the TB for a pitiful sum, signed an agreement never to print anything again, and went into retirement. Shortly thereafter he died. He had contributed substantially to the Nazi seizure of power; he had rejoiced in their success and in their use of force against the "Marxists"; he was broken completely by them.[38]

The struggle waged by the NSDAP to establish its own newspaper in a monopolistic position occurred even though both the TNN and the GHC printed only what the NSDAP wanted and printed it in the way the Nazis wanted it. From the very beginning of the Third Reich all the newspapers in Thalburg were active and effective instruments of propaganda for the Nazi dictatorship. In a similar way, almost all the organizations that were coordinated in the spring of 1933 were eventually made into instruments of Nazi propaganda. One group of organizations which had, in general, escaped *Gleichschaltung* during the first few months of the Third Reich were the veterans' and patriotic societies. This oversight was subsequently corrected. In November, 1933, all former veterans in the *Kyffhaeuserbund* and similar organizations were incorporated into the "second reserve" of the SA. Thus they were placed under direct Nazi discipline and used for demonstrations, parades, and so forth.[39]

Other nationalist societies that served the Nazi purpose were systematically promoted. This was the case with the "People's League for the Care of German War Graves." The result of Nazi aid was apparent in their annual collections which yielded 31 marks in 1930, 37 marks in 1932, but 187 marks in 1933, when the SA helped solicit contributions. Similarly the Society for Germandom in Foreign Lands was developed from a small group into a significant one. It was, of course, a perfect instrument for promoting Nazi claims in foreign policy.[40]

One of the main Nazi efforts went into expanding the glider group in Thalburg. By September, 1933, the town's second glider was built, and Aergeyz, in his dedicatory speech, laid emphasis upon the military importance of glider training. A Nazi glider group was created and a special flying show with mock bombing demonstrations was held. This was done by the express command of the government, though Thalburg's Nazis showed some initiative. The Thalburg Senate supplied close to 400 marks in financial aid.[41]

While gliders and air power were stressed, the NSDAP did not forget to promote civil defense. In September, 1933, an Air Defense Society was created in Thalburg under Nazi leadership and all the town's schools, clubs, and newspapers incorporated into it. Thalburg was divided into four districts and organized for civil defense. By November, 1933, the first courses began with 250 people attending lectures. Attendance was obligatory. The Civil Defense School was formally reorganized in May, 1934, with eleven teachers. Belief in a coming war had become a permanent aspect of Nazi rule.[42]

Another institution which was used for propaganda and then eventually incorporated by the NSDAP was the *Stahlhelm*. This organization began its career in the Third Reich in partnership with the Nazis. The Nazis were determined to bring it under control, however, since it represented an independent mass organization which could be a potential gathering place for dissidents. Through August, 1933, the Thalburg *Stahlhelm* spent much of its time trying to convince the NSDAP of its loyalty and friendliness. For that purpose a special "Comradeship Evening" was given, with much drinking and dancing. By September, it had been determined that the *Stahlhelm* would be unified with the SA, i.e., absorbed. The actual ceremony was turned into a source of propaganda for the NSDAP, with flags, bands, and a somewhat forced festive air. This process dragged into October, after which the *Stahlhelm* proper ceased to exist, being invoked occasionally in the next few months only for propaganda purposes. By incorporating the *Stahlhelm* into the SA, the danger of its becoming a rival group was obviated; moreover, additional numbers of Thalburgers were brought under direct Nazi discipline. But at the same time, whatever communal spirit and enthusiasm had existed in this organization were destroyed.[43]

In short, the mature totalitarian structure in Thalburg was monolithic and authoritarian, but also bereft of spontaneity. The terror system could evoke responses, but responses which were empty of inner enthusiasm. Propaganda became increasingly a matter of ritual. The Nazis were successful in stimulating genuine enthusiasm only in areas where Thalburgers had always felt enthusiasm—in civic pride, for example.

It is even possible that one consequence of the deadening of human relationships was a rise in crime. Police statistics for the years 1933 through 1935 show that crimes of all sorts tended to rise. The following table gives the figures: [44]

	1933	1934	1935
Total investigations by Thalburger *Kriminal-Polizei*	318	385	497
Misdemeanors: drunkenness, disturbance of the peace, etc. (excluding traffic offenses)	60	117	166

Crimes involving theft and betrayal of confidence rose especially sharply: [45]

	1933	1934	1935
Grand larceny	3	16	12
Petty larceny	57	69	76
Criminal fraud	11	17	14
Embezzlement	5	9	12

While the increases are relatively large, the numbers are still small. One can hardly speak of a crime wave in Thalburg in response to the establishment of the dictatorship. Nevertheless, the figures are suggestive, as was Kurt Aergeyz's somewhat bewildered letter to school and youth authorities in the spring of 1934, protesting the recent wanton destruction by children of shrubs (and even the burning of evergreens) in the town's parks.[46] The evidence suggests some kind of social disorganization, resulting possibly from the effect of living the life of insincerity required by the Nazi regime.

For all phenomena in Thalburg in the years after 1933 must be put into a general context. The context was one characterized by the general breakdown of trust and by the destruction or perversion of hitherto unifying social organizations. The response of the individual was generally withdrawal, sometimes aggression. Both were useful to the dictatorship: withdrawal removed threats to the new system; aggression could be channeled against internal or external enemies of the regime. But the type of inner unity that the NSDAP had promised did not appear. Instead of creating the ideal *Volk*-community the Third Reich launched an era of deceit, distrust, and progressive spiritual decadence.

CHAPTER 18

THE GREAT JUSTIFICATION

(Summer, 1933, to Winter, 1935)

> You hear people saying: "Now we have work again; now we can buy something again."
> —A THALBURG BUSINESSMAN

By 1935 Thalburg had overcome all external signs of the depression. A visitor to the town in the summer of that year would have been considerably impressed by what he saw, especially if he had also passed through three years earlier and thus had a point of comparison. Construction was booming; there were no unemployed; work and purposefulness dominated the scene. Furthermore, the city undoubtedly looked better. There was a new and unified system of parks, the houses in the old town were freshly painted and repaired, and the streets were cleaner. It might even be that the visitor came to Thalburg because of a new and vigorous tourist office which went out of its way to attract visitors to the small, charming town in the valley. All of these features must be credited to the Nazi record, and to a good extent to the imagination and energy of the Nazi leader, Kurt Aergeyz. The revival of the economy was the great and solid propaganda point of the NSDAP in Thalburg. It was also the main justification for the dictatorship, since Aergeyz could argue that economic revival was made possible through the unity imposed upon the town, and because of the conversion of the city government into an instrument of personal authoritarianism.

For the city bureaucracy the great lesson in the implications of the new system was the personal fate of Dieter Thomas. Thomas, the second highest administrator in the city government when the Nazis took control, was subjected to a kind of harassment which could only demonstrate Kurt Aergeyz's virtually unlimited power within Thalburg. This was not a result of Thomas's political views, but solely because he was a symbol of independent thinking. Throughout the summer of 1933 he was systematically stripped of his subsidiary offices. In August, 1933, he was removed entirely from the city administration and his place was given to a rival. Then the vendetta began. Wherever Dieter Thomas sought employment he was prevented from obtaining it by the personal intervention of Kurt Aergeyz. Aergeyz also let it be known that Thomas had two alternatives: he could leave Thalburg and sell his house at a loss, or he could find work as a ditch digger in one of the works projects under August Blanck.

To avoid either, the former *Stadtsoberinspektor* was driven to taking a job in a neighboring town as a news butcher at the railroad station. From this limbo he was ultimately rescued by the arrival of the Army in Thalburg. The Army was beyond the reach of Aergeyz and thus Thomas found decent work with it as a civilian employee. Though Kurt Aergeyz made an annual effort for the next five years to have Dieter Thomas dismissed as a security risk, the Army just as steadfastly defied him.[1]

Even though Aergeyz's campaign for the total degradation of Dieter Thomas fell short of success, it was enough of a demonstration of power to make the other members of the city administration his complete tools. By 1935 Aergeyz was able to demand that city employees not only carry out their regular jobs in accordance with his commands but that they place themselves at the full disposal of the NSDAP.[2] So far as it was possible, Thalburg's administration became the expression of Aergeyz's will.

Kurt Aergeyz's authoritarian position had only two checks against it: the NSDAP which gave him his power, and the City Council which had elected him. As long as Aergeyz could depend upon support from the higher offices in the Nazi party, he could control Thalburg's Nazi Group, and thus the City Council. By late summer, 1933, it was apparent to the forces opposing him within Local Group Thalburg of the NSDAP that Aergeyz did have the support of the higher offices in the party.

In September, Aergeyz took steps to weed out the opposition to him on the Thalburg City Council. On September 21, 1933, at the public meeting of the council, the first order of business was a vote of "no confidence" in the then Speaker of the Council, Tiere (the Nazi teacher and one of the leaders in the "Idealist Opposition"). Tiere asked in vain for reasons and then tried to speak to individual members of the council. When they refused to talk to him, he had no choice but to leave the meeting room. Shortly thereafter he was transferred away from Thalburg. At the same meeting it was announced that there would be no more meetings of the City Council, but that instead a committee of four members of the City Council would meet, in private, with the Senate.[3] The interim arrangement of the "Committee of Four" lasted until January 30, 1935, when the new uniform city code for Germany legalized the situation.

The new code (sections of which had been discussed as early as 1925) gave all power and responsibility to the Mayor. He was to be advised and aided by boards of consultants and advisers. These organs were completely subordinate to him, and in no way limited his power. Thus Kurt Aergeyz became the sole and authoritarian ruler of Thalburg.[4]

Aergeyz's absolute control over the city government was, of course, not the only weapon at his disposal for coping vigorously with the town's economic problems. Through his position as Local Group Leader of the NSDAP he could control all the various economic organizations in Thalburg which had come under Nazi domination in the course of the *Gleichschaltung*. In 1933 these various organizations were initially used for propaganda purposes. Thus the German Workers' Front, created to replace the Free Unions, limited its activities to holding mass meetings and enrolling members. The Artisan League provided an exhibition, demonstration, and parade. The retail merchants sponsored a week in which articles, advertisements, and editorials praised their function.[5]

While these activities were perhaps psychologically gratifying, they did little to end the depression.

The real usefulness to the Nazis of the "coordinated" economic associations was that they could provide the lever to pry the economy of Thalburg out of the depression. How the NSDAP proposed to do this became apparent by the fall of 1933. During the summer the town had been stripped of unemployed through a variety of public works projects. It was clear to the Nazis, however, that this was only a temporary expedient. The real need was to incorporate these unemployed persons into the regular economy. The Nazis seemed to be convinced that this could be accomplished if everyone in Germany did his part. If consumers purchased and employers hired, the depression would vanish. Thus the economic problem was viewed as one to be solved by organization and propaganda, fields in which the NSDAP felt it excelled.

The process began on October 5, 1933. On that date all employers, public and private, plus representatives of all clubs, met at one of the town's hotels. The city administration had composed a master list of all persons in Thalburg capable of hiring workers, and triple-checked it to make certain no one was omitted. In his speech on this occasion, Kurt Aergeyz told the assembled businessmen that now was the time when they would have to do their part. The government had hired the unemployed temporarily, and it had money on hand in loans and grants. Now the private sector of the economy would have to begin hiring. The Thalburg City Brewery would set the example by hiring four new men. The sugar factory had already agreed to keep its plant operating full time, with four shifts. Each employer would be visited in a few days and asked to hire as many new men as his situation permitted. There was no immediate response to this speech. Only a few people rose to comment afterwards. One suggested that the government should act firmly against illegal artisans. Another called on employers to hire old-time Nazi members first. But not a single businessman rose to pledge that he would hire a new worker.[6]

In subsequent days little was done publicly to realize the goals set forth in Aergeyz's speech. There were advertisements calling on people to buy more, to save more, and to patronize only legally licensed artisans. But by the end of October there were still 340 people employed in public works projects.[7] The situation remained relatively stable into the winter of 1933-1934.

In the spring the NSDAP began its drive in earnest. The new effort was to be called the "Battle of Work" *(Arbeitsschlacht)*. The kick-off date was March 21, 1934—the first anniversary of the "Day of Potsdam." But in Thalburg the propaganda effort began three weeks before that. Late in February letters were sent to all civil servants and heads of clubs and guilds, calling upon them to come to the *1910er Zelt* for a mass meeting. What Aergeyz would say to them would be the same thing that was being said all over the District, since a complete outline for material, contents, and presentation of speeches was forwarded to Thalburg from the Nazi District Propaganda Division. Nevertheless, Aergeyz's speech was an excellent one: forceful, convincing, and inspiring, with an aura of beneficial purposefulness. The message was simple. Every Thalburger must consume, hire, borrow, spend, turn the wheels of the economy. Employers were told to raise wages and hire new men. If they did not, the state would force them to. House owners were urged to have all repairs done now, when interest rates on loans were low. In short, the speech was a mixture of threats and cajolery. It left Thalburgers with the clear impression that the economy would revive and people would be rich and happy—or else! [8]

This mass meeting was followed by a second smaller meeting of employers, craft masters, and civil servants a week later. Involved were the same people who had been addressed by Aergeyz the previous fall. But this time the atmosphere was entirely different. In the first place, Aergeyz no longer talked *at* the assembly; instead there was a general discussion. In the second place, practically everyone in the room *believed* that an economic revival was in the making. The best reports were from construction. The Painters' Guild reported that a year ago there were only fifteen apprentices. Now there were forty. The Carpenters' Guild reported twenty new apprentices since January. Where there were gloomy reports, Aergeyz had positive things to say. The Shoemakers' Guild bemoaned the competition; Aergeyz promised that the Nazi Welfare Organization would order five hundred pairs of shoes to be made in Thalburg. The grocery owners complained of competition from the consumers' cooperative; Aergeyz promised that this organization "will not be with us forever." The bakers could not see improvement; Aergeyz swore it would come in a matter of weeks. But most of those present had learned over the winter that the new government was trying to help. The Tailors' Guild-Master reported that because of the sudden demand for uniforms, eighteen new apprentices had been hired. The Retail Merchants' head reported that the turnover in 1933 had been 11 per cent higher than in 1932 and that it was still rising. He promised that merchants would be hiring new people: "You hear people saying, 'Now we have work again; we can buy something again.' And I want to say that on the part of the NS *Volk*-Welfare much has been done for retailers."

After the initial discussion Aergeyz spoke in summary. He promised to attack illegal competition. He affirmed that Nazism was committed to the idea of decent profits. But he also swore he would crack down on anyone cutting wages, hoarding money instead of investing it, or working employees overtime. He set reasonable goals: sixteen new apprentices this month, a re-education course for employees who had forgotten their skills. Then came the most enjoyable part of the meeting. Aergeyz declared that money in abundance would be forthcoming from the government. What should it be spent for? Pet schemes poured forth. Old dreams were dredged up. The meeting ended in a burst of enthusiasm and plans. There is no doubt that, psychologically at least, the depression was over.[9]

The mood was sustained. A few days later there was a short but magnificent advertisement in the TNN: "Who still has no job? Report immediately . . . at the City Hall." On March 15 there was a countywide convention in the *1910er Zelt* with speeches outlining plans for the "Battle of Work," pep talks, and so on. On March 21 the "Battle" was officially begun. Parades, demonstrations, bands, flags, a radio speech by Hitler—all the Nazi trimmings went into making it a memorable event.[10] But more significant for Thalburg was the ceremonial ground-breaking for a series of new works projects.

Actually, despite all the discussion and propaganda, the depression was not defeated by every Thalburger doing his bit. Instead, the essential instruments were public works projects and a construction boom based on government pump-priming. The same week that Kurt Aergeyz was holding his remarkable discussion evening with Thalburg's businessmen he wrote a letter to the city engineer outlining in detail a new series of works projects for 1934. Since most of the money for these projects came from the central government, Thalburg paid no more for them than it would have paid in dole money for the equivalent number of unemployed.[11] Many of the projects undertaken were not spectacularly apparent. These included work in the town-owned forest, repair of the extant park system, and repair of roads. But there was one project which transformed the whole face of the town. This was the "park ring." Circling the medieval inner city was a series of defense works dating from the era of Thalburg's independence. By 1933 the wall was crumbling, the moats were filled, and the anti-artillery mounds covered with small vegetable gardens. Now, under the public works program, this was all rebuilt. The old wall was repaired where it could be and leveled completely in other spots. The moat was turned into a series of small swan ponds. The rest of the area was converted to pleasant parks, with grass, flower gardens, and playgrounds. As a result, Thalburg's park system was doubled in size and the town was given a delightful and distinctive aspect. Over eleven thousand workdays went into the creation of this "green belt."[12]

Thalburg was made more attractive in many other ways. The two town-owned taverns, both in the woods above Thalburg, were repaired and remodeled, and new roads were built to them. Several run-down sections of the town were cleared and refurbished. Under the guidance of the museum director, houses in the old section of Thalburg were repainted so that they again emphasized the medieval, half-timbered structural work. Much of this work was done by Thalburg's own unemployed, but much was also done by the Labor Service (Arbeitsdienst). This was begun as a voluntary organization, but soon became compulsory. It was admirably suited to take up the slack in the economy by removing people from the labor market. Thus, when the Thalburg sugar factory ended its seasonal refining in 1933, most of its three hundred temporary employees were taken into the Labor Service. Throughout 1933 the Labor Service undertook a number of random projects, from working on a football field and a shooting range to building paths in the town's forest. Beginning in 1934, however, they devoted full energies to creating a new asset for Thalburg. This was an open air theater, set in a natural declivity in the Thalburg Forest.

It was originally conceived of as a meeting place for Nazi ceremonies and was first called the *Thingplatz* (from the old Teutonic term for a tribal meeting place) and then, even more significantly, the *Weihstaette,* or "Holy Place." When it was completed it did create an almost holy feeling in the beholder, since it was dramatically incorporated into the natural setting of ancient and majestic oaks. Almost 23,000 workdays went into the construction of the Holy Place before it could be formally dedicated on June 7, 1936. The theater was useful for more than Nazi ceremonies, of course, and in 1936 alone lured more than sixty thousand tourists to Thalburg. Furthermore, Aergeyz arranged to have it turned over to the Nazi War Victims' Society which responded by making Thalburg its national headquarters and convention town. This drew considerable money into Thalburg.[13]

The Labor Service was also involved in the other main ingredient for the cure of the depression, the construction boom. As a result of its occupation of the old Army barracks, some seventy-five families who had been living there as "shelterless" had to be relocated. The problem of finding apartments for these displaced persons brought into sharp focus the housing shortage in Thalburg. The town had gone into the depression with a housing shortage, and the course of the depression only made it worse. From the beginning of 1930 to the end of 1933 Thalburg's net population grew by almost four hundred persons. At the same time construction lagged seriously. Thus the situation was ripe for a construction boom if only money were forthcoming.[14]

One of the first measures of the Hitler government was to make that money available. By November, 1933, close to 200,000 marks were ready for distribution in Thalburg, and more was yet to come. The money was made available through grants and loans under extremely favorable circumstances. For repair or division of apartments, for example, the Reich would pay 20 per cent of the cost and loan the rest at 4 per cent for six years. Similar terms were available for new construction. Under these attractive terms, more than 63,000 marks were allocated by March, 1934, for 728 different jobs. By 1936 over 1,300 applications had been approved totaling 175,000 marks. An additional 121,000 marks came from the government for new construction. This was increased again after the spring of 1934 when the Army returned to its old compound, forcing the government to erect new buildings for the offices previously located there and to build new barracks for the Labor Service. In short, by the spring of 1934 all the elements were at hand for a major construction boom in Thalburg.[15]

The situation was made even more favorable by the actions of Kurt Aergeyz. He was considerably embarrassed by the fact that he could not find enough housing for the "shelterless" displaced from the Army barracks. This forced him to locate them in old railroad cars, which was undesirable for the town in many ways. Furthermore, the response of many Thalburg landlords to his pleas for apartments for these people was to raise rents, which upset him greatly. For all these reasons Aergeyz sought to accelerate the construction of housing in Thalburg. By means of *Gleichschaltung* he already controlled the "Common Good Construction Club," which was now made to increase its building rate. To supplement this organization, Aergeyz founded a company called the "Thalburg Housing Construction Company" with himself as head. The city treasury was required to put up 100,000 marks for capital, and various Thalburg businessmen were induced to buy shares in the new company, with the City Savings Bank loaning them the cash for the shares. Thus organization was also at hand to push the construction boom. Beginning in the summer of 1933, but gaining full momentum only in the spring of 1934, a whirlwind of construction encompassed Thalburg. By the end of 1934, eighty-five new houses with 126 apartments were built. An additional hundred new apartments were fitted out in existing buildings. Over 1,200 were repaired. In the face of this effort, Thalburg's economic problems melted away. By the winter of 1934-1935, public works were continued only to complete projects already begun. By 1936 Thalburg had to import construction workers.[16]

The construction figures cited above do not include what the NSDAP considered the showpiece of its building projects—forty-eight new "settlers' " houses. Though the Nazis took full credit for this, the plans, money, and all other preliminaries were ready by the time the Third Reich was inaugurated. In fact, the main reason the settlement project was not begun in 1932 was that it had been blocked by the Nazis. This was conveniently forgotten in 1933. To the accompaniment of great ceremony, work was begun on the first two dozen houses in the project on August 16, 1933. Since these were simple houses to build, and since the project was also made a part of the public works program, these first houses were completed by early November. On the day of the opening of the "Battle of Work," the ground was broken for the second twenty-four houses in the "settlement." By the fall of 1934 those were also completed. Henceforth the settlement was commonly spoken of as the "Nazi Settlement." [17]

Since the depression was ended in Thalburg by means of works projects and a construction boom, what was the role of all the propaganda, the discussions, the "Battle of Work"? It seems clear that at the time this was considered an essential part of defeating the town's economic woes. Though its direct *economic* contribution was minimal, its *psychological* contribution was crucial. It convinced the townspeople that the depression was over, and it convinced them that they had been the ones to end it, under Nazi leadership. Whether deliberately or not, the Nazis took advantage of the fact that what men believe happens is sometimes more important than what actually does happen.

In addition to conquering the depression Thalburg's Nazis made great capital out of the fact that they also dealt with the side effects of the economic crisis: hunger, want, and the other aspects of poverty. In mitigating distress they pushed two concepts, both of which proved popular. The first was that everyone should help; the second was that contributions were not charity but rather a rightful obligation to fellow Germans caught in a situation not of their own making. This effort at social amelioration was the closest the NSDAP ever came to promoting the promised *Volk*-community.

The primary instrument for Nazi welfare work was the NSV (Nazi *Volk*-Welfare Society). As was the case with other Nazi sub-organizations, the main personnel for the NSV came from the ranks of the NSDAP itself: party members were simply required to join. But many Thalburgers, who would never have joined the NSDAP or any other Nazi sub-organization, found themselves willing to join the NSV because its work seemed so apolitical and beneficial.[18] The NSV was also able to make use of all the various clubs, societies, and other organizations which had come under Nazi leadership through *Gleichschaltung*. As in the case of the economic drive and the propaganda effort, the Nazis were thus able to use the entire social apparatus as a lever to move the masses.

The first project of the NSV began in September, 1933, and was called the "Winter Aid." The specific campaign was called "The Struggle Against Hunger and Cold." In newspaper advertisements Thalburgers were urged to give deeply. "Sacrifice" was the key word; those who contributed most generously were promised that their names would be inscribed in a special book of honor entitled *Thalburg Sacrifices*. In a very short time the campaign demonstrated again the Nazi penchant for thoroughness. A list was drawn up of all merchants in Thalburg, and each was expected to contribute. The merchants were also advised that "the lists will be examined closely and contributions which are too small will be rejected." By mid-October the town was divided into six districts for intensive collection. In the collection process, all clubs and other social organizations were given target sums and made responsible for their members. Nor were benefit evenings overlooked. One of the customary "German Evenings" with 30-*pfennig* admission turned its proceeds over to the "Struggle Against Hunger and Cold." The Hitler Youth was put to making special street collections. Finally, collection cans were set up in every public place, especially for small coins. They were marked with the slogan "When the *Pfennig* Wins, the Struggle will be Victorious."

But the most spectacular device was the *Eintopfgerichtsonntage,* or "Stew Sundays." The idea was that on selected Sundays (usually once a month) every person in Germany would eat stew instead of his regular meal and then contribute the difference in cost to the NSV. Stews were to be served in restaurants, homes, everywhere in Germany. By this means it would be proved that "all

Germans are prepared to suffer together when the least of us suffers." These measures brought in considerable money. Collections on "Stew Sundays" regularly totaled in excess of 1,200 marks and by January, 1934, the *pfennig* canisters alone brought in 342 marks. But from the Nazi point of view, the NSV work was even more important as a propaganda measure. Through it, every German was to feel that he had helped alleviate the misery caused by the depression. Nazi-imposed "unity" was again to be demonstrated as beneficial.[19]

The Nazis were also at pains to show the social direction of their government in other ways. Thus at Christmastime, 1933, a Christmas tree was put up in the Market Square "so that everyone in Thalburg would be able to enjoy one." Or again, articles appeared deploring the use of the term *gnaedige Frau,* in other words, opposing class distinctions.[20] Most Thalburgers approved of these concepts. They sensed the class divisions that had rent the town so much in Weimar days, and they felt that the Nazis were doing something about this by attacking the externals of the class structure. They were excited by the possibilities of "national unity"— even so superficial a unity as that imposed by Nazism.[21]

Nazi contributions to Thalburg's economy did not end with anti-depression measures. Kurt Aergeyz was convinced that much could be done to help Thalburg by promoting the tourist trade. One effect of the works projects was to make Thalburg a pleasanter place to visit, and this was frequently mentioned in explaining the repairs done on paths in the town forest and at the two town-owned taverns in the woods above Thalburg. It was for this reason also that Aergeyz arranged to have sixty "historical tablets" affixed to buildings of note and other appropriate spots in the town.[22] The beginnings of an active campaign to bring in tourists came early in 1934 when Aergeyz fused two existing clubs, the "Tourist Club" and the "Improvement Association," to form a new "Club for the Promotion of Tourism." In subsequent meetings and by the usual methods, the club's membership was increased to about five hundred. Advertisements in big city newspapers and brochures praising Thalburg's scenic location soon began to bring tourists to the town. In later years this added considerably to the town's income.[23]

Far more significant for Thalburg's economy was the re-occupation by the Army of the former compound north of the Muhle River. This was a project dear to the heart of Kurt Aergeyz and vigorously pushed by him. By the beginning of 1934, Aergeyz determined to begin negotiations with the Army and was prepared to expend up to 50,000 marks of the city's funds to buy additional land for the Army. The Army was also willing and a contract was signed in April, 1934. The main point of the contract was that the Army agreed to purchase the compound from Thalburg for 285,000 marks. This represented a loss for Thalburg, especially since the Army also demanded that the town's pool (located on land adjacent to the compound) be thrown into the bargain. Considering what Thalburg had originally paid for both the compound and the pool, the town lost close to 2,350,000 marks in the deal.

But this was more than compensated for by the Army. In the first place, by 1937 the Army spent over 2,000,000 marks in new buildings and repairs, most of which went to contractors and workers in Thalburg. Secondly, new buildings had to be erected by the central government to house the various offices hitherto located in the compound. Forcing an additional hundred-odd people out of the "shelterless" apartments also helped stimulate construction, especially since the Army granted funds for new apartments.[24] Most important of all was the economic gain to Thalburg from the simple presence of an additional thousand consumers who were not a burden on the labor market. The soldiers spent money in the town, their relatives came to visit them, and, above all, the Commissariat contracted for food and other items from local merchants. From every point of view the re-occupation of Thalburg by the Army was a first-class economic *coup* by the Nazis.[25]

Naturally the arrival of the Army had other effects upon Thalburg. While the soldiers had to be circumspect and the whole operation kept in disguise until 1935 (when Hitler announced to the world that he was defying the military clauses of the Treaty of Versailles), Thalburgers soon knew that a battalion was located in the old barracks. In view of Thalburg's great love for things military, as displayed in the pre-Hitler period, it can well be imagined that the arrival of the Army was greeted with joy.

Furthermore, as exemplified by the personal experiences of Dieter Thomas, the Army became a place of refuge for some Thalburgers. There they were immune from Aergeyz's wrath. Since many officers in the Army were unsympathetic to Nazism, there soon developed a fine feeling between the "Idealist Opposition" and the Army. Thus the Army made the Third Reich much more tolerable for many Thalburgers.[26]

In summary, the actions of the Nazis in the economic sphere did a great deal to redeem and justify Nazism in the eyes of the people of Thalburg. Those who had the time and inclination to assess the nature of Nazism by 1935 could set up a balance sheet. On the one hand, Nazism had apparently ended the depression, initiated an economic revival, beautified the town, provided vigorous and efficient leadership, and increased Thalburg's economic assets. On the other hand, it had vitiated and regimented social life, introduced a system of terror and authoritarianism, forced Thalburgers to participate in a constant round of dulling and ritualistic propaganda events, and tied the fortunes of the town to the personal whims and dubious personality of Kurt Aergeyz. Obviously the balance did not resolve itself into a simple equation.

By 1935 most Thalburgers again were unsure about Nazism. It is extremely hard to say what the results of a free election might have been. The odds are that in the minds of most Thalburgers the bad outweighed the good. Given the chance, they probably would have voted to end or alter the Nazi regime. But long before 1935 the decision had been cast.

CHAPTER 19

CONCLUSIONS

> *The repetition of conditions is the*
> *exception and not the rule, and*
> *when such repetitions occur, they*
> *never arise under exactly similar*
> *conditions.*
>
> —FRIEDRICH ENGELS *

After 1935 Thalburg continued to follow the lines laid down in the first years of the Nazi regime. Kurt Aergeyz continued to provide efficient and productive administration, the townspeople were herded into mass meetings and demonstrations whenever it suited the needs of Nazism, and rigid authoritarianism maintained its sway. The pace of economic expansion slowed considerably by 1937, but the town was still well off.

During the years after 1935 Nazism showed its true intentions on the question of religion. Aergeyz began a drive with the ultimate goal of making Thalburg the first town in Germany to be completely without church members. As his anti-religious campaign grew, the quiet opposition of the intensely Lutheran community also grew. Despite their use of increasingly threatening measures, Thalburg's Nazis were almost totally ineffective in their anti-church campaign. Resistance to Nazism thus increased as the Nazi era wore on, but the resistance was entirely passive. Even at the height

---

* Quoted in Edmund Wilson, *To the Finland Station* (New York, 1953), p. 187.

of the anti-religious campaign, when the Hitler Youth broke up meetings of confirmation classes and pelted the crucifix on the town church with snowballs, Thalburgers responded solely by increasing church attendance. The resistance clique around Walther Timmerlah showed its defiance of Kurt Aergeyz by singing in the church choir. On *Kristalnacht* in 1938, several Jewish stores and homes were ransacked, and while some Thalburgers protested, none tried to block the Stormtroopers.[1] The terror system retained its efficacy.

After the outbreak of the war, Aergeyz relaxed his anti-religious campaign but continued to keep a tight hold over the town. The only overt terrorism came in 1943 when three former Social Democrats were sent to concentration camps, apparently for no special reason. Even in 1945 Aergeyz retained enough authority so that as the Allied armies approached he was able to stake out the local militia on several county roads with orders to fight to the death, while he abandoned his Nazi uniform and drove off to the hills with a case of *Schnapps* in his car.[2]

Despite the militia, Thalburg fell to the Allies without a fight and thus escaped destruction. In 1944, American bombers completely destroyed the Thalburg railroad yards, but the town itself was hit by only a few stray bombs. While physically spared by World War II, Thalburg nevertheless underwent a radical change during and after these years. Refugees from the larger towns poured into Thalburg to escape the bombing and many stayed permanently after the collapse of the Third Reich. Even more refugees came to the little town from the areas occupied by the Russians. By 1950 the population of Thalburg had doubled. Of the inhabitants after 1945, probably only one of every three had been a Thalburger during the early years of the Nazi era. The old town was gone; it would never return.

Thalburg is not now, and never was, a "typical" German town. The composition of Thalburg in Weimar and Nazi days was not the same as the rest of Germany. There was an inordinate number of civil servants and the town was dominated economically by the railroad. Few places in Germany began the Third Reich with a two-thirds vote for the NSDAP, the national average being on the order of two-fifths. On the other hand, there were many places in Germany that saw more violence than Thalburg in the early days of the Third Reich.[3]

What, then, is to be learned from Thalburg's experience in the years 1930 to 1935, the years of the Nazi seizure of power?

In the first place, it is clear that an essential arena in the Nazi electoral surge and the seizure of power was on the local level. Thalburg's Nazis created their own image by their own initiative, vigor, and propaganda. They knew exactly what needed to be done to effect the transfer of power to themselves in the spring of 1933, and they did it apparently without more than generalized directives from above. Exactly how much was initiated locally and how much was promoted by the example of other Nazi groups in other towns or by the District and national Nazi leadership remains to be determined. It would be extremely interesting to know exactly what means were used by the NSDAP to instill the sense of purposefulness and initiative into its local groups, which were then used by the movement as a whole. It would be useful to know how coordination was combined with flexibility in this authoritarian instrument. The material available for this study of Thalburg did not supply answers to these questions. It has, however, made clear that there would have been no Nazi revolution in Thalburg, at least not of the totality that has been described here, without an active and effective local organization. Hitler, Goebbels, and the other Nazi leaders provided the political decisions, ideology, national propaganda, and, later, the control over the government which made the revolution possible. But it was in the hundreds of localities like Thalburg all over Germany that the revolution was made actual. They formed the foundation of the Third Reich.

As for the reasons behind the particular experience in Thalburg, the most important factor in the victory of Nazism was the active division of the town along class lines. Though there was cohesion in Thalburg before the Nazis began their campaigns leading to the seizure of power, the cohesion existed within the middle class or within the working class and did not extend to the town as a whole. The victory of Nazism can be explained to a large extent by the desire on the part of Thalburg's middle class to suppress the lower class and especially its political representatives, the Social Democratic party.

This is why Thalburgers rejoiced in the gains of the Nazis, and this is why they applauded the institution of the dictatorship. The antipathy of the middle class was not directed toward individual members of the SPD, but only toward the organization itself; not toward the working class as such, but only toward its political and social aspirations; not, finally, toward the reality of the SPD, but mainly toward a myth which they nurtured about the SPD. For a variety of reasons, Thalburg's middle class was so intent on dealing a blow to the Social Democrats that it could not see that the instrument it chose would one day be turned against itself.

Exactly why Thalburgers were so bitterly opposed to the Socialists cannot be answered on the basis of a study of this town alone; the answer lies in the history and social structure of Imperial and Weimar Germany, and possibly can be given only by a social psychologist. Nevertheless it seems clear that the nature of the SPD had something to do with the burghers' attitudes. Thalburg's Socialists maintained slogans and methods which had little correspondence with reality. They maintained the façade of a revolutionary party when they were no longer prepared to lead a revolution. They never seriously attempted to mend fences with the middle class and frequently offended bourgeois sensibilities by their shortsightedness and shallow aggressiveness.

Yet it would be wholly incorrect to place all the blame upon Thalburg's Social Democracy. The middle class responded to the existence of the SPD in ways which were almost paranoid. Its members insisted upon viewing the SPD as a "Marxist" party at a time when this was no longer so. They were determined to turn the clock back to a period when the organized working class was forcibly kept from exerting influence. They felt threatened by the very existence of this organization. This view of the SPD was not in accord with reality, since by any objective standard the goal of the SPD in Thalburg was to maintain the kind of town that Thalburg's middle class itself wanted.

Perhaps the behavior of the good burghers of Thalburg becomes more understandable when one realizes the extent to which they were committed to nationalism. The excess of patriotic feeling in the town during the pre-Hitler period was the great moral wedge for Nazism. In many ways the actions and beliefs of Thalburgers during the last years of the Weimar era were the same as if World War I had never ended. It was in this sort of atmosphere that the SPD might seem treasonable and the Nazi reasonable.

A similar effect was wrought by the depression. While Thalburg's middle class was not decisively affected by the economic crisis, the burghers were made desperate through fear and through an obsession with the effects of the depression, especially the sight of the unemployed. As for the effect of the depression upon the lower classes, it was equally large. There is no doubt that the progressive despair of the jobless, as reflected in the longer and longer periods of unemployment, weakened the forces of democracy in the town. It may be that this sapped the SPD's will to fight and led it into ritualistic responses to Nazism. It was hard for Socialists to bend all their efforts to combating Nazism when this involved defending a system which could produce this sort of economic misery. Had the SPD seriously undertaken to introduce democratic socialism in response to the depression, it seems likely they would have found new sources of strength among their own followers, and very likely might have won the votes of the many Thalburgers who cast ballots for the NSDAP simply because the Nazis promised to end the depression.

The depression weakened Thalburg's Socialists in other ways, too. The use of economic pressure at the sugar factory and at the railroad deprived the SPD of much of its prestige and power. If it could not even defend its own people when the chips were down, how could it defend democracy, and how could it bring about the socialist society? The success of the action at the railroad yards no doubt opened up several possibilities for the Nazis. It was there that they learned how economically vulnerable the workers were; it was there that they learned essentially that the SPD would not fight.

But the main effect of the depression was to radicalize the town. In the face of the mounting economic crisis, Thalburgers were willing to tolerate approaches that would have left them indignant or indifferent under other circumstances. Thus the disgusting and debilitating party acrimony and violence mushroomed in the years before the dictatorship. The extent of the violence in Thalburg was an expression of the radical situation, but it also added to it by making violence normal and acceptable. With the growing nationalism and increasing impatience over the depression, violence and political tension were significant factors in preparing the town for the Nazi takeover.

All these factors were exploited with considerable astuteness by Nazi propaganda. In the face of the senseless round of political squabbling and fecklessness, the Nazis presented the appearance of a unified, purposeful, and vigorous alternative. Their propaganda played upon all the needs and fears of the town and directed itself to almost every potential group of adherents. By their own efforts the Nazis captured the allegiance of the confused and troubled middle class.

This set the stage for the actual seizure of power, but the revolution itself was also conducted in such a way as to insure success. The fact that this was, in the words of Konrad Heiden, a *"coup d'état* by installments" kept the *Reichsbanner* from responding decisively at any one point. By the time the SPD had been broken, the terror system had been inaugurated, largely through social reinforcement.

The single biggest factor in this process was the destruction of society in Thalburg. What social cohesion there was in the town existed in the club life, and this was destroyed in the early months of Nazi rule. With their social organizations gone and with terror a reality, Thalburgers were isolated from one another. This was true of the middle class but even more true of the workers, since by the destruction of the SPD and the unions the whole complex of social ties created by this super-club was effaced. By reducing the people of Thalburg to unconnected social atoms, the Nazis could move the resulting mass in whatever direction they wished. The process was probably easier in Thalburg than in most other places, since the town contained so many government employees. By virtue of their dependence on the government the civil servants were in an exposed position and had no choice but to work with the Nazis if they valued their livelihood. Especially Thalburg's teachers—who formed the social and cultural elite of the town— found themselves drawn into support of the NSDAP almost immediately. As other Thalburgers flocked to the Nazi bandwagon in the spring of 1933, and as terror and distrust became apparent, there was practically no possibility of resistance to Hitler.

Beyond this, the Nazis took considerable action to strengthen support, especially in the early months. There were the constant parades and meetings which gave the impression of irresistible enthusiasm and approval. There was the vigor in the economic area which more than anything else seemed to justify the dictatorship. But in addition to Nazi efforts on their own behalf, there were other factors that favored them. Many signs indicate that the depression was slowly curing itself by 1933. Moreover, there was the public works money allocated under the previous regime, but available just as the Nazis came to power. And one should probably also take into account the fact that the essential work of establishing the dictatorship came during the spring—a time when enthusiasm seems appropriate and revolution not wholly unnatural.

Thus many factors combined to make Nazism a possibility for Thalburg. At the same time the town itself influenced the nature of Nazism as it manifested itself locally. It seems probable, for example, that the general lack of violence during the first months of the Third Reich was due to the nature of Thalburg as a small town. Much as the Nazis hated all that the Socialists stood for, both sides knew each other too well for cold and systematic violence to occur. The SA might be willing to pummel their neighbors in a street fight, but they seemed to shrink from attacking the Socialists when they were defenseless. This is not to say that no violence took place, but it does help explain the fact that no one was killed and no one sent to a concentration camp from Thalburg during the early years of the Nazi regime. On the one occasion when Kurt Aergeyz seemed determined to turn the Stormtroopers loose on Karl Hengst and his little tobacco store, it was not members of the Thalburg SA who were to do the dirty work; truckloads of Stormtroopers from another town were imported for the occasion. The subsequent relationship of Hengst and Aergeyz substantiates this again; it was hard for even the worst fanatic to be utterly ruthless against someone who had grown up in the same block with him.

The smallness of Thalburg, the fact that many families had known each other for generations undoubtedly modified the nature of the mature dictatorship. The Nazis could come and go but the "Club for the Defense of Old Thalburg Privileges"—composed of old city dwellers of every hue in the political spectrum—continued to meet and work together to make sure they would receive their annual ration of free beer, their 18 marks' worth of wood from the town forest.[4] There were other things that seemed to stay the same after Hitler came to power. While the Nazis claimed uniqueness for their charity efforts, it can be shown that Thalburgers gave just as much to their various separate charity organizations before 1933. While the Nazis felt they were doing something new by bringing the Army to Thalburg, it should be remembered that the love of the military was something that Thalburg had been noted for long before Kurt Aergeyz ever thought about it.

In fact, in many ways Aergeyz and his Nazi administration were simply the embodiment of the small-town chauvinism that Thalburg displayed in the pre-Nazi period. When it came to a choice between Nazi ideals and promoting Thalburg as a tourist center, Aergeyz had no hesitation. If important visitors came to Thalburg, he made sure they were lodged in the Hotel Georg-Friedrich, because it was the best hotel in town, even if its owner was a leading Nationalist party member and a master of the forbidden freemasons.[5] On the other hand, there were Thalburgers who saw nothing new in Nazism, except possibly the chance to put into effect policies they had hoped for over a long period. To several leading members of the Thalburg shooting societies, for example, the introduction of the Hitler regime meant simply that they could now have their 300-meter target range. To several of the town's businessmen, Nazism simply meant that now was the time to promote the concept that Thalburgers ought to do their shopping at home.

Finally, it is possible to construe the actions of Kurt Aergeyz after he came to power as expressive of the class divisions of Thalburg. Nothing is more difficult to discover than the truth about personal motivation, but many of the actions taken by Aergeyz and his closest friends suggest that they were a product of social resentment. Aergeyz was of the lower middle class and this undoubtedly made its mark upon him in a town where government and society were dominated by an elite which freely expressed its cool sense of superiority over the *petite bourgeoisie* as well as over the workers. When the Nazis came to power in Thalburg they destroyed the SPD and its sub-organizations and hounded Socialist leaders, but this is explicable because of the intransigent political opposition between Nazism and Social Democracy. What Aergeyz wanted of the Socialists was that they be rendered impotent, not degraded (except insofar as this would produce a sense of political futility). Thus he was capable of producing one of his rare smiles when a common worker defied him; when he attempted to harass Karl Hengst's brother, Hengst was able to stop this by telling Aergeyz: "Look, if you want someone to pick on, try me— but leave my family alone." [6] This Aergeyz respected; what he hated were the upper classes of the town. In this he was seconded by his clique. As Otto Made once said of Walther Timmerlah: "An honest Communist is more to my liking than such a *Scheiss-Akademiker*." [7]

As a result, Aergeyz did things to the town's elite which he never did to outright political opponents. The methods used in the long and sordid process of ousting Mayor Johns were as unnecessary as they were disgusting. The attempt to degrade Dieter Thomas falls in the same category. Aergeyz's treatment of the shooting societies and the Retail Merchants' Association went beyond customary "coordination"; they were a measure of his contempt. The same approach characterized all of his relationships with the town's upper crust, Wilhelm Spatel of the GHC being the most conspicuous example. The final expression of this attitude was in Aergeyz's struggle against the church, which was more bitterly pursued in Thalburg than in most other places in Germany. By attacking the citadel of the town's respectability with such extreme means and degrading methods, Kurt Aergeyz was possibly attempting to triumph over the environment in which he had grown up and which had condemned him previously to the condescension of his social betters.

This is not to say that the Nazi dictatorship affected only a few in Thalburg. Ultimately almost every Thalburger came to understand the Third Reich. Most Thalburgers learned what a dictatorship meant when they sensed the general breakdown of trust and social communication. All became aware of it when Hitler's policies brought war to them. Despite the super-patriotism in the pre-Nazi years, there was no cheering in the streets when the Thalburg battalion marched out of town in 1939. The war brought hunger with it, especially after 1945, and the sons of many Thalburgers learned to temper their love of militarism on the cold steppes of Russia.

But no one foresaw these consequences in the days when Thalburg's middle class was voting overwhelmingly for the introduction of the Third Reich. And that, perhaps, is the most significant lesson of all to be gained from Thalburg's experiences during and prior to the Nazi seizure of power. Hardly anyone in Thalburg in those days grasped what was happening. There was no real comprehension of what the town would experience if Hitler came to power, no real understanding of what Nazism was.

The Social Democrats failed to comprehend the nature of the Nazi appeal. So did the Jews and Lutherans, both of whom were to suffer bitterly under the Nazi whip, and even the convinced members of the NSDAP itself, such as Walther Timmerlah. Each group saw one or the other side of Nazism, but none saw it in its full hideousness. Only later did this become apparent, and even then not to everyone. The problem of Nazism was primarily a problem of perception. In this respect Thalburg's difficulties and Thalburg's fate are likely to be shared by other men in other towns under similar circumstances. The remedy will not easily be found.

Appendices

APPENDIX A

A DESCRIPTIVE LIST OF INDIVIDUALS INTERVIEWED
FOR THIS BOOK, WITH THEIR PSEUDONYMS

Order of information: occupation, political leanings, religion, age, chief activities, other.

Hans Abbenrode	Grade school principal, voted middle-of-the-road. Lutheran, aged 38 in 1930.
Franz von Altberg	County Prefect, 1932-45, member of the People's party. Lutheran, aged 42 in 1930. A professional government official of considerable ability.
Maria Armkerl	Wife of a high school teacher who was a member of the People's party. Lutheran, aged 35 in 1930. Her husband was a Freemason and a veteran of World War I.
Willi Brehm	Minor civil servant in the employ of the county, member of the Social Democratic party. Lutheran, aged 27 in 1930. Prominent leader of the local *Reichsbanner*.
Rudolf Fischer	High school principal, member of the Nationalist party. Lutheran, aged 42 in 1930. University graduate.
Karl Hengst	Small businessman (retail merchant), one of the local leaders of the Social Democratic party. Lutheran, aged 43 in 1930. Member of the City Council. Senator, delegate to the County Council. Veteran of World War I.
Erhardt Knorpel	Newspaper reporter for the *Thalburger Neueste Nachrichten* (a moderate newspaper), voted People's party. Lutheran, aged 38 in 1930. Veteran of World War I.
Heinrich Lamme	Assistant director of a private bank, voted for the Democratic party. Lutheran, aged 27 in 1930.
Hans Leidler	Semi-skilled railroad worker and union leader, active member of the Social Democratic party. Atheist, aged 31 in 1930. Leader of the *Reichsbanner* in a

	small suburb immediately adjacent to Thalburg, works council member at the Thalburg railroad station.
Otto Made	Owner of a dry goods store, member of the Nazi party and of the SS. Nominal Lutheran, aged 30 in 1930. Later a Senator for Thalburg. Veteran of World War I.
Ernst Meier	Semi-skilled laborer in City Gas Works, union leader, active member of the Social Democratic party. Nominal Catholic, aged 48 in 1930. Past member of Thalburg City Council. Veteran of World War I and holder of the Iron Cross, First Class.
Anna Moeller	Wife of the town's chief historian and author, Anton Moeller. Slightly right-of-center in political beliefs. Lutheran, aged 33 in 1930.
Gregor Rosenthal	Professional man, member of the Democratic party. Jewish, aged 45 in 1930. Veteran of and wounded in World War I.
Benno Schmidt	Unskilled day laborer, mostly for the city labor pool. Leftist, though never an actual member of the Social Democratic party. Nominal Catholic, aged 28 in 1930.
Eva Spatel	Wife of the owner-editor of the *Gräfische Hofs-Curier,* a rightist newspaper. Voted for the Nationalist party, of which her husband was an active member. Lutheran, aged 48 in 1933.
Hugo Spiessmann	Civil servant, director of City Savings Bank, rightist political convictions. Lutheran, aged 45 in 1930. Veteran of World War I.
Dieter Thomas	Civil servant in city administration, member of the Democratic party. Lutheran, aged 30 in 1930.
Walther Timmerlah	Owner of a bookstore, member of the Nazi party (first person in Thalburg to join the Nazi party, but left it after 1933). Lutheran, aged 43 in 1930. Former teacher in South America. An intellectual.
Kurt Zeisser	Printer's apprentice and member of the Hitler Youth. Nominal Lutheran, aged 13 in 1930.

APPENDIX B

TABLES, GRAPHS, AND CHARTS

Table I: Unemployment, Thalburg Employment Office District, 1930–1933

Table 2: Unemployment, City of Thalburg, 1930–1933

Table 3: Unemployment, City of Thalburg, 1930—1933
(Parentheses Indicate Incomplete Figures)

	Unemployment Pay	Emergency Pay	Welfare Pay	Total
1930				
January	313	16	?	(329)
February	297	18	?	(315)
March	264	18	?	(282)
April	200	19	?	(219)
May	159	19	?	(178)
June	175	15	82	272
July	(149)	(22)	82	(253)
August	151	36	47	234
September	178	33	(75)	(286)
October	271	31	102	404
November	189	26	97	312
December	298	42	97	437
1931				
January	296	61	103	460
February	281	69	110	460
March	313	78	114	505
April	304	87	114	505
May	224	101	125	450
June	191	102	107	400
July	162	115	111	388
August	152	143	114	409
September	159	143	113	415
October	147	145	126	418
November	147	152	136	435
December	159	141	165	465
1932				
January	219	186	202	607
February	231	199	222	652

Table 3 (cont.)

	Unemployment Pay	Emergency Pay	Welfare Pay	Total
1932 (cont.)				
March	250	217	237	704
April	239	220	282	741
May	168	202	273	643
June	132	207	288	627
July	(103)	(193)	303	(599)
August	73	179	328	580
September	61	160	283	504
October	53	152	298	503
November	65	128	273	466
December	69	112	306	487
1933				
January	?	?	317	(317)
February	107	199	321	627
March	?	?	317	(317)
April	88	160	296	544
May	56	159	266	481
June	60	163	245	468

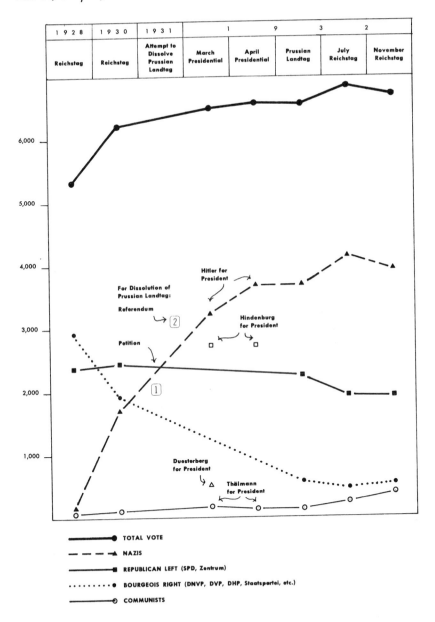

1 9 2 8	1 9 3 0	1 9 3 1	1	9	3	2	
Reichstag	Reichstag	Attempt to Dissolve Prussian Landtag	March Presidential	April Presidential	Prussian Landtag	July Reichstag	November Reichstag

For Dissolution of Prussian Landtag:

Referendum

Hitler for President

Hindenburg for President

Petition

Duesterberg for President

Thälmann for President

- ●— **TOTAL VOTE**
- ▲-- **NAZIS**
- ■— **REPUBLICAN LEFT (SPD, Zentrum)**
- ●····· **BOURGEOIS RIGHT (DNVP, DVP, DHP, Staatspartei, etc.)**
- ⊖— **COMMUNISTS**

Table 4: National Elections in Thalburg, 1928–1932

Table 5: National Elections in Thalburg, 1928–1933

Election	NSDAP	DNVP	DHP	Staats-partei	DVP	Zentrum	SPD	KPD	Other	Total
Reichstag 1928	123	475	455	505*	834	170	2210	28	572	5372
Reichstag 1930	1742	320	271	246	788	184	2246	115	275	6169

Petition to Dissolve Prussian Landtag
April 1931   Signers: 2246   Backed by NSDAP, DVP, DNVP, KPD, DHP, Staatspartei, and splinters

Referendum to Dissolve Prussian Landtag
August 1931   "Ja": 3333
              "Nein": 253 (not voting counts as "Nein")

	Hitler	Duesterberg	Hindenburg	Thälmann	Winter	Total
Presidential Vote #1 March 1932	3261	240	2789	182	22	6494
Presidential Vote #2 April 1932	3696	—	2777	127	—	6600

NSDAP-DNVP Coalition

Backed by DVP, SPD, Zentrum, Staatspartei, and splinters

Prussian Landtag April 1932	3620	202	62	105	154	175	2024	117	126	6585
Reichstag July 1932	4195	212	41	66	69	191	1639	285	32	6730
Reichstag November 1932	3928	301	51	34	136	176	1627	338	37	6628
Reichstag 1933	4268	406	62	67	101	183	1470	228	17	6802

* Includes Democrats who thereafter voted DVP, SPD, or NSDAP.
NSDAP—Nazis, DNVP—Nationalists, DHP—Hannoverians, DVP—People's Party, Zentrum—Catholic Center, SPD—Social Democrats, KPD—Communists

Table 6: Political Meetings in Thalburg, 1930–1933

	Nazis	Nationalists	Socialists	Others
1930				
January	1	0	1	0
February	2	0	0	0
March	5	0	1	0
April	1	0	1	0
May	2	0	1	0
June	3	0	1	0
July	0	0	1	0
August	4	0	4	0
September (Reichstag Election)	3	1	2	3
October	3	0	0	1
November	4	0	1	0
December	2	0	2	0
1931				
January	2	0	2	0
February	4	1	5	1
March	2	2	2	1
April (Petition to Dissolve Prussian Landtag)	2	1	2	2
May	3	0	1	0
June	1	1	4	0
July	2	0	3	0
August (Referendum to Dissolve Prussian Landtag)	3	0	2	2
September	2	2	0	0
October	2	0	0	0
November	3	0	0	1
December	2	0	2	0
1932				
January	2	2	3	0
February	2	2	2	3

Table 6 (cont.)

	Nazis	Nationalists	Socialists	Others
March (First Presidential Election)	5	2	3	1
April (Second Presidential and Prussian Landtag Elections)	5	2	4	4
May	4	0	1	0
June	3	0	1	0
July (Reichstag Election)	6	1	5	3
August	0	0	0	0
September	2	1	0	0
October	4	1	1	0
November (Reichstag Election)	1	1	2	0
December	3	1	1	0
1933				
January (Hitler Becomes Chancellor)	3	0	1	1
February	4	2	1	1
March (Reichstag and Local Elections)	12	1	0	0
April	6	1	0	0
May	6	0	0	0
June	6	0	0	0
July	4	1	0	0
August	5	1	0	0
September	7	0	0	0
October	5	0	0	0
November (Reichstag Election and Plebiscite)	7	0	0	0
December	2	0	0	0

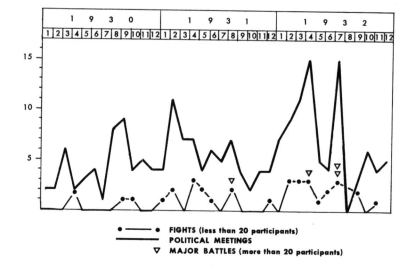

Table 7: Political Meetings and Political Fights in
Thalburg, 1930–1932

	JAN	FEB	MAR	APR	MAY	JUN	JUL	AUG	SEP	OCT	NOV	DEC
1 9 3 0	3	6 7	5 8 11 13 14	5	10 11	4 13 14		9 10 11 12	12 13 13	11 12 13	6 12 13 14	13 14
1 9 3 1	8 9	4 7 8 11	5 14	7 14	6 9 11	14	12 13	12 13 13	4 14	4 14	10 11 14	2 14
1 9 3 2	7 14	6 12	7 8 9 10 11	1 10 11 11 14	10 13 14 14	2 14 14	5 8 12 12 14 14		9 13	1 3 14 14	3	14 14 14
1 9 3 3	12 14 14											

Table 8: Topics at Nazi Meetings in Thalburg, 1930–1933
Numbers refer to subjects: 1—Pensions (2); 2—Christianity (2); 3—Capitalism (3); 4—Youth (4); 5—Jews (4); 6—Foreign Policy (4); 7—Civil Servants and Middle Class (5); 8—Militarism (5); 9—The Republic or "System" (5); 10—General Economics (6); 11—"Marxism"—the SPD (10); 12—History and Theory of Nazism (10); 13—Unclassifiable (12); 14—Pure Pageantry (26).

Table 9: Terror Activities in Thalburg,
January 31, 1933–June 31, 1933, As Reported by the Local Press

	House Searchings	Arrests
February 3	"at homes of Communists"	——————
March 1	"at Communists and Socialists"	one Socialist
March 2	"at a Communist's home"	one Communist
March 6	——————	seven Communists
March 14	——————	one Socialist
March 29	——————	one Socialist, one Communist
April 4	"at several homes"	four "Leftists"
April 8	"at several homes"	——————
April 10	"at several homes"	——————
April 19	"at several homes"	——————
April 24	"at one home"	one
April 28	"at one home"	one
May 5	"at several offices"	——————
May 9	——————	one "worker"
May 12	"at SPD offices"	——————
June 2	"at Liga fuer Mütterschuetz"	——————
June 17	——————	one SPD Councilman
June 19	——————	one woman "Communist"
June 21	"at a Rightist office"	——————
June 24	"at Union offices"	——————
June 30	——————	one "worker"
Total	14 different occasions	22 persons

Note: This table shows only those actions reported in the press. Actual arrests and searchings were more numerous.

APPENDIX C

THE THALBURG NSDAP

A Formal Statement to the *Gauleitung* in defense of the assertion that "Dreadful Conditions Prevail in Local Group Thalburg of the NSDAP."
Submitted by Party-Comrade Heinrich Trautmann, (Number —), in Thalburg, June 20, 1933.

On Friday, June 16, 1933, *Kreisleiter* Walter Eckstein and *Ortsgruppenleiter* Kurt Aergeyz demanded to know why I used the expression "dreadful conditions in the Local Group." In repsonse to this I am sending the following formal statement to the *Gauleitung*.

1) *Financial Matters.* I accuse the *Ortsgruppenleiter* of not having assured the necessary cleanliness and order in party finances. On the contrary; he attempted to hinder this in many cases.
a) In the case of the irregularities in the Women's Group Thalburg, Party-Comradess A, he made the statement "I shall permit no clarification in this matter." (Witness: Party-Comrade D)
b) The receipts demanded by Party-Comrades E and F when they were examining the books last December, concerning election campaign expenditures, contributions, receipts from membership applications, etc., were never made available. (Refer report of Party-Comrade F to the *Gau-Uschla*)
c) In December of last year many Party-Comrades met at the home of Party-Comrade C, discussed this, and laid the complaint before the *Ortsgruppenleiter*. He declared criticism to be healthy and asked for further cooperation in this sense. A few weeks later, on January 1, 1933, he expelled those Party-Comrades for plotting. (Witness: Party-Comrades C and Tiere)
d) In January, 1933, the *Ortsgruppenleiter* called together a commission for the purpose of examining ways of covering debts incurred. Present were Party-Comrades B, C, H, D, I, and J. The *Ortsgruppenleiter* was not present because of sickness, but was represented through his brother. The commission unanimously declared they would undertake nothing until a list of the debts, an explanation of how they were incurred, and a plan for the covering of them was presented. The commission was therefore never called again. The will to positive cooperation on the part of the members of the abortive commission is shown by the collections undertaken by them and the gifts made by them in connection with the election of March 5, 1933.

e) Concerning the holding back of registrations from the months of June, July, and August, 1932, and the incorrect acceptance of donations, see my complaint to the *Gauleitung* of June 11, 1933.

f) To cover the debts of the Local Group, the *Ortsgruppenleiter* raised the monthly dues by 50 pfg/mo. without having the approval of a Local Group meeting. In consideration of the financial misuses, many Party-Comrades refused to pay this.

g) The *Ortsgruppenleiter* demanded that every Party-Comrade in our Local Group make a special donation of at least RM 10.00 (see the enclosed). This was done arbitrarily.

h) On the same basis extra high entrance fees were demanded of new applicants, which were paid by most of them, since they feared that otherwise they would not be admitted to the NSDAP.

i) The present treasurer of the Local Group, Party-Comrade K, is reputed to have refused to do more than certify the amount of cash on hand when he took over that office because he did not want to be made responsible for his predecessor's malfeasance. I ask him to stand witness to this.

2) *Unscrupulousness in the Choice of Methods.*

a) On January 12, 1933, the *Ortsgruppenleiter* told the *Orts-Uschla* Chairman, Party-Comrade E, that he had been relieved of his post by action of the *Gauleitung* and the *Gau-Uschla*. This was untrue. (Witness: Party-Comrade E)

b) Twice, on January 19 and January 28, 1933, the *Ortsgruppenleiter* asked the *Orts-Uschla* chairman, Party-Comrade E, to sign the expulsion of Party-Comrades Tiere and C, and of Party-Comradesses L, M, and N, in spite of the fact that an *Uschla* trial had never occurred and in spite of the fact that he had already on January 12 declared Party-Comrade E removed from his office.

c) Shortly thereafter the *Ortsgruppenleiter* asked a member of the *Orts-Uschla* (Party-Comrade O) to sign alleged minutes of an *Orts-Uschla* trial according to which Party-Comradesses L and M were expelled from the Party, although such an *Uschla* trial had never occurred. Party-Comrade O refused to do this.

d) Later the *Ortsgruppenleiter* demanded that the documents concerning the case of Party-Comrade P be surrendered to him. This was refused. (Witness: Party-Comrade O) (See below)

e) The gravest suspicion exists that the *Ortsgruppenleiter* sets Party-Comrades to spying on other Party-Comrades who don't comply with his wishes. I ask the City Inspector, Party-Comrade Q, to say whether or not he was requested to spy on Party-Comrade R. But assure Party-Comrade Q that he won't lose his job, for the city employees stand under the constant dread of the dictatorial methods of the *Ortsgruppenleiter*, since, if they oppose him in any way, they will lose their bread. (See below)

f) At the election of the Senators, the City Councillors expressed objections to the choice of Party-Comrade Blanck because, owing to his fraudulent and illegal activities (of which I call Party-Comrade S to bear witness), he had a bad reputation. The *Ortsgruppenleiter* declared "I need Blanck as a fighter. The era of Mayor Johns is absolutely finished. Blanck will be the one to drive his fist to the Mayor's heart." And when the Councillors still refused to do as he wished, the *Ortsgruppenleiter* declared: "As *Ortsgruppenleiter* I declare that Blanck is Senator." (Witness: Party-Comrade G)

g) Shortly thereafter, the *Ortsgruppenleiter* said to the witness above, Party-Comrade G, a City Councillor: "If you won't obey, then you'll have to resign. You'll be surprised! I'll soon publish the first article against you in the newspaper. If you won't obey, I'll have your tavern boycotted and Tiere (Speaker of the Council) will be transferred to East Prussia" (Party-Comrade Tiere is a teacher). (Witness: Party-Comrade G)

h) A similar situation developed at the election for the Chamber of Industry and Trade. I refer to the complaint sent by Party-Comrade T to the *Gauleitung*.

3) *Untruthfulness of the Ortsgruppenleiter.* The *Ortsgruppenleiter* has a bad reputation for lack of truthfulness in Thalburg. He himself once said to Party-Comrade Tiere: "What is 'word of honor'? I recognize no word of honor." Here are some examples with evidence:

a) See cases 2 a, b, and c.

b) See cases 2 a, b, and c.

c) On January 30, 1933, he told Party-Comradess M that the *Gauleitung* had demanded her expulsion. The *Gauleitung* knows best that this is untrue.

d) A few weeks ago Party-Comrade P declared that the *Ortsgruppenleiter* lied not once but many times. He told Party-Comrade Blanck to tell that to the *Ortsgruppenleiter*. Thereupon the *Ortsgruppenleiter* sought out Party-Comrade P and struck this man, 25 years his senior, to the ground. (See the complaint of Party-Comrade P to the *Gauleitung*.) To me, the *Ortsgruppenleiter* said on June 16: "I shouldn't have just knocked P down. I should have beaten him across the Market Square with a dog whip. And those other pigs who are spreading vulgar rumors about me will get even worse. The next in line is D."

e) While he constantly protected the then leader of the Women's Group, Party-Comradess A, and declared: "I shall permit no clarification in this matter," he said privately to Party-Comrade U: "You're right, Frau A is guilty of everything."

f) An inner untruthfulness is at least extant if the *Ortsgruppenleiter* at the burning of the "Filth Literature" on the Market raged against the Jews while his own sister is married to a Jewish Lawyer in [a neighboring town] without the *Ortsgruppenleiter* having ever ceased his friendly traffic with her.

4) *The Ortsgruppenleiter Permits Corruption and Graft.* Since the *Magistrat*

in Thalburg has consisted of four National Socialist Senators one often hears the judgment: "The Nazis understand corruption and graft better than the reds."

a) The Senators voted themselves a salary of RM 50.00/month each, through the *Ortsgruppenleiter* previously declared the offices of Senator and Councillor to be purely honorary. The City Councillors have raised protest against this. (Witness: Party-Comrade C)

b) The *Ortsgruppenleiter* arranged to have his father-in-law, in whose leather goods store he works, get the contract for the boots for the Labor Service camp. (Witness: Party-Comrade D)

c) The *Ortsgruppenleiter* arranged for his brother, who has an iron goods store and who long ago ceased dealing in glassware, to be awarded the contract for beer glasses at the City Brewery. One of the *Ortsgruppenleiter's Dezernate* is the Brewery. (Witness: Party-Comrade Tiere)

d) The *Ortsgruppenleiter* arranged for his brother to be awarded the contract for garden chairs at the Brewery, although another ironmonger, Party-Comrade V, submitted a cheaper bid for the order. (Witness: Party-Comrade Tiere)

e) The *Ortsgruppenleiter* arranged for his brother to receive the order for caster-wardrobes for the city, although his brother does not stock such items and though other Party-Comrades in the town do. (Witness: Party-Comrade Tiere)

f) Senator Blanck arranged to have the city drop its milk delivery contract with Party-Comrade W despite the fact that the contract with W was very favorable for the town. Blanck's intention was to obtain the contract for himself.

5) *The Ortsgruppenleiter is not a True National Socialist.*

a) Party-Comrade Aergeyz has belonged to the Party for a long time but was never active until March 1, 1931, when he appeared at a members' meeting and immediately took upon himself the office of deputy *Ortsgruppenleiter*. The general judgment is that he is motivated solely by ambition. Evidence includes a statement of his made last year: "If I don't become *Ortsgruppenleiter* then I'll go over to the others and oppose the Nazis, and then I'll give the *Gauleitung* a piece of my mind." (Witness: Party-Comrades Tiere and Y) One assumes that the goal of his ambition is to become mayor.

b) Party-Comrade Aergeyz sees only the power and not the responsibility involved in the *Fuehrer*-Principle. He wants to rule in dictatorial fashion and considers any criticism as sabotage or intrigue. (Witnesses: Party-Comrades Tiere and C) He does not want capable men as fellow workers—only tools.

c) As a result of his power as Brewery Senator, the *Ortsgruppenleiter* fired 25 city employees at the Brewery because they belonged to the SPD, although the *Fuehrer* has said that membership in the SPD or *Reichsbanner* is not sufficient grounds for firing people. The *Regierungspraesident* objected to this move. (Witness: Party-Comrade Tiere) I put it to the *Ortsgruppenleiter* on June 16 that this action was not in the spirit of National Socialism which wants to see the *Volk*-community of all Germans. He replied that " '*Volk*-community' was just a nice word." It was much more important, he said, to provide bread for the SA people who had been lying in the streets for years; with the word "*Volk*-community" you couldn't fill their bellies. At a special meeting last night the *Ortsgruppenleiter* mentioned this and said there were groups who wanted to put the newly employed SA people back into the streets. The SA leaders should tell their men about this and then let them decide whether it should be handled in a Christian way. (Witness: Party-Comrade Z) I find this kind of inciting of the SA against their comrades and twisting of my statement to be in opposition to the spirit of National Socialism.

I respectfully request that the *Gauleitung* investigate these charges and clear up the situation in Thalburg.

Heil Hitler!
(signed) Heinrich Trautmann
Number, titles, etc.

NOTES

CHAPTER ONE

THE SETTING

1. Roger H. Wells, *German Cities: A Study of Contemporary Municipal Politics and Administration* (Princeton, 1932), p. 25.
2. *Thalburg, 700 Jahre Stadt, 1252-1952. Ein Festbuch zur 700-Jahrfeier* (Thalburg, 1952), pp. 17-18, 74-75; *Thalburg: Ein Fuehrer durch Vergangenheit und Gegenwart* (Thalburg, 1938); *Die wirtschaftliche Entwicklung der Stadt Thalburg vom Mittelalter bis zum ersten Weltkrieg* (Thalburg, 1960).
3. *Thalburg. Fuehrer durch Thalburg und Umgebung, herausgegeben vom Verein für Fremdenverkehr* (Thalburg, 1909), p. 41; *Thalburg 1933-36: Im Auftrag des Burgermeisters auf Grund der Berichte der einzelnen Abteilungen der Verwaltung dargestellt. Die Stadt Thalburg und ihre Verwaltung 1933-1936* (ms., Thalburg, 1936); *Chronik der Stadt Thalburg, 1932. Thalburg einst und jetzt* (Thalburg, 1932).
4. *Chronik des Standortes Thalburg* by Stabszahlenmeister Oessel and Zahlenmeister Borgholte (ms., Thalburg, August 26, 1939).
5. *Thalburg: Ein Fuehrer . . . , 1938*, p. 18.
6. *Die wirtschaftliche Entwicklung . . . ,* p. 12.
7. *Chronik des Standortes Thalburg,* pp. 27-33.
8. *Thalburg: Ein Fuehrer . . . , 1938*, p. 24.
9. *Thalburger Neueste Nachrichten*, March 1, 1932. (This newspaper will henceforth be cited "TNN.")

CHAPTER TWO

THE ANATOMY OF THE TOWN

1. *Thalburg, 700 Jahre* . . . , pp. 76-78; *Die wirtschaftliche Entwicklung* . . . , p. 14.
2. *Graefische Hofs-Curier,* October 7, 1932. This newspaper will henceforth be cited "GHC."
3. Interview with Franz von Altberg (County Prefect, member of the People's party, Lutheran, aged 42 in 1930; a professional government official of considerable ability). Also: Interview with Otto Made (owner of a dry goods store, member of the Nazi party and of the SS, nominal Lutheran, aged 30 in 1930; later a Senator for Thalburg; veteran of World War I).
4. Interview with Hans Abbenrode (grade school principal, voted middle-of-the-road. Lutheran, aged 38 in 1930).
5. TNN: April 25, 1930; January 1, 1933.
6. This and the table to note 12 were calculated from the town address book: *Einwohnerbuch der Stadt und des Landkreis Thalburg* (Thalburg, 1932).
7. TNN: September 10, 1931.
8. TNN: October 4, 1930; "Vorbericht," *Rechnungsabschluss der Stadtsparkasse Thalburg für den 31. Dez. 1930* (Thalburg, 1930), ms. in County Savings Bank archives.
9. TNN: January 10, 1930; November 1, 1930; May 6, 1931.
10. TNN: October 22, 1930.
11. Material on the economic structure of the town is derived essentially from sources cited in Chapter One, especially *Thalburg 700 Jahre* . . . Also, interview with Hugo Spiessmann (civil servant, director of City Savings Bank, rightist political convictions, Lutheran, aged 54 in 1930).
12. See above, note 6.
13. Notarized declaration made for *Entschädigungs Behörden* by Ernst Meier (semi-skilled laborer in city gas works, union leader, active member of the Social Democratic party, nominal Catholic, aged 48 in 1930, past member of Thalburg City Council, veteran of World War I and holder of the Iron Cross, First Class).
14. Notarized declaration made for *Entschädigungs Behörden* by Gregor Rosenthal (professional man, member of the Democratic party, Jewish, aged 45 in 1930, veteran of and wounded in World War I).
15. *Volksblatt:* November 13, 1930; November 21, 1932; TNN: November 18, 1931; October 18, 1933.
16. TNN: February 6, 1933.

17. Interview with Erhardt Knorpel (newspaper reporter for the *Thalburger Neueste Nachrichten,* a moderate newspaper; voted People's party, Lutheran, aged 38 in 1930; veteran of World War I).
18. GHC: December 1, 1931; March 6, 1932; April 6, 1932; TNN: January 13, 1932; *Volksblatt:* September 11, 1930; January 4, 1932.
19. Interview with the former chairman. Also, TNN: July 22, 1930.
20. Interview with Kurt Zeisser (printer's apprentice and member of the Hitler Youth, nominal Lutheran, aged 13 in 1930).
21. TNN: July 21, 1930.
22. TNN: February 3, 1930.
23. Interview with Erhardt Knorpel.
24. Interview with Hans Abbenrode.
25. *Ibid.*
26. GHC: October 7, 1930.
27. Interview with Kurt Zeisser; interview with Rudolf Fischer (high school principal, member of the Nationalist party, Lutheran, aged 42 in 1930, university graduate).
28. Interview with Erhardt Knorpel.
29. An invented name with which I have tried to capture the hopelessly antique impression given by the GHC's true name.
30. *Chronik der Stadt . . . ,* pp. 46-48.
31. Interview with Willi Brehm (minor civil servant in the employ of the county, member of the Social Democratic party, Lutheran, aged 27 in 1930, prominent leader of the local *Reichsbanner*).
32. *Hört! Hört!,* "Nachrichtenblatt der NSDAP Thalburg," No. 1, August 8, 1931. 15 *pfennig*/copy. The *Echo* sold for 20 *pfennig.*
33. Circulation estimates from Erhardt Knorpel and Eva Spatel (wife of the owner-editor of the GHC, voted for the Nationalist party of which her husband was an active member, Lutheran, aged 48 in 1933).
34. TNN: August 16, 1930; *Haushaltspläne der Stadt Thalburg, 1930-35* (ms. in City Archives, published yearly). For material on the city government see Wells, *op. cit.,* pp. 34-51, 119-129, 257-258.

CHAPTER THREE

ENTER THE NAZIS

1. Interview with Erhardt Knorpel, Hans Abbenrode, and Heinrich Lamme (assistant director of a private bank, voted for the Democratic party, Lutheran, aged 27 in 1930). On the SPD and the status quo, see Chapter Four.
2. Interview with Erhardt Knorpel, Otto Made, Hans Abbenrode, and Heinrich Lamme. *Rechnungsabschlusse der Stadtsparkasse Thalburg,*

1930-1933 (ms. in Kreissparkasse Thalburg). Also, *Thalburg 1933-36 . . .* , Tables: "Sparkasse 1 und 2" and Table to page 89 (no title).
3. Interviews with Heinrich Lamme and Hugo Spiessmann.
4. TNN: November 17, 1929; September 15, 1930.
5. Interview with Erhardt Knorpel, Heinrich Lamme, Karl Hengst (small businessman, one of the local leaders of the Social Democratic party, Lutheran, aged 43 in 1930, member of the City Council, Senator, delegate to the County Council, veteran of World War I), and Walther Timmerlah (owner of a bookstore, first person in Thalburg to join the Nazi party but left it in 1933, Lutheran, aged 43 in 1930, former teacher in South America, an intellectual). Also, TNN: January 16, 1930; February 15, 26, 1930; March 11, 1930; GHC: January 17, 1930; February 16, 27, 1930; March 2, 15, 1930.
6. Interview with Maria Armkerl (wife of a high school teacher who was a member of the People's party, Lutheran, aged 35 in 1930; her husband was a Freemason and a veteran of World War I).
7. Interview with Walther Timmerlah.
8. Interview with Dieter Thomas (civil servant in city administration, member of the Democratic party, Lutheran, aged 30 in 1930).
9. Interview with Maria Armkerl.
10. *Volksblatt:* March 26, 1930; Resolution of the Thalburg County Conference of the *Reichsbanner.*
11. TNN: April 16, 19, 1930.
12. TNN: March 20, 1930.
13. TNN: April 22, 1930.
14. GHC: April 26, 29, 1930; TNN: April 28, 1930.
15. TNN: April 29, 1930; *Volksblatt:* May 1, 1930.
16. TNN: May 17, 19, 1930; GHC: May 18, 1930.
17. GHC: May 16, 1930.
18. GHC: May 25, 1930; June 1, 14, 1930.
19. GHC: June 22, 1930; July 1, 2, 1930; TNN: June 30, 1930.
20. TNN: June 23, 25, 27, 1930; *Volksblatt:* June 27, 28, 1930.
21. *Volksblatt:* July 6, 19, 1930; TNN: July 5, 1930; August 29, 1930.
22. *Volksblatt:* July 9, 24, 1930.
23. *Volksblatt:* August 7, 1930; January 25, 26, 1931; TNN: June 26, 1930; August 5, 9, 12, 1930.
24. TNN: August 15, 20, 1930; September 26, 1930.
25. GHC: August 9, 15, 21, 25, 1930; TNN: August 18, 23, 25, 30, 1930.
26. TNN: August 18, 25, 1930; September 2, 4, 1930.
27. TNN: August 14, 25, 1930; September 13, 1930.
28. TNN: September 2, 6, 1930.
29. TNN: August 29, 30, 1930.
30. TNN: July 21, 1930; August 23, 1930; September 10, 1930; *Volksblatt:* September 10, 13, 1930. Interview with Ernst Meier, who was the object of one of the beatings.

31. TNN: September 11, 13, 1930, for the Socialist meeting; TNN: September 8, 10, 1930; GHC: September 17, 1930, for the Nazi meeting.
32. Though I have adopted a positive form of expression in giving the above voting analysis, so as to avoid cluttering sentences with qualifiers, it should be remembered that it is never possible to be absolutely sure where votes come from when the balloting is secret. The method I used to analyze these and other election returns was to calculate the total number of votes lost by all parties (and then by each party), the total gained by all parties (and by each), and then to subtract from the total gained by all parties those votes gained by the non-Nazi parties. The remainder I assumed to be the minimum possible number of votes gained by the Nazis from their opponents. The same process was applied to the "new" votes.

My basic assumption has been that there were no complicated vote shifts, e.g., from the DVP to the SPD or from the SPD to the DNVP. This assumption is based on the fact that the Nazis were the net gainers over the three-year period, and on general political affinities between the bourgeois parties and the NSDAP. For other examples of voting analyses in several other German districts, see Karl Dietrich Bracher, *Die Auflösung der Weimarer Republik. Eine Studie zum Problem des Machtverfalls in der Demokratie* (Stuttgart, 1957), pp. 645-656; and Alfred Milatz, "Das Ende der Parteien im Spiegel der Wahlen 1930 bis 1933" in *Das Ende der Parteien 1933,* herausgegeben von Erich Matthias und Rudolf Morsey (Düsseldorf, 1960), pp. 743-793.

Full figures and a graph of election returns in Thalburg are provided in the Appendix.

CHAPTER FOUR

EXPLOITING VICTORY

1. Interviews with Hans Abbenrode and Maria Armkerl.
2. *Volksblatt:* September 30, 1930.
3. Wells, *op. cit.,* p. 163; TNN: July 1, 1930; November 3, 1930; October 1, 1931; June 28, 1932. See also Erich Roll, *Spotlight on Germany: A Survey of Her Economic and Political Problems* (London, 1933), p. 188.
4. TNN: July 18, 1930; September 11, 24, 1930.
5. TNN: November 5, 1930.
6. *Volksblatt:* September 17, 1930; October 7, 1930.
7. TNN: August 1, 1930; September 9, 1930; *Volksblatt:* September 29, 1930.

8. GHC: September 14, 1930.
9. *Volksblatt:* September 24, 1930.
10. Bertram W. Maxwell, *Contemporary Municipal Government of Germany* (Iowa City, 1928), pp. 11-19; Wells, *op. cit.,* p. 64.
11. TNN: October 21, 23, 25, 1930; GHC: October 24, 1930.
12. TNN: October 24, 1930.
13. TNN: September 24, 25, 1930; October 3, 9, 1930.
14. TNN: October 18, 27, 1930.
15. TNN: November 7, 11, 13, 14, 29, 1930; December 16, 30, 1930; GHC: November 12, 1930; December 7, 1930.
16. TNN: October 6, 1930; November 1, 1930; *Volksblatt:* October 4, 1930.
17. TNN: October 11, 1930; December 12, 1930.
18. TNN: December 22, 23, 1930.
19. TNN: December 22, 1930.
20. *Volksblatt:* November 25, 1930; December 15, 1930; November 21, 1930; December 13, 15, 16, 1930. Also, interview with Willi Brehm.
21. *Volksblatt:* January 12, 1931.
22. *Volksblatt:* January 2, 5, 1931. The attack was unprovoked, the Nazis claiming that they were only trying "to shake the Hengst boy back to the present."
23. TNN: January 6, 1931; *Volksblatt:* January 5, 10, 1931. "Sitzt die Gesellschaft erst einmal drin, ist die Demokratie verloren." The speaker, Johannes Stelling, was subsequently murdered by the SA in June, 1933.
24. TNN: January 9, 1931.
25. TNN: January 16, 1931.
26. TNN: January 19, 23, 1931.
27. *Volksblatt:* January 26, 1931; TNN: January 26, 1931.
28. *Volksblatt:* February 3, 11, 1931.
29. TNN: February 3, 1931; *Volksblatt:* February 9, 10, 1931.
30. *Volksblatt:* February 17, 1931; TNN: February 20, 23, 1931.
31. GHC: February 19, 1931.
32. TNN: February 3, 7, 1931. The original title was "Die Bonzen im Speck, das Volk im Dreck."
33. TNN: February 16, 19, 1931.
34. *Volksblatt:* February 18, 23, 24, 1931; TNN: February 23, 24, 1931.
35. *Volksblatt:* February 14, 1931.
36. TNN: February 26, 1931.
37. GHC: February 27, 1931; *Volksblatt:* February 28, 1931. The original article was from the *Niedersächsische Tageszeitung,* No. 20, November 17, 1930.

CHAPTER FIVE

AUTHORITARIANS UNITE

1. Interviews with Maria Armkerl, Erhardt Knorpel, Heinrich Lamme, and Hans Abbenrode.
2. Interviews with Hugo Spiessmann and Maria Armkerl.
3. Interviews with Willi Brehm and Hans Leidler (semi-skilled railroad worker and union leader, active member of the Social Democratic party, atheist, aged 31 in 1930, leader of the *Reichsbanner* in a small suburb immediately adjacent to Thalburg and works council member at the Thalburg railroad station). Both noticed the prevalence of Nazi-inspired signs such as "Deutscher Kaufmann" in stores and also swastika buttons on store owners' lapels.
4. Interview with Heinrich Lamme and Erhardt Knorpel.
5. Interviews with Ernst Meier, Hans Leidler, Willi Brehm, and Benno Schmidt (unskilled day-laborer, mostly for the city labor-pool; leftist, though never an actual member of the Social Democratic party; nominal Catholic, aged 28 in 1930).
6. Interviews with Erhardt Knorpel, Ernst Meier, Willi Brehm, Hans Leidler, Hans Abbenrode, Benno Schmidt, and Karl Hengst.
7. Interview with Ernst Meier.
8. Interview with Erhardt Knorpel.
9. Interview with Franz von Altberg.
10. GHC: March 7, 1931.
11. TNN: March 12, 1931; GHC: March 22, 1931.
12. GHC: March 21, 1931.
13. *Volksblatt:* March 11, 12, 14, 1931; April 1, 1931.
14. GHC: February 19, 26, 1931; March 18, 1931; April 5, 1931; TNN: February 23, 1931.
15. TNN: March 23, 1931.
16. TNN: March 9, 1931.
17. Interview with Maria Armkerl whose husband was the leader in question.
18. TNN: August 5, 1931.
19. GHC: April 10, 1931.
20. April 13, 16, 1931; *Volksblatt:* April 18, 1931.
21. *Volksblatt:* April 22, 1931; August 12, 1931.
22. *Volksblatt:* March 24, 25, 27, 1931.
23. TNN: April 16, 1931; *Volksblatt:* April 17, 1931.
24. TNN: December 15, 1930; March 20, 1931; April 10, 1931; *Volksblatt:* March 16, 17, 1931.

25. *Volksblatt:* April 9, 17, 21, 1931; TNN: April 20, 1931. The *Jung-banner* wrote to the TNN on April 21 denying the incident of the children going to church: "Religious questions are outside their realm, since their membership includes all faiths. Fights between school children have nothing to do with the *Jungbanner* which has no school children in its ranks."

26. *Volksblatt:* April 1, 3, 1931.

27. GHC: April 16, 20, 1931; TNN: April 20, 22, 1931.

28. TNN: April 2, 9, 14, 1931; July 7, 1931; August 15, 1931; September 29, 1931; May 31, 1933; *Volksblatt:* December 22, 1931; January 5, 1932. Interviews with Hugo Spiessmann, Heinrich Lamme, and Erhardt Knorpel.

29. TNN: April 7, 1931.

30. *Volksblatt:* April 29, 1931; interview with Kurt Zeisser, whose father joined the NSDAP after a threat of boycott about this time.

31. TNN: December 11, 1930.

32. *Volksblatt:* April 11, 1931.

33. GHC: May 2, 1931; TNN: May 1, 1931.

34. GHC: May 10, 17, 1931; TNN: May 11, 1931; *Volksblatt:* May 22, 24, 1931.

35. GHC: May 21, 1931; June 7, 16, 1931.

36. GHC: July 10, 15, 16, 1931.

37. TNN: June 17, 20, 1931; GHC: May 6, 8, 1931.

38. TNN: June 1, 1931.

39. *Volksblatt:* June 3, 4, 9, 1931; TNN: June 3, 5, 1931.

40. TNN: June 8, 1931; *Volksblatt,* June 15, 1931.

41. TNN: June 15, 1931; *Volksblatt:* June 15, 18, 1931.

42. Interview with Heinrich Lamme.

43. *Volksblatt:* July 14, 1931; TNN: July 14, 1931.

44. *Volksblatt:* June 16, 22, 1931; July 8, 1931.

45. For the sickle incident, *Volksblatt:* June 15, 1931. Both the TNN and the GHC denied the story but the *Volksblatt* produced names in verification. See all three issues of June 17, 1931. For the *Reichs-banner* meetings, *Volksblatt:* July 15, 23, 25, 27, 1931; TNN: July 25, 1931.

46. TNN: August 1, 3, 1931.

47. TNN: August 5, 1931; GHC: August 8, 1931.

48. *Volksblatt:* August 7, 8, 1931; TNN: August 3, 1931.

49. Interview with Ernst Meier.

50. Interview with Karl Hengst.

51. *Volksblatt:* April 21, 1931; August 24, 1931; TNN: August 29, 1931. In pronouncing sentence the judge lamented that the law would not permit him to impose stiffer penalties. In December, 1931, the Nazis obtained a retrial before a sympathetic judge who acquitted ten of those previously sentenced and reduced the other sentences to token terms. This was jubilantly reported in the GHC on December 21, 1931.

52. TNN: September 20, 1930.
53. GHC: August 12, 1931; *Volksblatt:* August 14, 1931.
54. TNN: August 3, 1931.
55. *Volksblatt:* August 10, 1931.
56. Reprinted in *Hört! Hört!:* August 15, 1931.
57. TNN: August 10, 1931; October 21, 1931; November 6, 23, 24, 1931; May 13, 1932; GHC: August 11, 1931; November 25, 1931; May 14, 1932; *Volksblatt:* August 11, 1931; November 25, 1931; May 13, 1932. Also, interview with Hans Leidler, a witness on the *Reichsbanner's* side.

CHAPTER SIX

THE DEPTHS OF THE DEPRESSION

1. GHC: August 12, 15, 1931; *Volksblatt:* August 14, 1931.
2. *Hört! Hört!:* No. 1, August 8, 1931.
3. *Volksblatt:* August 8, 15, 1931.
4. *Volksblatt:* June 8, 1931; August 13, 1931; GHC and TNN: August 12, 1931.
5. TNN: August 28, 1931.
6. *Volksblatt:* September 28, 1931; TNN: September 23, 24, 28, 1931.
7. *Volksblatt:* October 22, 1931.
8. TNN: October 6, 7, 17, 1931; November 9, 27, 28, 1931; *Volksblatt:* December 14, 1931.
9. *Volksblatt:* January 28, 1930; February 5, 11, 1930; December 7, 1931.
10. TNN: September 15, 1931; October 8, 1931; January 4, 1932; *Volksblatt:* February 13, 1931.
11. TNN: January 6, 1931; February 12, 1931; September 29, 1931; October 22, 24, 1931; *Volksblatt:* March 31, 1931; December 30, 1931. The manager of the sack factory bought the plant and reopened it ten months later, an encouraging gesture of faith. See TNN: October 7, 1932.
12. TNN: January 4, 1932; December 2, 1932.
13. TNN: November 21, 1931; December 12, 1931.
14. *Rechnungsabschlusse der Stadtsparkasse, op. cit.,* 1930-1933; also, interviews with Heinrich Lamme, Hugo Spiessmann, and Erhardt Knorpel.
15. GHC: August 28, 1931; September 2, 12, 24, 26, 1931.
16. GHC: October 4, 18, 23, 28, 1931. Interviews with Erhardt Knorpel and Heinrich Lamme, both of whom remembered the Feder speech even after twenty-five years.
17. GHC: November 6, 26, 1931; December 23, 1931; TNN: December 9, 1931.
18. GHC: October 12, 1931; interview with Otto Made.

19. TNN: November 27, 1931; December 19, 1931; *Volksblatt:* January 23, 1932; February 24, 1932. Interviews with Otto Made, who claimed that the kitchen fed people without any questions, and with Benno Schmidt, who recalls being denied food because he was a "known leftist." The *Volksblatt* contended that the kitchen was run for profit.
20. TNN: January 9, 1933; GHC: January 6, 1932; April 15, 1932; *Volksblatt:* January 11, 1932; April 15, 1932.
21. Interviews with Maria Armkerl, Eva Spatel, and Benno Schmidt.
22. Interview with Kurt Zeisser. For the attitude of *Gymnasium* students, interviews with Rudolf Fischer and Erhardt Knorpel.
23. GHC: March 19, 1932; *Volksblatt:* August 6, 1932; November 9, 1932.
24. Interview with Kurt Zeisser corroborated by Otto Made.
25. Interviews with Ernst Meier, Otto Made, Erhardt Knorpel, Willi Brehm, Karl Hengst, Heinrich Lamme, and Benno Schmidt. Knorpel, the former newspaper reporter, made the most accurate estimate: forty.
26. Interview with Ernst Meier. "Unter diesen Zeichen wirst du rote Schwein verbluten."
27. Interview with Erhardt Knorpel. "Schmeiss die Juden raus! Die Juden sind unser Unglück!"
28. Interviews with Willi Brehm, Karl Hengst, Hans Leidler, and Erhardt Knorpel.
29. Interviews with Otto Made and Walther Timmerlah.
30. *Volksblatt:* June 12, 1931; September 21, 1932; TNN: November 28, 1932; GHC: September 20, 1932; December 20, 1932.
31. Interview with Walther Timmerlah.
32. Interviews with Erhardt Knorpel, Rudolf Fischer, Hans Leidler, and Dieter Thomas. Much of Eckstein's personal attitude was gleaned in conversation with his widow.
33. Interviews with Dieter Thomas, Erhardt Knorpel, Otto Made, Karl Hengst, Benno Schmidt, Walther Timmerlah, and Franz von Altberg. The quotation is from Erhardt Knorpel.
34. Interview with Dieter Thomas.
35. Interviews with Hans Abbenrode, Walther Timmerlah, Hans Leidler, and Franz von Altberg. TNN: December 8, 1931; GHC: December 10, 1931.
36. Interview with Otto Made.
37. Interview with Rudolf Fischer.
38. Interview with Kurt Zeisser.
39. Interview with Erhardt Knorpel.
40. Interview with Franz von Altberg.
41. Interview with Erhardt Knorpel.
42. Interviews with Maria Armkerl and Erhardt Knorpel. For the second statement, interviews with Gregor Rosenthal and Heinrich Lamme (whose employer was Jewish).
43. *Volksblatt:* February 4, 1932.

44. *Volksblatt:* August 19, 1931; February 6, 1932.
45. *Volksblatt:* January 14, 1932.
46. *Volksblatt:* November 20, 1931; March 26, 1932; August 8, 9, 1932.
47. TNN: October 19, 1931; *Volksblatt*, December 10, 12, 1931.
48. *Volksblatt:* February 17, 1932; March 1, 1932.
49. *Volksblatt:* January 21, 25, 26, 28, 30, 1932; February 2, 10, 17, 20, 23, 1932.
50. GHC: January 22, 26, 27, 1932.
51. GHC: November 14, 1931; TNN: 1932. By census count there were twenty atheists in Thalburg.
52. GHC: February 12, 1932.
53. TNN: February 13, 1932; GHC: February 11, 16, 1932.
54. GHC: January 14, 18, 1932.
55. *Volksblatt:* December 4, 1931; February 20, 1932; March 7, 1932.
56. GHC: February 27, 1932; TNN: February 27, 1932; April 9, 1932.
57. *Volksblatt:* April 23, 1932; August 4, 1932; December 21, 1932.

CHAPTER SEVEN

POLITICAL CRESCENDO

1. *Volksblatt:* December 4, 1931.
2. *Volksblatt:* February 23, 1932; TNN: February 26, 1932; GHC: February 27, 1932.
3. TNN: March 9, 1932; *Volksblatt:* March 16, 1932.
4. TNN: February 2, 3, 6, 8, 1932; March 12, 1932; *Volksblatt:* February 10, 21, 1932.
5. TNN: March 9, 26, 1932.
6. *Volksblatt:* January 16, 20, 1932; February 6, 1932.
7. TNN: March 7, 1932; *Volksblatt:* March 5, 8, 1932.
8. TNN: March 9, 12, 1932; *Volksblatt:* March 12, 1932.
9. TNN: March 11, 1932.
10. TNN and GHC: February 13, 1932; TNN: March 12, 1932.
11. GHC: February 17, 21, 1932; TNN: February 29, 1932; March 7, 8, 10, 1932.
12. GHC: February 12, 1932.
13. GHC: March 5, 9, 10, 1932; TNN: March 7, 1932; *Volksblatt:* March 9, 1932.
14. TNN: March 11, 1932; GHC: March 12, 1932; *Volksblatt:* March 10, 1932.
15. *Volksblatt:* March 14, 1932; GHC: March 13, 1932.
16. GHC: March 5, 1932.

17. See table in the Appendix for the statistics of this and the next two elections covered in this chapter.
18. Interview with Willi Brehm. For the police alert, see TNN: March 12, 1932.
19. *Volksblatt:* March 14, 15, 1932. Interview with Willi Brehm who was with the *Reichsbanner* "scouts."
20. TNN: March 16, 1932.
21. GHC: March 20, 22, 1932; TNN: March 18, 1932; April 8, 1932.
22. TNN: April 8, 11, 1932. The words were a variation of the customary "Juda Verrecke!"
23. TNN: April 9, 1932.
24. *Volksblatt:* March 18, 1932; April 12, 1932; GHC: March 16, 22, 1932; TNN: March 15, 1932; September 15, 1932. A lenient court subsequently found Tumpelmann guilty of assault but fined him only 10 marks. TNN: April 23, 1932.
25. GHC: April 2, 5, 7, 9, 1932.
26. TNN: April 13, 15, 21, 1932; *Volksblatt:* April 15, 23, 1932.
27. TNN: April 16, 19, 1932.
28. TNN: April 14, 1932; GHC: April 20, 1932.
29. GHC: April 25, 1932.
30. GHC: April 14, 19, 1932. Interview with Erhardt Knorpel.
31. *Volksblatt:* April 12, 19, 23, 1932.
32. TNN: April 25, 1932; October 27, 1932; November 9, 1932; GHC: April 26, 1932; *Volksblatt:* April 26, 1932.
33. TNN: April 18, 1932.
34. TNN: October 24, 1932.
35. Interviews with Dieter Thomas, Gregor Rosenthal, and Heinrich Lamme.
36. TNN: August 30, 1930; September 2, 13, 1930; August 4, 1931.
37. Tables in Appendix B.

CHAPTER EIGHT

THINGS FALL APART

1. *Thalburg 1933-36 . . . ,* Tables B-1, p. 76, and A-1, p. 27; also, *475 Jahre Städtische Gymnasium in Thalburg* (Thalburg, 1952), p. 12.
2. *Heimatblätter, herausgegeben von dem Museumsverein für Thalburg und Umgebung,* e.v., Nr. 4, Jhrg. 9, Mai, 1933: *"Jahresbericht."*
3. TNN: October 4, 1930; October 27, 1932. In July, 1930, there were 162 cars in Thalburg.
4. *Thalburg, 1933-36 . . . ,* Tables p. 8 and p. 62, and Table: "Städtische Warmwasserbadeanstalt."

5. *Ibid.,* Table p. 8; TNN: November 21, 1932; January 1, 1933; *Volksblatt:* November 21, 1932.

6. *Rechnungsabschlusse der Stadtsparkasse Thalburg, 1930-33.*

7. TNN: August 29, 1932; interviews with Hugo Spiessmann and Erhardt Knorpel.

8. TNN: June 15, 1932.

9. TNN: July 13, 1932.

10. *Haushaltsplan der Stadt Thalburg,* mimeographed and issued annually by the town. In the files of the *Hauptamt,* City Hall. Also, *Thalburg, 1933-36 . . . ,* Table: "Gewerbesteuer nach dem Ertrag und nach dem Kapital." Because of complicated formulae used in assessing taxes in German towns, the drop in the profits tax does not connote an equal drop in profits. Unless one examined each tax case, the most one could validly conclude from the figures cited is that profits were falling by some small and indeterminate amount in the course of 1932. A rapid drop in the *total* business tax yield would have indicated real trouble. In one sense, then, the tax returns simply show again that Thalburg was not decisively hurt by the depression. The *general* reduction in tax yield reflected essentially reduced spending, since the prime source of income for the town was, in addition to its various enterprises, indirect consumption taxes of various sorts. Thus the reduced budget does not mean that Thalburgers were actually suffering from the depression.

11. Wells, *op. cit.,* p. 170.

12. TNN: April 19, 1932; June 16, 1932; *Volksblatt:* May 19, 1932.

13. TNN: September 28, 1932; December 12, 1932; January 13, 27, 1933.

14. TNN: February 17, 1932; March 11, 1932.

15. TNN: August 26, 1932.

16. GHC and TNN: August 27, 1932.

17. TNN: September 30, 1932.

18. *Volksblatt:* April 13, 1932.

19. TNN: April 14, 1932.

20. GHC: April 15, 1932; *Volksblatt:* April 15, 22, 1932.

21. *Volksblatt* and TNN: May 2, 1932.

22. GHC: May 8, 11, 1932.

23. TNN: May 17, 1932; *Volksblatt:* June 13, 1932.

24. *Volksblatt:* December 10, 13, 1930; September 1, 5, 26, 1931.

25. *Volksblatt:* December 7, 1931. There is little doubt that students at the *Gymnasium* were Nazified, though most of them out of adolescent rebelliousness rather than political awareness, according to the former principal. (Interviews with Rudolf Fischer, Kurt Zeisser, and Erhardt Knorpel.)

26. *Volksblatt:* April 2, 1932; also interview with Hans Abbenrode, Tiere's supervisor in the school.

27. *Volksblatt:* April 7, 12, 1932; June 18, 1932.

28. TNN: April 29, 1932; GHC: April 30, 1932.
29. *Volksblatt:* June 6, 1932.
30. GHC: April 30, 1932; June 22, 1932; TNN: April 29, 1932; June 22, 1932.
31. GHC: May 15, 21, 24, 28, 1932; June 16, 19, 1932; TNN: June 13, 1932.
32. TNN: June 20, 1932.
33. GHC: June 21, 1932.
34. *Volksblatt:* May 15, 1930.
35. Interview with Hans Leidler.
36. *Ibid.;* TNN and GHC: September 8, 1932.
37. TNN: July 25, 29, 1932; *Volksblatt:* July 28, 1932.
38. GHC: October 11, 20, 1930; November 15, 1930; TNN: October 12, 17, 1930; none of these events was mentioned in the *Volksblatt.*
39. *Volksblatt:* July 28, 1932: *"Die Republikaner werden dafür sorgen, dass diese Geschäfte lebensfähig bleiben."*
40. Interviews with Karl Hengst, Ernst Meier, Otto Made, and Heinrich Lamme.
41. TNN: July 20, 1932; GHC: July 21, 1932.
42. *Kaufmännische Berufsschule Thalburg, Schulgeschichte 1887-1937.* Thalburg, January 1, 1937 (ms. in City Archives). Interviews with Erhardt Knorpel, Kurt Zeisser, Karl Hengst, Hans Abbenrode, and Heinrich Lamme.
43. Alan Bullock in *The Third Reich,* Beaumont, Vermeil, *et al.* (New York, 1955), p. 514.
44. *Volksblatt:* June 14, 1932.
45. GHC: July 1, 1932. Subsequent quotation from GHC: July 5, 1932; also TNN: July 4, 1932.
46. GHC: July 13, 16, 1932.
47. TNN: July 4, 7, 1932. The quotation is from *Volksblatt:* July 7, 1932.
48. *Volksblatt:* July 12, 1932.
49. *Volksblatt:* July 8, 11, 12, 1932.
50. TNN: July 11, 22, 1932; August 10, 1932; GHC: July 12, 1932; August 12, 1932; *Volksblatt:* July 11, 12, 13, 1932. The *Volksblatt* claimed that it had a witness who saw the Nazis making obvious preparations for the fight during the afternoon of the day. No such witness testified at the trial, however. The heaviest sentence was given to Benno Schmidt. At least one of the *Reichsbanner* men offered to testify against his comrades and also wept before the judge to get his sentence reduced (interview with Benno Schmidt).
51. TNN: July 13, 14, 27, 1932.
52. TNN: July 14, 16, 1932; August 12, 13, 1932; November 11, 21, 22, 1932; GHC: July 15, 16, 1932; August 14, 1932; *Volksblatt:* July 16, 1932; November 23, 1932.
53. GHC: July 19, 1932.

54. GHC: July 23, 1932. Interview with Kurt Zeisser.
55. GHC: July 21, 27, 29, 1932.
56. *Volksblatt:* April 2, 1931; August 29, 1932; *Hört! Hört!:* July 7, 1932.
57. TNN: July 27, 1932; *Volksblatt:* July 27, 28, 1932; August 5, 18, 1932.
58. TNN: July 25, 28, 29, 30, 1932; *Volksblatt:* July 28, 30, 1932.
59. GHC: July 31, 1932; TNN: July 27, 29, 30, 1932.
60. TNN: August 19, 23, 1932; September 8, 1932: GHC: August 27, 1932.
61. TNN: August 1, 4, 6, 1932.
62. TNN and *Volksblatt:* August 12, 1932.

CHAPTER NINE

THE LAST WINTER

1. TNN: August 13, 16, 18, 25, 31, 1932; September 5, 6, 8, 9, 1932.
2. TNN: November 4, 8, 1930; September 29, 1931; June 18, 1932; GHC: May 14, 1931; interview with Eva Spatel, whose son was a member of this Black Army unit.
3. *Volksblatt:* April 20, 1932; TNN: June 22, 1932.
4. TNN: August 20, 1931; GHC: August 21, 1931.
5. TNN: January 16, 1931; October 3, 1932.
6. *Volksblatt:* November 4, 1932.
7. GHC: September 17, 20, 22, 1932; *Volksblatt,* September 21, 26, 1932.
8. GHC: October 5, 6, 11, 1932; TNN: October 10, 11, 12, 1932.
9. *Volksblatt:* September 16, 1932; October 24, 1932; TNN: October 24, 25, 27, 1932.
10. TNN: October 10, 11, 1932; *Volksblatt:* October 10, 1932. The Town Band's conductor was very upset by this and wrote a letter to the TNN insisting on his political neutrality.
11. TNN: October 22, 24, 1932; *Volksblatt:* November 1, 4, 1932.
12. TNN: November 1, 4, 1932.
13. TNN: October 27, 29; November 1, 3, 5, 1932; GHC: November 1, 4, 1932.
14. TNN: November 7, 1932; *Volksblatt:* November 9, 1932.
15. TNN: October 22, 1932.
16. *Volksblatt:* November 28, 1932; TNN: November 1, 26, 1932; December 6, 1932.
17. TNN: October 22, 1932; November 21, 1932; January 14, 1933. Fourteen hundred free baths were taken in November and December, 1932, suggesting that the unemployed were possibly the cleanest citi-

zens of Thalburg. See *Thalburg 1933-36,* Table: "Städtische Warm-wasserbadeanstalt."

18. TNN: December 1, 1932.
19. Interviews with Ernst Meier, Hans Leidler, and Willi Brehm.
20. Interview with Benno Schmidt.
21. Interviews with Erhardt Knorpel and Hans Abbenrode.
22. TNN: August 13, 1932; January 27, 1933. GHC: November 3, 1932; *Volksblatt:* October 22, 27, 1932.
23. TNN: December 7, 15, 1932; January 19, 23, 1933; GHC: January 24, 1933. On internal squabbling, see Appendix C, paragraphs 1d, 2a, 2c, and 3c.
24. Interviews with Eva Spatel and Erhardt Knorpel.
25. J. K. Pollock, "Areal Studies of the German Electorate, 1930-33," *American Political Science Review,* XXXVIII, p. 93.
26. Nazi strength in Thalburg reflected the general area in which the town was located. From 1930 to 1933, Thalburg's electoral district was the eighth strongest, in percentage of Nazi votes cast, of the thirty-five electoral districts in Germany. In the second presidential election of 1932, Thalburg's electoral district gave the sixth highest percentage of votes to Hitler: 44.8 per cent, or roughly 8 per cent higher than the national average. *Ibid.,* pp. 60-63.
27. See tables in Appendix B.
28. For a graphic representation of this, see tables in Appendix B.
29. Nazi growth at the expense of the bourgeois right is portrayed in Tables 4 and 5, Appendix B. For a striking representation of this phenomenon nationally, see the graph on p. 119 in Richard N. Hunt, *German Social Democracy 1918-1933* (New Haven, 1964).
30. Tables 6 and 7, Appendix B, contain such a correlated distribution.

CHAPTER TEN

THE LAST ELECTIONS

1. TNN: January 13, 1933.
2. TNN: January 27, 1933.
3. TNN: January 26, 28, 1933.
4. TNN: January 28, 1933; February 2, 6, 1933; GHC: February 7, 1933.
5. TNN: February 2, 3, 11, 1933.
6. TNN: February 2, 3, 28, 1933; GHC: February 22, 1933.
7. TNN: February 18, 1933.
8. TNN: February 20, 21, 1933; GHC: February 21, 1933.
9. Interviews with Hans Leidler, Ernst Meier, and Willi Brehm.
10. GHC and TNN: February 24, 1933.

11. TNN: February 23, 27, 1933.
12. TNN: March 2, 1933. For the meeting, TNN: February 15, 17, 1933; GHC: February 18, 1933.
13. Interview with Rudolf Fischer, through whose pleadings the boy was ultimately permitted to graduate.
14. TNN: March 1, 2, 1933; GHC: March 3, 1933.
15. Interview with Willi Brehm; text from his *Entschädigungs* documents.
16. TNN: February 28, 1933; March 3, 6, 1933; GHC: March 6, 1933.
17. TNN and GHC: March 6, 1933.
18. TNN: March 6, 7, 1933. Apparently the Prussian Ministry of the Interior expressly ordered that there be no opposition to the flying of swastika flags from public buildings. Nevertheless there was some in Thalburg. When the janitor at the City Hall hung a swastika flag on the building's flagpole, the Mayor ordered that it be taken down on the grounds that it was improper to put a party symbol on a public building. The order to lower the swastika was actually delivered by Dieter Thomas, the Mayor's administrative assistant. This was later held against him by the Nazis. Thus on March 7, the only public building without a Nazi flag was the City Hall.
19. TNN: March 11, 1933.
20. TNN: February 6, 10, 11, 1933.
21. GHC: February 21, 22, 26, 1933. The GHC later announced that Senator Mahner and another Nationalist wanted it known that they had not authored the "Letter to the Editor." The announcement about the DVP's decision was *not* reported in its own paper, the TNN.
22. GHC: February 28, 1933; March 1, 1933.
23. Interview with Dieter Thomas.
24. TNN: October 23, 24, 1933.
25. GHC: March 14, 1933. All the speeches were printed in paraphrase, but since the Nazis were watching the GHC closely, and since they did not correct the account or otherwise comment on it, it was probably substantially correct.
26. TNN: March 11, 1933.
27. TNN: March 13, 1933.

CHAPTER ELEVEN

THE USES OF ELECTORAL SUCCESS

1. *Thalburger Beobachter:* March 15, 1933, for the distribution of seats in the Council (henceforth this new, Nazi-owned newspaper will be cited "TB"). Interview with Otto Made, for the operation of the "Leader Principle" in the Council; interview with Dieter Thomas and Karl Hengst on the disaffection of the SPD councilman.

2. Interview with Karl Hengst; TNN: March 29, 1933.
3. This account is drawn from interviews with three eyewitnesses (Otto Made, Dieter Thomas, and Karl Hengst) and from the extensive reports in the TNN: March 29, 1933; and GHC: March 30, 1933. Speeches came from the newspaper paraphrases, with the indented quotation from Aergeyz being a case where the two newspaper reports were identical. The difficulty in getting the exact words may be illustrated by the fact that Tiere's words to Hengst upon denying him the right to speak (quoted above from the TNN) were given by Hengst himself as: "For ten years you've made the people drunk with your tricks of speech. The people do not wish to hear you any more" —and by the GHC as: "Herr Hengst, in the years of your rule you plastered us with bile and scourges; we don't want to listen to you."
4. TNN: April 6, 1933.
5. TNN: April 7, 1933; GHC: April 14, 1933.
6. TNN: April 13, 1933. Actually these last two names were never used. The Nazis did go on to call the Market Square the "Platz der SA" and to create a "Reinhard Strasse" in honor of the Public Works Program director. Later street changes came as a result of the ousting of the Mayor ("Buergermeister Johns Strasse" became "Karl Dincklage Strasse") and attempts to discredit the church ("Kirchstrasse" became "Peter Hohmann Strasse"—even a "Tilly Strasse" was created). For a complete listing of the streets, old style, see election district lists in TNN: February 28, 1933. For all the new streets, see the map in *"Strassenverzeichnis Thalburg,"* Thalburg, 1938 (in town archives, no number). For typical names chosen before the Nazis came to power, see TNN: November 11, 1930. Through 1938 the names of eleven streets had been changed.
7. TNN: April 26, 28, 1933.
8. TNN: June 7, 1933.
9. TNN: June 27, 1933; July 19, 1933.
10. Interview with Franz von Altberg; TNN: February 25, 1933.
11. TNN: March 13, 1933. The prior County Council (old Thalburg County) had twenty seats: ten SPD, two "Middle," two NSDAP, five *"Bürgerliche* Unity," and one "Town and Country."
12. TNN: March 29, 30, 1933.
13. Interview with Franz von Altberg. Karl Hengst also remembered that von Altberg had sworn to him that he would never "change his shirt." Later, when Hengst twitted him about "having a new shirt" von Altberg simply replied that he could "do more good within the party than if he were outside and powerless." Interview with Karl Hengst.
14. Interview with Karl Hengst.
15. "It was at this announcement," said von Altberg later, "that I first realized that we were going to have a complete dictatorship." He had been sufficiently aware of the new realities to worry about the

phraseology of his own speech; so much so, in fact, that he took the extraordinary step (for him) of writing it out and reading it at the meeting. Interview with Franz von Altberg.

16. TNN: April 1, 3, 1933; GHC: April 4, 1933.

17. TNN: June 9, 1933; interview with Karl Hengst.

18. Interviews with Hans Abbenrode, Erhardt Knorpel, and Franz von Altberg. TB: January 30, 1936, *"3 Jahre N.S. Kommunal Verwaltung"; "Taetigkeits und Erfolgsbericht, 25. January, 1935, Nr. C, Buergermeister zum Landrat"* (ms. in City Archives).

19. For press accounts of the purge, see GHC: April 13, 27, 1933; TNN: April 27, 1933; May 5, 13, 1933; June 24, 1933. There is no extant document showing the number of persons employed by Thalburg immediately before the purge. In 1937 the town employed 221 persons of whom 105 were hour-wage workers, and the rest civil servants or *Angestellter*. Since new offices had been created in the interim (for example, the *Sippenamt*) and since there would probably be fewer workers at a time when the town was struggling to balance its budget, the probability is that there were about 180 persons on the city payroll before the purge. For the 1937 figures see *"Stand 18. IX. 37: Beschäftigte Arbeiter"* and *"Personalbestand am 17. IX. 1937,"* typescripts in City Archives, Thalburg.

20. GHC: April 13, 14, 27, 1933; May 5, 1933; TNN: April 27, 1933; May 5, 1933; June 24, 1933.

21. Interview with Erhardt Knorpel.

22. TNN: April 19, 1933; May 13, 1933; June 8, 9, 29, 1933.

23. TNN: May 10, 1933.

24. Interview with Dieter Thomas.

25. *Ibid.*

26. Interviews with Franz von Altberg, Erhardt Knorpel, Dieter Thomas, Karl Hengst, and Benno Schmidt.

27. TNN: January 13, 1933.

28. See Appendix C, paragraph 2 (f).

29. Interviews with Franz von Altberg, Dieter Thomas, and Erhardt Knorpel. For Blanck's *Dezernate,* TNN: April 7, 1933.

30. Interview with Dieter Thomas.

31. *Protokoll der Fraktionssitzung der Fraktion der NSDAP in dem Bürgervorsteherkollegium zu Thalburg, den 28 Juni 1933.* Carbon copy in private files of Walther Timmerlah.

32. TNN: June 7, 1933; August 15, 1933; interviews with Erhardt Knorpel, Dieter Thomas, and Hugo Spiessmann. After World War II, Aergeyz sued the City of Thalburg for a pension and thus the whole matter of how he became Mayor came before the courts. The suit was not successful. *"Ausfertigung. Streitliste Nr. AH II 176/54. In der Verwaltungsstreitsache des Bürgermeisters a.D. Aergeyz in Thalburg, Klägers, gegen den Rat der Stadt Thalburg, Beklagten, wegen Berück-*

sichtigung der Beamtenrechte," and *"Ante Nr. II OVG-A 30/56, 24. X. 56, Revisionsantrag."* Both in *Hauptamt Thalburg.* The formal clause used to dismiss Johns was section six of the law of April 7, 1933.

CHAPTER TWELVE

THE TERROR SYSTEM

1. Control over the police was actually secured by informal means. In the first place, both local judges were Nazis even before the March elections. Secondly, the effective administrative head of Thalburg's police, Police-Secretary Deuvelman, was vulnerable since he depended on an annual bonus from the City Council to cover his extravagant living habits. He had no choice but to conform to the will of the new all-Nazi City Council. Finally, individual policemen were simply required, about mid-March, to wear swastika armbands. Some had to be almost physically forced, but thenceforth they were compromised. Thereafter they risked losing their jobs if they did not obey Kurt Aergeyz's orders (interviews with Willi Brehm, Karl Hengst, and Franz von Altberg).

2. For example, in 1930 only nine hunting licenses were issued in Thalburg, all to business or professional men. TNN: January 8, 1930.

3. Interview with Willi Brehm and Benno Schmidt. The latter was seriously compromised when his friend sat on Schmidt's couch one day with a pocketful of bullets and let a few slip down between the cushions. When the police later searched Schmidt's apartment, there were the bullets, and it was only later and after conversations with his friend that Schmidt discovered how they came to be there.

4. TNN: March 6, 1933.

5. TNN: March 30, 1933; April 4, 8, 10, 19, 24, 28, 1933; May 5, 1933; GHC: April 4, 5, 1933.

6. TNN: July 11, 1933; August 2, 9, 22, 1933.

7. TNN: April 18, 1933.

8. For the distribution of these events, see Table 9, Appendix B.

9. TNN: March 14, 15, 29, 1933.

10. GHC: March 18, 1933.

11. GHC: March 29, 1933; TNN: March 30, 1933; July 12, 1933.

12. TNN: April 28, 1933; May 9, 1933.

13. TNN: June 17, 19, 30, 1933; GHC: June 20, 1933; July 1, 1933.

14. Interviews with Hans Abbenrode, Rudolf Fischer, Erhardt Knorpel, Karl Hengst, Hans Leidler, Dieter Thomas, and Walther Timmerlah. Otto Made himself denied any connection with the *Gestapo,* but as

Thalburg's highest SS official he was doubtless also part of the "V-Männer" system.

15. Interview with Maria Armkerl.
16. Interview with Heinrich Lamme.
17. Interview with Hans Abbenrode.
18. Interview with Maria Armkerl.
19. Interview with Hans Abbenrode.
20. Interview with Erhardt Knorpel.
21. *Ibid.*
22. Interviews with Hans Leidler, Ernst Meier, and Willi Brehm, from whose statement the quotation is taken.
23. Interview with Karl Hengst.
24. *"Kommunal-Politische Abteilung der SPD im Bezirk Hannover. Rundschreiben Nr. 6/35, Hannover den 23. März 1933. Von Wilhelm Hess an die Ortsvereinsvorstände im Bezirk Hannover."* Copy in files of Karl Hengst.
25. *Zeugnis* dated May 12, 1933. This and other documents cited for Ernst Meier's experiences come from his papers as submitted to the *Entschaedigungsbehoerde* of the Federal Republic of Germany in support of his application for monetary recompense for his loss of wages due to Nazi terror activities against him. The documents were verified and he received payments: *Der Beauftragte des oeffentl. Interesses beim Niedersaechsischen Landesausschuss fuer Sonderhilfssachen, Nr. o2/223, Hann. d. 17. Okt. 1952.*
26. Form letter from the *Magistrat der Stadt Thalburg,* May 12, 1933. In *Entschaedigungsbehoerden* papers.
27. *Ibid.* Notarized statement by a former police officer, Thalburg, January 5, 1953.
28. *Ibid. Der Buergermeister als Ortspolizeibehoerde an den Gasanstaltsarbeiter Herrn Ernst Meier, Thalburg, den 3. Januar 1934 (v 1505-35); Der Landrat des Kreis Thalburg an Herrn Ernst Meier. Thalburg den 6. Okt. 1934; Der Regierungspraesident Hildesheim an Herrn Ernst Meier, Hildesheim, den 28. Maerz 1935, I. v. 545.* The general point of these letters is that Meier could not have travel identification documents since he was politically untrustworthy.
29. *Ibid. Der Buergermeister an die Nat. Soz. Kriegsopferversorgung. z. Hd. von Herrn Fritz Kaeppke, Thalburg, den 9. III. 1934.*
30. *Ibid.* Notarized statement by a former police officer, Thalburg, January 5, 1953.
31. Interview with Ernst Meier.
32. Interview with Benno Schmidt.
33. *"Der Vorsitzende des Kreisausschusses an den Dauerangestellten Herrn Willi Brehm, Thalburg. d. 9. Mai 1933.";* "Der Preussische Minister des Innern an den Dauerangestellten Herrn Willi Brehm. Berlin. d. 20. Juli 1934." From *Entschaedigungsbehoerde* documents.

34. *"Willi Brehm an den Entschaedigungsbehoerde, Hildesheim,"* April 18, 1956.
35. Interview with Willi Brehm.
36. Interview with Karl Hengst.
37. Interview with Hans Leidler. This account and documents to substantiate it were certified by occupation authorities in 1946.
38. TNN: May 9, 19, 1933; July 15, 1933; GHC: May 12, 1933.

CHAPTER THIRTEEN

WHIPPING UP ENTHUSIASM

1. There was also a period between December 10, 1932, and April 6, 1933, when the paper was known as *Nationalsozialistische Beobachter.* TNN: July 18, 1933; TB: April 6, 1933; June 10, 1933; also, interview with Kurt Zeisser whose father printed the TB from October, 1932, to July, 1933.
2. *Runderlass der Kreisleitung Thalburg, an alle Ortsgruppenführer,* May 22, 1933, also letter, *Landrat,* to GHC, April 24, 1933, both from the files of the GHC, now in possession of Eva Spatel.
3. Interview with Erhardt Knorpel.
4. *Ibid.*
5. TB: April 6, 1933.
6. Interview with Erhardt Knorpel.
7. Interview with Walther Timmerlah.
8. TNN: May 9, 1933; June 7, 1933; July 15, 22, 29, 1933.
9. *Hört! Hört!:* April 16, 1932; October 22, 1932; GHC: April 26, 1932; May 1, 1932. The *Volksblatt* enjoyed this immensely, but continued to call the GHC a "Nazi organ" and demanded that it lose its status as official paper for the local governments. *Volksblatt:* May 4, 1932; July 2, 1932.
10. TB: May 21, 1933.
11. GHC: May 25, 1933.
12. Interview with Eva Spatel.
13. GHC: June 9, 1933; TB: June 10, 1933. Also, letter from von Altberg to Wilhelm Spatel, July 20, 1933, in files of Eva Spatel.
14. TNN: March 10, 13, 14, 1933; GHC: March 15, 1933; TB: March 15, 1933. It was on this occasion that Aergeyz tried to get the SA to smash Karl Hengst's shop.
15. TNN: March 11, 17, 18, 20, 1933; GHC: March 21, 1933. The actual title of the speech: *"Welch' ein Wendung durch Gottes Fügung."*
16. TNN: March 20, 21, 22, 23, 1933.

17. TNN: April 18, 19, 20, 21, 1933; GHC: May 21, 1933.
18. TNN: April 24, 1933.
19. TNN: April 24, 26, 27, 29, 1933; May 2, 1933; GHC: April 28, 1933; May 3, 1933.
20. TNN: May 24, 27, 1933; GHC: May 25, 1933.
21. TNN: March 23, 27, 1933; May 12, 15, 20, 1933; June 7, 1933; July 11, 17, 31, 1933; GHC: May 3, 1933.
22. TNN: April 22, 24, 1933; May 5, 13, 1933; GHC: May 4, 1933.
23. TNN: June 6, 1933.
24. TNN: April 22, 27, 1933; June 19, 1933; July 20, 1933; GHC: June 20, 1933.
25. TNN: March 17, 1933; April 28, 1933; July 20, 1933.
26. TNN: May 5, 1933; GHC: April 7, 1933; May 5, 1933; June 9, 1933. Interview with Rudolf Fischer, who joined the *Stahlhelm* at this time.
27. GHC: June 1, 20, 1933; TNN: June 27, 1933.
28. TNN: April 15, 28, 1933; May 2, 1933; June 28, 1933.
29. TNN: May 8, 29, 1933.
30. TNN: June 12, 26, 1933; August 7, 1933.
31. TNN: February 8, 9, 10, 1933; GHC: February 11, 1933.
32. GHC: June 22, 1933. Originally the glider group was sponsored by the Thalburg members of ADAC—the German equivalent of AAA. Auto owners in the early thirties in Thalburg tended to be both wealthy enough to finance a glider club, and nationalistic enough to want to do so, as a means of training pilots and circumventing the clauses in the Versailles Treaty which prohibited Germany from having an air force.

CHAPTER FOURTEEN

THE ATOMIZATION OF SOCIETY

1. TNN: January 1, 1933. The figure 102 is from 1900, when the town's population was approximately 8,000.
2. Interviews with Gregor Rosenthal, Heinrich Lamme, Benno Schmidt, and Erhardt Knorpel.
3. TNN: March 29, 1933; April 1, 1933. The fate of these forty individuals up to the outbreak of World War II was:

Died by natural causes	4
Left Thalburg	25
Taken from Thalburg to concentration camps	8
Committed suicide	2
Fate unknown	1

Of the 120 Jews in Thalburg in 1932, two returned to the town after 1945, both for economic reasons.

4. GHC: March 21, 1933; April 2, 1933. It was only in the farming communities around Thalburg that there were real feelings of anti-semitism, according to Erhardt Knorpel.

5. TB: April 6, 1933.

6. Interviews with Heinrich Lamme and Hans Abbenrode.

7. Interview with Gregor Rosenthal.

8. TNN: April 3, 1933; May 4, 1933. Interviews with Willi Brehm, Erhardt Knorpel, Heinrich Lamme, and Gregor Rosenthal.

9. Interviews with Eva Spatel and Heinrich Lamme.

10. Interview with Gregor Rosenthal.

11. Interview with Ernst Meier and Benno Schmidt.

12. A spark of the old way flared up in 1937 when Banker Braun died, of natural causes. Despite warnings, some sixty of Thalburg's leading businessmen attended his funeral. An SA leader photographed this scandal and the picture was published in the *Stuermer* under the caption: *"Judenknechte aus Thalburg!"* Apart from national publicity, the offenders received no punishment. Some of them were Nazis of the "idealist" group, described in Chapter Sixteen.

13. Interview with Franz von Altberg.

14. Interviews with Erhardt Knorpel and Rudolf Fischer.

15. TNN: March 20, 1933; April 8, 1933.

16. TNN: March 27, 30, 1933; April 24, 26, 1933; TB: April 6, 1933; GHC: April 27, 1933.

17. TNN: May 5, 20, 22, 1933; June 24, 1933; TB: May 6, 1933. The union officials temporarily rehired were dismissed on June 6, 1933.

18. TNN: May 22, 1933; July 18, 1933.

19. TNN: February 13, 1933; April 20, 1933.

20. TNN: April 18, 22, 26, 1933; May 4, 1933. Interview with Erhardt Knorpel.

21. GHC: May 21, 1933.

22. TNN: July 4, 1933.

23. TNN: April 18, 1933; May 24, 1933; GHC: April 23, 1933. Later teachers were also required to join the NSDAP. In the whole of Thalburg only one teacher refused to join the Nazi Teachers' League. She was an old maid who had been teaching in Thalburg long enough to have boxed Kurt Aergeyz's ears when he was a little boy. She declared that the whole thing was "nonsense" and refused to have anything to do with it. Perhaps as a result of ancient fears, Thalburg's Nazis never pressed the matter. But she was the sole exception (interview with Hans Abbenrode).

24. TNN: February 6, 1933.

25. TNN: May 16, 29, 1933; August 8, 9, 1933.

26. TNN: April 13, 1933; June 6, 1933; also, interview with Walther

Timmerlah. The outstanding rumor was that the consumers' cooperative delivery truck was used to carry a corpse.

27. TNN: March 25, 1933; April 3, 1933; May 8, 30, 1933; August 10, 1933; GHC: June 21, 1933.
28. Interview with Hans Abbenrode.
29. TNN: April 8, 19, 1933; *50 Jahre Volkschor: Festbuch* (Thalburg, 1955), p. 39.
30. TNN: May 18, 1933. After World War II several of the old clubs revived themselves.
31. TNN: May 16, 1933; June 24, 1933; July 1, 1933.
32. Interview with Walther Timmerlah. For an example of coordination from above, see *Heimat Blätter,* No. 5, June, 1933.
33. TNN: May 15, 1933; August 1, 3, 1933; GHC: May 12, 1933. Members of the football club "VfB" actually hid their club flag during the Nazi era. See *50 Jahre "Verein für Bewegungssport 1906, Thalburg, e.v.,"* Thalburg, 1957.
34. TB: June 10, 1933. The Bible passage is: "For of Him, and through Him, and unto Him, are all things. To Him be the glory forever. Amen."
35. GHC: June 11, 1933; also, TNN: June 15, 26, 1933.
36. TNN: June 10, 17, 1933; July 11, 15, 20, 21, 24, 1933. GHC: June 18, 1933.
37. Interviews with Karl Hengst, Hans Abbenrode, Rudolf Fischer, and Walther Timmerlah.
38. GHC: May 12, 1933.
39. TB: March 4, 15, 1933; TNN: July 3, 1933.
40. TNN: April 7, 19, 1933.
41. Interview with Rudolf Fischer.
42. TNN: May 20, 1933; *Thalburg, 1933-36,* p. 23.
43. TNN: March 9, 1933; April 15, 1933; May 13, 1933; GHC: April 14, 1933. Later, when the *Stahlhelm* was broken up, the band was also dissolved. See Chapter Seventeen below.
44. TNN: June 2, 1933.

CHAPTER FIFTEEN

THE POSITIVE ASPECT

1. *Stadtwohlfahrts und Jugendamt Thalburg, d. 25. Aug. 1936. Gesamtuebersicht ueber die Entwicklung der lezten 3½ Jahre.* Thalburg City Archives (No. 7/71/VII), p. 2. Also, TNN: January 13, 27, 1933; March 15, 1933; April 12, 1933.

2. TNN: July 20, 24, 25, 26, 27, 1933; also, letter and report from *Magistrat* Thalburg to the *Regierungspraesident,* August 17, 1933, in Thalburg City Archives.

3. TNN: August 29, 1933; September 1, 4, 1933. Also, letter to *Regierungspraesident* from *Magistrat* Thalburg, August 31, 1933, in Thalburg City Archives, No. 4.

4. TNN: June 17, 1933; July 20, 1933; interview with Erhardt Knorpel. In Thalburg there were only fifteen NSDAP members with numbers below 100,000, of whom five were unemployed. Many Nazis were given work at the time of the purge of city employees.

5. Letter from *Magistrat* Thalburg to *Regierungspraesident,* August 17, 1933. See also "Bericht ueber der Entwicklung des Fuehrerbegriffs in Thalburg, 1933-1937" (ms. in Thalburg City Archives), and TNN: February 9, 1933; July 25, 1933; TB: January 30, 1936 (special issue: "Drei Jahre N.S. Kommunalverwaltung").

6. TNN: July 14, 1933.

7. TNN: February 25, 1933; April 10, 26, 1933; May 12, 1933; June 3, 1933.

8. TNN: July 26, 28, 1933.

9. TNN: March 30, 1933; April 22, 1933; May 11, 1933; GHC: April 23, 1933. The soup kitchen also supplied some five thousand meals for various Nazi gatherings and to the standing SA guard kept at the kitchen in February and March.

CHAPTER SIXTEEN

REACTION AND RESISTANCE

1. TNN: February 25, 1933; April 29, 1933; TB: May 6, 1933.

2. Interviews with Dieter Thomas and Erhardt Knorpel.

3. TNN: May 22, 1933; interview with Franz von Altberg.

4. Interviews with Hans Abbenrode and Rudolf Fischer. Abbenrode candidly admitted this about himself and Fischer heard the same from one of his teachers. In the latter case the man actually was promoted.

5. Interview with Erhardt Knorpel.

6. Interview with Dieter Thomas.

7. Interviews with Heinrich Lamme and Maria Armkerl.

8. Interview with Erhardt Knorpel. The man in question lost considerable money since he had to let his workers march whenever there was a parade and had to pay them during that time, too. He was sure that if he refused to do either he would be boycotted.

9. Interviews with Franz von Altberg, Hans Abbenrode, and Maria Armkerl.

10. Interview with Maria Armkerl. Despite these doubts her husband voted NSDAP in March, 1933. He had been a local leader of the DVP.

11. "Report of the *Gau-Uschla* proceedings against Walther Timmerlah. Minutes for July 4, 1933," p. 2. See also Appendix C: "A Formal Statement to the *Gauleitung* in Defense of the Assertion that 'Dreadful Conditions Prevail in Local Group Thalburg of the NSDAP.' Submitted by Party-Comrade Walther Timmerlah (No. —) in Thalburg, June 20, 1933." This and other documents cited for the "Idealists' Conspiracy" are from the private files of Walther Timmerlah.

12. "Report of the *Gau-Uschla* proceedings against Walther Timmerlah. Minutes for July 1, 1933." Also, interview with Walther Timmerlah and Appendix C.

13. Mimeographed letter from Kurt Aergeyz to all NSDAP members in Thalburg. April 22, 1933.

14. *Ibid.* Also TNN: March 30, 1933; July 31, 1933. The former article speaks for itself: "The County Leader of the NSDAP has announced that collections, no matter what kind, without the written permission of the County Leader or approval of the Local Group Leader, are forbidden. Should collectors appear, their party card is to be immediately confiscated and the proper authorities immediately notified."

15. *Protokoll der Fraktionsitzung der Fraktion der NSDAP im Buergervorsteherkollegium, 28 Juni, 1933.* In all cases the reason given was that the individuals "no longer possessed the confidence of the City Council." In actuality the councillors were motivated mainly by fear of Aergeyz.

CHAPTER SEVENTEEN

FROM ENTHUSIASM TO RITUAL

1. TNN: August 7, 19, 21, 1933.

2. TNN: September 8, 11, 1933.

3. TB: September 20, 1933; TNN: September 18, 1933. The speeches given at other general meetings in Thalburg County were identical in content.

4. TNN: October 16, 17, 1933.

5. TNN: October 20, 23, 1933.

6. TNN: October 31, 1933; November 1, 3, 4, 6, 8, 9, 1933.

7. TNN: November 9, 1933.

8. TNN: November 10, 1933.

9. Mimeographed memorandum signed by Kurt Aergeyz (in private files of Walther Timmerlah).

10. TNN: November 9, 10, 1933.

11. TNN: November 11, 1933; GHC: November 12, 1933.
12. TNN: November 13, 14, 1933.
13. TNN: January 12, 1933; March 3, 1933.
14. Interviews with Maria Armkerl and Heinrich Lamme.
15. TNN: November 25, 27, 1933; December 25, 27, 1933; January 13, 1934; February 26, 1934. Also, interview with Walther Timmerlah.
16. Mimeographed circular of November 21, 1933, to all Thalburg NSDAP members; circular letter of the Local Group Leader to all party-comrades in Thalburg, July 30, 1935 (in private files of Walther Timmerlah).
17. Interviews with Otto Made, Hans Abbenrode, and Erhardt Knorpel.
18. TNN: August 29, 1933; September 2, 1933; November 25, 1933.
19. TNN: September 19, 22, 27, 1933.
20. TNN: August 10, 30, 1933; October 28, 1933; "Report to the City," August 24, 1936, by the *Stadtsoberinspektor*, No. 1/A in Thalburg City Archives. By 1936 about 1,500 Thalburgers had requested certification of ancestry.
21. Interview with Rudolf Fischer.
22. Interview with Karl Hengst.
23. Interviews with Heinrich Lamme and Erhardt Knorpel.
24. Wells, *op. cit.*, pp. 136-137; interview with Hans Abbenrode; and TNN: September 30, 1933; October 7, 1933.
25. *Thalburg, 1933-36 . . .* , p. 16.
26. *Ibid.*, pp. 17-19; "Report on the Development of the *Fuehrer*-Principle in Thalburg, 1933-37" by *Ortsgruppenleitung* (Thalburg, 1937) (ms. in Thalburg City Archives); interviews with Hans Abbenrode and Rudolf Fischer.
27. *Thalburg, 1933-36 . . .* , pp. 16-20.
28. "*Verwaltungsbericht der Katholischen Volksschule Thalburg. 2. Okt. 1936*" (in Thalburg City Archives, No. 6/54/V).
29. "*Bericht ueber die Hilfsschule Thalburg f. d. Zeitraum 1929-36*" (in Thalburg City Archives, No. 6/53/V). Also, *Thalburg 1933-36 . . .* , pp. 19-20.
30. Interview with Rudolf Fischer; also, "*Verwaltungsbericht des Gymnasium . . .* , Thalburg, September 16, 1936" (in Thalburg City Archives, No. 6/55/V). Also, *475 Jahre, . . .*
31. Interview with Hans Abbenrode.
32. Interview with Rudolf Fischer.
33. "*TB an alle Parteigenossen, Thalburg den 23. September 1933*" (mimeographed circular in private files of Walther Timmerlah).
34. "*Gaupresseamtsleiter an alle Kreis-und Ortsgruppenpressewarte, den Kreis-und Ortsgruppenleitern zur kenntnis, Hannover d. 5, April, 1934, Streng vertraulich!*" (copy in private files of Eva Spatel). Apparently there must have been a leak in the Nazi system, because the GHC obtained this illegally.

35. TNN: December 2, 12, 1933; interview with Erhardt Knorpel. The suppression coincided with the issuance of the "Law for the Protection of the Identity of Party and State" which might have made the masthead catch the *Pressewart's* eye. The TNN continued its independent existence until 1941, when it was merged with the TB as a "wartime economy measure."

36. TB: February 27, 1933; July 27, 1933; *"Gaupressewart an d. Herrn Wilhelm Spatel, Hanrover d. 14. XII. 1933"*; *"TB an GHC; 27. August 1934"*; *"RAD Ûnterfeldmeister X an Wilhelm Spatel, Thalburg d. 4.V. 1934"*; *"TB an GHC, 29. Januar 34"*; *"NSDAP Kreispressewart für Thalburg an GHC, 21. September 1934"*; *"TB an GHC, 25. September 1934"*; *"Reichsministerium fuer Voelksaufklaerung u. Propaganda, Hannover d. 26. Maerz 1935 an Wilhelm Spatel."* All from private files of Eva Spatel.

37. *"A. Schwertfeger an Wilhelm Spatel, X, den 2. Maerz 1935"*; *"Heinrich Sohnrey an die NSDAP Gauleitung X, 6. August 1934"* (enclosed in *"Heinrich Sohnrey an Wilhelm Spatel 8. August 1934"*). From private files of Eva Spatel.

38. Interview with Eva Spatel.

39. TNN: November 30, 1933; January 26, 1934; February 12, 1934.

40. TNN: January 21, 1931; September 13, 1933; November 27, 28, 1933; February 10, 13, 1934. Before the Nazis came to power the War Graves organization had 125 members and its collector was the Jewish banker, Braun (TNN: May 13, 1933).

41. *Regierungspraesident* to Thalburg *Magistrat,* October 9, 1933; in reply, Thalburg *Magistrat* to *Regierungspraesident,* October 16, 1933. In Thalburg City Archives, No. 5. Also, TB: October 8, 1933; TNN: September 23, 30, 1933; October 3, 9, 1933.

42. *"Taetigkeitsbericht der Luftschutzschule im Jahre 1935"* (in Thalburg City Archives, No. 121/XII). Also, TNN: September 7, 20, 1933; November 18, 1933.

43. TNN: August 31, 1933; September 4, 23, 25, 26, 28, 1933; October 3, 1933; TB: October 8, 1933; November 3, 1933; December 27, 29, 1933.

44. Table constructed from *Thalburg, 1933-36 . . .* , p. 33. Political crimes and "matters to be investigated secretly" are excluded.

45. *"Statistik ueber die bearbeiteten Kriminal-Polizeilichen Vorgaenge bei der Kriminal-Polizei in Thalburg"*; also, *"Schuetzhaft infolge Trunkenheit, Ruehestoerung, politisch pp."* No. 2/VII/c in Thalburg City Archives.

46. Speech of Buergermeister Aergeyz, 1. III. 34 (carbon copy) in Thalburg City Archives, No. 74/VII/6.

CHAPTER EIGHTEEN

THE GREAT JUSTIFICATION

1. GHC: May 17, 1933; TNN: August 7, 1933; interviews with Erhardt Knorpel and Dieter Thomas.
2. Order circulated among Thalburg city employees, June 26, 1935 (copy in private files of Walther Timmerlah).
3. TNN: September 22, 1933.
4. See Wells, *op. cit.* p. 62. For Aergeyz's installation as Mayor, TNN: March 27, 1934, and *Thalburg, 1933-36 . . .* , p. 2; also, "Report on the Development of the *Fuehrer* Principle in Thalburg, 1933-37." The new institutions were *"Ratsherrn"* (previously *"Buergervorsteher Kollegium"*) and *"Stadtrat"* (previously *"Magistrat"*).
5. TNN: August 3, 5, 1933; September 7, 13, 1933; December 30, 1933; January 20, 24, 1934 (for the DAF); October 12, 16, 1933 (for the artisans); November 18, 1933 (for the retailers).
6. *"Rede des Ortsgruppenleiter im Hotel X am 5. Okt. 1933,"* including a form letter and list of names dated September 30, 1933; all in Thalburg City Archives, No. 75/VII/b. Also TB: October 8, 1933; TNN: October 6, 1933.
7. TNN: October 14, 25, 29, 1933.
8. Letter and list of names dated February 27, 1934 (No. 74 in Thalburg City Archives) and *"Richtlinien fuer die Redner in der Arbeitsschlacht des Gaues . . ."* No. II 2640 hu-wk. (*ibid.*); *"Rede des Stellv. Buergermeisters Aergeyz ueber Arbeitsbeschaffung am 1. Maerz 1934 im 1910er Zelt zu Thalburg"* (in Thalburg City Archives, No. 74/VII/6). The entire speech, covering four whole newspaper pages was reprinted in TNN: March 2, 6, 1934.
9. *"Versammlung, betr. Arbeitsbeschaffungsmassnahmen, im Hotel 'Bismarck' am Do., dem 8. Maerz 1934, Abends 8:30 uhr"* (stenographic report in Thalburg City Archives).
10. TNN: March 10, 15, 20, 21, 1934.
11. *"Buergermeister Aergeyz an Stadtbaumeister X, Thalburg den 12. Maerz 1934"*; *"Rede des Buergermeisters am 31. August 1934"* (in Thalburg City Archives, No. B/IIa).
12. *"Merkmale ueber die Stadtforst Thalburg seit der Machtuebernahme durch unseren Fuehrer"* (January 10, 1935?), (in Thalburg City Archives, No. 8/91/IXc); "Report on the Development of the *Fuehrer*-Principle . . . ; *Thalburg, 1933-36 . . .* , p. 23; TB: January 30, 1936 (special issue).

13. TNN: November 29, 1933 (for the mass entry into the RAD from the *Zuckerfabrik*). On the theater, see *"Bericht ueber den Bau der Weihstaette in Thalburg, 1934-1936"* (ms. in Thalburg City Archives); *Thalburg, 1933-36 . . . ,* pp. 6, 26; TNN: February 5, 1934; June 7, 1936. Some Thalburgers profited more than others from the Holy Place; the land on which it was built had belonged to Senator August Blanck.

14. *Thalburg, 1933-36 . . . ,* Table *"Bevoelkerung der Stadt."*

15. *Ibid.,* p. 7, and TNN: November 7, 1933; March 2, 1934.

16. TNN: November 21, 1933; TB: January 30, 1936; *Thalburg, 1933-36 . . . ,* p. 7; *"Taetigkeits und Erfolgsbericht"* (*Buergermeister* to *Landrat*, January 25, 1935), (in Thalburg City Archives, No. C).

17. TNN: August 16, 1933; September 18, 1933; November 7, 1933; March 22, 1934; letter from *Buergermeister* to a list of Thalburg businessmen, civil servants, party officials, etc., dated March 22, 1934 (in Thalburg City Archives), and "Report on the Development of the *Fuehrer*-Principle . . ."

18. Interviews with Maria Armkerl and Karl Hengst.

19. TNN: September 21-26, 28, 1933; October 14, 25, 30, 1933; November 18, 24, 1933; December 1, 1933; January 8, 9, 1934; March 12, 1934. NSV meetings were also used to promote Nazi policy in explicit ways. A benefit evening held shortly before the November, 1933, plebiscite was used for electioneering purposes. Another, held in January, 1934, emphasized German claims to the Saar. TNN: October 25, 1933; December 15, 1933; January 13, 19, 1934.

20. TNN: December 18, 1933; TB: February 20, 1934. *"Gnaedige Frau"* is not necessarily a term of deference. It can also be used simply out of politeness. But servant girls were obliged to use it when addressing their mistresses and it was this the Nazis opposed.

21. Interviews with Heinrich Lamme, Hans Abbenrode, Maria Armkerl, and Erhardt Knorpel.

22. TB: January 30, 1936 (special issue); "Report on the Development of the *Fuehrer*-Principle . . ."; *Thalburg, 1933-36 . . . ,* p. 21.

23. TNN: February 3, 1934; TB: April 16, 1934. *"Versammlung des Vereins zur Hebung des Femdenverkehrs am 31. August 1934: Ansprache des Herrn Buergermeisters"* (No. B/IIa in Thalburg City Archives).

24. *Chronik des Standortes Thalburg,* pp. 29, 38-42, 59. Section 9 of the contract explicitly committed the Army to give most of its work to Thalburgers and to hire any extra personnel from the town.

25. *Thalburg, 1933-36 . . . ,* pp. 10-11. The Mayor was nevertheless greeted by many howls of protest when it was learned that the town was to lose its swimming pool. See *"Versammlung des Vereins zur Hebung, etc."*

26. *Chronik des Standortes Thalburg, op. cit.* pp. 40, 55; interviews with Erhardt Knorpel and Walther Timmerlah. Many *Wehrmacht* officers attended church conspicuously after the Nazi anti-church campaign began (see Chapter Nineteen).

CHAPTER NINETEEN

CONCLUSIONS

1. Interviews with Rudolf Fischer, Walther Timmerlah, Heinrich Lamme, and Erhardt Knorpel.
2. Interviews with Karl Hengst, Dieter Thomas, and Erhardt Knorpel.
3. For a comparative example, see Ernst-August Roloff: *Buergertum und National-sozialismus. Braunschweigs Weg ins Dritte Reich* (Hannover, 1961).
4. See Chapter Two for a description of this club.
5. Interview with Rudolf Fischer.
6. Interviews with Karl Hengst and Benno Schmidt.
7. Report of the *Gau-Uschla* proceedings against Walther Timmerlah, minutes for July 1, 1933 (in private files of Walther Timmerlah).

INDEX